D1155379

THE FIRST DUTCH SETTLEMENT IN ALBERTA

THE FIRST DUTCH
SETTLEMENT IN ALBERTA

Letters from the Pioneer Years
1903–14

TRANSLATIONS, INTRODUCTION, & NOTES
by DONALD SINNEMA

This book is volume XXV (2004) of the
Canadian Journal of Netherlandic Studies
and is being sent to all its subscribers.

caans ⋎ acaen

UNIVERSITY OF
CALGARY
PRESS

Published by the
University of Calgary Press
2500 University Drive NW
Calgary, Alberta, Canada T2N 1N4
www.uofcpress.com

We acknowledge the financial support of
the Government of Canada through the
Book Publishing Industry Development
Program (BPIDP), the Alberta
Foundation for the Arts and the Alberta
Lottery Fund—Community Initiatives
Program for our publishing activities.
We acknowledge the support of the
Canada Council for the Arts for our
publishing program.

Canada Council   Conseil des Arts
for the Arts   du Canada

Canadä

ALBERTA
LOTTERY FUND

caans · acaen

We also acknowledge the financial
support of the *Canadian Journal of
Netherlandic Studies*.

LIBRARY AND ARCHIVES CANADA
CATALOGUING IN PUBLICATION

The first Dutch settlement in Alberta :
letters from the pioneer
years, 1903-1914 / translations,
introduction and notes by Donald
Sinnema.

(Legacies shared ; 16)
Includes bibliographical references
and index.

ISBN 1-55238-173-0

1 Dutch – Alberta – Correspondence.
2 Dutch – Alberta – History.
3 Dutch Canadians – Alberta –
  Correspondence.
4 Dutch Canadians – Alberta – History.
5 Pioneers – Alberta – Correspondence.
6 Frontier and pioneer life – Alberta.
7 Granum (Alta.) – History.
8 Monarch (Alta.) – History.
9 Nobleford (Alta.) – History.

I Sinnema, Donald W., 1947–
II Series.

FC3700.D9F57 2005   971.23'0043931
C2005-902643-X

Cover design, Mieka West.
Internal design & typesetting,
    Jason Dewinetz.

∞ This book is printed on Eco Book,
a 100% post-consumer recycled,
ancient-forest-friendly paper.
Printed and bound in Canada by
HOUGHTON BOSTON.

Contents

Acknowledgments

I HAVE LONG BEEN INTERESTED IN THE HISTORY OF the Dutch community in southern Alberta where I grew up, where my grandfather and great-grandfather homesteaded. But this project began in the spring of 1995, when I stumbled across some printed letters in the Dutch-American newspaper *De Grondwet,* as I checked out a footnote reference in Henry Lucas's *Netherlanders in America.* Scanning the microfilm at the Joint Archives of Holland in Holland, Michigan, I noticed a series of correspondent letters sent to this newspaper by George Dijkema from the Dutch settlement at Granum.

This led to the discovery of many more correspondent letters in *De Grondwet* from Alberta settlers in the decade before World War I. On the hunch that such letters might also be found in *De Volksvriend,* the northwest Iowa paper, I checked microfilm of this paper at the library of Northwestern College in Orange City, Iowa, and found a good many more letters.

Then on visits to the Netherlands in 1996 and 2001, I checked bound issues of the *Twentsch Volksblad* at the Overijsselse Bibliotheek Dienst in Nijverdal and discovered a major cache of Alberta letters sent by Evert Aldus to this newspaper back home in the Old Country. In the *Nieuwsblad van Friesland* at the Provinciale Bibliotheek van Friesland in Leeuwarden I found the Schilstra letters promoting immigration to western Canada that led a large Nijverdal group to consider the move to Alberta in 1904.

I gathered genealogical information on various families from *Gemeentehuizen* in Nijverdal, Loppersum, and St. Annaparochie, and from the Rijksarchief Groningen.

At the Calvin College Archives I noticed several letters relating to pioneer church life in *De Wachter* and *The Banner,* periodicals of the Christian Reformed Church. The Reformed Church paper, *De Hope,* at the Joint Archives of Holland, supplied letters from that church perspective.

At the Provincial Archives of Alberta in Edmonton I gathered homestead records for all the Dutch homesteaders in southern Alberta. The Glenbow Archives in Calgary provided background information on the rush for homesteads. I was able to access ship manifests for Canadian ports at the Lethbridge Public Library and for New York from the ellisislandrecords.org Web site. The 1906 Census of Alberta is also available online.

All of these archives were most helpful in providing access to the materials I needed for this project.

Families of many of the original Dutch settlers have been very generous in sharing family information and, in some cases, personal letters of the early settlers and photos. Barend Bode of Giessenburg graciously shared a number of items from his collection of Bode family letters and he also helped with some translation issues.

Various others, including Dr. Henrietta Ten Harmsel, Florence Oosting, Dr. Harry Van Dyke of Redeemer College, and Henk Landeweerd of Raalte, offered valuable help in translating difficult expressions of the Dutch. Landeweerd was also gracious in lending me a hand to search for letters in the *Twentsch Volksblad.* Rev. Tymen Hofman helped edit some of my translations and shared his knowledge of early families of the community.

Thanks also to Ryan Olthof who did several searches for me at the Lethbridge Public Library and to Peter Sinnema who checked some records at the Provincial Archives of Alberta. Gordon Van Gaalen kindly offered his expertise to draw up the map of the Dutch homesteaders. Others willingly shared their photos of this early Dutch community.

Dr. Herman Ganzevoort, the leading scholar of Dutch-Canadian history, and Dr. Robert Swierenga, the dean of Dutch-American studies, each read versions of the manuscript and offered valuable suggestions.

I am grateful for the generosity of the Canadian Journal of Netherlandic Studies, which agreed to co-publish this volume, and of the Alberta Historical Resources Foundation for a grant to subsidize its publication.

Finally, a sabbatical from Trinity Christian College in 2001–02 allowed me time to concentrate on the translations and annotations for this project.

Introduction

THIS IS THE STORY OF THE BEGINNINGS OF ONE SMALL ethnic community in a rural district of southern Alberta – the Dutch community in the Granum-Monarch-Nobleford area – as narrated mostly by their letters. Yet it is much more. Though the focus is on this one small group, the story told in these letters casts significant light on broader themes and contexts.

This story is about *Alberta* history. It documents a slice of early life in Alberta just before and after the province was born in 1905, a time when the great land rush for free homesteads lured thousands of new settlers to the prairies from eastern Canada, the United States, and Europe.

This story is about *pioneer* life. It pictures the pioneer experience in elaborate detail from the lonely homestead on the bald prairie to a well developed rural community with new railroads and towns, new churches and schools, and even rural telephone service – all within the rapid course of a decade.

This story is about *immigrant* history. It tells how a group of European immigrants, rather poor but steeped in old-country culture, came to Alberta from the Netherlands or via the United States to make a new start and adapted to a very primitive setting on the Canadian prairies.

This story is about *Dutch ethnic* history. It is the story of the first Dutch settlement in Alberta, and the second enduring one in all of Canada.[1] In its first decade the Alberta settlement remained rather insulated from its non-Dutch neighbours; it found its identity as one far-flung Dutch "kolonie" in the broad network of Dutch immigrant settlements scattered across North America.

This story is about *popular* history. It is not about great Canadian historical figures, but about ordinary people, common immigrants, whose hopes and determination carved out a place for themselves in a new land and whose hands laboriously developed the Canadian west.

This story is about *local* history. In illuminating detail it sketches the rise and early development of the rural towns of Leavings (later Granum), Monarch, and Noble (later Nobleford), and their surrounding districts.

This story is about early *farming* on the Canadian prairies, the implements used, and the farming methods employed. It is about breaking the virgin sod, four good years, then three bad years devastated by drought, a hailstorm, and cutworms. It is about the wind and weather that so dictated life on the homestead.

This story is about *church* history. It pictures early worship life on the prairies as families crowded into homestead shacks for reading services and Christmas celebrations. It narrates the establishment in this community of the first Christian Reformed Church in Canada in 1905 and, four years later, the oldest Reformed Church in America congregation still in existence in Canada.[2]

Finally, this story is about *families*. It offers a wealth of genealogical information about the Dutch families who originally homesteaded, or soon arrived, in the settlement, many of whose descendants still live in the area. For most this was the traumatic moment of transition in their family history as they took the big step to emigrate from the Old Country and forge a new life in North America.[3]

---

1   Earlier a number of Dutch settled in Winnipeg in the 1890s. In 1893 two groups of Dutch immigrants landed in Winnipeg. Some stayed there; others dispersed to other places, including several families who went on to join a small rural group of Dutch at Yorkton in the district of Assiniboia (later Saskatchewan). There was a Dutch presence at Yorkton since 1885, but it never succeeded as a Dutch settlement; most of the Hollanders there moved to Winnipeg within a couple years. For the story of these early immigrants, see Klaas and Reindert De Vries, *Leaving Home Forever* (Windsor: Electa Press, 1995), and J. Th. Krijff, *100 Years: Dutch Immigration to Manitoba in 1893* (Windsor: Electa Press, 1994). For an overview of Dutch immigration to Canada, see Herman Ganzevoort, *A Bittersweet Land: The Dutch Experience in Canada, 1890–1980* (Toronto: McCelland and Stewart, 1988).

2   In the early 19th century the Reformed Dutch Church (later Reformed Church in America) organized a number of small congregations in Ontario, but all of them later became Presbyterian churches or disbanded.

THE BACKGROUND TO PRAIRIE SETTLEMENT

The district where the Dutch settled was part of the ancestral territory of the Blood tribe, a member of the Blackfoot confederacy. In 1670 the western prairies became part of Rupert's Land, created by a British charter granting the Hudson's Bay Company a trade monopoly in this territory. Yet the buffalo-centred way of life of the aboriginal peoples remained relatively undisturbed in the western part of the plains until the latter half of the nineteenth century.

After Confederation, the Hudson's Bay Co. ceded Rupert's Land to the Dominion of Canada in 1870 and it became the North-West Territories. In 1882 Ottawa divided the territories into four districts, one of them the District of Alberta, roughly the southern half of the present province.

Prime Minister John A. Macdonald's national policy basically envisioned the western prairies as a colony of eastern Canada. To establish Canada as a great nation from sea to sea and thwart American expansionism in the west, the national policy included several major elements imposed on the western interior: settlement of the prairies to provide a hinterland for the manufacturing interests of the east, Indian treaties to procure western lands for the settlers, an immigration policy to attract newcomers, a cross-country railway to bring in settlers and serve the western market, a police force to protect the settlers and prevent inter-tribal hostilities, and a tariff on imports to protect eastern industry.[4]

Before settlement the western plains first needed to be surveyed. Beginning in 1871, the Dominion Land Survey divided the prairies into townships and square-mile sections. In 1883 the survey of sections and quarters was completed in the area of Alberta where the Dutch would settle.

To attract settlers to the prairies, the Dominion Lands Act of 1872, following the U. S. Homestead Act, offered settlers a free homestead, consisting of a quarter section of land, for a filing fee of $10.

To get rid of American whiskey traders and establish law and order, Ottawa then sent the North-West Mounted Police into the west in 1874. Under Colonel James Macleod the NWMP established a post at Fort Macleod that year and then other posts throughout the territories, among them Fort Calgary in 1875.

---

3 Tymen Hofman, *The Strength of Their Years: The Story of a Pioneer Community* (St. Catharines: Knight Publishing, 1983), has told the story of the early years of the Dutch community in southern Alberta, especially from the perspective of the John Postman family. His account is based on family recollections and church records, not on the letters that make up this collection.

4 For background to the settlement of the Canadian west, see: Gerald Friesen, *The Canadian Prairies: A History* (Lincoln: University of Nebraska Press, 1984); Pierre Berton, *The Promised Land: Settling the West, 1896–1914* (Toronto: McClelland and Stewart, 1984); and *Alberta in the Twentieth Century*, vol. 1, *The Great West Before 1900* (Edmonton: United Western Communications, 1991).

To pave the way for settlement, the Canadian government also entered into a number of treaties with native Canadians. Treaty No. 7 was an agreement in 1877 with the five tribes of the Blackfoot confederacy in southern Alberta. By misunderstandings and misleading promises, the government officials took advantage of the tribes, whose survival and way of life was threatened by the rapidly diminishing buffalo. The government perceived the treaty as a legal document in which the tribes ceded and surrendered their rights to the land; it also set aside reserves for them. The five tribes, who knew no English, had a different perception. They thought they were entering a peace treaty with the government and agreeing to share their land with incoming settlers.[5]

By 1879 the buffalo disappeared from the Canadian prairies and the native way of life was gone. The next year the native peoples, now starving and dependent on government aid, began to straggle into their reserves.[6]

After the coming of the Mounties in 1874 and the signing of Treaty 7, southern Alberta opened up to white settlement. First came the ranching era. In the fall of 1877 the first range cattle were introduced in the area of Fort Macleod. Four years later the Macdonald government established a rangeland policy, which granted leases of up to 100,000 acres to huge cattle operations, such as the Walrond and Oxley ranches along the hills northwest of Fort Macleod. Smaller ranches also sprang up along the valleys of the Oldman River, Willow Creek, and other streams. About 1883, some twenty years before the homesteaders arrived, the first ranchers established spreads along the Oldman in what would become the Monarch district. Fort Macleod (which changed to its name to Macleod in 1893) soon became a ranching centre.

The Canadian government encouraged railway construction by offering the railways large land grants. After the Canadian Pacific Railway was incorporated in 1881 to construct a line to the Pacific, the CPR main line reached Medicine Hat by June 1883 and Calgary by August. Coalbanks emerged as an important centre around the coal-mining industry that had its beginnings there as early as 1870. It became Lethbridge in 1885. That same year a branch line opened from Dunmore, just east of Medicine Hat,

5   The recent volume by the Treaty 7 Elders and Tribal Council, with Walter Hildebrandt, Sarah Carter, and Dorothy First Rider, *The True Spirit and Original Intent of Treaty 7* (Montreal & Kingston: McGill-Queen's University Press, 1996) offers the aboriginal perspective on this treaty.

6   The letters of this collection are virtually silent about the native tribes living nearby on the Blood and Peigan reserves. In these letters the Dutch settlers neither understand nor give thought to the plight of the native peoples and the injustice done to them by the dispossession of their land. They simply think about the opportunity afforded to them of free land.

to Lethbridge, to move coal for the CPR, and in 1890 the line was extended from Lethbridge to Great Falls, crossing the boundary at Coutts. The next year a line opened from Calgary south almost to Fort Macleod. There was now easy access for settlement in southern Alberta.

However, the flow of people to the Canadian prairies remained a trickle until the late 1890s, for a variety of reasons – the preference of immigrants for the American west until the free land was gone, high tariffs, high CPR freight rates, international economic conditions, the resistance of ranchers, and bad weather.

Several factors then converged to create a climate favourable to prairie settlement after 1896. There was a rise in world wheat prices and an economic upturn in the Canadian west. There were breakthroughs in dry-land farm technology. There was a growing scarcity of free land in the western United States, and many American farmers now saw greater economic opportunity with free homesteads in the Canadian west. The CPR agreed, in the 1897 Crow's Nest Pass agreement, to reduce its freight rates for eastbound grain and westbound settlers' effects, making the economics of settlement more viable. Unfavourable economic and social conditions in Europe encouraged emigration from these countries.

The Canadian government also developed a more aggressive campaign for recruiting immigrants to the west. After the Liberals under Sir Wilfrid Laurier ousted the Tory government in 1896, Clifford Sifton became the new Minister of the Interior. He was a fervent advocate of western settlement and opened wide the gates to immigration. It was immigrant farm-folk that Sifton wanted as settlers. There was a massive proliferation of advertising for free Canadian homesteads, directed at the eastern provinces, northern Europe, and the United States (in seven thousand rural American papers by 1902), and the number of immigration agents abroad jumped dramatically.

THE LAND RUSH TO THE PRAIRIES [7]

The Dutch settlement in southern Alberta began as part of the great land rush that swept the Alberta prairies in the first decade of the twentieth century. Thousands came by wagon or rail to take up the free homestead

---

7 For the land rush to Alberta, see *Alberta in the Twentieth Century*, vol. 2, *The Birth of the Province* (Edmonton: United Western Communications, 1992), sec. 3. Background information on the Leavings (Granum) district is drawn from *Leavings by Trail, Granum by Rail* (Calgary: Granum History Committee, 1977), 7–54. For the Monarch-Nobleford district the best resource is *Sons of Wind and Soil* (Calgary: Nobleford-Monarch History Book Club, 1976), and for the Macleod district, *Fort Macleod – Our Colourful Past: A History of the Town of Fort Macleod from 1874 to 1924* (Fort Macleod: Fort Macleod History Book Committee, 1977). Each of these community histories also includes family histories.

land made available as Canada sought to populate its western plains. As a result, Alberta's population increased from 73,000 to 374,000 in the decade from 1901 to 1911. The largest group of homesteaders came from eastern Canada, but about 80,000 crossed the border from the United States, a third of them recent European immigrants. The rest were fresh immigrants directly from Europe.

The Canadian prairies were surveyed into townships of 36 square-mile sections, each consisting of four 160-acre quarters. In areas opened to homesteading, most even numbered sections were available as homesteads. For a filing fee of $10 any male over eighteen was eligible to claim a 160-acre homestead at a government land office. There was a district land agent in Lethbridge and a sub-agent at Macleod. The homesteader then had to "prove up" on his homestead by meeting certain basic requirements. He had to put up a home on the property and reside there for at least six months a year for three years, and he had to break at least thirty acres of prairie in those three years. After meeting these conditions, he received his patent or free title to the quarter.

A huge factor that made homesteading viable was the availability of a nearby railroad to bring in supplies and to ship farm products to market. In 1891 the Calgary and Edmonton Railway Company constructed a track south from Calgary to West Macleod, the end of the line several miles northwest of Macleod and north of the Oldman River. This line was then leased to the Canadian Pacific Railway. With the construction of the CPR's Crow's Nest Pass line in 1897–98, Lethbridge became connected to Macleod – or at least to Haneyville, the station two miles south of the town – and the C & E line was extended across the Oldman to link up with the Crow's Nest line at Macleod Junction just southwest of the town. To finance the building of its line, the C & E Railroad received a construction grant of over 40 per cent of the land along its track north of the Oldman River. After the homesteads were taken up, this C & E land – most of the odd numbered sections – was sold to homesteaders who wanted to expand their holdings and to other farmers. In 1903 the CPR bought the C & E line, but the grant lands remained in the hands of the C & E Land Company.[8]

The town of Leavings had its origins as a railway construction siding on the C & E line about thirteen miles north of Macleod. It is possible that there was a loading chute at this siding already in the 1890s for local ranchers to ship their stock to the Calgary market. The CPR whistle boards were painted

---

8 For the development of railway lines in southern Alberta, see Ronald F. Bowman, *Railways in Southern Alberta* (Lethbridge: Historical Society of Alberta, 1973).

"Leavings." Then in 1902 a box car was placed at the Leavings siding to serve as a station. In late 1902 Hans Ellison began constructing a small general store there, which opened the following May. The Leavings post office was then set up in the store. About that time a lumberyard was also established. After Leavings was surveyed on 15 September 1903, various other merchants soon set up shop there and in 1904 the first grain elevators were constructed. The town quickly blossomed into an important centre for homesteaders north of the Oldman River. On 1 October 1907, the name Leavings was changed to Granum.[9]

The period of homesteading in the Leavings area ran from 1888 to 1909, but the real land rush there occurred in the years from 1902 to 1905. First land closer to the track was snapped up, then land farther to the east.

The Dutch settlement originated as part of this land rush with the arrival of the first Dutch homesteader east of Leavings in early 1903. This first family came from the United States, and later that year other Dutch folk from there visited to check out land and claimed homesteads at Leavings. The first group directly from the Netherlands arrived in the spring of 1904, but they could only find homesteads farther to the east in what was later known as the Monarch district. Other families and single men soon followed, from south of the border and from the Old Country.

Those who arrived from the United States were usually more acculturated since many of them had lived for some years in the American context. Though they were usually part of a Dutch settlement in the States, they had learned some English. Some of them had also gained valuable farming experience there. They were a great help to the new immigrants from the Netherlands, who in most cases were not farmers and had to adapt quickly to a very different cultural setting.

The new Dutch settlement was not a particularly cohesive group. They were not part of any emigration society and had no specific leader. Though many in the Monarch district hailed from Nijverdal in the Dutch province of Overijssel, others were from Groningen, Friesland, Zuid-Holland, or another Dutch province. Though almost all grew up in the Reformed tradition, they represented several different church denominations. Family ties, however, were an important link, especially between earlier settlers and newcomers, as the settlement grew by what has been called "chain migration."

---

9 With the name change "Granum" was not the first choice. The *Lethbridge Herald* (5 April 1906) reported, "Our friends at Leavings have outgrown their present name, and have requested that the name 'Wheaton' be substituted for their present cognomen, and should they fail in securing the name of their choice, that any one of the following be given them: Millbank, Moreland, Jamieson, or Chinook."

THE FIRST DUTCH SETTLER

The first Dutch settlers to arrive in the Leavings area were Harm and Jantje Emmelkamp and their family, in January or February of 1903.[10] The Emmelkamps were not part of any immigrating group; they were an independent-minded family that for its own reasons sought the opportunity to homestead in Alberta after some trying years and experiences in the United States.

Harm was born on 20 October 1867 at Jukwerd, a small village in the northeastern clay-belt region of the Dutch province of Groningen. He grew up on the Jukwerd farm, where his father was a farm labourer, but his mother died just before his fourth birthday and his father a few years later when he was twelve. So at that age he began working as a farm hand on various farms in the general area.

To avoid the military draft twenty-year-old Harm immigrated to the United States, arriving on the *Edam* at New York on 4 June 1888. His destination was Holland, Michigan, but he soon worked as a labourer in Grand Rapids. There he met Jantje Roos, who had immigrated as a single woman to Grand Rapids a year earlier, and they were married there on 15 March 1890. In their first decade together they owned a thirty-acre mixed farm near Grandville and then a small truck farm in the Blendon township west of Grand Rapids. For extra income Harm worked in a stone quarry. In these years three children were born; one died.

Though Harm had grown up in the Hervormde Kerk in the Netherlands, in Michigan he and Jantje joined the Christian Reformed Church (CRC) as baptized members; they were married by the pastor of the Fifth Ave. CRC of Grand Rapids, then joined the Grandville Ave. congregation, and then the Jenison CRC in 1892. In 1897, however, Harm and his wife resigned from this church. They offered no reasons, but from church records it appears that they and others were not happy about the way the Jenison consistory handled the case of an elder of this church who was accused of stealing hay; he was hauling hay for another church member and was caught throwing down extra bundles to feed his own horses. Attempts by the consistory to get the Emmelkamps to return to the church failed, and in December of 1898 their membership was formally lapsed.[11] This experience left its mark on Harm; he never again joined a church, although he did attend services later at Granum.

---

10 Sources for the family stories that follow include family histories, Dutch population registers, ship manifests, homestead records, and church records. Family accounts differ on whether the Emmelkamps arrived in January or February.

In 1900 Jantje developed lung problems and doctors advised the family to go west to a drier climate. So in the latter part of the year they moved to northern New Mexico and settled at Raton just north of the small Dutch community of Maxwell City, where Bethesda Sanitarium drew Dutch folk suffering from tuberculosis. The Emmelkamps did not join the local CRC. Harm bought a dry-land farm of about eighty acres at Raton, but due to the arid climate and poor crops he could not make a living from the land and work was impossible to find. This left the family in heavy debt. One night in early December 1902 they abandoned the farm and quietly left with their debts unpaid.[12] The farm was claimed by creditors. Their destination was the Dearborn Valley, where a new government irrigation project was opening up farm land southwest of Great Falls, Montana. Nothing is known of their stay in the Dearborn Valley, but it was brief.

It was probably there that Harm heard about better opportunities in Alberta. A free homestead was appealing, and the dry climate would be healthy for Jantje. So in January or February 1903 the Emmelkamp family moved on to southern Alberta to make a new start. Harm went ahead, perhaps by a few days,[13] and landed at Macleod; Jantje and their young children Sienie, Jan, and Harm soon arrived by train. There at Macleod Harm had made arrangements for the family to stay in a log cabin with a sod roof and dirt floor for about a month. Harm was able to find some work with Thomas McLean who had a ranch on Willow Creek near the junction with the Oldman River, and the family then stayed in a log cabin nearby in the Oldman River bottom. It was located about six miles northeast of Macleod (on NE 33-9-25 W4).[14] They ended up staying there for two years. Their fourth child, Diena, was born there on Christmas day of 1903 – the first Dutch child born in the settlement.

Meanwhile Harm sought a homestead. On 21 April 1903 he filed on NE 28-10-25 W4, which lay five miles north of the cabin and eight miles east of Leavings. At this point Hans Ellison, the first merchant there, was just finishing his general store and was about to open it in May. Homesteads along the track at Leavings were already taken, and open homesteads lay to the east.

---

11 Membership records and consistory minutes of First CRC of Jenison, Michigan.
12 See 13 January 1903 letter from Maxwell City below.
13 A part of the family tradition suggests that Harm came to check out Alberta already in October 1902, but this seems unlikely. Had he done so, he would surely have filed on a homestead at that time and the family would not have headed for the Dearborn Valley in December. The 1906 Census of Alberta lists 1903 as their date of immigration.
14 This land location refers to the northeast quarter of section 33, township 9, range 25, west of the 4th meridian.

Harm and Jantje Emmelkamp family, *ca.*1913. (Courtesy: Dorothy DeBoer.)

While working occasionally for McLean, Harm was able to break fifteen acres on his homestead that first year, though none was cropped. The next year he broke another twenty acres and seeded fifteen acres of crop. By then he had six horses and four cows, and had worked on fencing the homestead. In February 1904 he built a two-room framed shack, twelve by twenty-four feet in size, which cost $150. But it was not till February of the next year that the family left the cabin in the river bottom and took up residence there. By the time Harm proved up on his homestead and received patent on it in May 1907, he had also built a granary, cattle shed, and chicken house, dug three wells, put up two and a quarter miles of fencing, and had broken a hundred acres, of which eighty-five were in crop the previous year.

Because Emmelkamp had become somewhat acculturated while living for almost fifteen years in the United States – he had learned English and had gained valuable farming experience, also on dry land – he was very helpful to the new and inexperienced Dutch homesteaders who arrived later.

EARLY DUTCH SETTLERS FROM MONTANA

In the summer of 1903 several Hollanders visited Alberta from the United States and claimed homesteads near Emmelkamp east of Leavings, but most of them came to settle only the following year. The connection between Emmelkamp and these new settlers – a link that enabled the development of a Dutch settlement – is not very clear. While these newcomers were not an organized group, the Dutch farming settlement at Manhattan, Montana, was a common staging point.[15]

In July 1903, it seems, Hendrikus ter Telgte and Arien Doornbos left from Manhattan to check out homestead possibilities in Alberta.[16] Ter Telgte had grown up in the Nijverdal area, in the Dutch province of Overijssel, and had worked in the cotton factory there. In May he, his wife Maria, and four children, immigrated to the United States and first stayed at Manhattan where his brother Jan Hendrik had a farm. How Hendrikus developed a contact with Emmelkamp is unknown, but after Hendrikus visited the Leavings area Emmelkamp, on his behalf, filed for an abandoned homestead three miles north of his own on 10 August. Ter Telgte probably returned to Manhattan for a few months and arrived with his family in late 1903; they built a two-room shack in January, and started living there the next month.

Arien Doornbos had grown up at Warffum in northwestern Groningen, and at age 18 he immigrated to the United States in 1900. After spending time in Chicago and then in Texas, which was too hot to suit him, Doornbos moved north to Manhattan, Montana. In mid-1903 it is probable that he visited Alberta with ter Telgte, and, though the records are missing, he claimed a homestead a couple miles northeast of ter Telgte's. After returning to Manhattan, he apparently changed his mind and decided not to settle in Alberta. This decision may have been related to the fact that in January 1904 he married Geertruida Vanderwal, then about two months pregnant. Whatever the case, in early March 1904 Doornbos declared his desire to abandon the homestead at Leavings.

Lubbert Van Dellen was another young man who came from Montana to check out homesteads in August of 1903. He filed entry on 18 August to a homestead right next to that of Doornbos; they had been friends in Montana.[17] Van Dellen had grown up on a farm at Burum in eastern Friesland. In about 1900 he immigrated to the United States, and first stayed with his uncle, Rev. Lubbert Van Dellen, a Christian Reformed minister in the Englewood neighborhood of Chicago. He did not feel welcome there so went west to Montana where he worked at various jobs in the Bozeman-Manhattan area and possibly elsewhere in the state. He worked in a coal

15   For Manhattan, see Rob Kroes, *The Persistence of Ethnicity: Dutch Calvinist Pioneers in Amsterdam, Montana* (Urbana: University of Illinois Press, 1992).

16   See Klaas Schuiling letter, 2 August 1903. I am assuming that the reference to "Bakker Bos" in this letter refers to Doornbos.

17   It is possible that the two had met even earlier, since both immigrated to Chicago in about 1900.

mine, delivered lumber by mule for a lumber yard, and helped local farmers with threshing. While in Alberta in 1903, he may have worked for a time at a ranch west of Leavings. But he returned to Montana that winter and worked again in a coal mine. In late February 1904 he came to settle on his homestead, this time with George Dijkema, with whom he had become friends in Montana.[18] Dijkema filed claim (on 9 March) to the homestead that Doornbos had just abandoned, and together they built a homestead shack on the property line – a clever but not uncommon way to meet the residence requirement.

Jan Hendrik ter Telgte, Hendrikus's brother, also visited Alberta in August 1903.[19] On 29 August he claimed an abandoned homestead two miles south-west of Emmelkamp's. It already had a good house (24 × 24 feet, with a 12 × 32 lean-to addition) that had been built by the previous homesteader Herbert Stewart. Ter Telgte (born in 1863) had grown up on a farm near Nijverdal, married Fenneken Willemsen, and immigrated to Paterson, New Jersey, in March 1892 with the Willemsen family. After working in Paterson for several years, the ter Telgte family moved west to the Dutch settlement at Manhattan, Montana, where they took up a homestead in 1897. After proving up on this homestead in early 1903, Jan Hendrik made his visit to Alberta in August and then returned to Manhattan for the fall and winter. In early March 1904 he arrived with his family to settle on the new homestead.

Another person who came to check out homesteads at Leavings in August 1903 was the bachelor Willem Feller from New Mexico. He obtained entry on an abandoned homestead next to that of Emmelkamp on 2 September. In this case there was a clear connection with Emmelkamp since both had come from the Maxwell City settlement.[20] Feller, originally from Venhuizen in the province of Noord-Holland, was one of the first Dutch settlers to farm at Maxwell City when that settlement began in 1890. He became a member of the Christian Reformed church there, but later he developed strained relations with this church. In late July or early August 1903 he was visited by the Maxwell City consistory for neglect of Sabbath observance.[21] This was perhaps a factor that led to his leaving for Alberta in August. Whether he then stayed in Alberta with the Emmelkamps is unclear. When Van Dellen

18 See Dijkema letter, 29 March 1904.
19 See Aldus letter, 3 October 1903.
20 Emmelkamp's homestead records indicate that he knew Feller since about 1896. That would suggest that Feller had gotten to know the Emmelkamps while they were still in Michigan. Feller seems to have spent some time in Michigan, since he had an "old flame" there. See Venhuizen letter, 25 April 1907.
21 Consistory minutes of the Maxwell City CRC.

Jan H. ter Telgte's house, where many of the 1904 immigrants first stayed.

and Dijkema arrived in late February of 1904, a bachelor – probably Feller – was already living there.[22] But in the spring of 1904 he also spent six weeks at Manhattan, and even became a member of the Christian Reformed Church there. Then in April or May he moved from there to Leavings with a railway carload of machinery and livestock. As he crossed the border at Coutts, Roelf Lantinga illegally entered Canada with him, as he lay hidden under the canvas of Feller's binder.[23] In July Feller built a dugout with a wooden front into the side of a bank and took up residence on his homestead.

George Dijkema, who arrived with Lubbert Van Dellen in February 1904, was one of the most educated persons in the Dutch settlement; he wrote many of the letters that make up this collection. Born on 1 October 1870, on a farm at Ten Boer in northeastern Groningen, Dijkema wanted to become a minister in the Gereformeerde Kerken, so in 1892 he entered the preparatory program of the Theological School of his church at Kampen. In advanced courses he studied under the distinguished Reformed theologian Herman Bavinck. However, he was a fun-loving student, and from March to

22 See Dijkema letter, 29 March 1904.
23 In April 1903 Lantinga had immigrated to Raton, New Mexico, expecting to work in a bank owned by a Van Houten relative. When he arrived there, he was not given a job, but only a horse and saddle, so he found work on a ranch and joined a cattle drive. While at Raton (where the Emmelkamps had lived earlier), it is likely that Lantinga came in contact with Feller, who lived at nearby Maxwell City. Homestead records indicate that the two knew each other since early 1904. Lantinga did not have the correct papers to enter Canada. In Alberta Lantinga first stayed for a while with the Emmelkamps in their river bottom cabin, and then he claimed a homestead at Leavings on 17 September 1904.

September 1900 he was temporarily expelled from the school for drunkenness and then was placed on probation for a year. But during the probation period his conduct only worsened, and he was permanently expelled in July 1901 at age thirty.[24] A shame to his family and to his fiancée, who broke up with him, he immediately immigrated to the United States in June of that year. He worked for a time on a tomato farm in Maryland, but by mid-1902 he was in the Dutch settlement at Manhattan, where his sister Klaassien and her husband Geert Venhuizen lived. There in 1903 he became friends with Van Dellen – also Gereformeerd in background – and in the fall of that year he was working for a Dutch farmer in the area.

Within a month after his arrival in Alberta, Dijkema sent his first letter to *De Grondwet,* a Dutch newspaper published at Holland, Michigan,[25] and then became a regular correspondent. He did not immediately join the Christian Reformed church when it was established in 1905. But as an excellent reader, he was often asked to read sermons for services, even though he was only a "friend" of the church. Later he joined the congregation in 1907 and soon became a leader of the Granum CRC.

Shortly after the coming of Van Dellen and Dijkema, two other families arrived from Manhattan, though the two parties were not aware of each other. On 3 March 1904, the families of Jan Hendrik ter Telgte and of Gerrit Jan Withage arrived by train at the Haneyville station, two miles from Macleod. Jan's brother Hendrikus was not there to meet them; apparently he had not received a letter about their arrival. While the women and children waited for Jan and Gerrit to come with the freight cars, they slept in the station. When the men arrived two days later, they all immediately went to the house on ter Telgte's homestead east of Leavings. The next day Withage led an informal service for the two families – the first worship service in the Dutch settlement.[26]

Having sold his quarter at Manhattan, Jan Hendrik came with some capital and was able to quickly develop his land. Already that first year he had ten horses and six cattle; he broke 60 acres and seeded 25 acres into crop. Two years later he had 130 acres broken, 105 in crop, and he owned twelve horses and forty-five cattle.

Like the ter Telgtes, Gerrit Withage (born in 1870) had come from Nijverdal, where he worked in the cotton factory. He married Theodora Schiebout, had two sons, and they were members of the local Gereformeede

24 Records of the curators of the Theologische School van de Gereformeerde Kerken at Kampen.
25 See Dijkema letter, 29 March 1904.
26 See document relating to 6 March 1904.

Kerk. Seeing no future there for their young sons, the Withages immigrated to the United States in June 1903 to join friends of theirs, two brothers named Scholten, in the Manhattan settlement. Gerrit worked there for local farmers until he linked up with ter Telgte and the families moved to Alberta in March. In many respects Gerrit became the spiritual leader of the early Dutch settlement in Alberta. When the Christian Reformed church organized in 1905, he was immediately elected an elder and usually led reading services in homes on the east side.

THE IMMIGRANT GROUP FROM NIJVERDAL

Till now the tiny Dutch settlement east of Leavings consisted of a rather disparate collection of four families and three single men who had come from the United States, most by way of Manhattan. They were joined, however, in early April 1904, by an organized group of forty-one persons who immigrated directly from Nijverdal.

Nijverdal was a small town in the centre of the province of Overijssel. The area was very rural, but one industry dominated the town – the local cotton-weaving factory. English owned, the Koninklijke Stoomweverij was a steam powered weaving mill that employed many local folk, including children over twelve. For those working in the mill the hours were long, from 6 a.m. to 6 p.m., and the wages were barely at subsistence level. There was no hope for advancement, especially for large families.

In early 1903 the Frisian newspaper *Nieuwsblad van Friesland* published a number of articles by S. A. Schilstra that promoted Dutch immigration to Canada. Schilstra was a minister of the Reformed Church in America, living in Passaic, New Jersey. These articles, especially a three part series that ran in May and June, titled "To Canada: Trustworthy Hints for Emigrants,"[27] seem to have stimulated an interest on the part of some families in the Nijverdal area to seriously consider emigrating.[28]

Everhardus (Evert) Aldus, a young Nijverdal teacher, took the lead in investigating the possibilities of immigrating to western Canada. Born 8 March 1874 at Barneveld in the province of Gelderland, Aldus followed in his father's profession as teacher, and from 1900 to 1904 he taught physics in the Christian National School at Nijverdal, where his father had been headmaster. In 1900 he married Christina Stotijn and the next year the couple had their first child. They were members of the local Hervormde Kerk.

27 *Nieuwsblad van Friesland*, 23 May, 13 and 27 June 1903.
28 See Aldus letter, 8 August 1903.

Koninklijke Stoomweverij factory, Nijverdal, *ca.*1895, where many of the
Nijverdal immigrants had worked. (Courtesy: Frits Calkhoven.)

But his father's vocation did not satisfy Aldus's adventuresome spirit and
he sought freedom from the class distinctions prevalent in Dutch society;
so he began looking into homesteading in Canada.

In the spring of 1903 Aldus began his investigation and wrote about
his findings in a series of letters sent to a local newspaper, the *Twentsch
Volksblad,* starting in August of that year.[29] These letters reveal that Aldus
very carefully explored prospects for immigrants in Canada. He not only
relied on Schilstra's information and asked further questions about it; he
also wrote for information from the Canadian government in Ottawa and
from the Canadian High Commissioner at London, from whom he received
various official government brochures and booklets. He obtained a large
Canadian map. He checked American newspapers for market reports. And
before August Aldus took up correspondence with a Hollander at Manhattan
– fellow-Nijverdaler Jan ter Telgte, or his brother Hendrikus who had just
immigrated there in May – about farming prospects in Canada.[30] In August
and September this correspondence continued with Jan ter Telgte after he

29 *Twentsch Volksblad,* 22 August, 5, 12, 19, 26 September, 3, 17 October, 7 November 1903. In the first four
    letters Aldus presents in several installments an extended quotation of an article by Schilstra in the
    Nieuwsblad van Friesland.
30 See Aldus letter, 8 August 1903.

had made his visit to Alberta to check out homesteading there.[31] During this time, probably by the influence of Aldus's *Twentsch Volksblad* letters and by personal contact, a group developed of persons interested in immigrating to Canada.

Aldus also sought information from D. Tréau de Coeli, the Antwerp based agent of the Canadian government for Belgium and the Netherlands.[32] Such immigration agents were hired by the Department of the Interior to recruit suitable immigrants and received an incentive bonus of about $5 a person. Tréau De Coeli suggested that he come and personally visit the group, so by October he met with ten of them at Nijverdal and discussed the pros and cons of immigrating to Canada.[33] Toward the end of the year Tréau De Coeli also ran an advertisement for three weeks in the *Twentsch Volksblad* about free farmland in western Canada.

From the information gathered from these various sources, it appears that Aldus and the Nijverdal group were rather well informed about conditions in western Canada before they left. Their situation certainly does not fit the common perception about misguided immigrants naively venturing into the unknown and being deceived by half-truths in advertisements and glowing reports about prosperity on the Canadian prairies.

Following the recommendation of the ter Telgte brothers, a group of forty-one persons – six families and two single men – decided to immigrate to Alberta and join the tiny settlement east of Leavings, where they could take up homesteads. Besides the Aldus family, this group included some of their relatives – Jacobus Nijhoff, his second wife Wilhelmina, and their three children. She was a sister of Evert Aldus. Jacobus, a baker, delivered bread around Nijverdal on a small cart pulled by a large dog. Willem Stotijn, a single shoemaker, was a brother of Aldus's wife. The group also included Hendrikus and Janna Veldhuis and their five children. Veldhuis worked as a stoker in a Nijverdal creamery. Johannes and Hendrika Huisman, with their five children, were also from Nijverdal, where Johannes worked in the cotton mill. From Heerde, some thirty kilometres to the west and just across the border in Gelderland, was the family of farmer Willem Van Lohuizen. Accompanying him, his wife Hendrika and their three children, were his

---

31 See Aldus letters, 3 and 17 October 1903.

32 A letter by an unidentified J. in the *Nieuwsblad van Friesland* (5 September 1903) mentions the type of information available from this agent: "You can obtain a beautifully done French description [of Canada] with pictures and maps from Mr. D. Préau [Tréau] de Coeli, agent of the Government of Canada, 88 Rue de Willebrord, Antwerp. There is also a less handsome description in surprisingly poor Dutch, also published by the Government of Canada; perhaps it can also be obtained from the above address."

33 See Aldus letters, 3 and 17 October 1903, and 31 December 1904.

sixty-six-year-old mother Hendrikje and his younger brother Jan. All these families were Hervormd in church background. Finally there was the large family of Jan Postman. With his wife Janna and their nine children, Jan was eking out a living on a small rented farm near Den Ham, just north of Nijverdal. He saw no future there for his seven sons. This family belonged to the Gereformeerde Kerk.

On 12 March 1904 this group left Nijverdal by train, traveled on a former cattle boat from Rotterdam to Hull, England, and then took the train to Liverpool. From there they sailed third class across the Atlantic on the steamship *Ionian*.[34] They arrived at Halifax on 27 March, and then headed across Canada to Macleod on a CPR colonial train. At Medicine Hat the group had to split up, some going by train via Lethbridge, others taking the longer route via Calgary. On 3 April both parties arrived at the Macleod station, at different times on that Easter Sunday.

As many as possible were taken in by the three Dutch families who already had homes. The Veldhuis family, in the first party that came via Lethbridge, was picked up later that day by the ter Telgte brothers – they had written to Hendrikus about when they expected to arrive – and they stayed for about three weeks with his family in their two-room shack. The next day the Aldus, Huisman, and Nijhoff families and Stotijn were all taken to the larger home of Jan ter Telgte. Since the Withage family was still living there, for several weeks there were twenty-six persons living together in that home. The men folk and boys slept in the cold attic.

Two of the families, the Postmans and Van Lohuizens, stayed for a time in the Immigration House at Macleod. Then the Van Lohuizens lived for several weeks in a tent near Emmelkamp's cabin in the Oldman river bottom. There on 21 April their oldest child, five-year-old Hendrikje, weakened by the trip, died of the measles and was buried on the lonely prairie.

Since homesteads were then no longer available in the Leavings area, Withage and the newcomers sought land ten miles farther east beyond the bend in the Oldman River. On 13 April the new families, except for Withage and Postman, filed for their homesteads at the land office in Macleod and obtained entry the next day – Withage and Postman did so the next month. Then the men helped each other construct simple homestead shacks. By May or June most of these families took up residence on their own homesteads, and the men folk began to break a few acres of land. Their homesteads, all

34 According to the ship manifest, Aldus arrived with $200, Nijhoff $1,000, Stotijn $30, Veldhuis $300, Huisman $500, Willem Van Lohuizen $400, Jan Van Lohuizen $400, and Postman $100.

within three miles of each other, formed the nucleus of the east side of the settlement; because of their background they soon called it Nieuw Nijverdal, but this was later known as the Monarch district.

The large Postman family, meanwhile, lived in a tent on the edge of Macleod for the summer while Jan found a job with a government bridge-building crew. He worked on the traffic bridge at Macleod, at Pincher Creek, and then on one at Morley, west of Calgary. His family spent the winter at Morley along the Bow River in a dug-out with a roof of driftwood covered by hay and dirt. To satisfy homestead requirements the first year, Postman hired Veldhuis to break thirty-three acres on his homestead in October and November. In April 1905 the family finally moved onto their homestead. Because of this year of work, Postman acculturated more quickly to Canadian society than others in the group.[35]

After arriving in Alberta, Aldus continued to send letters back home to the *Twentsch Volksblad*. He first described the journey to Alberta and then in ongoing letters he told the story of the pioneer experience and the development of the Dutch settlement over the next decade.[36]

THE TOUGH HOMESTEADING YEARS (1903–05)

After filing on their homesteads, the first thing these early Dutch settlers did was to buy two or more horses from local ranchers who lived along the river. These horses then had to be broken before they would pull a wagon or plough.

The next task was to build simple shacks on their homesteads. The one constructed by Hendrikus Veldhuis was typical of the shacks of the early Dutch settlers. In later years his daughter Gertrude described what she experienced as a nine-year-old when her family first took up residence on the homestead:

> My father bought a wagon, some lumber and fence posts and left early in the morning to travel the fifteen miles to our land. When he got there, he measured a piece of land 12 feet by 12 feet and put fence posts around it. Then he nailed boards all around it and after that the roof went on, without shingles of course. That would have to be fixed later.

35 See Hofman, *Strength of Their Years*, for the engaging story of the Postman family's pioneer experiences.
36 Evert Aldus (later known as Edward) and his family moved to Colorado in 1914 and later to Michigan, where he returned to teaching. He retired in Holland, MI, and died on 1 June 1948.

A day or two later Veldhuis moved his family to the homestead from the ter Telgtes where they had been staying:

> We arrived at our cabin in the late afternoon. It was getting windy and cold. Before anything else could be done my father cut an opening in the west wall for a door and a hole in the roof for the stove pipe. Then the stove was carried in, set up, and a fire started with cow chips. Our first home had neither a floor nor a window.... Can you imagine five children and two parents living in a twelve by twelve shack? There was a bench through the middle to sit on, the beds were against the north wall, and the stove stood in the southeast corner. The table was against the west wall and the south wall had a small window. This was our home for three years.[37]

Towards fall Veldhuis ploughed some furrows of sod near the shack and the whole family helped stack them around the boards of the shack right up to the roof, in order to provide insulation for the winter. Not all homesteaders put sod around their shacks; some simply put a layer of tarpaper over the boards to seal off the cracks.

At first the settlers fetched their water from nearby sloughs. Then they hauled it in wooden barrels from the river. The first well on the east side of the settlement was dug on the Veldhuis homestead. The other settlers hauled their water from there until they had their own wells.

As soon as they could, these homesteaders also began to plough up a few acres of prairie so that they could plant crops and a garden. But the summer of 1904 was dry and for three months the sod was too hard to plough. According to homestead records, in 1904 the Dutch settlers broke a total of 473 acres on their homesteads; Jan ter Telgte did the most – 60 acres – but on 11 of 28 homesteads in the settlement no breaking was done. That first year only 146 acres were planted to crop. Newly broken sod, however, was rough and unproductive. It had to be disced many times to make the soil fine. And the sod needed time to decompose, so only a full year after the prairie was first broken could one expect to receive a decent crop. For these

---

37 Gertrude (Veldhuis) Hofman, "I Remember as a Child," in *Sons of Wind*, 38–41. Written in 1970, this account presents a vivid recollection of the Veldhuis family's first year of pioneer experiences on the homestead.

reasons there was hardly any crop that first year. Since these settlers were not able to break much of their land before the summer of 1904, the crops were still meagre in 1905. Yet, there was cause for hope – earlier settlers in the area were getting good crops.

So the Dutch homesteaders had to eek out a subsistence living until the harvest of 1906. They grew what garden vegetables and potatoes they could. For most, whatever savings they had were spent on purchasing horses, harnesses, lumber, a wagon, a plough, a disc, and household necessities such as a stove. When their savings were depleted, they had to buy basic food and supplies on credit from trusting merchants in Leavings and Macleod. To earn a bit of money, some of the men took seasonal jobs with local ranchers or found work with a nearby railroad crew.

Later in 1904 more newcomers from the United States joined the settlement, especially from the Dutch settlements in Manhattan, Montana, Vesper, Wisconsin, and northwest Iowa. In May or June Roelof and Dina Van Dijk and their family arrived from Midland Park, New Jersey, to join their relatives the Jan ter Telgte family. In June the Geert and Klaassien Venhuizen family, relatives of George Dijkema, arrived from Manhattan. In September Teunis Bode and Thys Dekker from Vesper came to check out homesteads and then settled in November. They were the first of a number of single men and families who would come from Vesper over the next few years. Garrit Willemsen (my great-grandfather) filed on an abandoned homestead in November and arrived with his wife Hendrika and family from Manhattan the following February.

Also in September 1904 the first of a group of newcomers from Iowa came to claim homesteads. Brothers Leendert and Bastiaan Koole, part of a large farm family at Sheldon, Iowa, had spent three years working and seeking farming opportunities in the west, especially in Washington and Oregon. In the spring of 1904 they worked for ranchers in the Pincher Creek area of Alberta; then in September they filed on homesteads on the east side of the Dutch settlement and also bought several quarters of C & E Railway land. After spending the winter back in Iowa, they, with their brother Arie, returned to settle in March 1905 with two railway cars full of livestock and machinery.

Beginning in 1905 some related families from northwest Iowa settled south of the Oldman River to form a new Macleod branch of the Dutch settlement (later known as the Pearce district). In April Walter and Abel Vander Burgh came from Hull, Iowa (where they knew the Koole brothers) to check out land and claimed homesteads in this district for themselves and their brother Pieter. About the same time Gerard Schuitema, who had just arrived from Groningen in March, seems to have worked for local farmers of this district before he took up a homestead there in July. In December Johannes Gunst, a new arrival from Vesper, also claimed a homestead there. Then in early 1906 Pieter and Annette Vander Burgh, their family, and brother-in-law Jan Koole (cousin of the other Kooles) arrived from Iowa. In the next several years other families from northwest Iowa joined them – the Jacob and Leentje Leeuwerik family, and Jan and Piechia Zoeteman family[38] – along with other newcomers from the Netherlands and Nebraska.

Almost from the beginning there were attempts to develop a worship life in the settlement. After the first informal service led by Withage the first Sunday after the ter Telgte and Withage families arrived, some of the families gathered in homestead shacks on both the east and west sides of the settlement to hold home worship services. Though these Dutch settlers were from several different church denominations, almost all were Reformed in background. Most who immigrated directly from the Netherlands were of a Hervormde Kerk background, the mainline Reformed church in the Old Country. Others were from the Gereformeerde Kerken, the result of a nineteenth-century union of two conservative secessions from the more liberal Hervormde Kerk. Some of the settlers from the United States were from the Reformed Church in America (RCA), but more of them were members of the Christian Reformed Church (CRC), which had seceded from the Reformed Church in 1857. Then too there were some settlers who were not churchgoers, though they usually had some sort of Reformed upbringing.

The first visit from a minister occurred when the Jan ter Telgte and Postman families wanted to have their infants baptized. Since they were both members of the Manhattan CRC – Postman had transferred the family's membership there though they had never been to Manhattan – ter Telgte requested a visit from the minister of the Manhattan church, Rev. James Holwerda. In May 1905 he visited the southern Alberta community for two weeks, led services in homes on both sides of the settlement, and baptized the children. In August a Christian Reformed home missionary also visited, and on November 16 a Christian Reformed church was formally organized. Called the Nijverdal CRC, services were held once on Sundays at the Rocky

---

38 On 5 May 1915 Jan (John) Zoeteman was shot to death by a neighbour at Pearce in a quarrel about a discipline case at the local country school. See the *Macleod Spectator* (7 May 1915), *Lethbridge Daily Herald* (7, 11, and 18 May 1915), and *De Grondwet* (29 June 1915). A letter from Kipp in the latter paper reported: "Everyone is mourning the death of J. Soetema [Zoeteman], who was robbed of life by an assassin. Soetema was known as a decent and well-behaved man, and he leaves behind a wife and five children. Cocksen [D. F. Coxson] the murderer is known to be a disreputable person and already earlier he was accused of terrible things. We hope that his punishment will not be delayed because the crime was premeditated."

Coulee school on the west side for the first year, and twice when a visiting minister or seminary student was present. However, since the settlement was so spread out, the distance by horse and wagon to the Rocky Coulee school was a real burden, especially for east-siders. The east and west sides of the church were then permitted to worship separately, but when a minister or student visited, combined services were held in turn in the Rocky Coulee and Finley schools.

When the congregation was established, there were 40 charter members, including baptized members – about a third of the settlement at the time. However, there were many other "friends" of the congregation who attended the services in these first years. Some of them later became Christian Reformed members, but many others were of a Hervormd background and never joined – an omen of division that was to come.

THE YEARS OF GROWTH AND PROSPERITY (1906–09)

Beginning in 1906 most of the Dutch homesteaders had four good years of harvest, allowing them to move beyond the scarcity and struggle of the early years. By 1907, or a year or two thereafter, most of these homesteaders had proved up on their homesteads, having fulfilled the three-year requirements. In the end, fifty-seven of the sixty-six Dutch homesteaders (86 per cent) received patent on their homesteads, well above the general average of about 55 per cent for Alberta.

So now they owned their own land. At this point a number of them also began to buy an extra quarter or half-section of land – usually the C & E Railroad land that lay between the homestead sections. By the end of 1908 most farmers in the settlement had their homestead land broken and with the increased acreage they also harvested larger crops.

With greater prosperity most families made improvements to or put additions onto their original homestead shacks. By 1907 this trend is evident. Then in 1909 the Rense Nijhoff and Tijmen Hofman families were the first in the settlement to move into larger regular houses; others followed. In a number of cases families put up a good-sized barn, replacing a sod stable, before constructing a new house.

The 1906 Census of Alberta, enumerated in July of that year, lists 149 persons of Dutch descent in the community. This included 21 families and 28 singles, living in 48 separate households.

There was one trying experience in this period, the severe winter of 1906–07, but it did not prove to be a setback for the homesteaders. Instead of the usual Chinook winds that melted the winter snow, frequent snowstorms during that winter left a thick layer of snow on the ground from mid-November to mid-February. Temperatures were extremely cold, and brief thaws only left a frozen crust on the surface. This was a disaster for the many cattle that still ranged across the open prairie. They could not reach the prairie grass beneath the snow, and thousands died of starvation as they drifted in long lines from the north with feet cut and bleeding. This marked the end of the ranching era in this part of southern Alberta. The homesteaders were glad to be rid of the menace of range cows breaking into their crops and hay stacks, and the melting of the winter snow provided good moisture for their crops in 1907.

Meanwhile the broader area was also experiencing a burst of prosperity. Homesteads were all taken up by families or single men, and the quarters that could be purchased between the homesteads were being settled. The growing economy created by this increase in rural population led to the construction of new railway lines, and that in turn created new towns.

In 1906 the CPR purchased land for a new line between Lethbridge and Macleod which would replace the old high-maintenance line that wound through the coulees south of Lethbridge, over a wooden trestle bridge on the St. Mary River, and across the Blood Indian Reserve and the Belly River. While the high-level bridge was being built at Lethbridge, the new track was laid eastward from Macleod, and in the spring of 1908 construction of the track-bed began on the southern edge of the east side of the Dutch settlement.

When lots for the new town site of Monarch were sold at that location in July, a number of buildings were constructed immediately and the new town was born. A couple of months earlier the hamlet of Pearce began further west across the river with the building of a station on a siding on the same line. After the high-level bridge at Lethbridge was completed in June 1909, regular railway service began at Monarch in December. This was a major advantage for the Dutch farmers in the Monarch district; no longer did they have to make the wearisome day-long trip to haul their grain down the coulees and across the river to Lethbridge.

In the fall of 1908 a station was also constructed on this line at Kipp. This was the beginning of the new Aldersyde line that would run north from Kipp to Calgary. As this line was extended as far as Carmangay in 1909, a site for the new town of Noble (later changed to Nobleford in 1913) was designated on this line in May. It lay on the eastern edge of the Dutch settlement. Further north on the same line, lots for the town of Barons were sold at public auction in July; weeks earlier some eager merchants had already constructed buildings nearby to be moved onto the town site.

The church also benefited from the growing prosperity. Because of the distance both the east and west sides of the Nijverdal Christian Reformed Church had been worshiping separately; now each side decided to build its own sanctuary. The west side was the first to complete its small church building in February 1909. The east side dedicated its somewhat larger building in May. Both were constructed in the countryside in the midst of their respective settlements.

Once they had their own church buildings, the two sides of the Nijverdal congregation made plans to call a pastor. They decided to share a pastor since neither side was large enough to support a pastor on its own. But there was a bit of tension about where the pastor would live, on the east or west side. Finally, the Granum side went ahead and built a parsonage next to its church. It was sufficiently completed by the spring of 1910 so that a call was extended to Rev. Gilbert Haan from Michigan. When he declined, it was a big disappointment to the church.

In these years a second church was established on the Monarch side of the settlement – a congregation of the Reformed Church in America. In the spring of 1907 the Tijmen and Heiltje Hofman family arrived from Westfield, North Dakota, where they had been members of the Reformed Church. Hofman and other settlers from a Hervormde church background, who attended but did not join the Nijverdal CRC, took the initiative to request the Westfield RCA to help them start a church of this denomination. In early August 1909 the Reformed church was organized.[39] A year later this congregation put up their own church building, a half mile down the country road from that of the Monarch CRC. The ecumenical spirit that marked the early pioneering years was now gone as the Reformed and Christian Reformed went their separate ways, following the typical pattern in Dutch communities across North America.

Another sign of prosperity in this period was the fact that some of the early settlers began to travel. Several of them made visits back to the United States or the Netherlands. In November 1909 the Gerrit Bode family and two others left for the winter months to visit relatives at Vesper, Wisconsin. Toward the end of the same month seven men returned to the Netherlands to visit relatives or to seek wives. These visitors came with personal reports about prosperous farming in Alberta and convinced many newcomers to immigrate there. In mid-February 1910 the Bode family returned to Monarch

---

39 In letters in this collection the Monarch Reformed Church is often called the "Dutch Reformed Church," an earlier name of the Reformed Church in America denomination.

with four new families – relatives and acquaintances from Vesper. These families purchased land in the Monarch district and almost all of them joined the local Christian Reformed Church, a real boost for that congregation.

Then in March 1910 the seven travelers to the Netherlands returned, the three bachelors with new wives, but they were also accompanied by about sixty new immigrants from Nijverdal and fifteen from elsewhere in the Netherlands. Most of these new immigrants affiliated with the Reformed Church. They were able to find work in the district as hired men or carpenters for the summer, but since homesteads were gone in the area they had to look elsewhere for cheap land. They were still able to obtain homesteads near Carlstadt northwest of Medicine Hat, and in September most of these new immigrants took up residence there. So a new Dutch settlement was formed at Carlstadt, but the climate there was arid and eventually these people dispersed to other places after years of crop failure.[40]

THE YEARS OF ADVERSITY (1910–12)

The good years were followed by three years when the Dutch settlers received little or no crops. 1910 was a year of drought. Since the previous July there was no rain of any significance. Much of the grain did not even germinate in the spring, and there was no grass for the cattle. When the first rains came in August, it was too late. There was virtually no harvest. Established farmers had enough of a cushion to endure the loss, but it was devastating for the newcomers.

The drought also had an immediate impact on the Nijverdal CRC. After Rev. Haan declined their call in the spring, the church decided in August not to go forward with another call but to wait for a more opportune time when it was financially feasible. In February 1911 the Nijverdal congregation dissolved and reorganized as two separate churches – the Monarch CRC and Granum CRC. This was a natural development due to the distance, but the small size of both made it virtually impossible for either to afford their own pastor. It would be early 1914 before another call was made.

---

40 Carlstadt was a small town on the CPR line about forty miles northwest of Medicine Hat. The actual district of this Dutch settlement, about fifteen miles northeast of Carlstadt, was first known as Nijverdal and then New Holland. Several letters sent from Nijverdal (near Carlstadt) appeared in the 17 Dec. 1910, 11 Feb., 17 June, 9 Dec. 1911, and 17 Feb. 1912 issues of the *Twentsch Volksblad*. Beginning in 1912 a correspondent from Carlstadt sent regular letters to *De Grondwet* – the issues of 28 May, 2 July, 23 July, 1 Oct., 12 Nov., 24 Dec. 1912, 7 Jan., 18 Feb., 13 May, 22 July, 26 Aug., 2 Oct., 9 Dec., 30 Dec. 1913, and 10 Mar., 24 Mar., 21 April, 2 June, 11 Aug. 1914. When the town's name was later changed to Alderson in 1915, letters sent from Alderson appeared in the issues of 7 Mar., 16 May, 18 July 1916, 19 June 1917, and 2 July 1918. A letter from New Holland is found in the 22 Jan. 1918 issue. A Reformed church was established in the Carlstadt settlement in 1912. When this settlement dispersed in 1925, some of these settlers returned to Monarch.

The year 1911 started out well. There was plenty of rain in the spring. Though there was some problem with wind and cutworms, crops were reseeded and they looked good. Then on 15 August a crushing hailstorm swept through the settlement from the northwest. Crops in the centre of the Monarch district were almost all destroyed; the hail completely wiped out those near the town on the southeast side. It only spared some fields on the northeastern edge. Most gardens were devastated. The Granum settlers were not hit as badly, but a couple of families there lost everything as well. Whatever grain was left standing ripened late and suffered from early frosts, and an early snow storm covered what was still not threshed, so the quality of the grain was poor.

In 1912 the main enemy was the cutworm. The year began with a dry spring, so the crops came up unevenly. Then cutworms cleaned off large patches of crop. One day a stiff Chinook wind shelled out a lot of ripened grain, and an early frost also took its toll. In the end the harvest was very uneven – some received a fairly good yield and others next to nothing – and a lot of it was of poor quality. The price of wheat was also low that year.

With the successive crop failures, some families became disillusioned about prospects in southern Alberta and left the settlement. The country storekeeper Albert Rutgers sold his homestead where he had his store and returned to the Netherlands with his wife Francisca and family in the spring of 1911. Anthonie and Maria Gunst and their family, recent arrivals in 1910, returned to Vesper at the end of 1911. The Leendert and Gerrit Bode families, and Gerrit's father-in-law Klaas Van Schuur, all moved to Lynden, Washington, in the spring of 1912. Early that year the Geert Venhuizen family also returned to Manhattan, Montana. Jan Postman explored the possibility of moving his large family to the Peace River area. In 1910 he set out to scout for land there, but trails to this remote region in the north were impassable and he had to turn back. In 1912 he went again and selected land; most of the family made the move north in the fall of 1913. These families left for a variety of reasons – the Venhuizens wanted to send their children to a Christian school, Jan Postman had been excommunicated in 1912 from the Monarch CRC and he sought farming opportunities for his growing batch of sons – but the crop failures of these years were certainly a major factor. With families leaving, more land was available and land prices dropped.

These crop failures also led to a direct decline of the rural towns that so depended on the prosperity of the farmers. The town of Monarch that had so quickly mushroomed into existence now began to lose some of its services. The doctor, druggist, and a number of merchants left, leaving the town half depopulated with many empty buildings.

Another victim of the bad years was a proposed railroad that was to run through the Granum district. In the fall of 1911 the Canadian Northern Railway surveyed for a new line to run from Macleod to Calgary parallel to and in competition with the C & E track. It was to lie seven and a half miles east of Granum and a half-mile east of the Granum CRC. A new town site, called Stroud, was to be located a mile and a half northeast of the church. The Canadian Northern constructed a grade for this line in 1912, but later scuttled the project; the track was never laid and Stroud never became a town.

THE YEARS OF RENEWED STABILITY (1913–14)

The Dutch settlement was able to rebound in the following years which usually brought better harvests. In 1913 the crops were excellent, and land prices were again on the rise. 1914 started with a wet spring, but then came a dry summer and crop yields were down. Yet the advent of World War I at the end of July brought a rise in wheat prices to over a dollar a bushel.

These years were followed by three good years that brought prosperity back to the district. There was a bumper crop in 1915 with yields of 45 to 65 bushels of wheat per acre, and crops were also excellent in the next two years. Not until 1919 was there another dry year.

THE LETTERS

By far the majority of the letters in this collection were published in Dutch-language newspapers, both in the Netherlands and the United States. Some of the letters in the old-country newspapers focused on homesteading opportunities in western Canada and were written by interested parties and promoters especially for the sake of prospective immigrants; others were written by the new settlers in Alberta to describe pioneer life to the folks back home in Nijverdal.

The early Alberta settlers also sent letters to Dutch newspapers in the United States, to community newspapers as well as church papers. *De Grondwet,* the main paper of the Dutch community of Holland, Michigan, had the largest circulation of any Dutch-American newspaper. *De Volksvriend,* published in Orange City, Iowa, was the main newspaper of the northwest Iowa Dutch settlement. Both of these papers sought readers in the many Dutch communities throughout North America, and both developed a network of correspondents from these settlements. Such correspondents were expected to send in news from their community on a regular basis – in most cases it was several times a year. These correspondent letters became a major feature of these newspapers and sometimes extended over several pages. In this way these newspapers served as information centres that helped link together the many scattered Dutch immigrant settlements into one large ethnic network.[41]

The Schilstra Letters

Rev. Sybrandus A. Schilstra was an early and avid promoter of Dutch immigration to western Canada; he certainly stimulated the interest of the Nijverdal immigrants to Alberta. Schilstra was born in Ijlst, Friesland, on 31 August 1840, and as a young man he prepared for a missionary career in a school in Rotterdam. After being ordained, he served as a missionary to Java from 1870 to 1881. Then, due to sickness, he returned to the Netherlands where he promoted the cause of foreign missions and edited a mission paper. In 1892 Schilstra and his family immigrated to the United States, where he became the pastor of the First Reformed Church of Rochester, New York, from 1892 to 1901. He then retired to the Garfield/Passaic district in New Jersey, but made occasional pastoral visits to serve small groups of Hollanders in Maryland. After his wife died in July 1903, he moved to West Sayville on Long Island, where his son Elbert was a Reformed church pastor.[42] At Passaic and West Sayville Schilstra continued to be a frequent contributor to several newspapers, among them *De Grondwet,* for which he wrote columns on various religious themes.

Schilstra was also a regular correspondent to the *Nieuwsblad van Friesland,* a major Frisian newspaper that was published twice weekly in Heerenveen. He wrote letters reporting news about the Dutch in North America. In December 1902, however, he began to promote western Canada as a better destination for Dutch immigrants. From then until August 1905 Schilstra wrote twenty-three letters and articles for this newspaper, extolling opportunities in Canada.[43] All are simply signed S.A.S.

41 Donald Sinnema, "Dutch American Newspapers and the Network of Early Dutch Immigrant Communities," in *Dutch Enterprise: Alive and Well in North America,* ed. Larry Wagenaar and Robert Swierenga (Holland, MI: Association for the Advancement of Dutch American Studies, 2000), 43–56.

42 Information on Schilstra's life is found in the *Acts and Proceedings of the General Synod of the Reformed Church in America, June 1917* (New York: Board of Publication and Bible-School Work, 1917), 251–52. Later Schilstra moved to Preston, Maryland, to serve the small Dutch community there, and then to Telford, Pennsylvania, where he died on 26 July 1916.

43 *Nieuwsblad van Friesland,* 31 Dec. 1902, 21 Feb., 11 Apr., 9 May, 23 May, 13 June, 27 June, 15 July, 15 Aug., 2 Sept., 19 Sept., 28 Nov., 19 Dec., 25 Dec. 1903, 16 Jan., 5 Mar., 2 Apr., 9 July, 16 July, 13 Aug., 12 Nov., 19 Nov. 1904, and 23 Aug. 1905. The items of 31 Dec. 1902, 23 May, 13 June, 27 June, 19 Sept. 1903, and 19 Nov. 1904 are included in this collection.

In promoting Canada Schilstra does not seem to have been motivated by any personal gain. With a pastoral heart for his immigrating countrymen he appears to have been genuinely concerned for their best welfare, and so he researched opportunities in Canada and offered his best advice.

> What I offer is but a short summary of the many things that came to my attention about Canada, after months of investigation and a lot of study, but everything is faithful and true. To be sure, it is partly a hobby, but had I felt no compassion for my countrymen I certainly would have lacked the incentive to do constant study in many libraries and to read a mass of English periodicals. With care and without haste I have done this, with no self-interest at all, in order to possibly awaken my countrymen and give them the prospect of a better destiny.[44]

Having seen many immigrants disembark at New York and remain in the nearby Dutch settlement at Paterson, only to be locked into dead-end factory jobs, Schilstra saw the free homesteads of western Canada as a grand opportunity for new immigrants. He himself did not visit the Canadian west, and it is not clear what piqued his interest in the country. Perhaps the fact that his son Dr. A. J. Schilstra had gone to medical school in Toronto for five years was an influence.

For his information about Canada, Schilstra drew upon a variety of sources besides articles in newspapers and periodicals.[45] He mainly used official government documents that he received from the Department of the Interior in Ottawa. He also consulted library books and atlases about

---

44 S.A.S., "Canada," *Nieuwsblad van* Friesland, 15 August 1903. In an earlier letter Schilstra had also commented on his motives: "I have already sent a letter about Canada to Friesland's *Nieuwsblad*, and, if the editor approves, I hope to write a series of articles about Canada. These articles will form one whole and may be very important for immigrants. I must emphatically add here that I have no personal stake in it, and I do it only to make clear what is unknown. Also, I make no recommendation, but simply point out how things stand; and I do this on the basis of official documents published by the government. Convinced that there are many fine farmers and others now falling on hard times, who can become well off here, it is a pleasant task for me to be able to offer some guidance" (21 February 1903). The articles he refers to were the three-part series, "To Canada: Trustworthy Hints for Emigrants," published in May and June; they are included in this collection. Aldus and others also considered Schilstra's information reliable. See Aldus letter, 3 October 1903. In a letter to the *Nieuwsblad van Friesland* (31 December 1902), H. R. Rijpkema from Minnesota commented, "Insofar as I can judge concerning the diverse advice given from America, that of Mr. S.A.S. is certainly the most reliable."

45 For example, in July 1904 Schilstra referred to a six-part series on Canada in the *Grand Rapids Herald*, written by Rev. Charles Aubrey Eaton of Cleveland, formerly a Toronto journalist. These articles, which appeared in the *Herald* on 25 and 27 February, 3, 7, 10, and 14 March 1904, covered Canada's natural resources, its system of government, Ontario, the Northwest and its settlement, relations with the United States, and Canada's future.

Canada. He gathered testimonials, and later, when some Dutch immigrants began to settle in Canada, he contacted them to gather information on their perceptions of the country and its opportunities. Thus, after George Dijkema started sending letters to *De Grondwet,* Schilstra took up correspondence with him, published part of it, and even encouraged Dijkema to send letters to the *Nieuwsblad van Friesland.*[46]

Schilstra's letters offered a general introduction to Canada and so they often dealt with broad features of the country, its geography, climate, economy, living costs, homesteading opportunities, etc. He also offered practical advice to help immigrants adequately prepare. As for a specific destination, Schilstra considered the western prairies better than Manitoba because of the milder climate. He suggested the areas around Prince Albert, Regina, and Edmonton, but his preference was the Edmonton district. To alleviate the fears of prospective immigrants about languishing alone in the wilderness, Schilstra advised them to go together and form a colony. But they should first send ahead some capable young men to scout out the land and learn about farming conditions; then the families could follow.

The Aldus Letters

While Schilstra was definitely an enthusiastic promoter of immigration to western Canada, Evert Aldus was more cautious. Writing with a more objective bent, he not only described the positives, but he also did not hesitate to complain about certain aspects of homesteading in Canada.

His first letter was an inquiry to the *Nieuwsblad van Friesland,* with several questions for Schilstra – whom he only knew as S.A.S. – that had not been addressed in the latter's earlier letters and articles about Canada.[47]

Then in the course of the next decade Aldus wrote many letters to the *Twentsch Volksblad,* a local newspaper published at Almelo, near his hometown of Nijverdal. Reflecting his background as a schoolteacher, his letters are very descriptive, well written, and usually lengthy – some were printed in instalments. In great detail Aldus vividly describes the preparations, the journey to Canada, and the pioneer experience in Alberta – including the crops, the weather, the farm implements, the development of new railways and towns, early church life, and many other topics.[48]

---

46 See letters of 19 November 1904, 21 Jan., 6 May, and 27 May 1905.

47 See Aldus letter, 8 August 1903. Schilstra replied in the 19 September issue.

48 In 1918 Evert Aldus's younger brother G[erardus] A. Aldus published a children's book, *De Wildernis In: Twee Hollandsche Jongens in Canada* (Nijkerk: G. F. Callenbach, n.d.), which portrays two young men immigrating with others to Alberta in the spring of 1904 and their pioneer experience in the Monarch

In his first group of letters to the *Twentsch Volksblad,* appearing from August to November 1903, Aldus reported on the information he had gathered about Canada as he was making preparations to emigrate. His purpose was to share this information with those who were thinking about emigrating so that they would know what to expect. He denied that he was recruiting, but that was no doubt an effect. The first four items consist largely of a lengthy quotation of the Schilstra article printed in the June 27 issue of the *Nieuwsblad van Friesland.*

In this period before emigrating Aldus also entered into an exchange with Hendrikus Zandbergen of Enschede. Zandbergen had earlier been part of the ill-fated Dutch settlement in Colorado, established by an unscrupulous land company, and he wanted to warn Aldus and his readers about the possibility of similar deception in Canada. Aldus assured his readers that Canada was not Colorado, and that the Canadian government controlled the distribution of new land, thus reducing the possibility of exploitation.[49]

After Aldus arrived in Alberta in April 1904, he continued to write regularly to the *Twentsch Volksblad.* In these letters he aimed to share the immigrant experience in fine detail with those back home, including prospective immigrants. His first three letters describe the ocean journey and the train trip across Canada. Over the next decade Aldus sent twenty-seven more letters – some appearing in instalments – about pioneer life in Alberta. Some of these letters offer a year-end summary of what had happened in the Alberta settlement in the previous year.

Especially during the hardships of the first years, Aldus sometimes wrote in a rather pessimistic tone. He complained, for example, about the dirty train stations across Canada and the insufferable southwest wind that almost always blew and spoiled everything. The editor noted that Aldus had a reputation of having a dismal mood in cold or windy weather.[50]

The negative tone of his early letters initiated an exchange with Jan Hendrik ter Telgte, who took issue with Aldus's assessment of pioneer life in Alberta. These former Nijverdalers lived just fifteen miles apart in the

---

district. Though this is a fictionalized account, it is closely based on many of the Aldus letters. The story is told from the perspective of fictional Klaas Goekoop, who in real life was Willem Stotijn, Evert's brother-in-law. In later years Evert's son Paul Aldus, an English professor, wrote "Short and Simple Annals," a more literary account of his parents' immigration experience, published in G. H. Stotijn, *Loten van één Stam: 200 Jaar Hotijn-Stotijn, een speurtoch naar het verleden* (Drukkerskollektief Geule, 1996), 239–44.

49 See Zandbergen letters, 10 and 31 Oct.ober 1903, and Aldus's replies in the 17 October and 7 November issues. A final letter from Zandbergen in the 28 Nov. issue (not part of this collection) deals with the problem of maintaining viable church life in the small, far flung Dutch settlements in North America.

50 See Aldus letter, 15 Oct. 1904.

settlement, but this debate went on for three months of 1904 in the *Volksblad* back in the Netherlands.[51] It ranged over a variety of topics, from the treatment of immigrants on Canadian trains to the wind and weather conditions to the loneliness of the prairies and its lack of beauty.

Aldus also sent a number of letters to *De Volksvriend,* the Dutch newspaper from Orange City, Iowa. These are shorter than his *Twentsch Volksblad* letters and contain more personal references. Six can be identified as his,[52] but there are no doubt other unsigned letters from Monarch that were from his hand.

The Dijkema Letters

From the time he first arrived in Alberta George Dijkema was a regular correspondent to *De Grondwet,* the newspaper from Holland, Michigan. In the first decade he sent twenty-one letters to this paper, reporting on news from the Alberta settlement.

In contrast to Aldus, Dijkema tends to paint a rosy picture of life in the settlement.[53] Addressing the assumption of many Americans that it is so cold in Canada, he pointed out more than once that this is not really true in southern Alberta – a few days of cold are usually followed by a warm Chinook. In one letter he even claimed that "British Columbia has a tropical climate, and Alberta has taken over something of that" – an overstatement that prompted a retort from the editor.[54] Dijkema regularly reported the arrival of newcomers into the settlement and pointed out every sign of growth in order to portray the image of a growing and thriving Dutch community. In doing so he clearly sought to attract new Dutch settlers from the United States; on occasion he explicitly invited others to come and join the settlement where there was still opportunity to own fertile land.

In a similar vein Dijkema also sent a number of letters to *De Volksvriend,* the Dutch paper from northwest Iowa.[55] These letters have the same character and motive.

His three letters to the *Nieuwsblad van Friesland,* written at the urging of Schilstra, have a more general character. Instead of reporting news of

---

51 See ter Telgte letters 8 and 22 October and 12 November 1904. Aldus replied in the 3 and 31 December issues. In the 29 October issue George Dijkema also spoke out against Aldus's pessimism.

52 See letters of 16 Dec. 1909, 10 Feb., 23 June, 3 Nov. 1910, 26 Jan. 1911, and 16 Jan. 1913.

53 This is also evident in the one letter Dijkema sent to the *Twentsch Volksblad* (29 Oct. 1904) to challenge Aldus's pessimism.

54 See letter of 27 September 1904. This was before Dijkema experienced his first winter in Alberta.

55 See letters of 23 Mar., 15 June, 24 Aug., 21 Dec. 1905, 31 May, 20 Dec. 1906, and 9 May 1907. Not all of these are signed, but Dijkema is the probable writer.

the settlement, they describe various aspects of farming in Alberta, the climate, the availability of railway land, and the possibility of pre-empting a homestead. Two personal letters of Dijkema are cited as well in this newspaper.[56]

Dijkema also wrote some letters to *De Wachter,* the official weekly of the Christian Reformed Church.[57] These letters focus on church life, and deal with such matters as building the first church and the parsonage, visits by pastors and students, calling a minister, and the split of the Nijverdal church into two congregations.

Other Letters to De Grondwet and De Volksvriend

Most of the correspondent letters in *De Grondwet* and *De Volksvriend* are unsigned or are simply signed "Corr." (Correspondent). Hence it is not usually possible to identify the writers. The contents suggest that Aldus and Dijkema wrote a number of them, but many remain impossible to identify, partly because there was more than one writer from the Lethbridge (Monarch) district. Till 1909 Lethbridge was the address of those on the east side of the settlement. One Lethbridge correspondent to *De Grondwet* was from Vesper, Wisconsin, and of a Christian Reformed background – probably Teunis Bode.[58] Another was Jan Geleynse.[59] There may have been others. Tijmen Hofman sent one occasional letter.[60]

A few of the letters to *De Grondwet* report local news from the Macleod branch of the settlement south of the Oldman River. There are five such letters from 1907–08; the writer is not known.[61] In later years several letters appeared in *De Volksvriend* with brief news items from the Barons district. Arie Versluys was the writer.[62]

Letters to Church Papers

In addition to letters in the Dutch community newspapers, a number of letters were sent to church papers related to the Christian Reformed and Reformed churches. They report on developments in church life in these two church communities within the settlement.

---

56 In the 19 November 1904 issue of the *Nieuwsblad van Friesland* Schilstra cited a personal letter from Dijkema. Another is cited in the 13 January 1906 issue by E. Fennema from Illinois.
57 See letters of 24 Feb. 1909, 5 Jan., 7 Dec. 1910, and 12 Feb. 1913.
58 See letters of 5 Dec. 1905, 2 Jan., 23 Jan., 20 Feb., and 8 May 1906.
59 See letter of 4 December 1906.
60 See letter of 24 March 1908.
61 See letters of 16 July, 10 Sept., 31 Dec. 1907, 24 Mar. and 9 June 1908.
62 See letters of 10 Aug., 21 Dec. 1911, 9 Oct. 1913, and 29 Jan. 1914.

Twenty such letters appeared in *De Wachter*, the official weekly of the Christian Reformed Church, published in Grand Rapids. Apart from George Dijkema, other local settlers who sent church news to this paper were Gerrit Withage, Geert Venhuizen, and Roelof Kooi, as well as the young men Chris Schiebout and Jan Dekker, who commented on the Young People's Society. In addition, there were reports by home missionaries Meindert Botbijl and Menno Borduin, Rev. John Vander Mey of Manhattan, Montana, and seminary students Jacob Weersing and Karel Fortuin on their pastoral visits to the settlement.[63] Borduin also sent a report to *The Banner*, the English language weekly that served the CRC denomination.[64]

Two letters also appeared in *De Hope*, a church paper that served Reformed Church people in the west and Midwest. Rev. Barend Lammers reported on his visit to organize the Monarch Reformed Church, and Tijmen Hofman, an elder of this congregation, sent a later report.[65]

Personal letters

Besides the printed letters, this collection also includes a number of personal letters of Dutch people in the settlement. They present a more intimate glimpse of life as it was experienced by the early immigrants and settlers. Klaas Schuiling offers some insight into the very beginnings of the settlement. The letters of Hilje Mulder and Beert Nauta provide detailed travel accounts of the immigrant journey by ship and rail to Alberta. The Venhuizen, Dekker, and Poelman letters reveal interesting circumstances in the life of several pioneer families. Geert Venhuizen casts light on the personal character of the various Leavings settlers.[66]

Among the personal letters is a group of eleven letters from three related families in the Alberta settlement – the Bode, Hartkoorn, and Van der Werff families.[67] Leendert Bode wrote four of these; his son Teunis two. Gerrit

---

63 See letters to *De Wachter*, 14 June, 13 Dec. 1905, 10 Jan., 12 Sept., 12 Dec., 26 Dec. 1906, 24 Apr. 1907, 24 Feb., 21 July, 29 Sept. 1909, 5 Jan., 3 Aug., 7 Dec. 1910, 26 Apr., 8 Nov., 28 Nov. 1911, 13 Mar. 1912, and 12 Feb. 1913.
64 See letter of 23 March 1911.
65 See letters of 24 August 1909 and 28 June 1910.
66 See letters of 2 Aug. 1903, 25 Apr. 1907, 3 Jan., 22 May, 11 June 1908, 29 Aug., 29 Nov. 1909, 16 Sept., 26 Nov. 1910.
67 The original of the letter from Gerrit Hartkoorn to John Postman (late summer, 1912) is in the possession of Gertrude Hartkoorn of South Holland, IL. The originals of the following letters are in the possession of Barend Bode of Giessenburg, the Netherlands: Leendert Bode to Jan Bode, Lethbridge, 1 Mar. 1906; Leendert Bode to Jan Bode, Lethbridge, 27 Feb. 1907; Gerrit Hartkoorn to Jan Bode, Lethbridge, [December 1907]; Leendert Bode to Jan Bode, Lethbridge, 7 Feb. 1908; Teunis Bode to Jan Bode, Lethbridge, 3 Sept. 1908; Jabikje Hartkoorn to Jan Bode, Monarch, [Mar. 1910]; Leendert Bode to Jan Bode, Monarch, 15 Aug. 1910; Herbert Van der Werff to Jan Bode, Monarch, 16 Aug. 1910; Herbert Van der Werff to Jan Bode, [Granum], 9 May 1911; Teunis Bode to Jan Bode, Monarch, 7 Feb. 1912.

Hartkoorn wrote two; his wife Jabikje (a sister of Leendert Bode) wrote one. Herbert Van der Werff, a nephew of Leendert Bode and the Hartkoorns, wrote two. All but one of these letters were sent to the family of Jan Bode, a brother of Leendert and Jabikje, living on the family farm near Noordeloos in the province of Zuid-Holland. These letters provide a rare glimpse into the daily life of these related families. The Hartkoorn situation is interesting since Gerrit immigrated to Alberta in 1907 without his family; only three years later did his reluctant wife and two unmarried sons join him, and then they moved to Saskatchewan. In one letter Gerrit focuses on a family quarrel about a land sale. Van der Werff's letters offer the unique perspective of a single man working as a hired hand.

Unfortunately, none of the available printed letters from this community was written by a woman. So the women's perspective on pioneer life is rather invisible in this collection. One would wish there were letters about how the women went about their domestic duties, how they took care of the children, and how they coped with the loneliness of life on the prairies. The only exceptions are three personal letters, the two of Hilje Mulder and one of Jabikje Hartkoorn.

THE SIGNIFICANCE OF THIS COLLECTION

The year 2003 was the centennial of the origin of this first Dutch settlement in Alberta. This is a time to reflect historically on the beginnings of a significant Dutch presence in this province, at an important historical juncture – even before the province itself was born in 1905 – when the great land rush for free homesteads was opening up the Canadian west. The Dutch homesteaders of this settlement are part of the pioneer story. In its pioneer decade this community also became home to the first Christian Reformed church in Canada and the earliest still existing Reformed church in Canada.

The great majority of Dutch immigration to Canada occurred in the years after World War II, and the bulk of historical scholarship has focused on the post-war Dutch Canadian experience. The earlier Dutch in Canada have received some attention,[68] but the southern Alberta settlement deserves closer study. While the story of this community has been told, mostly from

---

68 See especially the works of De Vries and Krijff on the Winnipeg settlement, the first part of Herman Ganzevoort's *Bittersweet Land*, his *A Dutch Pioneer on the Prairies: The Letters of Willem De Gelder 1910–1913* (Toronto: University of Toronto Press, 1973), and his *The Last Illusion: Letters from Dutch Immigrants in the "Land of Opportunity," 1924–1930* (Calgary: University of Calgary Press, 1999). De Gelder was a homesteader in Saskatchewan.

later sources, by Tymen Hofman in *The Strength of Their Years,* it has not been told in the words of the Dutch pioneers themselves.

The letters of this collection are original sources from the founding decade of the settlement. Taken together these letters afford a wonderful insight into the early years of the Dutch settlement, as it developed from primitive homesteading conditions on the open prairie to a well-developed rural community.

The fact that there are so many letters and related documents just from the first decade makes possible a close look at the immigration and pioneer experience of these Dutch settlers, on a level of detail that is not often available. Especially the Aldus letters describe the immigrant experience in exquisite detail. The early Schilstra and Aldus letters reveal the actual sources of information used by the early Dutch immigrants to Alberta, sources that have been previously unnoticed. Also, the letters frequently mention when a new family first arrived in the settlement, so one can document the month, or even the day, of arrival for most of the early families. Though some details are mundane, even these help us understand the character of ordinary life as it was really experienced in the settlement.

The publication of these documents makes available for the first time letters that are highly inaccessible. In most cases the Dutch-language newspapers that printed most of the letters can be found only in one archives, in Michigan, Iowa, or the Netherlands. The personal letters are in family collections. All but five of the documents are originally in the Dutch language. By translating them I am making available primary source materials that should be of interest to scholars of Alberta history, pioneer history, prairie settlement, immigration history, Dutch-Canadian history, and Reformed church history, as well as to local history buffs, genealogists, and others.

One interesting feature of many of the letters is that they offer a distinctly Dutch perspective on pioneer life. This is evident, for example, in Aldus's comments on the lack of cleanliness in Canadian railway stations. Since he is writing to readers back in the Netherlands unfamiliar with conditions on the prairies, he also offers details and observations that would normally be assumed by Canadian writers.

The letters in this collection naturally fall into a preparatory phase and four periods in the course of the pioneer decade. Within this context the letters are presented in chronological order, even though this may at times interrupt a series of letters by one writer. The chronological sequence allows the letters themselves to tell the story of the community, its rise and development, as it actually unfolded.

CHAPTER 1

Preparing to Emigrate

DISCUSSIONS ABOUT THE PROSPECTS OF HOMESTEADING
in western Canada first appear in Dutch-language newspapers at the very
end of 1902. Then throughout 1903 there are a number of articles and letters
promoting, or sometimes warning against, Dutch immigration to the
Canadian prairies from the United States and the Netherlands.

This chapter includes a couple of early letters from the Dutch-American
paper *De Grondwet* expressing caution about immigrating to the Canadian
west. There are four articles of Rev. Sybrandus Schilstra avidly promoting such immigration. In seven letters Evert Aldus carefully explores the
prospects and challenges of immigration to Canada, before the Nijverdal
group, of which he was a part, immigrated to Alberta in the spring of 1904.
Hendrikus Zandbergen warns in two letters about immigrating to Canada,
on the basis of his experience with the Colorado fiasco a decade earlier, and
Aldus replies.

ARTICLE BY EDITOR JOHN MULDER
(*De Grondwet,* 30 December 1902)

Emigration to Northwest Canada

The emigrating of many western farmers across the line, and settling in northwest Canada, has taken on a great, and almost international, significance, says the *Orange Judd Farmer.*[1]

According to the Canadian [Dominion land] office in Ottawa, of the twenty-five million acres of land now owned by American farmers more than a fifth has been acquired in the past year alone. And, the spokesman for that office continues, probably more than a million acres are already in the full possession of actual settlers who came to us from the United States.

During the first six months of 1902 more than twenty-one thousand American citizens settled in Manitoba, and the movement still continues.

Our Canadian friends, the *Orange Judd Farmer* goes on to say, need not worry over the alien element crossing the borders today and settling in their midst. Because these industrious American farmers, who have gone there or will yet go there in the future to settle permanently in their territory, will undoubtedly become good citizens of Canada.

A word of caution may not be out of place, however, to our own people in Iowa, the Dakotas, and other states: We believe that the American farmer is making a mistake if he mortgages his farm in order to raise money to purchase these far-off lands. In general, says the paper, the safest rule to follow also in these matters is the old saying, "Stay where you are at home."[2]

1 This article, the first in *De Grondwet* to report on the land rush for homesteads in western Canada, is a loose translation of an editorial in the *Orange Judd Farmer* (30 August 1902). The *Orange Judd Farmer* was a major American agricultural weekly published in Chicago (about 70,000 subscribers). In 1902 an agent of the Canadian government placed in this newspaper nine advertisements for free homesteads in western Canada; in 1903 that number doubled, and there were also about sixty advertisements about western Canadian land for sale, placed by land agents from St. Paul, Chicago, Fargo, and Winnipeg.
2 An article in the 15 November 1902 issue of the *Orange Judd Farmer* was also critical of the movement of American farmers to Canadian homesteads, but after three editors of this newspaper made a two-week tour of the Canadian prairies in June of 1903, at Canadian government expense, they published a number of positive articles about agricultural opportunities in the Canadian west.

EXCERPT OF LETTER FROM S.A.SCHILSTRA
(Nieuwsblad van Friesland, 31 December 1902)

Passaic [New Jersey], December 1902
Dear Editor,[3]

... I would not like to give rise to deception; indeed, I do not present myself as a guide. When I give advice I do this completely in the interest of emigrants. For no money in the world would I want to bear the guilt of someone's misfortune, or even disappointment....

Farmers, who cannot rent a farm in the Netherlands, or can do so for too high a price, or clearly see that they are falling on hard times, certainly still have a future here. With complete frankness I can give them the advice: Go to *Western Canada* (English America). Vast fertile fields still lie there, where the plough can just be put into the ground; where coal can be obtained for almost nothing, as well as wood. Everything in Canada is under a very orderly administration, better than in America where the laws are sometimes poorly upheld. Even from western America many are going to Canada, naturally to make money, because the land there can be obtained for nothing. The government gives anyone 160 acres of land for nothing as a gift. Land that lies right next to the railway one can still buy for very little money. What I am writing here is not a loose thought or opinion; it is a fact, pure truth. Every possible official document, as well as maps and testimonies of persons, are in my hands, but all in the English language and rather detailed. However, I soon hope to find time to explain this further and to translate these items, in order to inform my countrymen who want to emigrate. Canada, of course, borders on the United States, as any educated school child knows.

The elderly will still remember how many Mennonites from Balk left for Canada about 45 years ago.[4] It would be worthwhile to hear something about these people in this paper. Is there any reader able and willing to do this? It would be very interesting.

S. A. S[chilstra]

---

3 As a correspondent from New Jersey, S. A. Schilstra often sent letters to the *Nieuwsblad van Friesland* with news about America. This is the first of many letters he wrote about Canada.
4 These Mennonites left Friesland in 1853–54 because of conscientious objection against military service and actually settled at New Paris, Indiana, not in Canada.

LETTER FROM MUSKEGON HEIGHTS, MICHIGAN
(*De Grondwet*, 13 January 1903)

In the next to last issue the editor of this paper struck a note of caution in his readers about overly hasty moves to Canada. And rightly so. Possibly the editor was aware that in 1892 some Dutch families settled in the vicinity of Yorktown [Yorkton], a small place about 200 miles north of Winnipeg, Manitoba.[5] They just wanted to become farmers on a 160-acre farm. The Canadian government supplied this land (free homesteads) for a few dollars on the condition of making good on certain requirements one had to fulfill.

The people who took part in this undertaking were sorely disappointed. After spending some time there on the prairies they later left to the city of Winnipeg and sustained themselves by finding work.

What the precise reasons were that the Dutch settlement failed is unknown to your correspondent, but the people explained that farms in the far north could not brag about prosperity. Naturally this is not intended to detract in any way from the really productive and prosperous areas of Manitoba. One would do well, however, to get completely reliable information before making a decision to move to Canada.

Corr. 3 Jan. 1903

We thank the correspondent, who made on the spot observations himself for the above information, and we hope that every Dutchman will carefully follow the advice of the esteemed correspondent and first go and see with his own eyes before moving with his family to the High North, trusting in his good luck. *Editor.*

---

5   This was the first rural Dutch settlement in Canada. Its roots go back to 1885 when Fredrik R. Insinger, a prosperous Dutch entrepreneur, started horse ranching on his homestead there. In 1892 and 1893 at least ten more families and single men immigrated to Yorkton, but within a couple of years most of them moved to Winnipeg. Yorkton is actually located almost 300 miles northwest of Winnipeg in the eastern part of Saskatchewan, then the district of Assiniboia.

6   Harm Emmelkamp and his family had farmed in the Maxwell City area since 1900. The Dearborn Valley is about 30 miles southwest of Great Falls. A government irrigation project was being developed there at the time and farmers were being recruited to the district. *De Grondwet* ran special articles on the Dearborn Valley in its issues of 2 February and 25 November 1902. So the Dutch community at Maxwell City would have been aware of this new development. In late 1902, when Emmelkamp arrived at the Dearborn Valley, there were few if any Dutch people there.

LETTER FROM MAXWELL CITY, NEW MEXICO
(*De Grondwet*, 13 Jan. 1903)

During the night of 10–11 December [1902] Mr. Harm Emmelkamp left secretly from here, leaving his debts unpaid. Our storekeeper laid claim to his farm, which will now be sold privately or publicly. As we understand it, he is at present in the Dearborn Valley, Montana.[6] Let everyone beware.

John Schoolland	John Klymma [Klijnsma]
Daniel Zwier	John Van Wijk
H. Westerman	B. Folkerts[7]

ARTICLE ON CANADA
(*De Grondwet*, 14 April 1903)

Enormous Growth of Wheat

In its fertile valleys and plains of the far northwest, Canada has the richest grain belt in the world. In 1902, 55 million hundredweight of grain of all sorts, including 33 million hundredweight of wheat, were grown here. So far only a tenth of Manitoba has come under the plough; the neighbouring district of Assiniboia consists of almost 15 million hectares, which can serve almost exclusively for the growing of wheat. Then Alberta, near the Rocky Mountains, is about 800 kilometres long and 480 kilometres wide, and Saskatchewan is a realm of the same expanse.[8] Mankind's hunger for land is apparent also from the flocking of people to these virgin lands. In 1902 there were already 50,000 immigrants, and in 1903 still more are expected, especially Americans.

---

7 Most Dutch farmers at Maxwell City were in debt (*De Grondwet*, 8 July 1902). Emmelkamp may have been indebted to these six. All were members of the Maxwell City Christian Reformed Church; Schoolland at this time was president of the consistory, Van Wijk the clerk. The Emmelkamps were not members of the church. The Emmelkamp family came to southern Alberta in early 1903. They were the first Dutch settlers in what would soon become a Dutch settlement east of Leavings. Emmelkamp's move to Alberta was first of all motivated by the availability of free homestead land, but perhaps he also wanted to escape the reach of his creditors in the United States.

8 At this point Alberta, Saskatchewan, and Assiniboia were still among the Northwest Territories. Alberta became a province in 1905.

If this vast wheat area is completely cultivated, it will easily produce between 1½ and 2 billion hundredweight, that is, more than whole world does at present. Canadians can rightly boast of the size of their native land, because it consists of 9,419,134 square kilometres, and is larger than the United States, if Alaska is not considered. Germany could be taken up in it 17 times, France 18 times, Spain 20 times, England 28 times, and Italy 33 times; and British India or the whole of Australia could fit within it 3 times. Canada forms a third of the whole English realm. The Hudson's Bay, 960 kilometres wide and 1680 kilometres long from north to south, could swallow up Sweden, Norway, Denmark, and Belgium. Canada easily has room for 100 million people.

EXCERPT OF ARTICLE BY S.A.SCHILSTRA
(*Nieuwsblad van Friesland*, 23 May 1903)[9]

To Canada: Trustworthy Hints for Emigrants I
by S.A.S., Passaic, New Jersey

Canada or British North America is a country on which many eyes are presently fixed. Thousands are flocking there, and because of favourable testimonies, the construction of railroads, and the fact that more steamships are being put into service on the Great Lakes and especially with Europe, this land has an extraordinary future.

Many speak highly of the fertility of Canada. The large export of all kinds of products to England and other countries, especially the excellent wheat, is proof that the soil is very fertile.

This is no new discovery, but what good is fertile soil when the means of transport are lacking? What value has land that is hundreds of miles from a railway? But now everything is changing. There are about four times as many railways under construction as there are in the Netherlands; they will run part way across Canada. Then also this huge country has a great advantage over the United States – the amazing Hudson's Bay on the north side penetrates deep into the interior of the country, so the largest ships can load products at ports lying on this bay, and they will soon multiply.

---

9   This is the first article of a three part series that S. A. Schilstra wrote under the title, "To Canada: Trustworthy Hints for Emigrants."

10 This article continues to give a general overview of the history of Canada, its government, its population, the climate, its trade and industry, the individual provinces, the Northwest Territories (including Alberta), and the principal railways.

So the distances to the coast are much less in Canada than those from the interior of the United States.[10]

... Many a time Canada is represented as a great wilderness, as a land of snow and ice, with only a habitable strip of land on the southern border. It is an undeniable fact that a large part of Canada in the north is uninhabitable, but it is also a fact that uninformed and bad reports have spread. On good grounds it is now assured that there is no healthier climate in the world than western Canada.... The climate of Alberta and part of British Columbia is very mild due to warm winds from the Pacific Ocean.

... The land in southern Alberta and Assiniboia is especially suited for raising horses and cattle. Immense expanses are occupied by ranchers and their herds. Only here and there has the plough been set in the ground. The land has still not been broken, so it is free from every obstruction, and is of the richest quality....

Addresses for information about Canada:

The High Commissioner for Canada, 17 Victoria St., London, S. W.
Mr. W. T. R. Preston, 17 Victoria St., London, S. W.
Mr. Alfred Jury, 15 Waterstreet, Liverpool
Mr. G. H. Mitchel, 15 Waterstreet, Liverpool
The Superintendent of Immigration, Ottawa, Canada

(to be continued)

ARTICLE BY S.A.SCHILSTRA
(*Nieuwsblad van Friesland*, 13 June 1903)

To Canada: Trustworthy Hints for Emigrants II
by S.A.S., Passaic, New Jersey

Canada's Future

The extraordinary fertility of the land and the sparse population – six million in such a huge area – offers a wonderful opportunity to industrious, responsible, and enterprising persons. There is no doubt that there is a future here. Already in a few years many have become well off, if not rich. Whoever chooses land today and settles on it will live in a developed area after a few years and then the value of the land will have risen considerably. In the beginning whoever is several miles from the nearest railway station will find that a lot has changed within a few years.

This has happened everywhere in the United States too. That is the general rule. There is no country in the world that is so intersected with railways as the United States. It is beginning to be this way already in the developed part of Canada; and it will be so in the still uncultivated part, where the ground is so fertile.

Canada is a very suitable land for farmers and farm labourers, and even for tradesmen. A growing country and growing cities need workers. As soon as agriculture flourishes and immigration increases, all sorts of industry come to be considered. Then factories are built and thousands earn a living without difficulty; that is, people do not run in each other's way as often happens in the large cities.

In the Netherlands in general there is certainly a desire for emigration, but little courage to do it. Many are held back by the fear that they will be lonely and abandoned in a strange land, without help in the middle of a wilderness, and so they trudge on while becoming poorer from year to year and their situation becomes more threatening. It may not be easy to separate from parents, family, and acquaintances, and to say farewell to friendly surroundings, perhaps with the prospect of never again seeing one's beloved town or village, but one ought to think about the future, especially of the children. And that is not very rosy in the Netherlands. If the separation is painful, no less painful is the thought of knowing that nothing but poverty is their lot, and it is always a matter of toil and struggle to get a scanty piece of bread. Then isn't it much better to move to a foreign land where the soil is rich and every responsible person can become well off in a few years, or has the assurance, in any case, that he can live comfortably there. Although one may have a subordinate position there, it is still possible to save money. In the United States, even in unfavourable areas such as the vicinity of New York, for example, the most responsible, thrifty workers come to possess their own houses.

Some will surely say: This is beautifully presented, but is it all so certain? Catastrophes and bad luck can happen anywhere. Now and then some things can turn out disappointing. One can occasionally entertain expectations that are too wonderful. Perhaps some also think that one can soon become rich in America with little work. To be sure, anyone in the world can be faced with things that he has not at all figured on, but, on the other hand, sometimes extraordinary advantages also present themselves. So, for example, I know a relatively poor man here who rented a farm for about $150 a year and last year he had $1,000 profit from it.

The General Rule in America

The general rule is that anyone who struggles in the Netherlands has it infinitely better here, no matter where he settles. The wages in America are much higher, the homes much more roomy and better – for example, the bedroom and kitchen – and the work time is shorter. Even here, nearby New York – in my opinion the most unsuitable place for immigrants since it is overcrowded – there is contentment because one has it much better. Yet the masses who come here and do not go inland are doomed to remain lifelong cutters of wood and carriers of water. To make headway and begin a business is almost impossible. One gets in the way of another. This is different and better in the western states, except, of course, in the large cities. There one should not go, except in growing cities that still have a future.

Already earlier in the *Nieuwsblad van Friesland* it has often been pointed out and recalled how unpleasant the situation must be of a Dutch farmer, for example, who is compelled in America to work in a factory for the long term or has to stand between Italians, Irish and other nationalities doing other subservient work. Although he then earns relatively much money, he can have no joy of life because he is not in his element. A farmer cherishes the land, views his cattle with joy and high spirits, sees the waving grain fields with gladness, and enjoys it when he can cut and gather the fruits of his labour into the barns or bring it to market. Then he feels he is a free man, which he is, and if all goes well, also the luckiest man in the world. Poot already sang: "How pleasantly rolls on the life of a contented farmer."[11] If this is not the case now in the Netherlands, there is no doubt that this can be the case after a few years in Canada. Whoever starts out there with hard work and business sense can say after only a few years: "I own my own farm; I have become a well-off man." Very many say this already in Canada. Many who came there poor a few years ago now live in a nice house, have a beautiful stock of cattle and the newest farm implements – and it is all their own property. Due to the unusual fertility of the land they have become prosperous. Hasn't it gone like this in the western States, for example, in South Dakota? So it happens everywhere, where the soil is fertile.

History has clearly demonstrated in the United States that especially Hollanders have transformed undeveloped areas into beautiful lands with thriving towns and villages, and rich farms. Whoever earlier came poor is now rich, and the children enjoy the inherited fruits of their labour and

11 Hubert Cornelis Poot (1689–1733) was a popular Dutch poet.

diligence. This has been the rule for all responsible, industrious people, and so it will ever remain in the future.

The great country of Canada that can take in millions of people is waiting for hardy, enterprising persons, and has this advantage – one does not need to take along any capital. The government willingly welcomes such people and paves the way for them in every way. How fortunate that every immigrant has the assurance that no private land agent can cheat him, but that the government accommodates and protects him in every way.

Investigate and Take a Risk!

If there are in the Netherlands enterprising persons, who perhaps for a long time already have fixed their eyes on America, they should doubt no longer, but investigate and take a risk. Every year that goes by is a lost year. Not that Canada will fill up, or that the land will be taken up within a few years; no, that cannot happen – it is too extensive for that. Yet, it is also true that other nationalities can come before our people and occupy the most suitable places first. Many Germans and Finns have already flocked there and many will follow before long. There needs to be no fear in the least that one will not succeed. People with little knowledge but with sound understanding are always making headway, and most become persons of fortune in the growing towns. You can't gain a foothold in an existing business, but you simply start a new business, and the growing population guarantees success. So whoever does not wish to be a farmer can settle in a suitable place, for example, where railroads meet. Whoever has no money seeks simple work in order to begin something after one or two years when he has saved some. The farmers, whose numbers in the area are increasing more and more, need everything and come to buy their wares in such towns or villages.

In the province of Manitoba there are 27 million acres of suitable and fertile land, and this is offered free by the government. I ask you: Isn't this attractive? The best sorts of grain are grown there. Of all that land only three million acres have yet been cultivated. What a lot of room yet. In winter, however, it is colder in Manitoba than the more westerly regions. Apples, pears, plums, and grapes grow there.

In the Northwest Territories there are still 195 million acres, of which only one million have been brought into cultivation. So there is room for millions of people, even for our descendants. New discoveries are continually being made. Everything is officially investigated carefully. Also, here and there so-called experimental stations are set up, in order to find out which products can most suitably be grown in the different regions. This is a wonderful thing, since many a time it has happened that newcomers first had trouble with crops and finally by long and hard experience arrived at a favourable result. This now is precluded by the government, and those interested are informed about everything. Government appointed experts even go around and give the necessary information. They also try to encourage the population with awards at exhibitions. In my possession is a report of the nineteenth annual exhibition of every possible product of the farm, ranch, and industry, held at Prince Albert in Saskatchewan Territory on August 5, 1902.

Without going further into specifics, be it said with emphasis once more, that everything stands under the orderly control of the government, and deception is impossible. In Canada there are no land agents without a conscience who buy up available land and often cheat others. The land is under the authority of government personnel, and everything that I have written here comes from official sources, directly received from the Ministry of the Interior in Ottawa. The government does sell land, to the railway companies, among others, but on the condition that it be sold again at a fixed low price. In St. Paul, a large city in the United States, a company was formed which bought five million acres from the Canadian government for 50 cents an acre. The conditions, however, are these: The land must be sold in ten years to immigrants, but never for higher than $3 an acre, thus amazingly cheap. On this purchased land there is a place for 18,750 families, calculated at 160 acres (a homestead) for each family. In regard to this land, it is strongly recommended to stay as close as possible to each other. The fact that this company was established and bought land also confirms that all eyes are fixed on Canada, and that this country is heading for an extraordinary future.

The rule is that the land, 160 acres, is offered free, but one can also buy it from one or another railroad company, or from the above-mentioned company. The regulations for the railway companies are that they may sell it for $1.25 to $5 an acre. They give credit at 6 per cent interest. Of course, the price depends more on the location of the land than its quality.

When so many flock to the fertile areas, there is also need of a work-force. In 1892 more than two thousand people went from eastern Canada to Manitoba and the Northwest Territories to help with the harvest. This shows what a wonderful opportunity there is for the worker. A Dutch farmer, who does not immediately wish to take possession of land, as well as farmhands, can find enough work here and gain some experience in order to begin on their own later and be their own boss. For one who owns nothing it is necessary first to earn something, although a trustworthy person can certainly get everything on credit. Without money you can do little with 160 acres of land. Although in the first year a little of the 160 acres is broken up, you must be able to live for some time before you can gather the fruits; besides, a house must be built and implements must be bought, however few. But whoever is willing and able to work, will certainly make it. From the many examples that I can point out, I will take one to show how it goes for many. Someone from Prince Albert wrote the following in the *Manitoba Morning Free Press* (a daily paper):

> In order to show how things have gone with me, I can state that I came here in 1882 and settled on 360 acres of land. I had basically no capital, except for a team of oxen and a wagon with which my wife and I arrived. Without any help from others I have continually worked and now have (in 1898) 75 acres in cultivation; I own 9 horses, 15 milk cows, 10 sheep, 30 pigs, a good two story house, sheds, and horse stables. Barns are not necessary, though I have a good storage shed for grain, and also all modern farming machines. Last year I harvested 1,300 bushels of grain and a lot of vegetables of various sorts. It went very well with my cows, sheep, pigs, and chickens. Sicknesses among the cattle are unknown here. I have a lot of hay, good water, and wood. I am very satisfied with the land. The area is very healthy and I can work every day in the winter. Never has the harvest failed.

This quoted example is certainly not the most favourable, but one can see how far one person can go in sixteen years. Little soil was brought into cultivation, yet everything is his property, and soon he will be helped by his children whom he still has to care for now. The man came poor. Now he is well off. How then would it be, if a father would take along a couple of sons and a little capital? Undoubtedly this man had to work for someone else and so he could do less on his own farm. So it happens also in the United States. Thus I know many who came here poor and first worked as farmhands, but now, after a few years, have farms themselves; that is, they have bought on instalment. There are those who already after ten years have everything paid off, and may be called well off. More than once I have heard it said that Dutch farmers can make more from the land than Americans can, because they pay more attention to the small details and are more accustomed to thrift. If that is true, then everything is in favour of our countrymen. And because it is a fact that almost all who have beautiful farms came here poor, then the same can certainly happen in Canada, where conditions are more favourable than the United States and where, according to experts, the choicest soil is found.

Why Canada is Still Not Populated

Perhaps this or that person will ask: If Canada is such a huge, beautiful, and fertile country, why didn't more people go there earlier?

In the first place, people then were not as familiar with the interior as now. There were almost no railroads. Whoever traveled through the country a few times spoke highly of the soil, but what use is fertility if one cannot transport the products? That Netherlanders did not think of Canada, but of the United States, is certainly based on the fact that they had already settled there in earlier centuries and continued to maintain communication with the Netherlands.

The real immigration began in about 1847 with Rev. Van Raalte and other leaders.[12] In the main these people went to the state of Michigan, now a thriving Dutch colony. Many stayed along the way due to the difficult journey in those days, and settled elsewhere with good success, for example, at Rochester and its environs. Others went still further than Michigan. Whoever was well settled sent money to relatives in the Netherlands (as still happens today) and so attention remained fixed only on the United States. And because large states, like Iowa and others, were almost unpopulated, had rich soil, and the land there could be obtained very cheaply, attention remained confined to them. And when so much gold was discovered in California, the far west even more became the destination. The journey remained focused on the United States, especially after the trip became easier and shorter thanks to the steamship. Going to Canada was not considered; it didn't need to be considered. There certainly was immigration to Canada, but on a limited scale – French and Irish, and then mainly to the eastern part. Just as many stay near the city of New York, so they remained close to the large cities of Montreal and Quebec. If they were too close to each other or didn't like it there, they even crossed the border to the United States, and did not go further into Canada, simply because the way was not yet paved. Slowly this has changed, especially when one could go across by train. Railways clear the way for an orderly immigration, as the discovery of goldfields in the Klondike has once again demonstrated.

---

12 Starting with the large group led by Rev. Albertus Van Raalte to the Holland, Michigan, area and another large group led by Rev. Hendrik Scholte to Pella, Iowa, there was a steady flow of Dutch immigrants to the United States in the 19th century.

The regions of Canada that especially come into consideration for immigration are the provinces of Ontario, especially the western part, and Manitoba. In both provinces there is a lot of fertile land, but in West-Ontario still a lot of forest lands. Although the wood here and there has great value, it requires a lot of effort to turn woodland into farm land.

No doubt the soil is very good, but one still has to toil over the remaining stumps and roots. The custom is to cut off the trees about a foot above the ground and then the land is put into use. It takes years before everything is cleaned up. Nonetheless, many do not find this so difficult. However, there is other land in abundance, especially in the already mentioned Territories of Saskatchewan, Alberta, and Assiniboia. As far as I can judge, the best places where Netherlanders can start a mixed farm are the area around Prince Albert, a growing city in Saskatchewan where there is a large fertile valley, or the area around Regina, a thriving place in Assiniboia, or in the neighbourhood of Edmonton in Alberta. The territories of Alberta and Assiniboia border directly on the state of Montana; Saskatchewan lies north of Assinibioa. The shipping of products from these lands of the future is much easier than from the United States, due to the Hudson's Bay that penetrates deep into the country. I could name many other favourable places, but these seem to be the most favourable for Netherlanders.

I have already pointed out the very small number of inhabitants in these lands, and their amazing size.

(to be continued)[13]

13 Part III of this series appeared in the 27 June issue of the *Nieuwsblad van Friesland*. This last article was submitted by Evert Aldus to the *Twentsch Volksblad*, where it was reprinted in the issues of 22 August, 5, 12, and 19 September 1903. See translations below.

14 This letter from Klaas Schuiling to his relatives in Friesland is preserved in the Hoogland collection at the Rijksarchief in Leeuwarden. Schuiling had farmed in the Dutch settlement west of Belgrade (near Manhattan, Mont.) since 1898.

15 The Frisian newspaper was the *Nieuwsblad van Friesland*, which had been running articles by S. A. Schilstra about immigration to Canada since December 1902.

16 There is no record of a Bakker Bos taking up a homestead in the Leavings area. The name likely refers to Arien Doornbos. He took up a homestead east of Leavings probably in 1903 – the records are missing – and later abandoned it in March 1904. George Dijkema then claimed this homestead.

17 This name certainly refers to Hendrikus ter Telgte. He had emigrated with his family from the Netherlands in May 1903 to the Dutch community at Manhattan, Mont., where his brother Jan H. ter Telgte farmed. It is probable that Hendrikus and Doornbos visited southern Alberta in July of that year to check out the possibility of homesteads in the Leavings area. By early August Hendrikus returned to the Manhattan area without having filed for a homestead for some reason. On 10 August 1903 Harm Emmelkamp filed for a homestead on Hendrikus's behalf.

18 Schuiling never did immigrate to Canada.

19 S. A. Schilstra replied to Aldus's questions in the 19 September 1903 issue of the *Nieuwsblad van Friesland*.

EXCERPT OF LETTER FROM KLAAS SCHUILING
(2 August 1903)[14]

Belgrade, [Montana], 2 August [1903]
Dear Brother and Sister,

… Are you reading the Frisian newspaper,[15] and have you heard if there are people there near you too who want to go to Canada? At present many are going there. One can take up a homestead there for $10, that is, 160 acres of land. And according to what they say and write, it's very good land. Here also two Hollanders have gone there to have a look. It seemed very good to them there, and both have also taken up 160 acres of land (Bakker Bos[16] and Totelten[17] are the names, according to Koning).… I think if I can sell the farm for a good price, we will go there too. It always appeals to me so much to have a good farm for nothing.…[18] In Canada one does not need to irrigate.…

Greetings, Klaas [Schuiling]

LETTER FROM EVERT ALDUS
(*Nieuwsblad van Friesland,* 8 August 1903)

Nijverdal [Netherlands], Aug. [1903]
Dear Editor,

In connection with the articles about Canada that appeared in your paper on May 23, June 13 and 27, the undersigned would like to use the opportunity to ask some questions.[19]

1 Must the land (offered by the Canadian government) be irrigated, or is the amount of rain sufficient? (A Hollander from Montana wrote me that this is the case in large stretches of Canada, namely, that it is irrigated, resulting in huge costs for the immigrant.)[20]
2 Must the land be fertilized with manure, so that cattle raising is necessary?

20 This correspondent from Montana was probably Jan Hendrik ter Telgte, or possibly his brother Hendrikus, or Gerrit Jan Withage, all fellow Nijverdalers. Jan H. ter Telgte immigrated to Paterson, New Jersey in 1892, and then moved to the Dutch community at Manhattan, Montana, in 1897. Hendrikus ter Telgte immigrated to Manhattan in May and Withage in June 1903.

Evert Aldus, 1909. (Courtesy: Frieda Dekker.)

3 Can one get land that can be ploughed the first year, or is a lot of time lost with preliminary work?

4 Can the grain that is grown always be sold, without having to go too far to market?

5 When a small family arrives at the beginning of the year, how much money do they have to bring along to live until the harvest with a thrifty way of life? And how much for necessary implements, draft animals, seed-grain, etc.?

6 Would Mr. S.A.S. be willing to inform us in the *Nieuwsblad van Friesland* about the prices of necessities of life, such as food, furniture, clothing, and also what the prices of livestock, implements, etc., will be in more remote areas where the immigrant settles?

I also tell you, Mr. Editor, that we are not making use of your paper out of curiosity, but because some people here have serious plans to emigrate and therefore are eager to be as well informed as possible.

Yours faithfully, E[vert] Aldus

LETTER FROM EVERT ALDUS
(*Twentsch Volksblad*, 22 August 1903)[21]

Nijverdal, [Netherlands], 19 August 1903
Dear Editor:

Recently in our area of residence much has been said about moving to another country or emigration. Time and again one of our fellow-villagers has already left for America to seek a better future there. In this connection I kindly request a place for this article in your paper. Perhaps there are those who are interested in emigrating and who therefore will be served by information about it in your newspaper.

What I wish to state is in large part taken from an article that appeared in the Extra Bijblad of the *Nieuwsblad van Friesland* of June 13 and 27.[22] In this piece a Hollander who lives in the United States shared information about Canada, a very suitable country for emigrant farmers.

Till now people from Nijverdal have gone to Montana, Iowa, or Minnesota.[23] If one has family or friends there, this is the best place to go. If not, then emigration to Canada is preferable, because conditions there are more favourable, as is evident from the following.

Canada is the northern half of North America. It is more than 300 times as large as the Netherlands, and has six million inhabitants, a few more than the Netherlands. Canada has a Governor General appointed by the English king. Otherwise it has complete self-rule. It has its own government, its own [government] departments, and has a universal right to vote. It is divided into provinces, each with its own provincial government.

In the eastern part the temperature is lower than here. In the middle and in the west winter lasts from December to April. Winter there is colder, and summer is warmer than here.

In the west people leave the cattle in the pasture in winter; little or no snow falls there. In general the sky there is clearer, the atmosphere drier and more healthy than here. There is almost never foggy weather there. There certainly is in the eastern provinces, but for emigration these are left out of consideration.

---

21 This is the first of a long series of letters that Evert Aldus sent to the *Twentsch Volksblad* about Canada.

22 The articles in the *Nieuwsblad van Friesland* were written by S. A. Schilstra from New Jersey. The extensive quotations from this newspaper in this and the following articles are taken from the 27 June issue.

23 Nijverdalers who had gone to the Dutch community at Manhattan, Montana, included the families of Jan Hendrik ter Telgte and Garrit Willemsen, both of whom had first immigrated to Paterson, New Jersey, in 1892. In 1903 the families of Hendrikus ter Telgte (in May) and Gerrit Jan Withage (in June) immigrated directly to Manhattan. Johan Ten Harmsel and Christiaan Schiebout immigrated to the Dutch settlement in northwest Iowa in July 1903. All except Ten Harmsel later moved to southern Alberta.

The land designated for farming consists mostly of heavy clay soil. It is extraordinarily fertile and never needs to be manured. It is prairie land covered with long grass or woods. In the province of Manitoba there are ten million hectares of such fertile land that is being offered *free* by the government. In the western regions there are even much larger areas. If the whole population of our country went there, not all of the land by far would yet be occupied. Moreover, there are large forests in Canada, so lumber there is cheap. Coal and metals are found in abundance in the ground. Wheat, oats, rye, barley, flax, tobacco, peas, beans, potatoes, carrots grow there, and all other fruits that grow here. One sows grain in April and reaps it in August, so fertile is the ground. Fruit trees grow there just like here; grapes, etc., ripen better since the summer is warmer.

In Canada there are various railways so that one can ship products. Seldom does one come to live more than four or five hours from the nearest railway station. Naturally this is true only in areas suited for farming, not in the less habitable northern regions.

English, French, Germans, Irish, Hollanders, etc., live in Canada. The dominant language is English. Also French is spoken a lot.

You can buy land there for a small price from railway companies or others. You can also get it free from the government. There are persons appointed by the government in every place that is not too small, who are in charge of caring for immigrants. They offer information about the location and suitability of land, and show it, etc. Further, someone officially comes to meet immigrants as much as possible and offers them advice.

The big question, however, is:

How Does One Become a Landowner?

To answer this question I will let the writer in the Extra Bijblad of the *Nieuwsblad van Friesland* have the word. He writes:[24]

> "Everything in this matter is determined by law. The head of
> a family, man or woman, and every person over eighteen, can
> request from the government and select 160 acres for free, *i.e.,*
> 72 hectares of land. If a family with three sons eighteen settles
> somewhere, then 4 × 160 acres can be applied for. Yet they must
> obey the regulation and begin to work each 160 acres, and not

---

24 The rest of this letter is taken from an article about Canada by S. A. Schilstra in the 27 June 1903 issue of the *Nieuwsblad van Friesland*.

work just on 160 acres and leave the other land wild. However, they can live and work together. Whoever applies for and receives land is required to live on it three successive years, each year for at least six months, and begin to work it. One must put the land to use, begin to cultivate it or let cattle graze on it.

This regulation is a measure to prevent arbitrariness. Six months of absence is allowed to attend to matters that come up, if the family is called away or works for someone else. Whoever wants to be absent longer than six months must give notice and can get the time extended. Arbitrary absence will lead to trouble and suspicion that one has left the land. In such a case the government then has the right to give the land to someone else. If everything is done in the proper way, then during an absence the land is protected by the government.

One cannot be absent eight months one year and four months the next. Whoever stays away for more than six months forfeits that year, and is then obligated to the present regulation for four years instead of three.

As soon as someone is eligible by age [eighteen] to apply for a 'homestead' – a dwelling place – and desires land, there is a favourable regulation for him – he may stay living in the house of his father. And whoever once owns a homestead and also wants a second does not need to build a house on the new land.

Whoever has plans to settle somewhere has to apply to the local land office of the district in which he intends to settle, but he can also apply in writing to the Minister of the Interior in Ottawa or to the Commissioner of Immigration in Winnipeg. This makes it evident how land agents are completely excluded. One has to deal only with the government and thus fraud is impossible.

But there can be circumstances when one would rather have a different homestead. In that case one applies to the Land Commissioner in Ottawa with the request to make an exchange. For proof of ownership ten dollars is due.

In order to settle in Canada no special papers are required. Whoever wants a homestead must become a citizen of Canada in three years. For a Netherlander it is enough to be able to show a regular change of address certificate as proof that a person and his family have left their fatherland in an honest way. Whoever is under obligation of military service, be sure to comply with the law. Many who have not done so have later regretted it, since the old country is then closed to them; that is, [it offers] no secure residence.

But we have still not finished talking about the homestead, and need to say more about it. If anyone has lived for twelve months on his land and has brought 30 acres into cultivation, he may also buy that land from the government for a proportionate price and then he immediately receives the title deed. Also anyone can buy from the government 160 acres of land that lies next to his land, if it is still vacant. He is then required to pay a quarter of the purchase price right away and the rest in similar instalments. Then interest is charged at six per cent. The payment must be made to the agent of the land office; if one lives rather far away, then this can also be done by a bank draft.

Persons who do not have a homestead and want to buy land from the government can apply to the Land Commissioner at Ottawa who decides these matters. If it is necessary to send money there, then the draft must be made payable to the Deputy of the Minister of the Interior.

The taxes are very reasonable and for each quarter section, *i.e.,* 160 acres, a homestead, they only amount to $2 to $2.50. The total tax seldom amounts to more than $7 to $8 per year, namely when the homestead falls within a school district. As soon as a few families have twelve children between five and sixteen, an opportunity for education is available and then the taxes increase to the named amount. The government gives $300 to $350 per year for each school. Only certified teachers are allowed, and the required knowledge is the same for large and small places. The regulation about the required number of children is not the same everywhere, but this is of no consequence. In general it is a fact that in Canada everything is well regulated, and the laws there are upheld just as well in distant areas as in the developed regions; this is not generally the case in the United States."

(to be continued)

LETTER FROM EVERT ALDUS
(*Twentsch Volksblad,* 5 September 1903)

(continuation)[25]

How the Land is Divided

"Now I am going to clarify how the land is divided. Given below is the plan of a township. (Town is the name of a small city; city is the name of a prominent place.) The wilderness lands are divided into large square blocks, so every homestead is also perfectly square, and all roads are straight. A township is divided into 36 parts; each part, or section, is a mile long and wide. A township is thus six miles square, and if we reckon one mile as 20 minutes, it would take 12 [8] hours to walk around the boundaries. The diagram below makes everything clear.

The whole is a township. Each part is a section consisting of 640 acres of land; thus one section is 4 times 160 acres, or four homesteads. A whole township can thus contain $36 \times 4 = 144$ families.

31	32	33	34	35	36
30	29	28	27	26	25
19	20	21	22	23	24
18	17	16	15	14	13
7	8	9	10	11	12
6	5	4	3	2	1

However, the government has taken wise precautionary measures and keeps some sections for community purposes, usually two, which are called school sections. For the future, when everything is occupied and more of an influx arrives there, when trade and industry expand, and the land rises in value, this measure offers great advantages for the community. Parts of these lands can only be sold by public auction, for the purpose of forming the centre of the community and building churches, factories, stores, etc.; also private homes. Then there is still enough land left for parks, etc., because 640 acres is an area of considerable size.

25 This letter is a continuation of the extended quotation from S. A. Schilstra's article in the *Nieuwsblad van Friesland* (27 June 1903).

Since all these lands cannot be used for the time being, there are regulations about renting this land from the government for a very small price for hay land or pasture; for example, in Manitoba for 6 cents an acre per year, and in the North West Territories for 4 cents. Whoever buys a piece of school land may pay a fifth of the purchase price cash and the rest in four instalments, at 6 per cent interest.

It is very important for the immigrant to know how he can manage to build a house, barns, etc., and how he can get the necessary materials. We already saw that Canada is very rich in lumber, so one can get it reasonably at the railway line at every place of some significance, but in case one needs lumber and does not have it on his own homestead, then the government gives permission to ask for wood from the local land agent for a house, barn, fence, and firewood. The following amounts by dimension are provided free:

- 3,000 feet of lumber, no thicker than a foot (12 inches) at the lower end.
- 2,000 poplar trees for fence rails, no thicker than 5 inches at the lower end.
- 500 posts for fences, 7 feet long and no thicker than 5 inches at the thin end.
- Fallen trees for firewood, fences, or other purposes, with no further stipulation.

The certificate for permission costs 25 cents.

I could still dwell on many things, because I have lying before me many official brochures and maps, beautiful pictures of the cities of Winnipeg, Vancouver, Victoria, etc., and of prosperous farms. In the brochures the produce of the land is shown, as well as the average temperature. After all that has been said already, however, I consider it unnecessary to go further into it here. Though the statistics are trustworthy, the fertility of the soil and the ease in procuring land must be the deciding factor for the immigrant."

(to be continued)

LETTER FROM EVERT ALDUS
(Twentsch Volksblad, 12 September 1903)

(continuation)[26]

Whoever Wishes Ask

"If there are persons who want to improve their position and are seriously thinking about coming over [to North America], then the way is open for them to send various questions to the editor of this paper. I am ready to answer all questions, if I can, as quickly as possible.[27]

If someone asks whether Canada is much better than the United States, the answer is affirmative, because land in Canada is available for free. In the United States there is land in abundance. Millions can still live there, because it is very thinly populated. To give one example, there is the great state of Montana on the border of Canada, but as soon as there is some influx of people, the land immediately goes up in price and they ask $15 an acre. Several years ago this was still the price in the fertile state of Iowa, but now it is sometimes worth $90 there. That's how it is everywhere.

And Canada has the advantage that the government alone has everything under control, and it cuts off any opportunity for monopolies and trusts, the cancers of the United States. In Canada they have clearly seen the reefs on which many run aground in the United States. Though there may be some speculation with land sales to the railway companies, etc., we have seen how everything is regulated by very fair laws and [private] land agents are excluded.

After all I have written, I know very well that it is difficult to make a choice in a land that is much larger than all of Europe, even though one is eager to go there. If you go, there must, of course, be a place of destination where you can settle for the time being and go to work, unless you take along some capital and immediately wish to begin [farming]. That beginning can be done on a small scale. You learn by doing, and also by watching

---

26 This letter is a further instalment of the extended quotation from S. A. Schilstra's article in the *Nieuwsblad van Friesland* (27 June 1903).

27 The newspaper was the *Nieuwsblad van Friesland,* and Schilstra was ready to answer questions about Canada.

how others do things. The mode of work may differ, but in many cases you can also raise cattle and poultry. Everything depends on the circumstances, especially the size of the family.

Whatever the case may be, one receives for free all possible information about the provisional place of destination. One finds large maps of it, with railways, rivers, and the lay of the land. There it is made clear what land is most suitable for the interested party, in accordance with his wishes and plans, whether he wants to go into farming or cattle raising, or desires a mixed farm.

It would be a wonderful thing if some reliable, friendly, industrious, enterprising men would put their hands together in order to establish a colony and stay together. Then – I have no doubt – many would follow.

In 1902 50,000 people from the United States went to Canada to request a homestead, and now there are 150,000 more ready to go to the same region. In England there are 10,000 ready, persons with some capital, it is reported, who want to go together to become farm folk.

Dare to Take a Risk

The weakness of our Dutch people is that they hardly dare to take a risk. When a lot is explained in the newspapers and it is mentioned that whoever is able and willing to work will certainly succeed, almost no matter where you go in the United States, then people will still ask all sorts of questions in private letters; from this it appears that there is still apprehension about every-thing. Why is that? Doesn't one take along his bodily strength, his will power, zeal, understanding, knowledge, yes everything? Is there no self-confidence? Will he who is able and willing to work in the fatherland be clumsy here? Indeed, no! Everything is certainly not the same, but this means nothing.

Already it has been said that a Dutch farmer gets more from his land than an American, and that whoever learns a good trade in the Netherlands never needs to be ashamed before anyone.

But it is so easy not to take such a decisive step and leave everything with one's wife and children. Well, if you do not dare to do so, perhaps still do not trust it, and you lack all self-confidence, even though the prospect still appeals to you, then I will point out a way that is not so difficult, though decision and self-confidence still enter into it.

Aren't there sturdy, capable young men in your vicinity? Let some of them join together – farmhands or farmers' sons and tradesmen, with a good head on their shoulders – who can make an informed judgment after a short stay in Canada. They will find work in the small, rapidly growing towns, or with farmers. They will quickly become informed about everything in the surrounding area, and will be able to prepare everything; if need be, even select the land. In this manner they pave the way and make it easy for others. The costs are calculated. One can then know what should or should not be taken along. And these forerunners, who are slowly becoming familiar with the English language, can serve as guides for those who want to come later (if possible as a colony).

As was said, tradesmen no doubt have a future there and can be assured of higher wages. A surprising amount is being built. Also, for a manual labourer nothing at all stands in the way for him to seek a homestead. In this respect they are not choosy in America. If there is a shortage of workers, little is asked about what a person did earlier. One simply tackles a job. Shoemakers and tailors are transformed into carpenters, and I have now and then met farmers who were coppersmiths and bakers in the Netherlands. Whoever is able and willing to work never stands in need in this land and easily finds his way, especially now in Canada. Large cities that are no longer expanding have no definite need for people. Some are stuck there, but must worm their way through it and have no future. There conditions are, or are slowly becoming, European.

I dare say that sturdy, well-behaved young men will earn enough extra money after a relatively short time to be able to make the return trip to the fatherland, in case they don't like it.

In Canada there is also a great shortage of female personnel, in more than one respect, because there are thousands more men than women. Domestic maids are welcome and as a rule they earn a lot of money."

(to be continued)

LETTER FROM EVERT ALDUS
(*Twentsch Volksblad,* 19 September 1903)

(continuation)[28]

The Trip

"After having hastily pointed out one thing or another, I would add that a person or family who comes to Canada with the goal of seeking a homestead receives for free a certificate from the government agent. On presenting this certificate, which has the name of the family, a railway ticket to the place of destination is given at the station for a significantly reduced price. If, for example, you arrive at Montreal, all kinds of information is available, and no one needs to doubt whether he will be helped in a friendly manner. You will have no difficulty importing and transporting the goods brought along for your own use. The less cargo you take along to a civilized country where everything is available, the better, because there are always a lot of extra freight charges for transportation to the boat, across the city to the station, and later for picking it up from the station.

When anyone first goes alone to seek land and then returns for his family, he may travel back on the same favourable terms, and likewise, his family also may later go to the destination.

The travel costs to Canada are comparable to those to the United States. If you take the passenger boat that sails from Rotterdam to Montreal, this is the easiest way. Otherwise, take a boat at Rotterdam or Harlingen, and in England one of the boats to Montreal.[29]

---

28 This is the final instalment of the extended quotation from S. A. Schilstra's article in the *Nieuwsblad van Friesland* (27 June 1903).

29 At this point Aldus omitted the following paragraphs that are part of Schilstra's original article in the *Nieuwsblad van Friesland*:
"It takes no longer when you go with a Dutch boat to New York, but then you cannot directly take advantage of the favourable offer of the Canadian railway company, and must first take the train at full fare about 800 miles from New York to Buffalo, to get to Canada. Arriving immediately at Montreal is thus more economical, and also much easier, when you take along possessions. There a certificate is issued and on presenting it a cheap ticket is received for the whole family, for a third of the usual cost, I think.
The distance from Montreal to Regina is about 1600 miles. If the fare in Canada is 2 cents a mile, then this amounts to $10.65 [$32], but if it is 3 cents, then $16 [$48]. That difference of one cent sometimes exists, especially due to competing lines."

Final Thoughts

Now I come to the end. There will still be those – I have no doubt – who after reading this, remain unsatisfied. But this will be the case, even though one has read volumes about Canada. And these are abundant. The well-known writer Bancroft wrote a work of 774 pages that runs to 1886 just about the province of British Columbia.[30] As far as it went, he pretty well visited everything and praises that land as an inexhaustible source of riches. There are large coal fields, gold fields, and petroleum sources – a lot of fertile land and magnificent kinds of lumber. But there were no finished roads. Now there are more there.

In my possession is also a small book of 150 pages, closely printed, and published in Ottawa by the government, containing letters of various persons who have lived in Canada for a shorter or longer period of time and have become prosperous; or are very satisfied with their adopted land.

Yet – emigration is viewed as a risky venture.

That may be, but then not like a fire, when out of necessity and in danger to life one must jump out of the window with the chance of serious injury. I know very well that one forms an idea for himself, makes a rough sketch or plan, according to which everything will work out; and yet a lot happens that will not fulfil expectations. This is already the case in one's own situation. Not everything happens according to our idea. Yet not everything is therefore a disappointment. In Canada it may well be that one has to live meagrely for a year with housing and such things, but the gold – the prosperity – comes from the ground before long and then beautiful houses will spring up there, like you see everywhere in fertile areas in America. Whoever comes here and acts cautiously, practically, and with discretion, will soon say: 'I had expected many things to be different, but the reality far surpasses my expectation. I was not told the half of it.'[31]

There is plenty of bread for everyone. Whoever does not want to be a farmer can soon open a store in a rapidly growing place, almost no matter where, and he will succeed, because of the farmers in the area; everyone needs everything. Enough, the matter is clear.

---

30 Hubert Howe Bancroft, *History of British Columbia, 1792–1887* (San Francisco: History Company, 1887).
31 This is an allusion to 2 Chronicles 9:6.

However, one thing is necessary – don't think too much, but act. One has to believe, dare, take a risk, surrender oneself, have self-confidence and courage, and also keep heart in a bit of adversity and don't immediately be at a loss.

But, also a warning. Canada needs persons who want to work. No lazy thinking: that is a land of golden mountains. The treasures are in the ground but must be brought out with effort and perseverance. Especially those who get into a bad situation in the Netherlands by their own fault will not succeed in Canada, unless they do away with the cause of their situation.

Age also comes into consideration. Whoever is elderly can no longer undertake great ventures, unless they go with their family, especially with industrious sons. Whoever can go with well-behaved children goes easily, since their roots have not grown too deep in the soil of the fatherland.

It's too bad that many, who indeed want to go, are not able, because they cannot pay for the crossing. Therefore it would be good to form a society and help each other on terms to be agreed. For example, one could live together for the time being, and help each other break 160 acres very quickly, etc. Whoever has no means and can borrow the money needs not become deterred. Whoever is well-to-do and places trust in persons can safely lend such a small amount of capital. No one can invest his money better than in this way.

So then, I have reported what Canada has to offer, not on the basis of my own ideas, but on the basis of facts. My goal was only to call attention to it, in order to work if possible for the outward success of my countrymen who have little future in the Netherlands.

The population in the Netherlands is growing, and the struggle for existence is not improving there. One crowds out another, and instead of being able to have a restful old age, many become old and poor. In the United States, and in the part of America that bears the name of Canada, this is completely different for decent people. Even here [in New Jersey] in such districts as Paterson, Passaic, etc., where there are large Dutch churches, there are almost no diaconal poor. And yet this area is the least favourable for Hollanders. The masses work in factories. One can begin to do this at a young age and end at old age. It is better than in the Netherlands, but it is changing into a semi-European condition. Some are beginning to think about wresting themselves from that situation. At Paterson some are thinking about Alabama. A few have already gone. Others will follow. Here eyes are also opening toward Canada. It is my wish that thousands may stream into Canada.

If there are extensive fertile fields that lie ready and can be obtained on favourable terms, why then hesitate and wait until the youthful years are past and need at last is pressing. Don't wait until your youthful vigor is squandered for a scanty wage; don't wait until your ever diminishing bit of capital is completely consumed, but spend it rather on passage to a land with enormous, rich resources. You will never regret it.

Whether you decide to go or stay, keep your attention focused on Canada; read what the newspapers will report about it, and the outcome will show that I have not said too much about it – yes, that I have not been *able* to say too much about it.

With this I lay down the pen, with the hope that I myself may one day call out to you: Welcome to Canada!"

S. A. S[chilstra]

LETTER FROM S.A.SCHILSTRA
(*Nieuwsblad van Friesland,* 19 September 1903)

West Sayville, Long Island, N.Y.
27 August 1903

Answer to E. Aldus, Nijverdal[32]

1 In Canada, especially close to the border with the United States, a lot of land needs artificial watering, like in some states of America, but you do not need to go there, though no doubt it is very good there too.

2 In my article I have clearly stated that the Canadian government cooperates and helps with everything, and especially has

---

32 This letter is a reply to Evert Aldus's questions published in the 8 August 1903 issue of the *Nieuwsblad van Friesland.*

experimental stations, and thus you know beforehand what the land is most suited for. There are terribly large stretches of fields with black earth, so the land never needs to be manured. There is no more fertile land in the world. Nowhere is better wheat grown, and nowhere is the production per acre as large. Years of experience indicate this with statistics.

3 In Canada there is oh so much forest land; thus you cannot immediately plough there, but there are fields, much larger than Germany, where you can just begin ploughing.

4 Certainly the grain can be sold; otherwise no one would want to live there. It may well be that you need to ride some miles to deliver it, but after a short time, with some immigration, villages appear and everything becomes easier. It depends on what land you choose, close to or far from the railway.

5 You can take along a lot of money or little. Whoever wants to put 160 acres immediately into cultivation may well have a couple thousand dollars, but I am convinced that whoever begins slowly, and works 6 months for himself and 6 months for someone else, will have enough to live on from the earned wages; you can also grow daily necessities on your own soil.

  I have given an example in my article. There are many examples of those who came with nothing, with $200, $500, $1,000, or more. Whoever has no money does not need to ask for land immediately. No doubt in such a country there is abundant work everywhere for good wages. Just take into consideration that at the moment four times as many railways are being constructed as there are in the Netherlands. What a lot is built there! That requires hands, so any handy man can come prepared for anything, even though he is not a carpenter. No Jack-of-all-trades and master-of-none exists in America. One does what he pleases, and simply tackles what is there, no matter what.

6 Necessities of life, etc., are cheap here if one compares American cents with Dutch cents. In the far remote areas everything is generally somewhat more expensive; yet, as soon as a place is accessible by rail, this cannot be very much.

Before me lies a newspaper of 21 August with the market prices in Michigan and in the city of Chicago. This will not be much different than in Canada;

for example, 1 barrel of flour (100 pounds) $4.40, a bushel of wheat 77 cents, 1 bushel of rye 45 cents, 1 bushel of potatoes 35 cents, 1 pound of butter 16–20 cents, eggs 16 cents a dozen, chickens (cleaned) 11 cents, live 8 cents, turkeys (live) 10 cents, fat 10, lard 11, meat 5–6, bacon 6½, mutton 7, veal 6–7 cents a pound. Coffee, tea, sugar, etc., is very reasonable in price; clothes also.

Implements vary so much in price that no answer can be given. Draft animals will probably not be cheap since there is a lot of demand for them. However, there are horse farms on a large scale. Seed grain, I think, is not expensive in a land of plenty.

Let no one who wishes some self-denial (no suffering from poverty, but making do in the beginning with living conditions, etc.) torment himself with all kinds of questions, but remember that here it is completely different and better than in the Netherlands. Because the earned wages generally go up from week to week. Today I received a report from an acquaintance in Michigan, a young man of 17 years, that he is earning $1.75 a day. He pays no more than $3 a week for board there. Craftsmen earn much more. Thus whoever is frugal soon has $100 saved. This is simply the rule here. Well-behaved married men buy a piece of land and build a fine house on it.

A land that is as fertile as Canada and is on the rise must be blessed, and whoever is able and willing to work need not be worried. You can well face things very different than you expected, but this is the lot of every emigrant.

Since Canada is much larger than the United States, and one state (or province in Canada) is much larger than Germany, yes even Russia, everyone will grasp at once that this does not begin to answer all questions exactly.

Thus those who have an interest in it should keep this in view: Canada is very fertile. Canada is extraordinarily large. Canada has only six million inhabitants. Eyes for Canada's riches are now opening. The government promotes immigration and helps as much as possible. There is a need for many workmen. The railway company charges just 1 cent a mile for immigrants; otherwise it is 3 cents, etc., etc.

Where to? I will mention three main places that are in the process of formation and growing quickly. (There are certainly many more, but I will mention only three for this purpose.) These are west of Winnipeg, namely, Regina, Prince Albert, north of Regina, and Edmonton, west of Prince Albert. These places are hundreds of miles apart, and between them there are many villages and hamlets on the railway lines. Although Edmonton lies the furthest west, it would be my choice. I think one first ought to settle, as humbly as possible, in one of these places, work there and become well informed, in order to make a choice for land later. Winnipeg (see my article)[33] is becoming a very important centre, and already has 50,000 inhabitants in a few years. However, it is very cold there in the winter. But this does not seem to hinder many; it hinders them even less than the Hollanders at St. Petersburg.

The climate is very good, according to the unanimous testimony of experts in the three mentioned places, and in general they promise a lot for the future. That the land near such cities is already taken is understandable, but there is abundant room in and around the villages that are slowly forming in the vicinity of the cities.

I think that all who want to go should take notice of each other, so that they may possibly travel together and remain together.

Recently someone asked me by letter whether boats go from Rotterdam to Montreal. I read in a Dutch newspaper that a young man hid in a boat at Rotterdam and went along on the trip to Montreal.

This is all I can write this time. My wish is that I may make many happy by offering good advice without personal interest on my part. Also, I kindly request that people closely read my article about Canada once again before asking for further explanations.

S. A. S[chilstra]

LETTER FROM EVERT ALDUS
(*Twentsch Volksblad,* 26 September 1903)

Still More about America

In the previous issue of this paper the article about America concluded with a piece quoted from the Heerenveen paper[34] from the hand of S.A.S. I still want to share some information that is important, in my opinion. I think it is clear to everyone that you cannot begin to do anything with such a large piece of land as you receive in Canada without money.

You have to build a house, have horses and tools, etc.

Anyone who would want to convert his 160 acres immediately in the first year into a fresh farm would certainly have to take along 4,000 guilders. Not

---

33 Schilstra's article, "To Canada: Trustworthy Hints for Emigrants I" (*Nieuwsblad van Friesland*, 23 May 1903), contains a section on Manitoba and Winnipeg.

34 The *Nieuwsblad van Friesland* was published in the Frisian city of Heerenveen.

only for a house and farm machinery, but also to hire workers who must be paid a high wage there. However, it is not necessary to develop everything immediately; one can begin small. If one is alone, he can buy enough to get started for 800 to 1,000 guilders. If, however, someone goes with three or four families and they help each other, then each head of the family needs less since they can work together.

If A ploughs on Monday he can sow on Tuesday, and B can use the plough that day, etc. Thus six people can well manage with one seeder the first year. It is not necessary for each to have a wagon. Together they can buy foodstuffs, such as potatoes, sugar, flour, etc., in larger quantities, which is more economical. They can help each other build a house, butcher a cow together, etc.

If, however, someone has absolutely no money, it doesn't work to immediately begin on his own land. When someone comes in the spring, he can still immediately ask for land. Then he can work, for a farmer, for example, in the summer, *i.e.,* the first half year. Then he still has time remaining to plant some potatoes, beans, etc. on his own land; thus he has some provisions for the coming winter. And from the extra money earned after one or two years he can begin. If anyone has worked a year or two for someone else and people see that he wants to get ahead, then he can get horses and machines on instalment and become a farmer himself. Unmarried men and women always find work. A man and wife without children very easily find work, often on one farm. This still works with one child who is not too young. But when the family is larger it becomes more difficult and one must live from the wages of the husband. This is not a drawback; one can well manage, because a worker who knows no trade always earns $2 a day and he who knows a trade earns more. But when a man and wife both work they can earn $100 in a short time. For a family with many children, without money, it is therefore the most difficult to become independent in Canada, that is, to get oneself a farm. One should not think too lightly about the difficulties for such a family.

If someone has some money and has chosen land (preferably pick out land without trees; then one can immediately plough), he begins to build a (temporary) house. He can do this from the trees that he gets free by laying them lengthwise on each other, thus making four walls. This goes very quickly and costs nothing. If you have to haul the free wood far, this may not be so good for then you lose too much time. People also build a house by ploughing the tough sod from the ground and piling pieces on each other. When the clay-sod becomes good and hard, you have a strong wall. And for 150 to 200 guilders you can buy boards as well as finished doors and windows. For about 200 guilders you can build a house 4 by 9 metres from these. The walls are made double by nailing boards on both sides of the posts.[35] When the house is finished, you can begin to work. To break the hard, tough ground you need a strong plough and three horses at first.

You walk behind the plough. When you plough the ground the second time, you then sit on the plough. You sit also on the seeder and binder and all other implements. The first ploughing is the most difficult work. The second time you can use a wider plough and also do not need to have three horses for that. When you have ploughed the 160 acres once, you have won. Then the prairie is converted into farm land, and you can say, "Now I am where I have to be." When one has done this much, then one man can work the 160 acres, each year a half, alternately. Threshing takes place on the land as soon as the grain is ripe. For this someone comes around the farmsteads with a (steam) threshing machine, for payment in cash or grain. After a year or two one builds a better house.

You immediately need three workhorses, which are rather high in price and cost about 200 guilders apiece. Also a plough that costs about 50 guilders, a harrow about 50, and a seeder about 200.

Then in the summer you need a rake (an implement for haying) that costs about 200, and a binder that mows and binds the grain and costs 250 to 300. A disc (an implement to make the ground fine) costs 70 to 80 guilders. Most of these implements, however, you can buy together with three to six men. You can get them on a five-year instalment plan. In the fall you can plough and sow winter wheat, or sow in the spring.

A milk cow costs 100 to 150 guilders. A small pig about six weeks old roughly a rijksdaalder.[36] Chickens are about the same as here in Holland. Cattle prices naturally go up and down with the market, so they can somewhat vary from the listed prices. With government approval, you can get money by mortgaging your land, up to $500. This can be done as soon as you have received the land, thus immediately. Clothing and furniture cost about the same as here. Fuel, *i.e.,* wood and coal, are generally very cheap. Petroleum is expensive. Groceries also do not cost much. Thus a pound of sugar costs 5 to 6 dollar-cents, a pound of pork or bacon 6 to 10, veal 8, beef from 10 to 18 cents a pound. Bread and potatoes cost much less than here, butter and cheese also. Tobacco and cigars, as well as strong drinks, are very expensive. Home-grown tobacco is cheap, but not very good.

---

35 Homestead shacks were often constructed by nailing boards to four fence posts at the corners.
36 A rijksdaalder is equivalent to 2½ Dutch guilders.

In the areas suitable for immigration the religion is mixed, that is to say, there are Protestants and Catholics. There is no state church in Canada. Sunday laws are rather strictly enforced there.

And now something about the trip. If you go from Rotterdam to Quebec, the city where the ships arrive, that costs 72 guilders for an adult third class, 36 g. for a child from 1 to 12, and 6 g. for a child below 1 year. The train from Quebec to Winnipeg costs 30 g. for an adult, to Edmonton (*i.e.,* at the other end of Canada) 60 g. For a child 5 to 12 half of that, and under 5 free. So for an adult the whole trip from Rotterdam at most costs 132 guilders. For that you are taken to the furthest region of Canada that is suitable for immigration. For a child between 5 and 12 it would cost 66 guilders, between 1 and 5 years 36 g., and below 1 year 6 guilders. In addition there is the trip from here to Rotterdam. It is possible, however, that the trip may cost less from Antwerp. You may take along a lot of baggage on the boat and train, so you can easily pack bedding, clothing, etc., and take it along without cost. But aside from the items mentioned it is better not to take much along; you can better buy it later in Canada. Also you may easily take along new blankets or clothes if you do not intend to sell them on arrival.

Now I am at the end of the story. I am writing about Canada not to advise anyone to go there, only to inform. Because, although it is no doubt better there for the labourer than here, since there is a great shortage in the human workforce and consequently wages are higher, and since foodstuffs are very cheap, yet life will certainly bring a lot of disappointments and burdens before one is well established in Canada.

Therefore each person himself has to know what he wants to do. With hearty thanks, Mr. Editor, for the space you have so readily granted in your paper, I end with the hope to be of service to those interested in immigrating to America.

A[ldus]

LETTER FROM EVERT ALDUS
(*Twentsch Volksblad,* 3 October 1903)

Mr. Editor:

I kindly request a place for the following in connection with my letter about America in the last issues of your paper. I do so because of the question asked by some: "Is that letter really trustworthy?"

One should know that what I wrote I had read in brochures and literature about Canada. I received them in response to a letter that I sent directly to the Canadian government in Ottawa, and by writing to the High Commissioner for Immigration to Canada, living in London. The brochures in question were printed by the government printing office in Ottawa and published by order of the Canadian government. They include all sorts of things worth knowing about Canada, in various territories. They are provided with maps and pictures. One is written only in Dutch, the others in the German or English language. Anyone can get these booklets free if he applies in writing to Mr. D. Tréau de Coeli, Agent of the Government of Canada for Belgium and the Netherlands, at Antwerp. The part I copied out of the Heerenveen newspaper[37] from the hand of S.A.S. agrees completely with what can be read in the official brochures. If this were not the case, I would not have copied it. Who S.A.S. is, I don't know. I only know his place of residence, namely, Passaic, New Jersey, the United States.

Also that he is a Hollander. In one of the later issues of the Heerenveen newspaper he says that he only wrote about Canada in the interest of his countrymen who can have a better future there.[38] If anyone wants to know who S.A.S. is, Mr. Hepkema, the publisher of the Heerenveen newspaper, will perhaps share that; he knows, of course. Since his letter squares with what stands in the brochures, I have not inquired about his name or person.[39]

Finally I wrote to one of our fellow-townsmen who has lived for several years as a farmer in Montana, U.S.A. I did this all the more because everyone who earlier knew this person here is convinced that he is an honest and trustworthy man, who will say too little rather than too much. He answered me that he had just returned from a trip to Canada (Alberta). He had investigated everything there that relates to farming, because he himself has made up his mind to settle there.[40] His letter confirmed for me completely what I had read in the brochures. If anyone would like to know this person, or read his letter to me, he can ask for my address at the office of this paper and inspect this letter at my home. And so I end.

My hearty thanks to the Editor for the readily granted space.

A[ldus]   Nijverdal, 1 October 1903

---

37 This is the *Nieuwsblad van Friesland.*
38 This passage in Schilstra's letter of 15 August 1903 in the *Nieuwsblad van Friesland* is quoted above. p. 30.
39 This letter clearly reveals the main sources of information that Aldus and the others in the large group of forty-one emigrants relied on when they left for Alberta in March 1904.
40 The fellow-townsman Aldus wrote to was Jan Hendrik ter Telgte, who left Nijverdal in 1892 and settled in Paterson, New Jersey, before taking up a homestead at Manhattan, Montana, in 1897. It appears that in

LETTER FROM HENDRIKUS ZANDBERGEN
(*Twentsch Volksblad,* 10 October 1903)

Enschede, October 1903

Dear Editor,

As a faithful reader of your esteemed paper I make a friendly request to place in the *Twentsch Volksblad* a short summary of my view of America and emigration.

I did not want to interrupt the correspondent of the letters about Canada,[41] but I thought I must say a short word now, since his argument greatly arouses the strong inclination to risk undertaking the trip and since one has to be so cautious in these matters, so that later one does not have to hear that a brother or sister is languishing abroad over there. The correspondent also might regret advocating this matter without convincing himself, hoping perhaps that many countrymen may move there.

This is not narrow-mindedness on my part, because I too am a great lover of emigration, even today. The fact is, I spent two full years, not in Canada, but in the United States, in the state of Colorado which lies quite deep in the heart of America. Now I am ready, if it does not demand too much of the editor, to relate a little of my experience with a short yet sound note of my findings. First I want to identify myself as belonging to the Gereformeerde church here at Enschede; my name is H[endrikus] Zandbergen. I left in the year 1892, on the advice of a distinguished man of our Gereformeerde churches, and came back in 1894. I shall, however, conceal names in order to harm no one. With some emigrants we were to establish a colony there on land already bought for that purpose. Large fields were already purchased, so it was said. Immigrant houses were ready, which also seemed to be true, but mind you, dear readers, on arrival we were surprised to set foot on about a foot-thick layer of loose sand instead of fertile ground. And truly, if you had seen the printed booklets with all the calculations with large figures, you would have said with us, that can produce a good living. We saw already at Amsterdam the rich stalks of barley and oats, so we went on cheerfully, with a happy outlook of having our relatives also come over soon, all the more because we fully trusted those who took this move on their conscience.

August 1903 Jan Hendrik made a trip to the Leavings area; on 29 August he obtained entry on a homestead there, and then returned to sell his land at Manhattan and to fetch his family. The correspondence between Aldus and ter Telgte then must have occurred in August and September; it took about three weeks for a letter to travel between the Netherlands and Montana.

41 He is referring to Evert Aldus's letters in the *Twentsch Volksblad.*

The men who fetched us from New York and had a large role in the game, as we understood it, then tried to make us also believe that the sand was all mineral material and thus made the ground all the richer. And although the most prominent among us shook their heads, we still decided to go ahead and buy the land. Soon they learned yet in the bargain that these gentlemen owned not a foot of property there and, as it turned out, even the immigrant houses were built on forbidden land. Then all kinds of discontent arose; the land owner (who later could supply no title deed but certainly wanted his pennies) and the mayor and higher-ranked persons stepped in, and things occurred that I would rather not tell. We lived through that also.

In any case, the gentlemen who guided us from New York were completely untrustworthy, and I would not recommend their leadership; this I soon grasped.

And so it happened that the most prominent among us selected land, as best they could, a couple of hours from there, from the just mentioned owner, and the younger ones looked for work. Some with a farmer, others about 40 hours back in the coal mines, among them this writer. To put all my experiences on paper I would reach no end at present. I am not the only one who again sought the Motherland. If anyone thinks I wish to maintain that there are no prospects in all of America, he is very mistaken; and if anyone supposes that I think the leading persons of the Committee or those who also had a hand in it had knowledge of this, he is also mistaken. We even had a guide along from Holland, who from experience had a love for us and was interested in where we were being led.[42]

My only intention is to warn anyone who is enchanted or is making plans, about the many, many deceptions in America, and therefore to be extremely cautious and not trust people too much without knowing them very well, though they sound so convincing. Put no trust in princes, says the Psalmist.

Everyone should also overestimate the costs. If a well-off labourer's family should wish to go, after selling their belongings here for 1,000 guilders, then they have 600 guilders left over on the other side of the ocean and still have travel costs in America. If the household consists of four or five persons, then they have as good as nothing left when they arrive in Canada. And if they claim for the 1,000 guilders only 600 dollars or rijksdaalders, I tell

42 See Peter De Klerk's article on the fiasco in the San Luis Valley of Colorado, "The Ecclesiastical Struggles of the Rilland and Crook Christian Reformed Churches in Colorado in 1893," in *Perspectives on the Christian Reformed Church*, ed. Peter De Klerk and Richard De Ridder (Grand Rapids: Baker, 1983), 72–98.

you that nowhere can one do more with that [dollar] there than here with a hundred Dutch cents and he receives only a homestead on reasonable terms. There will be many things that you don't expect. And that happens immediately if there is no food for your family. This must be grown when that land (that has been wild since the creation) is properly broken up, which does not happen in a couple of days, also not without a plough and horse and a full stomach. I think that beside the beautiful face the dark backside also has to be pointed out a little. If anyone is interested in these matters, I would be able to give some good advice, by letter or however.

With greetings and thanks for the space, I am your friend and faithful servant,

H. Z[andbergen]

LETTER FROM EVERT ALDUS
(*Twentsch Volksblad,* 17 October 1903)

Mr. Editor:

Once again I kindly request to make use of your paper, in connection with what Mr. H. Zandbergen wrote in last week's issue.

First I say that I am completely convinced that this man wrote his piece with good intentions and on good principle. Yet I would like to point out the following for your readers.

That my argument arouses "the strong inclination to risk undertaking the trip" you will at most be able to find in the part I copied from S.A.S. out of the Heerenveen newspaper. This man occasionally moves into reflections and he holds forth quite a bit. The facts and figures that he gives, however, are in complete agreement with what may be read in the official brochures of the Canadian government, etc. And it is the facts alone that anyone will take into account when he wants to emigrate, I think.

Then Mr. Z. should know that I wrote only to inform those who were thinking about emigrating. I communicated what came to hand by an extensive investigation of about a half year, and I named the sources I had used, so everyone can judge for himself.[43]

---

43 This letter reveals Aldus started investigating the possibilities of emigrating in the spring of 1903. It seems that the Colorado fiasco may have helped confirm Aldus's choice to emigrate to Canada rather than to the United States.

As I said at the beginning of my article, I wrote only to inform, without intending to recommend anything to anyone. I have no interest in the least whether people leave for Canada. Also I am not persuaded by nice words or numbers. No one has ever advised me to move to Canada; no one has even spoken to me about it.[44]

Wanting to emigrate myself, I have investigated, read, written letters to trustworthy persons in America for information, taken market reports from American newspapers to get to know prices, etc.[45] Thus I came to the conclusion that it is better in Canada than in Montana, for example, and I wrote my "information."

What happened to Mr. Z. in Colorado is sad indeed. In my opinion he was a sacrifice in the well-known Colorado story, in which so many were disappointed and swindled.

But Colorado is not Canada. If it is bad in Amsterdam, it can certainly be good in Paris.

A single glance at a good map indeed shows that there is little good land in Colorado, but a lot in Canada. In my possession is a map of Canada 2×1 metres large on which everything is indicated. The map is printed this year, so it is completely up to date. Anyone who wishes can inspect this map if he asks for it at the office of this paper.

It seems to me that Mr. Z. was swindled by agents of some business enterprise. This is something that has often happened to other people as well. The Canadian government, however, is no business enterprise and has no agents. It continually warns against unscrupulous persons who swindle others to benefit themselves, and it advises that one should apply only to the officials it appoints. Now more on this. Some time ago Mr. Tream [Tréau] de Coeli, representative of the Canadian government at Antwerp, was here. He came at the request of some residents who wanted information about Canada. Before he came, he wrote: "I find it better to visit and inform you personally, not to advise you to persist in your plan, but so that you yourself can judge whether you can seize the opportunities that are presented in Canada. It very often happens that persons have a much too exaggerated notion of what can happen in a foreign land, and if they leave with these thoughts they become very disappointed. It is completely to the advantage of the Canadian government that everyone who goes there succeeds and

---

44 By saying he has no interest in whether people emigrate to Canada Aldus appears to be less than candid. Also his contention that no one spoke to him about Canada is questionable since he was among the ten Nijverdalers to whom Canadian immigration agent Tréau de Coeli had talked.

45 This letter reveals additional sources of information that Aldus investigated.

possesses the necessary qualities to do so; hence a personal visit is opportune. Your party is much too important for you not to know the pros and cons well." Let everyone judge this letter for himself. It is available to read, along with the whole correspondence of the said gentleman, for everyone who has interest in this matter. The ten persons who spoke with Mr. Tream [Tréau] de Coeli here will also assure you that this man recommended nothing, and also pointed out in all seriousness the difficulties as much as the positives.

That one can get good land for nothing, and also wood, I know for certain because acquaintances of mine from Montana have traveled to Canada and they received it. You can read their letter, if you wish, and also inquire about the trustworthiness of their person here, and then judge for yourself.[46] When Mr. Z. says that a labourer's family has not much left over after the money for the trip is gone from the 1,000 guilders that they have, that is true; yet, in my article, especially in the last instalment,[47] I very clearly said that a person with 1,000 guilders, if he has it there, can still only begin very small. Also that someone without money can begin to do nothing with the land since he needs draft animals, tools, a small house, and food until harvest time. If one has nothing, he first has to make some money. For single people or people with one child that goes well, but for a larger labourer's family it is not easy; that is why I emphatically also pointed out that such a family has a lot of difficulty becoming independent in Canada. But several persons who help each other will be able to begin with less money because a lot can be bought communally. If Mr. Z. will read over my article once again, he will see that I wrote just what he is pointing out.

Now something yet about the buying power of the money.

That one with a dollar there does no more than here with 100 Dutch cents is partly true and partly not. It is true in that the money there (to say it simply) is cheaper. Silver there has absolutely less value; merchandise, labour, etc. have greater value than here. A man who earns two guilders here will receive 2 dollars (5 guilders) or more for the same work in wages there. If he has the 5 guilders here, he can spend 500 cents, but there only 200 cents because a dollar has 200 [100] dollar-cents. Such a dollar-cent is worth 2½ of our cents, but in America it has the buying power of only one cent.[48] On the other hand, it is not true that a person with a dollar there does no more

---

46 Aldus's acquaintances from Montana were Jan Hendrik ter Telgte and his brother Hendrikus. Both had already filed on homesteads in Alberta. The letter is the one of Jan Hendrik that Aldus had already mentioned in his 3 October letter.

47 See Aldus letter in *Twentsch Volksblad* (26 September 1903).

48 Aldus's references to America obviously mean North America. He is referring to the Canadian dollar.

than with one guilder here. For one guilder one here gets about 3 pounds of meat, or 4 pounds of sugar, or 2 pounds of butter, or 25 pounds of salt, or a third of a hectolitre of potatoes, etc. In Canada for one dollar one buys 6 pounds of meat, or 18 pounds of sugar, or 3 to 4 pounds of butter, or 100 pounds of salt, or 1 hectolitre or more of potatoes. So the labourer can live better from his dollar than he can here from his guilder.

The difference in value of the money is, however, very disadvantageous for those who come to America with their Dutch money and have to buy something with it there. Thus an American pays $100 for a workhorse, which for him is as much as 100 guilders for us, because he just as quickly earns one dollar as we earn one guilder.

If someone buys this horse with the money he has taken along, then he also has to pay $100, *i.e.,* 250 guilders. So if a pound of meat costs us 15 dollar-cents (at arrival, for example), two and a half times 15 is 37½ cents. But as soon as one earns American money, he is beyond this and again lives in the usual situation. And now I end. If anyone, for good reason, can show something untrue in my writing, or has received reliable information that makes it undesirable to go to Canada, then please share this in this paper, because it is also my intention to tell the truth about such a serious matter. And I am in complete agreement with Z. on the point that above all caution is necessary. Nevertheless, it seems to me that it is not desirable to place over against the "beautiful face" of Canada the "dark backside" of Colorado, because Canada is not Colorado. But if anyone is be able to place the dark backside of Canada over against its good side, more so than I have done, then I will very thankfully accept this. With kind thanks for the willingness of the editor, I am your faithful servant.

A[ldus]   Nijverdal, 14 October 1903

LETTER FROM HENDRIKUS ZANDBERGEN
(*Twentsch Volksblad,* 31 October 1903)

Enschede, October 1903
Mr. Editor,

I kindly request a small place for this piece, in connection with the response of Mr. A[ldus]. I'm glad that Mr. A. is well familiar with the Colorado affair, and I think his letter seems to give a little more warning to observe caution than he did before. I'm also glad that, with good intent, he has rightly understood the intention of my letter. Yet I wish to say a short word, the more so because I understand that friend A. also feels personally attracted to Canada, and then I want to tell you that you have given good advice. I along with many Hollanders had my hopes deceived [in Colorado]. Now you may well think that we did not just stay sitting there, but also made inquiries into other places, also Canada. I was then advised to write to a Hollander in Iowa, who was a trustworthy person. I did that. The letter was long delayed because it went astray and finally was received by the man, who moved to Texas. He answered that he would not advise me to go to Iowa or to Texas, and that, in short, there was a great shortage of money in the whole of America. Others inquired about Canada. Finally, I did so myself, and according to this inquiry it is perfectly correct what you write. The land is available for free when strict conditions are followed. If you do not fulfill these, then you have prepared the land for someone else. But that aside. You should also know that it is cold in Canada and the winter is severe, and you have to take that into consideration in regard to the crops; and that it is not easy to break up that land, with trees that have roots deep in the earth because of their age and because the whole land is a wilderness. But an immigrant who can stick it out there and can do without until he has broken some [land] and finally all of it, – well I would have little objection to that if someone feels called to do this for the sake of his descendants, because, I would say, for himself such a person doesn't need to go if he can do all of that, as long as he runs no immediate danger of becoming destitute here or the Lord does not visit him with calamities. But you well know that this can well happen there, because, generally speaking, Nature rages more severely there than it does in our Fatherland. A cyclone is not news there, but if a good cyclone would come here we would think it extreme, wouldn't we?

Now a word yet about the dollar. It is true, as Mr. A. says, that sugar is a cheap article, which is easy for a family, and salt and meat and potatoes are also cheap. However, sugar is no staple and salt is not very necessary for a family, but when you eat there from your own potatoes, you will agree, that you would gladly see the other items fetching somewhat higher prices on the market, and when you have a cow for the butcher and have a pig or so left, you no longer desire cheap meat or bacon. I helped deliver [a cow] for my farmer to the fairly large town of Alamosa [in Colorado] for four cents a pound and have seen a fairly fat cow for which an American farmer got $12. And I believe that there is no less business in Colorado than in Canada, because Canada is unpopulated and Colorado has its good qualities as much as Canada does.

Hence in America profit has to come from quantity and size. A farmer with eleven or twelve cows and nine or ten pigs does not get very far. A small parcel of land or some potatoes is not very beneficial; there it must be 40 to 50 acres, and an acre is about as much as 20 spint here, a spint reckoned at 200 square yards, thus 4,000 square yards for an acre.

I could still write of more experiences, but enough. In my opinion, one can do no better, when some people wish to leave, than to select one person with sound judgment from their midst to go ahead, before some families themselves venture forth together; preferably a young man who can manage for himself in every respect. Incidentally, a blue linen pants that costs about 1 guilder here cost us 90 to 95 dollar-cents there; a pair of fine work shoes cost me about $3. Now I will end by saying that I am not against emigration, provided that there is very good deliberation and an invoking of God's help and his blessing; not a goal of pursuing riches, because that kingdom will fall into many temptations.

With a friendly thank you, Mr. Editor, for granting the space, I am your friend and faithful servant,

Z[andbergen]

LETTER FROM EVERT ALDUS
(*Twentsch Volksblad*, 7 November 1903)

To America

May I be allowed once again to make use of your paper, to write about the above-mentioned topic, in connection with the letter of Z[andbergen] in your previous issue. The Homestead law requires a three-year residence by the colonist, at least six months per year, and that each year 10 acres be ploughed, *i.e.*, 30 acres in three years. At the end of the three years with two witnesses (neighbours, for example) one has to prove that he has satisfied the regulations, and become a Canadian; then he receives the title deed for a payment of $5. If in that time someone cannot satisfy these regulations, he has not worked for nothing. Also not for someone else. If someone, for example, has resided for one year, and then would like to be away for a year or two, he can request this of the government. Then, however, he must wait one or two years longer for the title deed. Likewise when one cannot get 30 acres ploughed. Of course, there must be a valid reason for requesting such permission.

If one has not satisfied the law, for example, by leaving after residing for two years, then too one has not worked for someone else. If one leaves in such a case, then the land is given to someone else. Before this person gets it, however, the value of the labour that one has done on it is appraised and the new owner must pay this value before he can take possession of it. All the money is handed to the one who first occupied the land. The homestead law states this clearly. In the future I hope to place some articles of this law in this paper, if the editor approves.

Now something about the cold in the areas where there is room for immigrants. In Manitoba it is very cold, in winter certainly as cold as St. Petersburg in Russia. In the summer it is warmer there than here. It is one of the most fertile provinces in Canada, and is already fairly populated, so the cold does not seem to bother. Almost as cold is eastern Assiniboia, Saskatchewan, and northern Alberta. In southern Alberta and western Assiniboia the winter is much milder.[49] There the snow seldom lies longer than a few days. The cattle that are native there stay on the land in the winter. Sometimes one can plough there in the winter. What Z. writes about natural phenomena is true; they are more severe there than here. The average summer temperature for Winnipeg (Manitoba) is 66 degrees; for Prince Albert (Saskatchewan) 59.5 degrees; for Calgary (southern Alberta) 58.8 degrees. The average winter temperature respectively for these places is 0.9 degrees, 2.1 degrees, 13.9 degrees, and the average annual temperature is 33.3 degrees, 30.7 degrees, and 37.4 degrees. These observations were done over 10 years. What Mr. Z. writes about uprooting trees, which one has to work at for years, is not true. There are tens of thousands of acres to be obtained, prairie land, which one can immediately plough. There is more land without bush than with it. And one can choose. Certainly there are areas where everything is covered with bush, but one does not have to take these.

It is certainly true that the prices for butchered cattle are lower there than here. But not as low as Z. states; he is possibly naming a couple of particular cases. A milk cow costs from $36 to $50. A fat cow I don't know, but never much less. Nevertheless, if one knows that feed there is very cheap for pigs, and for cows it costs the farmer nothing, and that there is no tax on meat there, then everyone understands that a farmer there can very easily have a large number of animals. Also because one has at his disposal a lot of land. Also grain there yields much less than here. The great quantity must do it.

---

49 At this time the District of Alberta consisted of the southern part of what became the province of Alberta in 1905, and the District of Assiniboia consisted of what was later southern Saskatchewan and eastern Alberta.

And this is possible, because the farmer, by possessing a lot of good land that he can cultivate without manuring and by use of modern implements, can produce a large quantity. Also, the fact that feed for horses is cheap is to the advantage of the American farmer. I have already written earlier myself what Z. says about the prices of clothing. Cotton is cheaper there than here, linen is largely as expensive, wool and baize materials much more expensive. Shoes and leatherwork a little more expensive, or for some articles as expensive as in our country. Here I will leave off.

My sincere thanks to the Editor who so kindly granted me space.

Your servant, A[ldus]   Nijverdal, November 1903

ADVERTISEMENT IN *TWENTSCH VOLKSBLAD*
(28 November 1903)[50]

CANADA   FREE FARMLAND AND PASTURE

The government of CANADA is giving f r e e 160 acres (64 hectares) of very good farmland or pasture, in MANITOBA or N. W. CANADA, to Netherlanders who plan to go to CANADA. Such people will be put into contact with each other, if they so desire, in order to enjoy all the benefits of a trip together and to obtain a fertile district.

Information concerning the land, the climate, etc., as well as brochures are available from Mr. D. Tréau de Coeli, Agent of the Canadian Government, at Antwerp.

Concerning passage and fares contact the office of the CANADIAN PACIFIC RAILWAY, 209, Leuvehaven, Rotterdam

50   The same advertisement appeared in the issues of 5 and 12 December 1903.

CHAPTER 2

The Tough Homesteading Years
1903–05

THIS CHAPTER CONTAINS THE EARLIEST LETTERS
that the Dutch settlers wrote from Alberta. They describe the journey of
the large group that emigrated from the Netherlands in the spring of 1904
and the early development of the Dutch settlement with the challenges of
homesteading and pioneer life.

These years include fourteen letters of George Dijkema describing the
early progress of the settlement. In four letters Evert Aldus reports in detail
on the journey by ship and rail to Alberta. Then in fifteen later letters Aldus
carefully describes various aspects of the pioneer settlement: the geography
and climate of the area, the means of transportation, the social situation,
farming prospects and costs, farm implements and early crops, gardening,
house moving, Christmas celebrations, and the beginnings of church life.
In four letters Jan Hendrik ter Telgte and George Dijkema complain about
Aldus's portrayal of pioneer life, and Aldus replies. Finally there are a couple of letters from Gerrit Withage describing the origins of the Christian
Reformed Church that was established in 1905.

LETTER FROM MACLEOD, ALBERTA
(*De Grondwet,* 29 March 1904)

Dear Editor,

I have just received your paper and now I'll take the liberty to send some news once as your correspondent.[1]

The Dutch colony in Alberta was very small when we arrived (my friend and I). All we met there were two families, consisting of twelve persons, with a bachelor for company.[2] Yet we were there only a short time when to our joy it was reported that other households were on the way.[3] And behold, in the beginning of March, Mr. J[an] H. ter Telgte with his family and G[errit] J. Withage with his wife and healthy boys arrived, all from Manhattan, Montana. And now a report is spreading around the country that three families are on their way directly from Holland.[4] So the colony is slowly becoming larger.

The climate here, as far as we know from experience and from what we have heard, is not very cold. To date not much snow has fallen. And if a little sometimes falls, the climate [chinook] winds quickly melt it again, so the snow here actually covers the ground no more than three or four days.

Everything is expensive here, a result, no doubt, of the war between Russia and Japan. Well-broken horses which anyone can handle are rare, so people must make do with horses that are still untrained.

Enough for now.

Geo. Dykema 17 March 1904

---

1 This is George Dijkema's first letter as regular correspondent of *De Grondwet.* Such correspondents were expected to report on the news in their local Dutch community.

2 The two families already there were those of Harm Emmelkamp and Hendrikus ter Telgte, each with four children. The ter Telgte family came to Alberta in late 1903 from Manhattan, Montana. The bachelor was most likely Willem Feller, whose homestead was next to Emmelkamp's.

3 This letter implies that Dijkema probably arrived in late February 1904, a "short time" before the ter Telgte and Withage families arrived on 3 March. Dijkema's friend was almost certainly Lubbert Van Dellen. He had come to Leavings the previous year and had filed on a homestead on 18 August 1903. He then left to work in a mine in Montana for the winter, and returned now with Dijkema. It seems that they did not come directly from Manhattan, since they did not have previous knowledge of the coming of the Withage and J. H. ter Telgte families.

4 The "three families" reported to be on their way from Holland were actually six families and two single men, a total of forty-one persons. They arrived on 3 April.

THE FIRST WORSHIP SERVICE, 6 MARCH 1904
(Excerpt of Speech by Chris Withage)[5]

It was late at night on March the 3rd 1904 that the ter Telgte family and our family arrived in Macleod. On Saturday morning, March 5, Mr. ter Telgte and my father arrived with the freight cars (by the way, we had been sleeping on the floor in the old Macleod station then for 2 nights).[6] The freight cars were unloaded, and towards evening we started from Macleod. That evening at around 11 o'clock we arrived at a house 2 miles south of this church, where the Hillebrands now live.

On Sunday, March 6, my father led the first religious meeting of Christian Reformed people in Alberta. How well I remember singing, "Geloofd zij God met diepst ontzag," and "Hoe lieflijk, hoe vol heilgenot," and at the close, "Heer, ai! maak mij uwe wegen, door uw woord en Geest bekent."[7]

LETTER FROM EVERT ALDUS
(*Twentsch Volksblad,* 26 March 1904)

Canada

In the hope and expectation that you will be interested, dear readers of this paper, I wish to tell you from time to time something about the above-mentioned topic.[8] I will begin by communicating something about our

---

5   This is part of a speech presented by Chris Withage in 1955 on the occasion of the fiftieth anniversary of the Granum Christian Reformed Church.

6   Chris Withage was eight years old when he arrived in Alberta in March 1904 with his parents Gerrit and Theodora Withage and older brother Cornelis. They came from Manhattan with Jan Hendrik and Fenneken ter Telgte and their four children. The previous August ter Telgte had come to Alberta to claim a homestead that had been abandoned east of Leavings. There was already a moderate-sized house on the place. In early March the men accompanied their belongings on a freight train while the families arrived earlier by passenger train. The railway station at that time was not in Macleod but in Haneyville, two miles south of Macleod.

7   At first both families stayed together at the ter Telgte home. (This house is still standing two miles south of the present Granum Christian Reformed Church). The first worship service, held in that home, probably included only the Withage and ter Telgte families, although by this time there were two other Dutch families and three single men in the area. Gerrit Withage took the initiative to lead the first worship service and quickly became a religious leader in the Dutch community. In 1905 he would become an elder when a Christian Reformed Church was organized. The songs sung in that first service were Dutch Psalms 68 vs. 10, 84 vs. 1, and 25 vs. 2.

8   This is the first of many letters that Evert Aldus would send to the *Twentsch Volksblad* in the next decade to describe for people back home what it was like to emigrate to Canada. In March 1904 Aldus, his wife and young son were part of a group of forty-one emigrants (six families and two single men) to leave the Nijverdal area to settle in southern Alberta. Aldus had been a Christian school teacher in Nijverdal, and tried to present a fair account of what he experienced—the good and the bad.

experiences on the journey. On the whole I will limit myself to short pieces of information; and I want to report especially on things that are of interest to the emigrant and that can be of use to him on the journey to the new country. In everything I hope to remain faithful to the truth. In order to give a good survey I will first tell something of

The Trip to Hull

On Saturday March 12 we left our home. No one will be surprised that it was hard for us to part with our family and friends, especially since so many said a last farewell to us at the station. We reached Rotterdam without incident. We were met by someone from the Müller firm (head-agent of the Boot-Mij)[9] and were taken to the boat. At the same time two wagons were available for our hand luggage. (We had already sent our crates a few days earlier.) On one of the wagons room was made also for some of the small children, since the distance from the station to the boat pier was rather far. When we arrived at the boat we had to wait for about an hour before we could board since everything was still not ready. In itself this was not bad, but it was a little unpleasant for the women and children because they were tired. So I advise every emigrant who is married to take his family to a hotel until he goes to the boat and is convinced that it is ready to receive passengers. Everyone also should take some food along, because if the departure is in the evening, one goes to the dining hall only the following morning.

Our boat, the "Swallow," was an English vessel with an English crew. So, for those of us who had learned a little English it immediately came in handy. I advise everyone who wants to emigrate to learn at least enough of the English language that he can refer to the simplest things. It's a very great convenience. Moreover, the crew of the boat was very polite and friendly.

The boat was 72 metres long, built of steel and lighted electrically the whole night, also in the bedrooms. We were taken into a very neat second-class cabin and bedrooms. The bedsteads were of mahogany; the seats were covered with thick cushions. Everything was very beautiful and also very clean. In each little room there were wash-stands with all the necessities of a nice bed-chamber. However, there was not enough room; some of us had to sleep in the cabin. But this was no difficulty in the least. On this boat, as in general, there were also contrasts.

While we were so neatly billeted there, we took a peek into the steerage. There we saw a large number of Romanian [Russian] Jews, men, women, and children

---

9   The Boot-Mij was a Dutch transport company.

in a room that I think was otherwise used for transporting horses or cows. They were dirty and unsightly and lay like a herd of animals on straw sacks. Sometimes even five or six on a sack. Some of us shared from our bags cookies and oranges that we had taken along for the trip; also the raisin bread that we had. They accepted everything eagerly and showed that they were very thankful. Yet we could not understand them; they spoke no Dutch or English.

At 9:30 in the evening the rope was untied and the boat slowly began to move. It was a splendid evening, and the sight of Rotterdam with its thousands of lights was uniquely beautiful. Imperceptibly they receded into the distance, at least so it seemed. Again and again we saw new lights at places along the waterway. Finally at 11:30 at night we passed the lights of the Hook of Holland. Yet we stared a long time from the North Sea at these last points of light of our fatherland, until at last they disappeared before our eyes. Indeed, these were sad, deeply sad moments.... Perhaps there is an eternity between us and our Fatherland!

That night most of us slept well and awoke in the morning on the North Sea. Nothing to see but water and sky, only a passing steamship from time to time. Our breakfast consisted of bread with butter and wurst and coffee. In the meantime the sea began to be more turbulent so that the boat danced bravely up and down. A couple of times the waves lashed right across it. Many of us then became seasick. This is very unpleasant and distressing. Yet, though I myself was also very sick, I could not control my laughter when I saw a short row of lads bending over the railing to relieve their stomachs of the water they had just drunk.

At noon we received some food that looked much like pea-soup and was very good. In it there was a large portion of meat for everyone. When I finished eating I saw below in the ship the meal of the Russian Jews. They received unpeeled baked potatoes which they scrambled for with their dirty hands out of a pot; each also received a salt herring and a slice of bread three English inches thick.

At three o'clock Sunday afternoon the lighthouse from the English coast came into view and soon we could see both shores of the wide mouth of the Humber. This river at its mouth is as much as an hour wide. After we had sailed for a half hour, we saw the docks and harbours of Hull, and the ship soon lay ashore. At Hull the Humber is no broader than the Rhine at Arnhem. Before we went ashore a customs officer came to ask us whether we had tobacco, cigars, or Dutch gin in our handbags. But when we assured him that we did not have more than the allowed amount he let most of us go without unpacking.

From the boat we were taken to the hotel for emigrants. Our baggage was carried on a wagon. In this hotel we were treated to coffee and bread of good quality, with margarine of poor quality; unlimited sugar in coffee and on bread. This residence, and especially the sleeping accommodations, were very unsightly and far from clean and neat. I advise every emigrant to take a pair of sheets with them to cover the bedding. I had also done this. On Monday morning we were treated to the same as the previous evening, and afterwards we were taken in buses with our baggage to the Railway. Here we received a third-class ticket to Liverpool.

We did not see much of Hull since we spent only one night there. What we saw were large ships in the harbour, warehouses and factories in the vicinity. Everything was very dirty and black from smoke and coal. More about it I cannot say. But I can tell of the train trip to Liverpool; about that next time.

The same person who earlier in our paper wrote some pieces about Canada, as far as he got to know it by word and picture, has himself now left with some others to that country, and has promised us, by means of our paper, to give a faithful report of his experiences and findings for all who are interested. The above article is the first of the series that we hope to receive from his hand. The second, Lord willing, he will send from Halifax, the first city he arrives at in American territory. *Editor.*

LETTER FROM EVERT ALDUS
(*Twentsch Volksblad,* 23 April 1904)

As you may remember, Mr. A[ldus] promised in our 26 March issue to give a description of the next part of his journey as soon as he arrived at Halifax (in America). This promise he fulfills today. Mr. A. makes no mention of a collision of his ship with another, sinking the other ship, so the rumours that have spread here about that are simply unfounded. Now to Mr. A.'s words:

The Train Trip from Hull to Liverpool
On Monday morning we were taken on large buses to the Railway. At nine o'clock we took our place in the third-class compartments of the train that would bring us to Liverpool.

How neatly the third-class coaches are equipped. Just as good as the second class in Holland, with thick cushions on the seats. Also the crew of the train was very helpful and friendly. The train was made up of about forty coaches with emigrants; most went to America, others to Canada, all from Liverpool.

After we left Hull we first saw flat grassland with trees, as in Holland. Soon, however, the terrain became hilly. We passed rocks through which the train track was deeply carved out; sometimes we also sat completely in the dark for a few seconds when the train passed through a tunnel. High hills were visible; many a time the railway lay along the side of a hill so that when we looked out of the windows to the right we looked up to a height, and at the same time to the left we looked into a deep valley. For as much as a half hour we had at the side of the train track a valley with a broad river or small lake, where towns and villages lay along the slopes of high hills rising on the other side of the valley. O, this was so beautiful!

Every now and then we passed coal mines and huge ironworks with many high black smokestacks from which the bright fires stood out sharply against the slowly rising black smoke columns, mixed with clouds of white steam. In that area almost everything was built of stone – houses, roads, train bridges, walls around gardens and between farmlands. Halfway through the trip the train stopped for a few minutes; the passengers could get some supplies in the station (Penistone). At the same time buckets of fresh water were placed alongside the coaches so that everyone could get a drink. Before continuing on the trip the gas light was lit. Why we didn't know. Soon, however, this became clear to us, because shortly thereafter we rode through a tunnel that was very long. The train went on at full speed and was in the tunnel for six minutes. The air in the coaches then was unpleasant since smoke from the locomotive penetrated into the coaches. Until close to Liverpool the land remained mountainous. Wild bubbling brooks poured their water from the heights, while rock was always visible on the surface when we drew near to Liverpool, hills and valleys giving way to flat land. As for house construction we noticed that homes all along the way were erected plainly and uniformly. The windows were small and without shutters or blinds. The roofs were mostly covered with flat red stones that are laid not like tiles over each other but next to each other.

The chimneys mostly stand at the ends of the houses and are always supplied with clay flues. For the most part all buildings were black and dirty from coal and smoke.

After a journey of five hours we reached

Liverpool (*Our stay there*)

When we left the train we heard loud shouting! "White Star Line," "Cunard Line," "Allan Line," "Pacific Line," rang out. It was the agents of the various boat companies who came to fetch the passengers. Here it was necessary to pay attention very well if one wanted to end up in the right place, especially since the names of the Lines were called in English. After the agent of the "Allen Line" had gathered his passengers we went in buses drawn by two horses to the emigrant hotel. Arriving there we soon received a good meal. This hotel at Liverpool was much better than the one at Hull. It was clean and as neat as one can expect from such lodging. The food provided to us was very good and also in sufficient amount. But the margarine was of such bad quality that no one could eat it, just like at Hull.

Moreover, one should not have too high a notion of these hotels. They are unpleasant barrack-like residences, consisting of some half underground dining rooms and a number of large and small bedrooms stacked up several floors high. There is no large room or place where people can comfortably be with each other, read, or write, and where one can buy refreshments.

Yet one can spend a few days very well there at Liverpool. The innkeeper is a very friendly man who will gladly help anyone. He is also willing to go along to buy something for the trip lest one be haggled or cheated.

Now something about Liverpool. It's a very large city; the streets and wharves are hours long. The railway station is larger than Central Station in Amsterdam. Electric trams ride through the whole city. Every twenty seconds one passed by our hotel. To describe the large stores and warehouses, in addition to the splendour and wealth that one sees there, is impossible. Yet beside great riches one also sees acute poverty; young boys clothed in rags run through the streets barefoot at a trot to sell newspapers. At the corner of one street an old blind man stood playing a mouth harmonica in order to get a handout from passersby.

In Liverpool there are many large buildings. We visited one of them, the museum. To say what could be seen here is not possible. There were stuffed examples of all known animals, and also many skeletons. A complete skeleton of a whale, one dorsal vertebra of which is as large as a blacksmith's anvil while the ribs are several metres long. Also a mammoth and a skeleton of such an animal. Furthermore, land animals and their skeletons, idols, weapons and clothing of all sorts of peoples, antiquities, mummies, stones and catafalques with written symbols from Egypt and Babylon, old coins and medals. I advise anyone who stays in the hotel at Liverpool to visit this museum. It is easy to find and it costs nothing.

Bread was cheap at Liverpool and of excellent quality. Butter, cheese, and sugar also were not very expensive there. One can get very cheap clothing there, for less money than in Holland, so one can get for himself clothes that he has forgotten to take along. Also tools were low in price there. But a bottle of spirits for which we paid 30 cents in Rotterdam cost 60 cents here.

The traffic in this city is especially busy. Trams, autos, electric trains, large wagons drawn by heavy horses such as are used at the factory in Nijverdal.

Large street locomotives draw heavy loads. The street cleaning carts are powered by a steam engine in front.

On every church stood a sign on which was written who would speak there on Sundays and on what topic. Thus on the sign of a church was the following announcement which read: On Sunday morning Rev. X will preach. Topic from natural science: "Light." At noon Rev. Z will preach. He will speak about a gospel topic: "God is Love."

A cemetery was 40 metres deep, in a low area carved out of the rock on which the city is built.

On Wednesday a doctor came to examine the emigrants. In five minutes he did a hundred. He looked at the eyes and hands of some, but the whole examination amounted to nothing. If, however, someone has consumption or suffers from an infectious disease he is rejected. So Thursday morning drew near, when we were taken in buses to the docks where the boat lay. The docks and landing places are several hours long. At ten in the morning we went on board where we were once again inspected by a doctor. Before I tell about our stay on the boat, I will first report a thing or two about the boat.

The Yonian [Ionian]

This is the name of the vessel that took us over the ocean. It is 160 metres long, 17.5 metres wide and 7.5 metres deep, and has a tonnage of 9,225 tons. It is built completely from steel, also the masts and topmasts. Two propellers driven by a gigantic steam engine move it forward. At the same time the engine moves the rudder, four large pulley apparatuses for loading and unloading, and the capstan that winds and unwinds the anchor. The rudder, however, can also be moved by hand, if the engine is out of order. Below in the ship is the large engine-room and the boiler-room, the storeroom for coal, the hold where cargo is loaded, and a space filled with fresh water for drinking and washing. Further, there are two floors above the hold, the first and second decks, both taken up by third-class cabins and dining rooms. At the same time on the first deck one finds the bakery, the butcher shop (there are cows on board, some of which are slaughtered each day), the kitchens, and the laundry rooms.

Then there are the residences of the ship's crew; in addition, the first- and second-class cabins and apartments on the top deck. High above these is the bridge with the cabins of the captain and helmsmen. At the same time the whole ship is supplied with a water-works. It is divided into watertight compartments.

The third-class cabins contain sleeping accommodations for two, four, or six. Everyone receives a room in proportion to family size. The Hollanders were placed near each other.[10] Each sleeping accommodation contains a straw bed, a pillow, and two blankets. Under each pillow lies a cork life-belt that one can use in time of emergency.

(On the boat there were 22 smaller lifeboats, which together can hold 325 people, thus not enough by far.) The beds and little rooms were clean, also the eating utensils and tables. The food provided to us was very good and of sufficient quantity. Only, the potatoes were not peeled. That did not much matter, since meat, bread, and soup constituted the main dish, so one could easily let them lie.

Meals consisted of: fresh or salted meat in large quantity, fresh bread, soup, pea soup, fish, eggs, potatoes, different kinds of jelly, rice, grits, oatmeal, coffee, tea, butter, cheese, sugar, and once preserved gherkin. All of very good quality. On Fridays there was no meat, but fish and eggs; this was done for the sake of the Catholic passengers.

The crew in general was very kind, with a few exceptions. If these people, however, are a bit impudent, then it is best to respond to them in the same way; one has a right to good treatment.

In general, treatment was good and so was the furnishing of the boat for the passengers. Seasick travellers and children were cared for by two female employees. Such persons received milk, soup, grits, and rice. Dirty linen of babies the parents themselves have to clean, in the room intended for that. Hot water is available four times a day. You receive no soap or towels.

In my opinion, it was not good that seasick persons were not given an indispensable object, namely, a water pot (so to speak, as everyone understands). When you are seasick, sometimes you suddenly have to vomit. There was nothing to put this in; every seasick person had to lie in bed clothed and with shoes on so he could get up in time to reach the toilets or at least the corridor. Not by a long shot did he always succeed, so the little rooms were sometimes very filthy, and lying clothed in bed also did not promote cleanliness.

In the corridors the smell was mostly very foul. Perhaps this could hardly be helped, since the portholes of the ship could not be opened due to the storm. The washrooms and toilets were together in one room. This, in my opinion, was a dumb way of construction; with no extra cost and space it could have been improved.

10   On the *Ionian* the group of Hollanders traveled third class.

S.S. *Ionian* at Halifax, 1905. (Courtesy: Library and Archives Canada, H.J. Woodside collection, PA-016385.)

LETTER FROM EVERT ALDUS
(*Twentsch Volksblad,* 30 April 1904)

The letter of Mr. A[ldus] was mistakenly broken off the last time. As one may remember, it was about the steamship *Yonian.* The last part of the article was about the fact that toilets and washrooms were together in one room, which Mr. A. called a dumb way of construction that could have been improved with no extra cost and space. With this he continues:

It is very unpleasant to have to wash yourself in a room constantly filled with stench.

The essentials, the food, and the sleeping accommodations were, however, very good. The number of crew members was about 200; that is, all the seamen, engineers, etc., servants, cooks, bakers, butchers, and the doctor.

There were 787 passengers on board;[11] but a seaman informed me that there could be 1,400, though to me that number seems greatly exaggerated.

Now that I've said a little about the boat I will also share something about our trip.

As I said, we came aboard the ship at around ten o'clock Thursday morning. Then after some time loading cargo the *Yonian* was towed from the dock

---

11   The ship manifest records a total of 988 crew and passengers on board the *Ionian.*

by two tugboats. A little further it stopped again and took on passengers and cargo. Friday morning the boat was north of Ireland. The coasts of this country rise steeply from the sea or gradually slope higher. We saw many picturesque little villages along the coast; villages with white houses and small churches surrounded by dark fir forests and farm land, and behind that mountain tops covered with snow.

Also moss-covered ruins appeared before our eyes. Perhaps the remains of the castles of robber knights which one reads about. Here also the boat took on passengers who were brought on board by small steam boats. At four in the afternoon the boat received mail on the north coast of Ireland. Afterward a musician played a melody (perhaps the English anthem) on a horn, the steam-whistle sounded, the propeller began to turn and the water rushed backwards with thunderous force; and soon we sailed on the great Atlantic Ocean. Thus far everything went well. The weather was nice. But already on Friday evening it began to blow hard and we had stormy weather. The effects were inevitable – seasickness for almost all passengers. The wind increased on Saturday and we had it until the following Saturday.

I had well imagined the sea to be rough and the waves large, but not as much as they really are. Our large boat was tossed up and down like a nutshell, and constantly danced and staggered like a drunken man. The front rose eight to ten metres when it went up against a wave only to fall just as much later. From that I concluded that the height of a wave amounted to no more than ten metres. The wind was almost always against us. If, however, the wind was from the side, then the ship rocked violently, that is, the starboard goes high in the air, the port-side drops almost to water level, and vice versa. On the deck ropes were stretched out to hold yourself up; otherwise you could not keep your feet. I myself do not believe we were in danger; the storm was not that bad. When such a large strong ship does not have a collision or catch fire, it can easily endure a storm, unless the rudder or propeller breaks. I, at least, and many of us, slept calmly in spite of the storm. The worst, however, is the seasickness and the fact that passengers, at least women and children, cannot go on the deck. Because to go there in the fresh air is the best way to get better. On our trip the waves often struck from in front of the ship over the deck, and if the high bridge was not in the middle of the ship it would have been knocked over before long. Many a man who did not take sufficient cover got soaked in a second from such a wave.

For most the seasickness was gone again after two or three days; one got used to the boat. Small children had the least trouble with it.

On our trip we passed a steamship and a shipwreck. On Friday we saw a great number of flying fish, sometimes as many as twenty-five together. They surfaced, fluttered on for 50 metres, and then fell down again. Every day there were sea birds by the ship. On Saturday morning the sea became calm; the wind dropped. We were delighted, thinking that the last day of the trip would be a beautiful one. But we were very mistaken. During the noon meal all of a sudden we heard the steam-whistle. "Land!" many called out and went up on deck. However, there was no land but a very thick fog so you could not see 50 metres ahead. The fog was so thick that on the deck a drizzling rain incessantly fell, so that you could not be there. Every two minutes the sound, or rather roar, of the steam-whistle rang out as a warning for other ships, while three men continually stood on the lookout. This lasted till 4:30 Sunday morning. Then the fog receded. And when morning came at about six o'clock we saw in the far distance the coast of Nova Scotia, of the new country.

Everyone was happy, but most, I think, because they would soon leave the boat.

About nine o'clock the boat was in the harbour at Halifax. The land before our eyes consisted of hills overgrown with fir trees all covered with snow, and on the shore and against the hills the houses and towers of the city. Immediately a man came on board with apples to sell (16 for 60 cents), and on Sunday, 27 March 1904, at about ten o'clock in the morning we left the vessel that had carried us through the storm and in which God had safely protected us, and we set foot on Canadian soil.

Due to the heavy head wind our sea journey had lasted ten days. The booklets of the Allan Line state a six day average for the sea journey. If one means the trip from Liverpool to Halifax, I believe that 7 to 7½ days would be closer to the truth.

I want to point out one thing yet: If you are not vaccinated, this must be done on the boat, also for children. Otherwise you will not get through the quarantine. Since I refused to have my child vaccinated, the doctor informed me of this personally. It is difficult though for an opponent to stand before the choice: be vaccinated or go back. Still, one of us managed to get his children in unvaccinated.[12]

I deliberately wrote a few things about our sea journey so that anyone who plans to make the trip knows what can happen. Yet the ship's crew assured me that one can well make a dozen trips without striking it as bad as we did.

12 Aldus and other Dutch families probably objected to vaccinations for religious reasons.

It almost never happens that one has rough weather and storm for nine days. Also it is better to travel in February or in the summer than in March.

I want to say yet that the passengers of our boat included Hollanders, Belgians, French, English, Irish, Danes, Germans, Norwegians, Swedes, Finns, Russians, and Poles. Next time I hope to tell a little about the train trip in Canada.

LETTER FROM EVERT ALDUS
(*Twentsch Volksblad,* 7 May 1904)

Before I tell about our trip on the train I will report something about the railway trains, etc., in America. The locomotives and the coaches are larger than in the Netherlands; the former have ten wheels, the latter eight or twelve. Besides the usual parts found on the steam-boiler, one also notices a bell of respectable size. This is lustily sounded by the engineer as a signal when the train will leave, or as a warning when the train goes through towns. The coaches are longer, wider, and higher than in Holland. There are ventilation windows at the top; the side windows are large, of double glass and provided with Venetian blinds. They are completely draft-proof. From the platform you step onto the coach from either end. Throughout the length of the coach runs a corridor with seats on each side for two passengers. There are second and first class coaches. In first class there are red cushions and backs on the seats, of so-called mock-velvet. They are very soft to sit on. You can turn the seats around so that the seating is backward and vice versa. In that way you can turn two seats toward each other; then you can easily sleep on them. However, a space always remains between the seats. It is best to place a suitcase or some such thing in between or lay a board over (you can easily pick one up here or there); then you can lie down better.

In second class the seats are supplied with leather cushions or are only made of wood. These seats are easier than in first class insofar as you can pull them out just like an extension table, so that the space between the two seats is filled and in this way you get very good sleeping places. Usually you can screen off these sleeping places from the others by partitions. If you then put a cloth or piece of clothing along the corridor side with a pair of pins, then you lie pretty well hidden from view. Also in these coaches you have better storage places for luggage. Besides, you find in each coach a large heating unit, two toilets, a tap with drinking water, and a washroom with a water supply. One of the coaches has a large cooking range with fuel nearby, for the use of passengers. But since there is only one in the whole train, it is a real feat to set a coffee pot there because it is heavily used. While riding you can always walk through the whole train. If the train is standing still, the engineer will offer some hot water that he lets run from a tap from the steam-boiler. Moreover, everyone makes himself as comfortable as possible in the coach and does the best he can. Some of us tilted the back of the seat in order to sleep better at night. (You ought to try that in Holland!) In the coach apples, oranges, grapes, bananas, tobacco, cigars, chocolate, books, raisins, and sometimes bread are offered for sale. Usually rather high in price. Never is anyone forced to buy something. The vendor walks up and down through the train, loudly calling what he has to offer, and no more. You can, however, buy enough bread, etc., at the stations or in the stores when the train is stopped.

Every now and then when a conductor comes on duty he comes through the train to check tickets. These conductors are very genial and calm officials. Usually with a wooden pipe in their mouths and no other uniform than a cap with gilded letters they ask for tickets. If the conductor comes on duty at night, then it is a real job for the man to get tickets from sleeping passengers. With great patience he awakens a sleeping passenger until he shows the tickets and then repeats the same with the next person. And so through the whole train. Never did I see these officials become angry or even impatient.

The stations in Canada are small and constructed of wood. Just like the railway cars, they are dirty and unsightly on the outside. They consist of two waiting rooms; but no first and second class. Beggar and millionaire wait in the same room. There is, however, a separate waiting room for women. Then there is a compartment where an official sells tickets. (You can also get them on the train.) Not through a chicken hatch, as in Holland, but behind a sort of counter. In most stations there is a restaurant where you can buy food for a moderate price, and in the large stations I sometimes saw a store with books, shoes, etc.

Moreover, everyone in the station can freely walk around, on the platform and on the railway. The platform is not closed off; neither is the railway. Barriers or guardhouses I have never seen. When the train leaves the station, the engineer rings his bell, and if you are not in then you climb in on the go. Everyone can do or not do as he pleases, but each person himself must take care that the train does not crush him; an official does look out for that. The train track makes sharp curves, has steep slopes, and goes through and over rocks and mountains. If the train goes down a slope, it then goes at great speed. When you ride so fast for the first time it's a very unpleasant feeling, especially when it is night and the rocking of the coaches tells you that you are not riding but flying along the track. When the train stopped for some time, some passengers entertained themselves by shooting a revolver or gun next to the track. You may freely do that, and also carry a firearm uncovered.

And now something about our trip, although there is not very much to tell about it. At ten o'clock Sunday morning we went from the boat to the St. John station close by. There we stayed till seven in the evening; then we rode off in the train. In this station a doctor had a look whether the passengers were healthy (like on the boat), and we received train tickets. At the same time we were asked there what we wanted to do in Canada and how much money we had. You can state what you wish, because it was not checked. In general we did not have much help here and we had to do a lot of asking ourselves. Also there was little space, so it became pretty crowded. Each one could go look in the cargo shed whether his baggage was there; for each item we received a receipt that we had to hand over again upon receiving it (at Macleod). In this station all sorts of things were for sale: 1 pound of sugar 10 cents, 1 p. butter 30 cents, 1 p. cheese 18 cents, 1 p. coffee 18 cents, 1 loaf of bread 7 cents, 1 twig basket to take along bread, etc., 15 cents, 1 meal consisting of two eggs, ham, bread, and tea 25 cents. (These statements are in dollar-cents. 1 cent is 2½ Dutch cents. When I indicate money values from now on I'll do so in dollars and cents. 1 dollar is 1 rijksdaalder. 1 dollar is 100 cents.)

The first five days to Winnipeg we rode in a first-class coach. The trip mostly went through fir and birch forests, over hills and mountains, sometimes along steep rocks. The towns and villages that we passed were mostly built of wood. The main form of the houses is a house with gables, or a cubical form with a flat roof. In Ottawa, the capital city of Canada, the train stopped for some time. The conductor advised us to buy bread, etc., there for three days since perhaps we would have no opportunity in that time to acquire any. We then bought a large amount from vendors who stood on the platform with carts loaded with bread, wurst, etc. The scoundrels had certainly counted on the fact that we would buy much and in a hurry, because a lot of the bread was old and stale.

Up to Ottawa the timber thrived. Sometimes we saw gum-trees [maple trees] with buckets down on the trunk to catch the sap. Once the train was delayed four hours because a freight train was derailed by a falling boulder. The following night we rode along the terrain of this accident. One of the derailed cars stood next to the track on fire; people said the fire was lit to provide light for the workmen repairing the track. Sometimes the train stopped in the middle of the forest; then they were repairing the track and this had to be completed first. For two days we rode through, in my opinion, infertile Ontario. The plant growth there was very poor. Thursday morning we passed Lake Superior. Along this lake the region is very desolate and rocky. There were some coal mines. That day we reached Port Arthur on the northwest point of the lake, a large city with workshops, etc., of the Canadian Pacific Railway.

On Good Friday we arrived at Winnipeg, where we stood still for a few hours and where some Hollanders, as well as many other immigrants, stayed.[13] The government agent was at the station and advised us well. Winnipeg is a large city with many large stores, broad dirty streets paved with timber, many electric trams, and many wooden houses. Here there was a thick layer of snow and it was very cold. Indeed, from St. John until a half day by rail from Macleod the ground was covered by a layer of snow everywhere. People rode by sled everywhere, nowhere by wagon. From this city the trip went through regions that mostly seemed very fertile. The snow, however, prevented us from seeing the ground. Trees and rocks disappeared to make way for flat land, prairie. Farmsteads and large herds of horses and cattle were the main things we saw.

Some of us rode directly to Macleod and reached this place on Sunday morning. Due to lack of space others had to make the trip via Calgary. Long before we reached this city we saw on that Easter Sunday the snow-covered tops of the Rocky Mountains glittering in the sun. Yet we were 200 English miles away. (An English mile is 18 minutes.) In Calgary where we had to transfer to another train and wait a few hours we were treated in a very friendly way and well advised by the land agent. This man was helpful to us in every way. Finally, after a train trip of a full week, we reached our place of destination, Macleod, at nine o'clock in the evening.[14]

---

13 The ship manifest of the *Ionian* indicates that there were six Dutch people on board whose destination was Winnipeg.

14 This letter makes it clear that this group of forty-one Dutch immigrants was split up en route at Medicine Hat, some (the Veldhuis, Postman, and probably Van Lohuizen families) going from there directly to Macleod via Lethbridge on Sunday morning, the rest (including the Aldus family) taking the longer route via Calgary and arriving Sunday evening. Willem Stotyn, who was in the latter group, gave a somewhat different version later in life (at age 70), in an interview in 1955 (Jacob Dekker, "Monarch, A Little Bit of Old Holland," *Lethbridge Herald*, 25 June 1955). According to Stotyn, "The party was at Medicine Hat and was advised that there would be a twenty-minute stop. Being short of food they decided to purchase some bread, cheese, etc., and their train pulled out before they got back, leaving them stranded. Mr. Aldus, who could speak English, was informed by the station agent that the next train would not leave for two days, 'but,' said the agent, 'there is a freight train leaving for Calgary in a half hour and you can get a train from Calgary

Our friends who were to meet us did not expect us so late, and so we lay down to sleep in the waiting room as best we could on the benches and on the floor. The stove and lamp were left on for us.[15] And on Monday morning, to our great joy, we saw our friends come; they picked us up with a buggy and two wagons.[16] And on that day our long trip ended. It lasted three weeks and a day.

In general the train trip is very good. If one has many children, then it is certainly difficult now and then. Treatment by officials is very good in general. On the last part of the trip we sometimes had to move to another coach suddenly because the train continually lost passengers. This is not always pleasant, especially when it happens during the night. Also one can sometimes get into company with rude and dirty people in a coach. Then one must pay close attention. Because going aboard each person creeps in where he can and will. This happens in a very disorderly way. Because of this it is difficult for some families to get into the coach together. Neither the government agents nor the railway officials take any care to deal with this. Nothing is done, though in my opinion this is very necessary and also can be done very easily. Now I will end this description of the trip with the following short summary: the boat trip to Hull very good; the stay in the hotels in England mediocre; the ocean trip to St. John [Halifax] in the main very good; the train trip good, except for a few things. The help of the government agents is usually satisfactory, not always.

---

to Fort Macleod tomorrow and thus arrive one day sooner.' The party decided to do this and thus arrived in Fort Macleod the following day." Aldus's precise account is more reliable. He indicates that the splitting of the group was due to lack of space on the Crow's Nest line train, to which the families who took the direct route to Macleod transferred at Dunmore Junction near Medicine Hat. In his letter of 3 December 1904, Aldus adds that the Dutch families had been on a colonist train until Medicine Hat, and then those who went via Calgary took the regular passenger train.

15 The Macleod train station was at Haneyville, then two miles south of the town.

16 The friends who picked them up at the Macleod station were the brothers Hendrikus and Jan ter Telgte and probably Gerrit Withage, all of whom had originally come from Nijverdal. Gertrude (Veldhuis) Hofman's account (*Sons of Wind*, 39) seems to indicate that the Veldhuis family, who arrived on Easter Sunday morning, was picked up later that day; they were taken to Hendrikus ter Telgte's two-room shack. The second group who arrived at Macleod on Sunday evening had to wait till the next morning to be picked up. If this is the case, some reached their final destination on 3 April and the rest on 4 April; that would explain the different dates found in family histories. The Postman and Van Lohuizen families at first stayed in Macleod at the Immigration House while the others were taken in by their friends the ter Telgte families. Since the Postmans were from Den Ham and the Van Lohuizens were from Heerde they were not an immediate part of the network of "friends" from Nijverdal. Aside from lack of space, that probably helps explain why these two families first stayed in Macleod. The Van Lohuizens, however, soon went to the Emmelkamps, staying in a tent near their log cabin in the river bottom. The Aldus, Huisman, and Nijhoff families, along with Willem Stotyn, were at first taken into the larger house of Jan H. ter Telgte, with whom the Withage family was already staying. Until their homestead shacks were built, this group of twenty-six people—all Nijverdalers—shared this one roof.

No one should think, however, that he will meet no unpleasantness on such a big trip. Even if everything is very well arranged and in order, there will always be something left to be desired and everything will not come up to expectations.

In regard to the trip I offer the following suggestions:

1 Be calm in going on board, etc., and never push, because everyone gets a turn. Yet each should pay attention that he is not too slow and another person takes the best or all places.

2 On the trip do not put on your best clothes. Take an old suit or new work clothes to wear. If one has a good Sunday suit on, it will be spoiled at the end, because one's clothing has to endure a lot along the way. Especially take care that you are heavily clothed, because sometimes you have to wait for hours at places where it is cold and drafty, at least when you travel in the spring. This is true especially for children as well.

3 For babies take along a large number of old pieces of cloth, etc. for their daily change of diapers. These must no longer have any value, so that you can if necessary throw them away when they are dirty, because you don't always have the opportunity to wash these cloths.

4 If you go with a family, then take along metal cups to drink from, a spirit-lamp with a small water kettle to heat water in the train for coffee and tea, and a bottle of spirits. Also take along some coffee, tea, and sugar, and a piece of smoked meat or wurst. You can get condensed milk in cans at the stations; you can also buy good butter there. (Milk 25 cents a can, butter 20 cents a pound). You can buy bread also at the stations or in the stores. It is good and not expensive.

  For single people it is sufficient to take along a little meat or wurst; for the rest they can shift for themselves. When you have small children it's necessary to take along an enamel chamber-pot.

5 Take along as little luggage as possible, in no case more than one or two suitcases or travel bags. If you have more pieces, then you have a very large burden when transferring, etc. It is better to have one or two large heavy packs than a large number of small or lighter ones. Pack whatever you don't definitely need along the

way in the large boxes, and take with you only what is absolutely necessary. For example, I would mention a set of linen and for small children a blanket to cover them up at night.

6   Be on your guard for thieves. Never talk about your money and pack it away well. Never leave anything in the open, because a wallet, knife, etc. is easily taken away. Also some things were stolen from us. It seems that you can easily lay clothing down beside yourself without it being taken.

Now something about baggage. On the boat every adult is allowed 10 cubic feet of baggage, a [child at] half-fare half of that. According to this I [with wife and child] could take along free on the boat 25 cubic feet. But I had 45 cubic feet, and most of our people had more than they were allowed to have. Yet nothing was said about it. In this matter they are very generous on the boats of the Allan Line. On arrival in Canada the baggage has to be inspected by officials. When we entered the station an official stood at the door writing on every suitcase or travel bag a mark with chalk as proof that nothing prohibited was in it. However, he did not look in one single suitcase and did not ask what was in it. One of us did not even notice the inspection of his bags, so quick it was; so at that point he walked right on.

Also we did not need to open our large crates. Except for one of our people, we were not even asked about the contents. On the Canadian Pacific Railway you may take along 300 pounds (an English pound is about 4½ Dutch ounces) for each full-fare person, half of that for half-fare. If you have 500 pounds too much, then you may be asked to pay fare for one [more] person. It does not always happen, however; at least some of us had excess baggage and they did not need to pay for it.

Usually you receive your crates a few days after you arrive. Ours came ten days later than we did. Also make the crates extraordinarily strong. They are very roughly thrown around. Do not neglect to nail strong supports in the inner corners; otherwise there is a chance that the sides will collapse.

Now I am at the end of my story of the trip. Next time I hope to communicate something about the country where we now live.

A[ldus] Macleod, 18 April 1904

LETTER FROM ALBERTA
(*De Grondwet,* May 31, 1904)

The Dutch colony in Alberta is expanding more and more. A couple months ago there were only twelve souls;[17] now there are sixty-eight. A few weeks ago seven families came directly from Holland.[18] They had heard of Alberta's beauty and fertility, and that attracted them so much that they chose to live as strangers in a foreign land rather than to tread any longer the ground that their fathers had trod. Most of them were families of the better class in Holland, and yet they exchanged their fatherland for what is, we hope and trust, a better land.

Several days ago the weather was sometimes cold and gloomy and many hoped it would snow or rain, but that didn't happen. For a few hours a little rain was all that came, and now the weather is as beautiful as one can wish for. The prairie is so innocent and beautiful that it is almost a pity to plough it, and yet it must be done because it will be this fertile ground that will make the population prosperous and Alberta a flourishing country. For hundreds of years this virgin prairie has been as it is now; no wonder that it produces fruit 30- and 60-fold, yes sometimes 100-fold.

Houses are rising here also in goodly numbers, and it is not only Hollanders who are here, but also English and Scots, Belgians and Germans, Swedes and Norwegians, even Russians. Many nations are represented, many languages are spoken, and yet the country is still not full. No, a great amount of land still lies untouched by anyone, excellent land, rich soil, that is just waiting for people to inhabit and farm.[19] That land is now controlled by "cattlemen," but I believe there will come a time when every quarter will be managed by its own owner.

Corr. [George Dijkema] 19 May 1904

---

17 Before George Dijkema and Lubbert Van Dellen arrived in late February, the only Dutch settlers were the Emmelkamp and Hendrikus ter Telgte families, each with four children.

18 The six, not seven, families coming directly from the Netherlands arrived at Macleod on 3 April. These included the families of Everhardus Aldus, Johan Huisman, Jacobus Nijhoff, Jan Postman, Hendrikus Veldhuis, and Willem Van Lohuizen and his mother, as well as two single men Willem Stotyn and Jan Van Lohuizen. The sixty-eight Dutch people now in the colony included this group of forty-one as well as the Emmelkamps, H. ter Telgtes, J. H. ter Telgtes, Withages, Lubbert Van Dellen, George Dijkema, Willem Feller, and Roelf Lantinga. Actually, as of mid-May, I can account for only sixty-six persons.

19 When the group of forty-one arrived almost all homesteads in the Leavings area were already taken up, so the Withages and these families took up homesteads farther east in what would become the Monarch area. Only every other section was homestead land; the other sections were C&E Railway land, school land, and Hudson's Bay land, which was sold to settlers a few years later. Dijkema's reference to areas of open land probably refers to the railway lands and to homestead land still available to the east.

LETTER FROM EVERT ALDUS
(*Twentsch Volksblad*, 2 July 1904)

The River

Before telling about anything else I want to communicate something about the "Old Man River" near where we live.

Every Hollander may think, "Nothing needs to be said to us about a river; we know enough about that here." Yet no Hollander can imagine the "Old Man River" if he has seen nothing but the Rhine, Maas, or the Waal.

This river comes from the Rocky Mountains. It is fed by melted snow. That's why the water level can be high in the summer since a lot of snow melts then. I think this river flows into one of the streams that carries its water into the Arctic Ocean. I don't know for sure, since I have no good map of Canada in my possession.

Now to the point. The river does not flow like the Rhine, between dikes that have to hold back the water. Rather, the water surface is 80 to 100 metres below the surrounding land.

In order to descend into the river bottom one has to climb down steep embankments. Sometimes one of the banks is almost perpendicular or over-hanging and made of thick boulders. On these rocks some sort of swallow has built its nests. Usually the location of these nests is inaccessible.[20] Alongside and in the water lie huge rocks that have fallen from the banks. In Drenthe large boulders lie on the prehistoric grave sites (*hunnebedden*). At Havelte I measured one 5 1/10 metres long. Here, however, they are much larger.

In some places the river runs between high narrow rocky banks; in other places the river valley is almost a mile wide and the banks are not as steep and are overgrown with grass. There one can sometimes get to the water with a horse and wagon to haul water. Here live mostly cattlemen who need water from the river for their cattle. Some of them have hundreds of cows and horses. These animals grow up on the prairie where they roam around freely. That's why the young horses must first be tamed before they are suited for work.

The descent of the river is very significant. The water tumbles quickly forward over boulders and rocks that cover the riverbed. Alongside and in the water lies a lot of course gravel and rocks. We can hear the murmur of the water from our homes, though we live more than a half-hour away.[21]

---

20 Near Aldus's homestead the high south bank of the river rose sharply from the water and was home to hundreds of swallow nests.

The plant growth in the river bottom is more lush. Plenty of willows and poplars stand there. From the plains one does not see the trees; they stand too deep.

One cannot get a homestead near the river; this land has been taken up by cattlemen. Also the ground there is no good for ploughing. It is poorer than on the prairie, full of boulders and rocks and is hilly.

The Plant World

The variety of plants here is much less than in Holland. On the prairie various kinds of grass grow, also a kind of sage. Then in the river bottom and also on the prairie one sees plants grow and bloom in the wild which seem to be grown in Holland. Here are the names of some: willows, poplars, cherries, plums, gooseberries, roses, strawberries, tea bushes, lilacs, all along the river. Further, there and on the prairie: lupines with yellow and purple flowers, primrose, cactuses, yarrow, vetch, and many other plants, sometimes with very beautiful flowers. Especially papilionaceous flowers are strongly represented.

As for the crops grown here, there is wheat, oats, barley, potatoes, and almost all the vegetables, etc., that grow in Holland. Rye is little or never raised here, though it will grow very well.

The Animal World

Like plants there are also fewer representatives of animals than in Holland. Among domestic animals there are horses first of all. They are totally indispensable. Someone without horses cannot do much. Also, cows, and on occasion sheep and pigs. There are no goats here. Dogs and cats certainly. But it is not as easy to get a young cat here as in Holland. Cats here do not have litters as often. This happens not because cats are less productive here than elsewhere. I think this phenomenon can be explained by the greater distance of people's homes, and consequently also of cats. Hence the animals of both genders cannot often pay each other a visit. Result: fewer young kittens. Furthermore, when one builds a house one quickly gets a visit from mice. As in other places a cat can drive them away, however. The largest wild animal that shows up here is the prairie wolf or coyote.

This beast of prey belonging to the wolf family is as large as a sheep dog. It likes to visit the chicken coop at night and eat some cacklers, or it snaps one away that has wandered far from home. For people this animal

21   Aldus's homestead was just over a mile north of the Oldman River.

is absolutely no danger; it is even very afraid of them. That's why it is very difficult to shoot such an animal. Some people kill coyotes with poisoned meat. They are rather numerous here and many an evening and morning one hears them howl and yelp at some distance from home.

A beast of prey [lynx] the size of a fat cat, belonging to the cat family, also lives here. People say it is useful for catching and eating very harmful gnawing animals, the prairie dogs [gophers]. These small animals are quick underground animals the size of a rat. They live in large numbers on the prairie. Like both of the previous animals they make holes in the ground. They destroy crop seed and carry it away, like the hamsters found in Limburg. These prairie dogs are not shy; sometimes one can kill them with a stone. Boys hunt them by catching them in snares.

Also, there is a good supply of "swarming" animals here, flying grasshoppers, mosquitoes that sting very smartly, etc. Insects that remind people of one of the Egyptian plagues do not seem to exist here much. Also, so far here I have not heard of the quick brown little animal that one can no more easily root out of a land than the strong lion. They say that many people here have trouble with the so-called bed-bugs, which is perhaps caused by the wooden houses.

Birds are rather plentiful here on the prairie. Very large eagles catch and eat the prairie dogs. A smaller kind is harmful since it catches young chickens. Also, crows and magpies, large owls, and a bird with a beak about 15 centimetres long, a stilt-walker [curlew] that is also found in the Netherlands and I think is called a "welp" there. Geese, ducks, prairie chickens (gallinaceous birds), and a number of smaller kinds. Tame pigeons I saw in Macleod. Sparrows and starlings, those faithful companions of mankind, I have not yet met here. They say the number of birds increases when the land is cultivated.

Songbirds are few here. One [meadowlark], however, the size of a thrush, breaks the dead stillness of the prairie with its lovely song. Early in the morning, sitting on a fence, post, or other high point, it resounds its merry tones, which is really refreshing for us who heard so many birds singing in Holland. People here have chickens a lot. I believe the same kinds as in the Netherlands. There are almost no hares and rabbits here; the coyotes eat them, so there are not many left for a shotgun.

The Weather

The weather is very disappointing here. It seems to me that the beauty of the weather, which the brochures about these areas speak so highly of, is awfully exaggerated. When we arrived here, on April 4, there was about two feet of frost in the ground. In the same month we had days with warmth like the middle of summer in Holland, but it froze at night with ice two fingers thick. Usually days are very warm, nights very cold. In April it snowed considerably a couple of times. Until late in May it froze most nights. On Pentecost Monday we had a heavy snowstorm.

Here it is either hot or cold; so far never the lovely mild weather that can be found in Holland. To be sure, it does not rain here as often as in Holland, and it is almost never foggy. But when, instead of many rainy days, one has a very *annoying* and *strong* wind almost every day, a wind that can be warm and then again very cold, then to me it seems no better – indeed worse – than rainy weather. A day of completely still weather without a strong wind we have not yet seen here. If one has to plough, harrow, or disc, and the ground is dry, then the wind blows up a cloud of dust so that many here wear goggles for work. If one is building a house, then one can't keep control of any board due to the wind.

Perhaps someone will say: "You are only there for one spring; you know nothing about it." That is true. But when one considers that everyone I asked who has lived here longer assured me that this spring is much better and more beautiful than the last, and that southern Alberta has the most favourable and mild climate in Canada, then I believe that what I said about the weather can stand the test of truth.

People tell me the following about the weather: A late spring, a short hot summer, a long beautiful fall, and a very severe winter from January to April. Hard frost in the winter and not much snow. We shall see, and if we stay healthy, I hope to tell something about it later.

There is no doubt that the climate here is healthier than in Holland. It is drier. Less rain falls, and the humidity level of the air is lower. This is evident from the fact that wooden objects taken along from Holland pull apart and crack, the rings on chisel handles come loose, shoes shrink, etc. On polished or rubbed objects the polish lets loose and flakes off.

Yet till now the amount of rain is sufficient to germinate the seed. From this perspective the snowstorm of Pentecost Monday was very helpful. The snow quickly melted and moistened the dry ground.

LETTER FROM EVERT ALDUS
(*Twentsch Volksblad,* 30 July 1904)

In connection with what I wrote the last time about the weather, I will share a couple more facts about it.[22] It freezes some nights until the end of May. The morning of 6 June there was ice about 1 centimetre thick on the water. Then the freezing stopped until the night of 25 June. That night our beans and potatoes froze. On oats and wheat this frost did no damage. I have been told that last year it froze here first on the night of 31 August, and then not again till late in September. So it seems that here only two to three months are completely free from night frost. At present the weather is mostly warm, as in Holland in the middle of summer; but it usually blows hard. Yet on 26 June it was so cold in the afternoon that one shivered from the cold sitting on a wagon with a thick coat on. A wind blew like the east wind can blow in Holland in March, but the wind was much stronger. Yet this month [June] after warm days we sometimes have had very beautiful evenings, though not as many as in Holland.

With this I conclude my information about the weather. I hope in the future to report some more details about it; then each can judge for himself.

The Roads and Means of Transportation

The roads here are all natural trails. There are no hard constructed roads, not even in the towns. Only in Winnipeg we saw streets of wooden planks, which were placed side by side on the ground. Like the sand trails in Holland, here also a road is formed from the wagon tracks. However, between these tracks there is no horse path. This happens because here there are always two or four horses pulling the wagons and they walk in the tracks. Also, the roads run over hills and through valleys.[23] A slope of 45 degrees is not unusual. Sometimes the trail is cut through by a creek or river. When the water is not too high the farmer drives his horses across as easily as a farmer in Holland rides over a small bridge. When you do it for the first time, it is a scary sight, especially when the water flows wild; sometimes right up to the seat of the wagon so you have to lift up your legs to keep them dry. If

---

22 This is the first part of a lengthy letter that Evert Aldus apparently wrote late in June 1904. The same letter continues in the 6 August issue.

23 By this time the roads were no longer just trails across the prairie but, with homesteads being rapidly settled, trails were now beginning to follow the straight road allowances between sections of homestead land. This also meant that at times a trail went directly over a rise or across a coulee.

the water is too high, then sometimes you have to make a long detour to reach your destination.[24]

If the weather is dry, then the roads here are as hard and smooth as a good gravel road. The clay then becomes so hard in the tracks that the heaviest load can easily roll over it. But when it rains for a day, the clay becomes so slithery and soft that no horse can keep its feet.

But since it rains here less than in Holland, and the ground dries up much faster, and also because here in winter it freezes more regularly and longer, the roads are usually pretty good to ride on. Bridges over the "Old Man River" are being built by the government. The one at Macleod is finished; at Lethbridge the bridge is half done and people are ferried across with a flying-bridge until the time the bridge is ready.[25]

The chief means of transportation is along the railway lines. Everything that people buy in the towns is not manufactured here, but is transported mostly on the Canadian Pacific Railway from the large warehouses of Winnipeg. From Macleod one can travel by rail in four different directions. Each day one train goes in each direction and one comes from each direction, so passenger transportation is not very busy. There are a lot more freight trains. The transporting of freight is very busy. Among these goods I can mention lumber, fence posts, thousands of pounds of nails and barbed wire, coal, farm machinery, etc. At harvest time trains transport grain every day.

The passenger trains are not as regular as in Holland; it can very well happen that one leaves an hour or two later than the previous day. From the railway to the countryside and to the station all transportation happens by horse and wagon.[26] There are no boats here.

Post Offices

[Post offices] are in places along the railroad. Letters, etc., are only delivered to the towns. Whoever lives on the prairie must fetch his letters and newspapers from the post office, and also letters that people want to send have to be brought there. Telegrams also are not delivered, and must be fetched.

24　Aldus's main experience with river crossings would have been the Oldman River south of his homestead on the way to Macleod, and Willow Creek north of Macleod.

25　These were steel traffic bridges over the Oldman at Macleod and at Lethbridge. The bridge at Lethbridge was opened in August 1904.

26　From Aldus's homestead on the east side of the Dutch settlement the distance to Lethbridge would have been about 21 miles, including a ferry crossing of the Oldman River. The most direct route to Macleod for Aldus would have been 19 miles, also across the Oldman River; the longer route across Rocky Coulee, Willow Creek, and the Oldman River would have been about 27 miles. The new village of Leavings (1902) would have been about 21 miles away, across Rocky Coulee. These were the nearest towns at this time.

The distances you have to go are mostly very great. This is a burden, but the difficulty is removed in large measure if you have a pair of good horses. Due to the lack of objects in the terrain and the clearness of the air, things appear to be closer than they are. Thus if you see a house an hour distant, it is really four hours away. You can understand that one can very easily get lost on the prairie.

Therefore when one is on his way he pays close attention to the position of the sun, moon, and stars, and to the direction of the wind, etc. Also, people here tell distances in miles, never in hours, as happens in Holland. This is because the land is divided into sections a square mile in size.

The Inhabitants

[The inhabitants] of this district are, as far as I know, Hollanders (12 families and 8 young men),[27] Belgians (who speak Flemish), English, many people from the United States, and also many from other parts of Canada.

In and around the towns one sees red Indians with their many-coloured shawls around them, long black hair, and ugly faces;[28] Chinese, who make a living doing laundry for the townspeople and are considered very sly; Negroes, who do all kinds of work and usually are dressed as nice as any citizen. In Lethbridge I once saw a couple of Japanese, small, nimble and peevish-looking fellows.

Churches

[Churches] are not out in the country. In Macleod and Lethbridge there are Protestant and Catholic churches. In the latter place there is also a large building of the "Salvation Armee." Protestants and Catholics live here. As in Holland, I have met people here who do not hold to any religion, and also others who are religious people. Certainly, when one lives far from town, one has no opportunity to attend a church; but that does not mean that one has to become a person who never worships. When one lives nearby some fellow countrymen and people of the same religion, one can also come together on

27 By the end of June 1904 the twelve families on both sides of the Dutch settlement included the families of H. Emmelkamp, H. ter Telgte, J. H. ter Telgte, G. Withage, E. Aldus, J. Huisman, J. Nijhoff, J. Postman, W. Van Lohuizen, H. Veldhuis, R. Van Dyk, and G. Venhuizen. The single men were L. Van Dellen, G. Dijkema, W. Stotijn, J. Van Lohuizen, W. Feller, R. Lantinga, J. Bannink, and B. Nijhof.

28 These people would have been from the Blood and Peigan Reserves south of Macleod.

29 The reference to home worship services suggests that from the beginning of this Dutch community at least some families got together on Sundays in someone's homestead shack to hold a worship service; this probably included singing of psalms, prayer, and reading from a Dutch sermon book. The first such home service, led by Gerrit Withage, took place on 6 March 1904 in the house of J. H. ter Telgte.

Sundays to hold a home worship service.[29] You should not forget that the differences that form a division between Protestant Christians in Holland here fall to the background or disappear.[30]

Here also, as in Holland, there are church denominations that one can join, in which case one is visited on occasion by a minister. This is the case, for example, with the American Reformed Church.[31]

Schools

[Schools] are built when there is a sufficient number of school children, and when they are requested.

(to be continued)

LETTER FROM EVERT ALDUS
(Twentsch Volksblad, 6 August 1904)

The Laws

So far the laws of this land have not given us much trouble. I'll tell you what I know of them. Theft, especially of cattle, is very heavily punished. This is necessary since it would take very little effort to steal a dozen horses or cows in one night. Yet the thief would soon get into trouble since each of the cattle is branded. These brands are registered by the government in the name of the owner. So by investigation the theft can come to light. However, one never hears of robbery. I believe that almost no one here locks the door when he leaves the house. At night one never does. One does not think about such things. Beggars, peddlers of paper or matches, or other people who collect interest, never come here. So wherever you want to, you can safely

---

30 Some of the Dutch settlers had belonged in the Netherlands to the Gereformeerde Kerken, others (including the Aldus family) to the Hervormde Kerk. In this early period of the settlement Aldus suggests that families from these different backgrounds had no difficulty worshipping together. The differences re-emerged, however, in the next few years, after a Christian Reformed Church was organized in the settlement in 1905 and then a Reformed Church in 1909.

31 Aldus's reference to the "American Reformed Church" actually refers to the Christian Reformed Church, a Reformed denomination of Dutch heritage in the United States (see his 3 December 1904 letter). At this early stage of the settlement no minister from this denomination had yet visited these families. The first such visit occurred in May 1905 when Rev. James Holwerda from the Manhattan, Montana, Christian Reformed Church came to do baptisms for families whose membership was with the Manhattan church. Here Aldus is only referring to the possibility of joining such a church and of receiving a visit. At this point he could have had such information from the Withage or Jan H. ter Telgte families or from Willem Feller, who were still members of the Manhattan Christian Reformed Church.

set down your horses and wagon and leave for a few hours. Never does anyone ride away with them, nor is anything taken out of the wagon. We never have trouble with the Indians. Also, for setting a prairie fire there is a heavy penalty.

Anyone can go hunting here wherever he wants, except on settled land. There is no privilege here that permits men with money to enjoy the pleasure of the hunt and prevents the poor farmer from killing harmful rabbits which come to eat up his grain. I mean the hunting law, the perverted right.

Furthermore, there is no tax here on meat, sugar, springs on wagons and buggies, bicycles, furniture, horses, dogs, income, etc. When you tell people here about all these burdens, they shake their heads and cannot conceive of such plunder.

But perhaps the reader may ask: Don't you pay any tax there, and if so, where does it come from? Certainly, a municipal tax is paid here. It is used to improve roads, for schools, etc. If one has no school in the district, one pays nothing for it.

The expenses of the realm are covered by import duties on tobacco, liquor, etc. Also machinery and hardware from the United States are subject to import duties to promote the manufacturing of these things in Canada and in England. Hence one doesn't have to pay a state tax.

Freedom, equality, and Brotherhood

[Freedom. Equality, and brotherhood] taken in a good sense, are found here more than in Holland. That there is more freedom here is evident from what I wrote above about laws and taxes. The childish and ridiculous things that are sometimes caused by the law in Holland do not occur here. If one does not steal, set fires, or murder, one is free to do anything. Also every farmer is his own boss in everything, and the workman is not a kind of machine who has to produce so much work each day. The conductor in the train is not the military model of Holland; he does not rush in front of his superiors, but talks ordinarily with them. The engineer smokes his pipe in the locomotive, where he is located in a larger compartment that can easily be closed when it is cold. Not like the open locomotives in Holland where the wind and rain can come in.

Also, the workman in the workshop and in the mine is much freer than the factory worker by you. He works and does his duty, but he is not a slave who is anxious and afraid to do something displeasing to his employer. Not that this is always the case in Holland, but it often is. Here you hear little about higher and lower classes. When you tell people that in Holland the shopkeeper, baker, and carpenter think they stand a little higher in society than the factory worker, and he thinks he is something more than the farmer, etc., and also that people must observe an almost servile courtesy before a higher-placed civil servant, etc., then they shake with laughter about such foolish ideas and customs.

Everyone, the negro who washes windows in town, and the black worker who digs coal in the mine, as much as the doctor, the lawyer, the land office official, are all addressed as "Mister."[32] One bares his head for an old man, no matter what he is in society, and for women. That is, not only for a "lady," but for the wife of a farmer or workman as much as for the wife of a high-ranking person. It seems to me that people here are of the opinion that everyone who does his best to fulfil his duty, and thus does something useful, has the same rights and deserves as much respect, no matter what work he performs. Anyhow, people here are too sensible to take up a class concept like in Holland, a class concept that can only exist in the imagination, a "fixed idea" that can be defended on no single good ground. So, when you get to the bottom of it, equality here is for those who are equal.

One finds brotherhood here in the sense that the hospitality is great, and people help and guide each other more than by you. By this I am not saying that people here are better; that I don't know. When one realizes, however, that almost everyone here came as foreigners and at first needed help and guidance, then it is natural that they want to help others who come after them. They know the difficulties and know how pleasant the help is. Also the distances require that people often need each other.

Fuels

In areas such as these you can get no other fuels than coal; that is, you can't buy anything else. If you are not far from the river, you can haul fallen and dead trees... as long as the supply lasts. Coal costs $5 for 2,000 pounds in Macleod and Leavings. In Lethbridge where the mines are, $2.25 for the same amount, or if you want to have small pieces, $1. And if we want to spend nothing for it, then we go three hours from our homestead. There in hills on the prairie layers of coal lie two feet thick. Anyone can haul as much as he wants for nothing. It is of moderate quality. But it is heavy work to knock loose the coal with a pick and load it on the wagon. Two of our people went on their way at 7 a.m. with one wagon. At three o'clock they were back with at least 2,500 pounds (12 hectolitres) of coal. And if you have no coal

32   Aldus uses the Dutch term "Meester" meaning *master*. "Mister" in English is a weakened form of *master*.

or wood on hand, then you go to work like in the Transvaal and Hungary. You look on the prairie for, yes, dry cow dung. It lies there in abundance, it burns just as well as white peat, and gives off absolutely no smell in the house. Many a housewife by you will pull up her nose if she reads about the use of this prairie peat.

Before I end my short description, I will give the prices of foodstuffs, etc., that is, the main items. These are the prices, as we have paid them:

Coffee, 20 to 40 cents a pound
Sugar, 5 to 6 cents a pound
Salt, 4 cents a pound
Wheat flour (very good), $2.50 to $3 per 100 pounds
Tea, 50 cents a pound
Butter, 30 cents a pound
Beans, 10 cents a pound
Dried apples, 10 cents a pound
Vinegar, 10 cents a bottle
Kerosene, $2 a can containing about 22 liters
Potatoes, from 50 cents to a dollar for 100 pounds
Matches are very cheap, also soap and such things.

A cooking stove costs from $17 to $60. One for $20 is not as nice as a Dutch stove for 20 guilders but it is much better designed. You can bake bread in it. Stove pipes are 15 cents for one and a half feet.

Tools are rather expensive but are very much better and more practically designed than in Holland. A shovel or handle costs about $1, a hammer 75 cents, a saw $2, an ax from 75 cents to $1.50. You buy everything completely finished, with handles.

Clothing is expensive, except cotton goods which are pretty cheap. Shoes are not expensive. A pair of fine work-boots is $1.50 to $2.50. Tobacco and liquor are very expensive. The former is bad; the latter I don't know.

LETTER FROM LEAVINGS, ALBERTA
(*De Grondwet*, 2 August 1904)

Every month the Dutch population in Alberta is growing in numbers. Each month new people come, either from America or from Holland.[33] And why not? The land is good and the climate leaves nothing to be desired. At present the days are warm here, pretty warm sometimes, but the nights are always fresh and cool.

Leavings, a small place consisting of three or four houses last year, is now larger and every day people are busy building new houses.[34] All sorts of machinery that people need can be obtained there. Soon, this summer or in the fall, people say, it is getting an elevator and a flour mill, and there is also talk of a new railroad from Lethbridge to Leavings. This railroad will greatly benefit the Hollanders since it will be laid through land only a few miles from the Dutch colony, while now some are 10, others 15 miles away from the nearest town. Therefore, though at present not everything here is as one might wish in this new colony, yet we can say with the poet De Genestet: "The future is smiling upon us."[35] And so we also take heart, and we are working with all our might to become a flourishing Dutch colony as quickly as possible, so that Alberta may keep its good name and many more Hollanders may yet come to share in the blessings and prosperity that is our lot here.

Geo. Dykema July 1904

33 The latest Dutch people to come to Alberta were Willem Feller and Roelf Lantinga from Manhattan, Mont. in April or May, the Roelof Van Dyk family from Midland Park, N.J., in May or June, the Geert Venhuizen family from Manhattan, Mont. in June, and Jan Bannink and Berend Nijhof from the Netherlands in June. Mrs. Dina Van Dyk was a sister of Fenneken ter Telgte (Jan's wife), and Mrs. Klaassien Venhuizen was a sister of George Dijkema. In a letter to his friend Hendrik Veldman, dated 24 January 1904, Geert Venhuizen wrote from Manhattan: "I am an elevator man again, my previous work. The other man went away and I knew of nothing better to do than take up my old work again under somewhat more favourable conditions, among others, a $15 per month raise in wages. I have committed myself to stay until June 1; then I can go where I wish. They wanted me to promise to stay longer, but I didn't want to do that." Geert was working at a grain elevator in nearby Belgrade, Mont. After working there until June 1904, as he promised, the family moved to Alberta, where Geert could begin farming on a homestead of his own.
34 The town of Leavings began in 1902 at a siding on the C & E track and rapidly developed in 1903 and 1904. The *Macleod Gazette* (1 July 1904) reported: "Even the new burg of Leavings has a fine hotel, two big general stores, several livery stables, blacksmith shops, restaurants, and numerous other institutions."
35 This is the Dutch poet Petrus De Genestet (1829–1861).

LETTER FROM EVERT ALDUS
(*Twentsch Volksblad,* 20 August 1904)[36]

(continuation)

I want to conclude with the following about the land in general.

Is This a Pretty Land? A Land With Natural Beauty?

No, the land is very lacking in beauty. Except for a few places in the river bottom, there is nothing that captures the eye, nothing one is attracted to.

Is the Land Lonely?

Yes, very lonely. There is no village, no church tower, no windmill, no factory smokestack, no tree or bush that meets the eye; nothing but grass, and nothing but posts and some wooden dwellings give an appearance of human activity. One hears no train, no rumbling of wheels, no clap of hammers, no sound of a church clock, no merry babble of school children. Compared with a village like Nijverdal, here it is almost as lonely as a church cemetery.

Is There Freedom in the Land?

Yes, everyone here is much freer than in Holland. The relationship between employer and worker is infinitely better. In most cases the lot of the subordinate is not much different than that of the owner.

Is There a Good Future for One who Begins to Farm?

To answer this question would require a year of experience.

These are the answers you get when you ask those who have been here longer. One says, "This is not a pleasant land, but in a few short years you can make a lot of money." A second person says, "Some years you get a good yield, other years it is too dry and you lose what you gained in the good years, and you remain a poor man." A third answers, "Though it is dry you can also have a moderate harvest."

And so I get all sorts of answers. What is the truth? I don't know. Only experience can tell.

But perhaps someone may ask, what are your thoughts? I think that if it doesn't freeze too late in the spring or too early in the fall and if there is sufficient rain one can grow a good yield here. This year the last frost was late in June. It has not rained for some weeks, so the ground is too hard to

---

36 The first part of this letter, which appeared in the 13 August issue, is not extant. In the archives at Nijverdal the page containing this letter is missing.

break. That it is dry here is evident from the fact, among others, that you can get hay from good seeded grass once every two years; in Holland twice a year. And that the frost-free time is short here is proved by the fact that you can grow beans but cannot harvest dry beans for planting. You have to plant them too late for that and it freezes too early. If it froze here no more than in Holland and the amount of rain was the same, then this would be the most fruitful land in the world.

How is the Climate?

Very healthy, but very unpleasant and variable. Nights are cold and days are hot in the summer. Almost never mild weather.

And then there is the wind, the insufferable annoying wind. The wind which almost chokes you with dust when you are ploughing, discing and harrowing, which makes it necessary for you to use a seeder, and which forces you to haul your hay in a wagon with large racks. And yet, when you load your hay onto the wagon, the always troublesome wind blows your hay from the fork or drives it through the bars of your hayrack, so that it flies like a rain shower over the prairie where it blows away like chaff before the wind. This wind, which covers everything in your house with dust, no matter how good you store away and close everything, which prevents you from keeping your hat on in the sunshine; in short, the wind which almost always blows and spoils everything here.

How Much Money is Necessary to Begin Farming Here on a Small Scale?

This is what we spent:

- 3 horses, $150. This is half the price, because you can usually get horses with a half down payment. The other half you pay later with 6 to 8 per cent interest.
- 1 cow, $50.
- 10 chickens, $7 to $10.
- 1 shack, $30 to $60.
- 1 cook stove and other necessities, $50.
  Fence posts and barbed wire, $50.
- 1 wagon, $65.
- 1 plough, $25.
- 1 disc, $45 and up.
  Harnesses for 3 horses, about $55.
  Altogether, $400 to $500.

If you have a lot less, then you are taking a big risk to come here to farm.

I have mentioned only the most necessary items. Some money in addition is needed for oat seed, oat straw, also for seed-potatoes and eating potatoes. You should also save some money to live on until the second harvest. Certainly you make a little from eggs and butter, but not enough to live on.

But, the reader may say, can't you get money as a mortgage on your land? The government allows you to get a $500 mortgage, doesn't it? That is true. But what help is it that the government allows this when no one or nothing will give you money on the land, not $500, not $5, not 5 cents.

"Can't you soon earn a little money?" another may ask. Listen to how it has gone with us so far. One of our people found immediate work on the bridge at Macleod.³⁷ He's still working there and earns $2.50 to $3 a day. That is very good. Later three others looked for work. With a lot of difficulty and after asking around for a long time they got work on the rail line to the United States border. Very hard and difficult work, ten hours a day, for a dollar and a half. If you take $4 off for board, then $5 is left over. Some stayed for several days, others several weeks. You can better do polder work in Holland.

Still others found work with ranchers for a few weeks during the hay season to help harvest the hay. They earned their food plus $25 to $30 a month. The work was good, but the pay was poor.

Soon harvest time will be here for a few weeks. Then I expect there will be more work. Yet, it is very hard to find good work here and to earn a decent wage. I hear that in Manitoba and northern Alberta there is enough work, but it is too far to go there from here. One has to spend too much money to travel by rail.

So I say once more: You should be very cautious, especially when you have a wife and children, about coming here with the intention to farm with little or no money. You would probably have lots of troubles.

Are There Good Signs for the Future of This Land?

Yes. In the first place the land is very quickly being taken up or sold, also by people from Montana, Ontario, etc., who know what life is like here. Second, the dealers are willing to give you machines and tools on extended credit. If they placed no trust in the land, they would not do so. Because if you don't pay them when you get no harvest, they can only collect the tools that are then of little value anymore.

---

37 Jan Postman is the one who worked on the crew to build the traffic bridge over the Oldman River north of
    Macleod. Meanwhile his large family first stayed in the Immigration House in Macleod and then lived in a
    tent near the river.

Now I am at the end of my story for the time being. Later I hope to report something about the way of working on farms, etc. If anyone wants to ask questions about this land, I am ready, if I can, to answer them in this paper. One should bring a request to the editor whether he wants to take up these questions.*

A[ldus]   Lethbridge, 19 July 1904

* We will gladly do so. *Editor.*

LETTER FROM LEAVINGS
(*De Grondwet,* 27 September 1904)

In the last while no Hollanders have come to Alberta. But there are again a few families coming, families whose relatives left Holland this spring and sent reports to the old Fatherland about Canada that urged others to exchange the Netherlands for Canada. But it is not only people directly from Holland who are increasing the population here; no, I hear also that there are families from the United States of North America ready to leave for Alberta.[38] And why not also from the United States? Old Holland suffers, so to speak, from overpopulation. Aren't there places in the United States that have the same problem? Aren't there places, yes even states, where newly married couples cannot obtain a farm simply because there are no farms for them? They cannot carry out the work for which they are qualified. Why then not look for land where it can be found? Why do the sons of farmers seek other work than that for which they are trained? Why not look for a spot where they can remain farmers? Well then, let such people go to Alberta; there they can farm. Ja, people say, it is so cold in Canada. Certainly, it is cold in Canada, but not in Alberta. Alberta borders on British Columbia; British Columbia has a tropical climate, and Alberta has taken over something of that. [If the writer actually means this, tropical is plenty strong for me. *Editor* of *De Grondwet*]. Alberta lies nearby or up to the Rocky Mountains, and if they were not there, then Alberta would be much warmer still and would perhaps share an almost tropical climate. Certainly in northern Alberta it is colder than here, but not as much as in eastern Canada where

---

38 The people Dijkema heard were coming from the United States were probably Teunis Bode and Thys Dekker from Vesper, Wisc., and the Koole brothers from Iowa. The Rense Nijhoff family would arrive from Nijverdal the following spring.

the winters are definitely severe. Many people in the United States think that it is as cold here as in Winnipeg, but if they think that, I can assure them that they are very mistaken. No one has ever frozen to death here, as many in the United States think.

Hoping, Mr. Editor, that it is not too much to ask of you to include this article, I sign my

Geo. Dijkema 11 Sept. 1904

LETTER FROM JAN H. TER TELGTE
(*Twentsch Volksblad,* 8 October 1904)

Leavings (Alberta, Canada), Sept. 1904
Dear Mr. Editor,

Will you be so good as to take up these few lines in your paper, for which we thank you in advance.

From what I hear and also read in your paper, Mr. Aldus, former teacher at Nijverdal, occasionally writes a piece in the newspaper. I have nothing against that, but then he should write the whole truth.[39]

That there is wind here on some days is true, but that there is so much wind that you cannot control a board is true only insofar as this happens very seldom. I have always been very able to keep working in the wind, and in the time I have lived here I have been able to build ten houses in the wind.[40]

That we have a hard, cold winter here, and a short, hot, dry summer, as Mr. Aldus writes, should also be corrected somewhat. The truth is, we have had a dry summer. Yet there are farmers around Leavings who, I hear, are getting 30 bushels of wheat to the acre. Now I think, and yes know, that this is not bad. This is spring wheat.

We also have winter wheat here; I hear that people got 40 bushels an acre. That also is not bad, though it could be better. That we have a hot summer here is definitely not true. If Mr. Aldus had lived three or four years in New Jersey or New York, then he would know a little more about hot summers.

Here you do not hear about sun strokes. It is occasionally warm; if it were not warm in the summer, how would the grain grow? Writing about large

---

39 Ter Telgte wrote this letter in response to Evert Aldus's letter in the 2 July 1904 issue.
40 The ten houses ter Telgte helped build since he arrived in March were likely homestead shacks of other Dutch settlers.

rocks, Mr. Aldus gives the impression that he has not yet seen large rocks. Then he should go to New Jersey. I mean New Jersey in America. Also the scarcity of cats is not that bad, since I think that Mr. Aldus has more than one kitten. I have delivered a kitten to at least five families (there must be a tom cat).

What I really mean is this: I hear that in Nijverdal there are some households or families (perhaps three) who sold their belongings in order to go to Canada, but now on account of Mr. Aldus's letter they no longer venture to go to Canada.[41] In my judgment, these people are making a mistake in going to Iowa, from what I hear – at least to become a farmer.

I hope to be able to get hold of your paper, and then I will try to refute Mr. Aldus's writing in every respect where it is not completely the pure truth. It is not my intention to criticize or carp at Mr. Aldus, but through his writing I and others are shown up to be liars.

J[an] H[endrik] ter Telgte

LETTER FROM EVERT ALDUS
(*Twentsch Volksblad*, 15 October 1904)

The Summer

July, August, and September, the summer months, are behind us. The hay and also the wheat are for the most part harvested. At present everyone here is busy breaking the land that will be seeded next spring. The weather in these last three months was better than in the very cold unpleasant spring. Many days were warm. However, not as warm as people in Holland often imagine. I cannot remember a day when the heat was more troublesome for work than in Holland. The nights are usually cooler here than there. Also some days are cooler than they ever get by you in the summer.

We had thunderstorms pretty often, also severe ones. Usually the thunderclouds brought little or no rain. The wind did not blow as much in the summer as in the spring. Yet it blew more than in Holland and it was sometimes very annoying and unpleasant. As I wrote earlier, we had our

---

41 The emigration lists at the Nijverdal city hall indicate that three related families—those of Cornelis Van Egmond, Ferdinand Schiebout, and Antoon ten Harmsel—left for northwest Iowa in August 1904. Ter Telgte makes it clear that their original intention was to join their fellow Nijverdalers in Alberta. Several years later, in 1910, the Van Egmond and Schiebout families moved from Iowa to southern Alberta. Antoon ten Harmsel, who happens to be my wife's grandfather, stayed in Iowa.

last strong night frost on 24 June. In July and August it sometimes froze a little at night, but did no damage. The night of 12 September, however, it froze rather hard, and in the morning there was ice on the water about as thick as a guilder.

Naturally the potatoes, beans, etc., froze to the ground. Thus we were free from hard frost from 25 June to 12 September, that is, 11 weeks and 2 days. At the end of August a thin layer of snow fell at High River, about thirty miles from here. The night of 22 September it snowed here a little.

This summer it rained very little. Other years, people tell me, it was not as dry. For us beginners, this is a very unprofitable year. Our oats and potatoes were a total failure, so we will have to buy them till next fall. The drought, however, is not the main cause. It is mostly due to the fact that we seeded and planted and had not ploughed and worked the ground well enough. The reason for this is that we had little time to plough, and that some of us who had never ploughed before were not able to do it very well right away. The drought, however, did us most harm by making the ground so hard that we couldn't plough (for next year) for about three months. Because a year of previously ploughed ground offers more chance for a good harvest than ground that is ploughed in the spring and directly seeded.

By ploughing I mean what people here call prairie-breaking, the working of prairie ground on which nothing had ever been done before, not ground that was ploughed already earlier.

The reader may perhaps ask: "How then was the harvest on well worked ground in such a dry year?" To this I can with pleasure reply: "Our expectations were exceeded by far." I will share a couple of details. A man whom I know very well seeded 47 acres of wheat. He received short straw but a lot of seed. I saw his harvest and helped him bring it in.[42] He told me that each acre had yielded at least $15 of grain for him, thus not less than $750 in total. This man worked his land alone and he has four workhorses. Last year he got about $30 an acre from 20 acres, thus $600.

I saw the harvest of three other farmers. They are getting no less than $15 an acre and are making a nice sum of money. These people came here last year in July. They broke sizable pieces of land before winter, however.

Certainly it is encouraging for those who have been here a short time to see these good results in an unusually unfavourable summer with respect to rain and heat. I myself think that this certainly confirms the great fertility

---

42 This may have been local rancher John Wright, whom Aldus had helped with haying that summer, or more likely, some other early farmer.

of the ground. Then also people generally say that the growing power of the soil becomes better and increases when it is well worked for several years. To me this seems very plausible.

Also, many who have well worked their ground grew pretty good potatoes, though not as good as last year. They now cost about $1.25 for 100 pounds. I also saw good cabbage, carrots, peas, beans, and onions in some gardens. The early frost, however, has done a lot of damage to such plants.

Now that the summer is past I will not be able to write much news for the next few months. The next time I hope to report something about the hay and wheat harvests, the working of the land, and also what the cost of an acre of wheat is for seed, labour, and wages for threshing, etc., and what the net profit from it is. For this, however, I first have to collect reliable data. I wrote this piece with joy because I could mention something positive.

Now I wish to say something yet to my former fellow-townsmen. No one should think: "One cannot live in that cold, windy, unpleasant land." That is absolutely not the case. Thousands are coming here and are able to live here.

I believe that anyone can be here who: (1) can adapt himself and get used to a number of unpleasant things that he has never seen or experienced in Holland; (2) possesses enough courage, patience, and perseverance (I would say toughness) to overcome many burdens and difficulties which never happen or affect us in Holland, and which people there cannot imagine. You should not forget that, besides many unpleasant and difficult things (especially in the earliest period), there are also many good things from this land that should be mentioned, which I think I showed in my earlier writing – such as the unlimited freedom, the better relationship between those who possess more and those who possess less, the more appropriate and just laws, in my opinion, and especially the greater earnings of the working class. I have never much noticed poor people, those who cannot obtain meat or bacon. And if it is possible most years to get a good harvest – an assumption to which the results of this summer give some certainty – then without doubt a worker who can make it through the first years has a carefree future in store for him here. You should not forget, however, that it is very difficult here in southern Alberta to begin farming with little or no money.

Because it is "new" here, the wages are too low to earn enough money quickly. In other earlier populated parts of Canada, however, the wages are twice as high as here. But the most important thing – a large piece of good land – the government gives free to anyone. In places where there are forests you can get permission to cut down wood. When you have lived somewhere for two years the government gives 500 young trees for free, on condition that you plough five acres to plant them. An official – an expert – is first sent to see what sort of trees best grow in that ground. I would say, no government does so much as the Canadian to provide the worker an opportunity for a prosperous existence. And finally this: if you work for an employer, be it a manufacturer or someone else, you get paid for part of your work; the other part (sometimes the largest perhaps) is for the employer. If you succeed in getting a farm going here, then you work for yourself and reap all the fruit of your own labour.

I wrote the foregoing not to talk nice about what is bad, nor to talk badly about what is nice. I did it to show that Canada has a lot going against it, but also very much going for it. I hope that my writing may serve not to misrepresent this land but to do it justice for the reader.

A[ldus] Lethbridge, 27 September '04

On a superficial level you would perhaps think that this letter of Mr. Aldus is a response to the piece submitted by J. H. ter Telgte in our previous issue. On closer reflection, however, you will understand that this cannot possibly be the case. Mr. Aldus naturally knew nothing yet about that piece that was submitted.

We are glad with Mr. Aldus that this letter can be more cheerful than the previous one. Whoever is acquainted with Mr. Aldus knows that a dismal mood in cold or windy weather was always his weakness, also in Holland. *Editor.*

LETTER FROM JAN H. TER TELGTE
(*Twentsch Volksblad,* 22 October 1904)

Leavings, Sept. 1904
Dear Mr. Editor,

A previous week I wrote something about Canada, actually a few things to counter Mr. Aldus. I now want to cite a couple of points about the travel account that Mr. Aldus offered at the time.[43] He then made a remark about the dirty waiting rooms at the train stations. Now I do not want to maintain that here they are completely clean; yet it requires a lot to keep them clean, since the train traffic here is not as regular as in the Netherlands – due, first of all, to the great distances, and second to the snow (in the winter and spring). Now you may ask: What does that have to do with the cleanliness of the waiting rooms? This – it can well happen, and does often happen in

43 Ter Telgte wrote this letter in response to letters from Aldus in the 7 May and 30 July issues.

the winter and spring, that trains arrive three to six or ten hours late. It is not seldom that some people chew tobacco and spit the extra juice there on the floor. Also it happens all too often that some have sacrificed a lot to Bacchus, and then throw it up on the floor. Also in the spring it is often muddy on the street, so all that dirt together makes a dirty mess.

Then there was another remark. Mr. Aldus thought that the railway crew could well arrange things so that all immigrants, that is, every family, would get a good place together in the train. Well, I don't agree with Mr. Aldus.

Surely it would not be fair, would it, for the railway officials to push me and anyone else who pays the full fare (I think three times as much as the immigrants) over into a corner for the sake of the immigrants? Immigrants pay, I think, one third of the full price; can they then expect to have the best place? They are treated just as politely as other travellers.

Now I jump over to the issue of Saturday, 30 July, since I have not seen some issues and so do not know what they contain.

That it was so cold the afternoon of 26 June that one sat shivering from the cold on the wagon with a thick coat on is a bit exaggerated, it seems to me. And then once again the wind! I have not had much trouble with it.

Next, when it rains for a day, the roads become so slippery that no horse can keep its feet. But there is a reason for that. People here use horses without horseshoes – that is the reason. From Macleod you can travel, as far as I know, in three, not four, different directions – east, west, and north. I have not yet seen the fourth direction. Also, there are not only Hollanders and Belgians and Englishmen and others from America here, but also Scotsmen, Irish, Swedes, Norwegians, and Italians, and who knows what others. What the writer meant by the American Reformed Church I don't know. Probably the Christian Reformed Church of America.

About the letter that appeared in the issue of 6 August I have no comment to make, and so I will end this time, and, if the editor will include it, next time I will examine what Mr. Aldus says in the 13 August issue.

Hoping to have this included, and thanking you in advance for the space, I am yours,

J[an] H. ter Telgte   Leavings, Alberta, Canada

LETTER FROM GEORGE DIJKEMA
(*Twentsch Volksblad*, 29 October 1904)

Mr. G. J. Sybrandy, Editor-in-chief of the *Twentsch Volksblad* of Almelo
Dear Mr. Editor,

Mr. A[ldus] of Lethbridge writes in your 20 August paper about Canada. I too would very much like to say a few words about it in your well-read paper.

Mr. A. writes about Canada, but I believe, Mr. Editor, that he writes about it with too pessimistic a viewpoint. He views everything from the dark side without seeing things in their full light.

He writes: "Is it a pretty land? A land with natural beauty?" "No," he says, "the land is very lacking in beauty. Except for a few places in the river bottom there is nothing that captures the eye, nothing one is attracted to."

Mr. A. thus finds woods and bushes beautiful, and he must have thought that we have woods upon woods here. But if the land here was like it is in the river bottom, then no people would come here, because to convert woodland to farmland takes at least 40 to 50 years and you still always have the stumps. But the land is completely different here. There is no tree or bush to be seen on the prairie, so one needs to do nothing but set the plough down and plough, and he has very good land, if not the best land in the world. If Mr. A. had wanted woodland, then he should have gone to the United States, for example, to the state of Wisconsin, where people abandon their woodland and come to Alberta (Canada) to get good land without bush. They have enough of woods, bushes, and stumps, enough of Mr. A's natural beauty.

He also writes, "Is the land lonely?" And he answers, "Yes, very lonely. No village, no church tower, no windmill," etc., nothing of anything. Of course not! Because a year ago there was nothing but a vast plain, at present varied by a little house here and there. Yet there are nearby places with several thousand inhabitants, but large cities like New York and Chicago do not come like mushrooms out of the ground. They rise gradually. Leavings, a little place with four houses a year ago, is now a place where you can do all the business you want. Rome also was not built in a day. Mr. A. should have known in advance that the prairie was more lonely than living in a village like Nijverdal. If he had wanted to enjoy more variety and not live so lonely, why not go and live in a town like Lethbridge?

What he further writes about whether the land is free and whether there is a good future for the person who begins to farm, about that he has heard the same things that I've heard. But then he goes further: "How is the climate?"

When he writes about it, Mr. Editor, his view again becomes too gloomy. He again becomes too much of a pessimist. "Very healthy, but very unpleasant and variable. Nights are cold and days are hot in the summer. Almost never mild weather. And then there is the wind, the insufferable annoying wind, etc., etc." Here the nights are cool and the days warm, sometimes a hot day in the summer.

That is the difference between some states in North America and here. There the days are hot and so are the nights, which is unpleasant for man and animal and especially dries out the crops. If it were that way here, the climate would definitely be unpleasant and it would make the land completely unfruitful some years. But precisely because the nights are cool, the climate is pleasant and healthy and it provides the cultivator of the ground food for himself and his cattle.

As for the wind, Mr. Editor, there Mr. A. definitely goes too far. "The wind," so he says, "which almost chokes you with dust when you are ploughing, harrowing, and discing, which makes it necessary for you to use a seeder, etc." Och, Mr. Editor, the wind is not so bad. Certainly it blows sometimes, but does it never blow in other parts of the world? Has Mr. A. never seen dust fly up in Holland when farmers there are seeding and harrowing? Has he never travelled by train through Drenthe or over the Gelderland Veluwe and has he never looked at his black jacket, how it was covered with dust? As it blows and is dusty there it never is here. And how the wind can make it necessary for someone to use a seeder, Mr. Editor, I have no idea. According to experts, one uses a seeder because it is quick, easy, and reliable, but never due to the wind. Also the wind does not force you to haul your hay in a large wagon with racks. No, that is because the prairie hay is so short and one man must usually manage on his own, and if he has a large wagon with racks he can also manage it alone. But not on account of the wind. And as for wind that drives the hay through the bars of the hayrack so that it flies over the prairie like a rain shower, has Mr. A. never seen or heard how farmers in Holland do it when they haul in grain, how when it blows there are two men on the wagon and one putting the sheaves onto the wagon, and that the two men on the wagon are busy holding the heavy sheaves of wheat or rye down on the wagon, simply and solely because the insufferable and annoying wind blows so much?

"And this wind, which covers everything in your house with dust, no matter how good you store everything, which prevents you from keeping your hat on in the sunshine; in short, the wind which almost always blows and spoils everything here." Och, Mr. Editor, in regard to houses here, they are not yet as they should be. Mr. A. himself writes, "a shack for $30 to $60." You understand that one cannot build a house for $30 to $60 that satisfies all requirements, but I assure you that if Mr. A. would go to farmers who have lived here for several years and ask them whether the wind covers everything with dust, also how well they store things and shut it out, then they will answer: No, not at all. It doesn't hinder us at all.

And as for your hat blowing off, one can ask, why do all the farmers wear hats, even straw hats, and why don't they buy caps for themselves? For the rest, Mr. Editor, I have the same experience as Mr. A.

Thanking you in advance for the space, I remain respectfully yours,

Geo. Dijkema ⸱ Leavings, Alberta, Canada 1 Oct. 1904

LETTER FROM JAN H. TER TELGTE
(*Twentsch Volksblad,* 12 November 1904)

Leavings, Alberta, Canada, 9 Oct. 1904
Dear Mr. Editor,

Regarding the letter appearing in the 13 August issue I only want to touch on a couple of things. (1) The friend of Mr. Aldus had lived here only three weeks, that is, he was here three weeks earlier than Mr. Aldus.[44] (2) The name of Mr. Aldus is not pronounced Elds but Oldus; and the name of Mr. Withage is not Oewidheedjz but Withake.

The letter of Mr. Aldus appearing in the 20 August issue. "Is it a nice land? A land of natural beauty? No, the land is very lacking in beauty." Now, in my opinion that is a bit beside the truth. It is a land of flowers, growing here in the wild. Many of them people in the Netherlands have in their gardens. Also the highly praised cactus grows here freely on the prairie. We have flowers here from the middle of April till now. Then there is another beauty here, at least to my eye – fields of wheat and oats.

Then: "Is the land lonely? Yes, very lonely.... No village, no church tower, no windmill, no factory smokestack, no tree or bush; one hears no trains, no rumbling of wheels, no clap of hammers, no sound of a church clock, no merry babble of school children." No village. But Mr. Aldus surely didn't expect, when he left Nijverdal, to get 160 acres of land for nothing in a village or town, did he? In what village or town does such a piece of land lie for

---

44 The friend was Gerrit Withage who arrived in Alberta in early March.

the taking? No church towers…. In Macleod there are three churches. In Lethbridge, that I don't know. No windmills…. No, one doesn't need them here. No smoking factory smokestack…. If Mr. Aldus looks in an easterly direction, he can see smoke seven days a week.[45]

One hears no trains…. Yet I hear them every day, also some from Mr. Aldus's direction. No sound of church clocks. First people have to build a church on the prairie. In my opinion, Mr. Aldus could well have known that in advance; also: no merry babble of school children. Is there a good future for one who begins to farm? This question Mr. Aldus answered very well, in his last point: Are there good signs for the future of this land?

"That it is dry here is evident from the fact, among others, that one can get hay from good seeded grass once every two years." That is definitely a lie. People mow good seeded grass every year. Also, that one cannot grow beans here for planting the next year is not true; at least I can well show Mr. Aldus those that I have grown here this year. And if the amount of rain was as much as is usual in the Netherlands, then people here would not get a bushel of ripe grain but only straw that would lie flat on the ground.

And then the climate. "The insufferable wind." I don't know what Mr. Aldus means by insufferable wind. "The wind which almost chokes you with dust when you are ploughing, discing, and harrowing." I've had almost no trouble with the wind while ploughing, discing, and harrowing, and yet I've done a lot more ploughing, discing, and harrowing than Mr. Aldus. "The wind which makes it necessary for you to use a seeder." That is not true. Mr. Aldus knows better than that. Just read his letter that appeared in the issue of 13 August; one uses a seeder because one has to seed too much to do by hand. "Which forces you to haul your hay in a wagon with large racks." That is also not true. Even the farmers who grow nothing but alfalfa (a kind of grass or hay that always clings together) use such a wagon, even when there is never a wind. It is for the sake of convenience, since one man alone can then do a load of hay without help and in less time.

"Then the always troublesome wind blows your hay from the fork and through the bars of your hayrack, so that it flies like a rain shower over the prairie." That is also not true, unless the wind always concentrates around Mr. Aldus. "This wind, which covers everything in your house with dust." Well, I have not yet seen everything covered with dust in our house. I know nothing of that, and we still have no cupboards or anything like that to store away and close things up.

45 This was smoke from the Lethbridge coal mines.

"The wind which prevents you from keeping your hat on in the sunshine." Now for me, this summer my hat has blown off once already (once, I say) and yet I have a hat on every day, without tying it on. Also, I have yet to see anyone go bareheaded.

"The wind which almost always blows and spoils everything here." Now, the wind is not always blowing and it spoils nothing, literally nothing; rather, it does a lot of good instead of bad.

Then: "You can get $500 as a mortgage," says Mr. Aldus, but that is definitely not true. The government does not allow that. When you do not pay your debts, the government only allows the debt to be levied against the land, but not for more than $500. But that is not a mortgage and also not a loan.

I will now end and have no intention to write again for your paper, unless it so happens that Mr. Aldus later strays again too far from the truth.

J[an] H[endrik] ter Telgte

If anyone would like to ask anything of me personally I will answer him if possible. My address is: Leavings, Alberta, Canada.

EXCERPT OF LETTER FROM S.A.SCHILSTRA
(*Nieuwsblad van Friesland,* 19 November 1904)

Preston, Maryland, Nov. 1904
Dear Editor:

... A friend of mine[46] who lives at Leavings, Alberta, Canada, sixty miles from the border of the state of Montana, and has a homestead (160 acres) there, speaks highly of the climate and the fertility of the land. At the beginning he also had difficulties; four of the five wells that he himself dug were dry, but the other one produced enough water. His brother-in-law dug one and immediately had plenty of water.[47] The land consists of the best clay; here

46   Schilstra's "friendship" with George Dijkema seems to be based on a mutual interest in promoting Dutch immigration to the Canadian west, rather than on any contact in person. There is a slight possibility that Dijkema may have met Schilstra in New Jersey or Maryland after he immigrated to the United States in 1901. In a letter in the *Nieuwsblad van Friesland* (16 July 1904), Schilstra noted that in Canada "there is already a Dutch colony of sixty-eight persons, and the reports are favourable." This is clearly based on Dijkema's letter in the *De Grondwet* (31 May 1904). After reading this, it seems that Schilstra took up correspondence with Dijkema to gather information from someone actually living in western Canada. Dijkema, who evidently considered Schilstra a useful contact person in attracting more Dutch immigrants to the Alberta settlement, then wrote him a personal letter on 22 June 1904.

and there it is a bit stony. In the worst homesteads there can be thirty to forty acres that are not worth ploughing up, but this is good for pasture.

He recommends, for those who are at all able, to *buy* land from the railway company.[48] You pay in five instalments: one dollar in the first instalment, thus $160 immediately for 160 acres. You are then immediately the owner, and can do with it as you please and are also free to live anywhere on it.

There are many small houses there, which are multiplying quickly; thus there is certainly an influx of people. The small houses are usually 24 feet long and 12 feet wide, 10 feet high in the front and 7 feet in the back. There are also larger houses, but they are first built when one is there a couple of years or longer, though this happens to the extent that circumstances allow. He writes: "There are still no palaces, as farmers in eastern America have. Everything is still too young and too new to immediately have all the best, but that is no reason not to come here. When one makes enough money, luxury comes early enough."

The climate (he continues) is dry and healthy, but not too dry, so one can grow grain well without irrigation; this is what those who have lived here thirty to forty years say. Wheat and oats, barley and potatoes grow very well. In the winter sometimes a lot of snowfalls, sometimes little; last winter little. The snow usually stays no longer than three, four, or five days before the warm Chinook winds quickly melt it; then it is almost summer weather again. It is cold now and then in the winter as well as in the spring, but for a very short duration. In the summer the days are warm, the nights cool. The sky is almost always clear; sometimes there are thundershowers, but generally they stay hanging over the mountains. June is called the rainy season. On 22 June (the date of the letter) little rain had yet fallen. In May it had already rained so the crops were fine. The prairie grass was also good and could soon be mowed.

It is not my business now to communicate all that my friend wrote about Canada. So as not to be too lengthy, I now wish to conclude this letter with how he concluded his letter: "If anyone in your area wants to know more about Canada, it would be good to write me. I'm ready to serve you as much as I can. I would gladly like to see many Hollanders here, the more the

---

47 George Dijkema's brother-in-law was Geert Venhuizen, who had married Klaassien Dijkema. This letter indicates that the Venhuizen family had already moved to Leavings from Manhattan, Montana, probably in early June 1904.

48 In each township in the Leavings area the Calgary and Edmonton Railway had been granted almost every other section in a checkerboard pattern. The C & E Land Company then sold this land to settlers to finance the construction of railway lines.

better. Would you be so kind as to give my address to people who desire to know anything else about Canada? If they want to know more, certainly let them write, so that later they may not cast at my feet the accusation, 'You have deceived us.'" The address is: Mr. Geo. Dijkema, Leavings, Alberta, Canada.

Whoever is seriously thinking about emigrating can certainly go with the Holland line; but I suspect that if you go directly by boat to Montreal (Canada) and take the train across Canada, you can make the trip much more economically, because in Canada a substantial reduction is given to immigrants. In any case, the trip via Montreal is just as suitable. On the boat you will immediately be thrown into the English language; but this presents no difficulty because many have made the trip. And everything will turn out all right in any case.

S. A. S[chilstra]

LETTER FROM EVERT ALDUS
(*Twentsch Volksblad,* 3 December 1904)

Today when I received the 22 October issue of this newspaper I read in it a second piece from Mr. J[an] H. ter Telgte that purports to show the falsehoods in my letter. Point by point, but very briefly, I will reply.

1. Ter Telgte agrees with me that the waiting rooms in the train stations are filthy. He tries to excuse this by blaming the uncleanness on tobacco chewers, drunks, and people with muddy shoes, all in connection with a sometimes long wait for the train.

In Holland, however, there are ten times more people in the waiting rooms than here. There are also plenty of tobacco chewers among them. Also intoxicated people now and then, and often people with dirty shoes. Yet the waiting rooms are much cleaner there than here. Why is that? Well, because they do a better job of keeping them clean.

What do I mean when I write about the uncleanness of the stations? This. In all the stations we saw on the trip across Canada the windows were so dirty that you could hardly see through them; also, the walls that originally appeared to be whitewashed were grey or black from dirt and dust. In short, everything looked very unclean. I call all this, great uncleanness. I hope Mr. ter Telgte will be so good as to give a better sounding explanation of it.

2. Further, Mr. ter Telgte would not like it if he, as a full-paying passenger, would have to vacate his seat for a half-paying immigrant. Fear not, Mr. ter Telgte. You will never have trouble with that. You do not seem to know that immigrants in Canada are transported in separate trains, if their numbers are not too small. We rode in such a separate train to Medicine Hat, for six days. The seventh day we were placed in a regular train, where we naturally had the same rights as the other passengers.

What I meant, however, and also wrote is this. The brochures about Canada say that the railway company takes care that in the immigrant trains families or companions can have seats together. On our trip, however, the railway company did nothing of the kind. When it was time to get on, hundreds of immigrants rushed like madmen into the coaches. The quickest found places to their liking, while large families had great difficulty getting two or three benches together, which they had a right to. Also, it was not right that once we had to leave our seats and find others, because a group of rude dirty immigrants made it so difficult for us that we almost had to defend ourselves with our fists. I myself went to complain to the train officials three or four times, but they did nothing for us.

Therefore I wrote what I did, and with full right. The officials of the C. P. Railway did nothing for the immigrants, whatever the brochures say.

3. On 26 July [June] it was so cold that one sat on the wagon shivering with a thick coat on. Ter Telgte finds that exaggerated. He does not thereby prove it was untrue. To be sure, he wanted to do this to point out the false-hoods in my letter. That he had no trouble with the wind on that day is even less proof that no strong wind was blowing. Had I worked that day in the cellar, I would have had no trouble with it either. Riding on the wagon from Lethbridge I certainly experienced it, and so did my companions.

4. Mr. ter Telgte confirms what I wrote about the horses slipping on wet roads. But he adds that the cause is that the horses are unshod. Yet the whole summer I used a shod horse and it also slipped. I also think that in Holland shod horses slip when it rains a lot. Here also Mr. ter Telgte does not prove a falsehood.

5. From Macleod one can take the train in three directions. And I wrote four. Certainly by mistake, because I knew full well that to take the train south from here to the United States one should go from Lethbridge. But that doesn't matter. Congratulations, Mr. ter Telgte, for your success. Here you have pointed out a gross lie, a terrible falsehood. How shall the readers ever thank you for that! It is of utmost importance for them to know this.

6. Here there are not only Hollanders, Belgians, English and Americans, as I wrote, but also Scots, etc. My word, what a liar I am. To conceal such important things as this – that besides the ones I named there are still other nationalities here.

7. I wrote "American Reformed Church" instead of the Christian Reformed Church of America. Here ter Telgte proves two things for me. First, that I made a mistake with the name of this church. Second, that he, Mr. ter Telgte is a great hair-splitter and nitpicker. This is indeed evident from this letter and from his whole preceding one. Any truth loving reader will have noticed that Mr. ter Telgte pointed out and proved not one falsehood *of any significance* in my letter. All sorts of insignificant remarks about cats, rocks, small mistakes, etc. And wonder of wonders! What do I read there? – I have no comment on the letter of Aldus in the newspaper of 6 September [6 August]. How is that possible, Mr. ter Telgte, no comments on this piece! I have written various pieces in the newspaper about my life, and I thought that not one of them was without fault. But now I know for certain that in the one of 6 August no letter stands crooked; in a word, it is perfect. My word, Mr. ter Telgte, I read it over once again.

Here I will leave it, hoping that Mr. ter Telgte in his next letter will point out to me significant falsehoods in my letters, so that our writing may be a little more fruitful for the readers of this paper.

E. Aldus Lethbridge, 8 Nov. 1904

LETTER FROM EVERT ALDUS
(*Twentsch Volksblad*, 31 December 1904)

Dear Editor,

I kindly request that you include the following.

In your issue of 12 Nov., I read a third letter from Mr. J[an] H. ter Telgte, about which I would like to touch on the following points.

1. Ter Telgte says that I wrote that my friend had lived here only three weeks, and he says that means: "He was here three weeks earlier than me."

Now I ask: What difference is there between these two statements? Let Mr. ter Telgte make that clear. That is beyond me.

2. Mr. ter Telgte says: The name Aldus in English is [not] Elds (which I also did not write) but Oldus, and Withage is not pronounced Oewidheedjz in English, but Witheke.

Well, Mr. ter Telgte! The English lady at the English post office in Lethbridge pronounced these names that way when she read the addresses of the letters to me. Be so kind as to scold her; and will you give the lady, who perhaps learned her language as a child, a little lesson in pronouncing English language? Indeed I have never heard the English say anything else than Oewidheedjz or Oewidheege. Witheke I have never heard.

3. Mr. ter Telgte was not pleased that I wrote that there is little natural beauty here, because, he says, nice flowers grow on the prairie. That is true. Beautiful flowers are found on the prairie, of many kinds. Imagine, dear reader, a region where you find plains larger than the whole Netherlands, without one tree or large bush, covered with short yellow grass, where at certain times and places nice flowers grow. Tell me, reader, is such a land lacking in natural beauty or not?

And then the highly praised cactus grows here, exclaims Mr. ter Telgte in admiration. Tell me, Mr. ter Telgte, for what is this plant so highly praised? Its false prickles, its short thick stem – branch – leaves, or its dirty yellow flowers? (The reader will understand that this is not the flower cactus grown in Holland, but a completely different insignificant kind.)

4. I wrote that it is very lonely here, and before I came I did not expect anything else. This, however, does not hinder me from saying once again: "Here it is so lonely that you cannot imagine this in Holland." That was also the intention of my letter. You cannot see factories here; only the smoke of the Lethbridge mine works.

5. Mr. ter Telgte says: "It is definitely a lie" that from seeded grass one can hay only once every two years. It may well be, Mr. ter Telgte, that I do not know this from experience. This summer, however, I worked for Mr. Wright, a nearby rancher.[49] I helped him bring in the hay. This man has large pieces of seeded grass around his house. When we hayed this, I told him that in Holland one can mow grass twice a year from the same land. Well, he said, here I can usually mow only once every two years. Now is it true that Mr. ter Telgte, who has not yet been here a year, knows much better than Mr. Wright, who has lived here over twenty years already and who knows from experience? That's what I think.

6. The wind, says Mr. ter Telgte, he has no trouble with the wind. That one uses machines to be able to work better and faster I well know, and I think everyone else knows it. That one has a lot of trouble with the wind

---

49 Rancher John Wright owned land along the Oldman River, south of the future town of Monarch. His was the nearest ranch to the east side of the Dutch settlement. According to the 1906 Census of Alberta, Wright had 125 horses and 400 head of cattle. The ranchers along the river were the first white settlers in the district.

while doing almost all work, I also know. That it would be very difficult, and even impossible on many days, to seed without a machine, to haul hay without a rack, is also true. That the dust penetrates even into well-built houses, has been shown to me many times by residents. Every Hollander who comes into this area will experience what a plague the wind sometimes is. That the wind "spoils nothing" we have seen this summer when it took all the moisture out of the ground in a few days, and made the last traces of a heavy rain shower vanish in a few hours.

It is true that the wind does some good. Among other things, it quickly dries hay and mowed grain, and since it is a warm (not very cold) wind, it quickly melts the snow, so that cattle can again find grass.

7. The government, Mr. ter Telgte says, does not allow you to take a $500 mortgage on the land. In the brochures written about Canada anyone can read that the government does allow this. Also Mr. Tréau de Coeli, agent of the Canadian government at Antwerp, informed me about this, and the other Nijverdalers who are here, before we left.

And since some of our people, having saved up the $500, arrived here – and more should still be able to do so – I wrote: "You can get no money on the land" (before you are an owner after three years, when you no longer need permission from the government). I kindly request Mr. Tréau de Coeli, whom I have always known to be a truthful and helpful man, to state in this paper what the truth is in this matter: Does the Canadian government give permission to borrow money or not? And with this I conclude, leaving the reader to answer the question: Did Mr. ter Telgte's letter consist of profound comments, or was it mostly a search after insignificant things?

With thanks for the space, yours truly,
E[vert] Aldus   Lethbridge, 8 Dec. 1904

LETTER FROM LEAVINGS
(*Nieuwsblad van Friesland*, 21 January 1905)

Mr. Editor:

I was asked by a friend from the United States to place some letters in your newspaper.[50] I am residing in Canada and wish to write about it. However, I will not focus on Canada as a whole, but on one of its territories, Alberta.

---

50 Dijkema's American friend was almost certainly S. A. Schilstra from Maryland. See the latter's letter in the issue of 19 Nov. 1904.

Incidentally it may be observed that Canada is 250,000 square miles larger than the United States, and that it has only a twelfth of the population.

Alberta is one of the states or rather territories of Canada.[51] It lies to the east of the Rocky Mountains and to the north of the American state of Montana. It covers an area of 120,000 square miles. Yet this land is not everywhere suitable for cultivation. If you go to the far north, it is very cold and only some fishermen live there, but farther to the south it is good for both agriculture and cattle-raising. The grass that grows there is outstanding, though it is only prairie. (For explanation may it be said that prairie grass is the sort of grass that is not sown, but is really natural grass.) You can see how good it is from the cattle that get nothing else to eat, neither in summer nor winter, and yet they are very fit to be butchered. In the summer the steers that roam around the prairie are fat. These cattle certainly belong to some owner, though one never sees them. Every ox or cow or horse or whatever is given a brand by which the owner can always recognize them, no matter how far the animals stray, sometimes 40 to 80 miles.

But someone may ask, is Alberta then such a place that cattle can graze everywhere? Don't any people live in the area?

Only a few years ago very few people lived in Alberta. Here and there near a river or small creek stood a house and there lived a large horse rancher or large cattleman, who let his horses or cattle graze on the prairie and once or twice a year went out to check up on them. But that has now changed.

Several years ago the land of Alberta was opened up to homesteaders. A homesteader is someone who can receive a piece of land 160 acres large for a sum of 10 dollars. He must be a man over eighteen years old (no woman can get a homestead; that is possible in America). The government enacted a law that each can get 160 acres of land for $10. And then Englishmen, Scots, Irish, Swedes, Norwegians, Danish, Germans, French, Hollanders, Belgians, and even Russians, came to take 160 acres of Alberta's rich prairie. The Canadian Pacific Railroad Co. laid a railway line through Alberta and for this it was granted a large area of land – I cannot say how many hundreds of square miles in size. But yet there was enough land left that was available for $10. Now, after the course of a few years, that free land has already been taken up and it belongs to owners, to farmers, who have ploughed up the land and have grown lovely, excellent, choice wheat on it. So this prairie has been converted into excellent farmland. However, there is still land enough to buy, but to get 160 for almost nothing – for $10 – belongs pretty much

---

51 When Dijkema wrote this letter Alberta was still a territory; it became a province on 1 September 1905.

to the past. To be sure, such a piece of land can still be gotten, but here it is like almost everywhere: "not all wood is lumber."

Farther north from where we Hollanders live there is still land, but it's not good for agriculture. It rains there too much and it freezes too early. Also, the soil is not so good. But all the land that the government granted to the railroad company can be bought and it is not yet expensive. In a couple of years that also will be 50 per cent more expensive. But beautiful rich prairie can still now be bought for $6, $7, and $8 an acre.[52] That money, however, does not need to be immediately paid in full. No, one pays $2 per acre immediately and the rest over 5 years; each year a fifth plus the interest. The closer to a town, the more expensive, of course.

Geo. Dijkema   Leavings, Alberta, Canada, Dec. 1904

LETTER FROM LEAVINGS
(*De Grondwet*, 24 January 1905)

Some weeks ago we had the pleasure here to make the acquaintance of some gentlemen from Wisconsin, namely Mr. [Teunis] Bode and Mr. [Thys] Dekker from Vesper, Wood County.[53]

These gentlemen had also heard of Alberta, and thought it was well worth coming to inspect these beautiful flat prairie fields. So they bought a ticket and on a certain morning arrived at Leavings. But they were not satisfied to see only Leavings. No, they wanted to see more; they wanted to go into the countryside. And they went. After a few hours of riding around the prairie,

---

52 By comparison, a letter in the same issue of the *Nieuwsblad van Friesland* from the Dutch settlement in Bonhomme County, South Dakota, noted that in seven years farmland prices there had risen from $15–$20 to $30–$40 an acre.

53 Before coming to Alberta, Teunis Bode, Thys and Arie Dekker had spent some time in Montana exploring land possibilities. On 11 April 1904 they sent the following letter from Great Falls to *De Grondwet* (26 April 1904): "We have now been here four days, have seen much of the country, and are very well satisfied. Never before have we seen such fine land, and besides, it is government land, not far from the railroad. The climate is a delight, such beautiful weather; if it is always like this, then it couldn't be better. The farmers are busy ploughing and seeding. We can get work here for $35.00 a month plus room and board. We will first do that, and when we have some more experience we hope also to write later about the crops that grow here. Other Hollanders have also come here, but they have a farm close to Great Falls and will farm there this year. Mr. R. E. Werkman of St. Paul went with us and has treated us very well. We can recommend him to our Dutch people. We all come from Vesper, Wisc., and are readers of *De Grondwet*." Reinder E. Werkman was a land agent for the Great Northern Railway, with an office in St. Paul, Minn. He actively promoted new Dutch settlements in Montana, and organized frequent excursions for potential settlers to see these areas. He regularly advertised in *De Grondwet*.

they went to Lethbridge and each took a homestead for himself and also for a brother and a brother-in-law.[54]

They, however, went back to Wisconsin to put their affairs in order, in order then to return and establish themselves here. And now having arrived a couple of months ago, they are already living in their own houses and are as good as at home here.

So the Dutch settlement is slowly but surely expanding. Not only are there more Hollanders from the Netherlands, but also Wisconsin is letting itself be heard. Thus the Dutch colony here is becoming larger. This spring still more will come from the Netherlands, and off and on people still come from the United States. In a couple of years we hope there will be a fairly large colony here. That the Dutch settlement in Alberta may grow and flourish and that Hollanders may come from the north and south is the wish of your faithful correspondent.

Geo. Dykema 16 Jan. 1905

LETTER FROM EVERT ALDUS
(*Twentsch Volksblad*, 11 February 1905)

What do you do, now that it is winter? asks the reader. Well, to answer this I should first say something about the weather. The snow that fell in October did us a lot of good. It made the ground wet and soft, so that we could break the sod better. I think we could plough for the last time late in November. Then the ground froze too hard. After October we still had nice days. Also days with a lot of wind, and sometimes a little snow, but never more than two to three inches. Never rain or more dreary weather, as in Holland. The last half of December it froze very hard. We could work outside, *e.g.*, digging wells and such work, otherwise not. I believe it froze much harder than in Holland, because the river, which flows perhaps six times as fast as the Rhine or Waal, was thick almost everywhere. On some places the ice is almost a foot thick, so that we can safely walk over it. During Christmas week the Chinook began to blow, so the cold decreased, and the freezing almost stopped.

---

54 Teunis Bode and Thys Dekker arrived in Alberta probably in September. On 16 September 1904, Bode filed on homesteads for himself and his brother Gerrit, and on the 21st for his brother Barend. On 16 September Thys Dekker filed for himself, his brother Arie, and his brother-in-law Johannes de Puyt, who had married his sister Maartje on 22 April 1903. De Puyt never did settle in Alberta.

As long as possible we worked on the land, ploughing and discing. After that we have been busy fixing our houses, stables, chicken coops, wells, hauling firewood, etc. So far each of us has abundant work. Each of us owns a plough, some a disc, a harrow, or a hay mower with a hayrack.

We still have not bought seeders and binders, because we do not need them yet. One uses a harrow here for the lumpy pieces and to make the ground more level, not to cover up the seed; this is done by a seeder.

And now another topic. I think many readers will certainly ask: How are they feeling, our former fellow townsmen and countrymen, there in a strange land, different in many ways from the old Fatherland?

Well, the answer to this question can be very satisfying. In general, everyone is cheerful and in high spirits, and good harmony prevails. To be sure, it may happen that two people do not agree on a certain point, but usually everything goes on in good unity. Indeed, you get used to everything. Also the monotony and loneliness of the prairie quickly becomes little felt any more. I think in general that we are as cheerful and contented here as in Holland. In the evening and on Sundays people still have a chance to talk.[55] As anyone can understand, Sundays and holidays are less attractive here than in the Netherlands. On Sundays one usually begins by taking care of the cattle, milking the cows, providing water, etc. The day differs little from any other day; only the plough is not driven in the fields. Yes, here too Sunday is still recognizable by something. Our children, 14 of them, are instructed from God's Word. We have a Sunday school.[56] Certainly small and simple in every way, but yet beneficial, we hope. This Sunday school, begun by [Gerrit] W[ithage], is now led in turn by W[ithage] and A[ldus] in their homes.

Also, our children celebrated Christmas. "What are you saying," the reader may ask, "Christmas celebrated on the prairie?" Certainly, why not? To be sure, the party room was no church or school, decorated with a Christmas tree, dotted with little lights, and hung with gifts, but only a small wooden shack, 12 by 14 feet. Certainly the number of students was not hundreds, as in N[ijverdal], but only fourteen; but the children still had a Christmas program. And not an American Christmas celebration, where (I am told)

---

55 Apparently Sunday was a time for families to visit each other. But this letter makes it clear that, apart from the Sunday school, no regular organized worship services were yet held in this Dutch community. One reason was the lack of a nearby facility large enough to hold everyone. The homestead shacks were too small. As yet there was no local schoolhouse. On the east side, the Rose Butte school opened in the spring of 1905, the Finley school in January 1906; on the west side, the Rocky Coulee school was built in May 1905.

56 This Sunday school was only for children on the east side of the settlement.

they combine into one this event and Santa Claus (Sinterklaas),[57] but a real Dutch celebration, roughly like in N[ijverdal].

It went like this. A few weeks earlier the parents talked about preparing a small program for the children. Everyone contributed a quarter (25 cents). All were faithful in doing so. Also the widow van L[ohuizen] and her unmarried son [Jan], as well as the young man B[erend] N[yhof], gave their 25 cents, though they had no children to send. With this money chocolate, sugar, currants, candy, and apples were bought.

The baker (that is, he was a baker in N[ijverdal])[58] baked currant buns, one of the women baked cookies, and some gave a half pail of milk for the chocolate. So we could give the children chocolate, buns, cookies, apples, and candy.[59] The first day of Christmas dawned. The previous day a thin layer of snow had fallen. The sun shone brightly, but it froze so much it snapped (as they say in Holland). Real Christmas weather. The program was held at Mr. W[ithage's] house. W[ithage] lives a little at the edge, at some distance from the others.[60] Many a person would say it was an excursion, to walk part of the way through the snow with the children. The snow and distance were no hindrance, oh no. Toward noon (at twelve o'clock the program began) sleds drawn by one or two horses approached the W[ithage] house at a good pace, occupied with parents and children. It was quite a sight, those small low sleds gliding over the prairie, so fast that the snow flew up high, the horses with ice covered hair and steaming nostrils, and well wrapped children with noses red with cold. Just as in N[ijverdal] the Christmas story was told to the children, as well as other nice stories. The little ones ate and drank as much as they liked and had a good time. Many a little verse learned in the Nijverdal school re-echoed in the shack on the prairie. And I think that "Eer Zij God in den Hooge,"[61] sung by these few children, sounded pleasing to the great Friend of children, who when he was on earth took children into his arms and blessed them.

It was a pleasant sociable day, also for the parents. At four o'clock it was all over, and the return trip began by sled.

Old and New Year went by "as usual;" that is, on January 1 we wished each other well in the new country.

---

57 In the Netherlands the traditional St. Nicholas (Sinterklaas) Day is celebrated on 5 December, several weeks before Christmas.

58 This was Jacobus Nijhoff.

59 Since there was no money for Christmas presents, the children were each given a calendar donated by merchants at Leavings.

60 Actually the Withage home was within three miles of the other families on the east side of the settlement.

61 "Eere Zij God" (Glory to God in the Highest) was a very popular Dutch Christmas carol.

And now to jump from one thing to another, I still want to say some things of a different nature. Sometimes you can see the very beautiful northern lights here, with bright beams shooting out the top, just as it is pictured in the books.

This fall some of us shot a few prairie chickens. Also, rabbits appear more numerous than before, but it is a trick to shoot them.

Here also there are sometimes less pleasant encounters, as the following makes apparent. During these days two of our people went over the ice to chop wood on the other side of the river. There they saw a porcupine under a pile of branches. Not a hedgehog, as in Holland, but a real specimen, one and a half times the size of a rabbit, and with quills like darning needles on its body. One of the two men (I will not say who)[62] wanted to grab this sweet little animal by the tail to take it along. Slap! went the porcupine, and struck the reaching hand with its tail. He immediately pulled it back, but it was filled with a couple dozen quills, which penetrated so deeply and firmly that it was a lot of trouble to remove them. Blood streamed along the hand. One of the quills broke off, and gave the porcupine hunter a swollen and painful hand for three or four days. This made him solemnly promise never again to try to grab a porcupine by the tail, and to kill it without ado, if he ever sees the aforementioned specimen again.

Van L[ohuizen] went to Lethbridge some time ago. On the way, near the city crawls a snake which makes a peculiar rattling sound. He strikes the beast dead. A couple of passersby have a look at the dead reptile, and explain that it's a rattlesnake, a very poisonous beast. People say these kind of snakes are found close to Lethbridge in fair numbers.

Now I'm at the end of my story. In my story there is not much order, not much tidiness. But then it was not my intention to write anything of significance. I only tried, at the end of 1904, to relate something about our situation. I hope I was successful.*

A[ldus] Lethbridge, 2 January 1905

* We do not doubt that all our readers will read it with great interest. *Editor.*

62 This incident happened to Aldus himself.
63 In the middle of his first full winter in Alberta Dijkema focuses on the weather at some length to counter the assumption of American readers that it is so cold in Canada.

LETTER FROM LEAVINGS
(*De Grondwet,* 21 February 1905)

The month of January with its mild weather and bright sunshine is again past. The first days of January were beautiful here. In general each day was fine, but on a couple of occasions there were three or four days that were fairly cold, compared with the others. There is a little snow on the ground. When it snows here, it is not cold, but when the snow lies on the ground and the sky is bright, then one can count on it that it will become colder. Yet that usually doesn't last long. For two, three, four days, sometimes five, the snow lies on the ground and then a Chinook comes – the warm west wind – and the snow melts in one day, sometimes even faster. A few days ago, at the end of January, there was about two inches of snow; in the morning the wind changed direction, the sun shone bright and clear, and by noon the snow had almost disappeared.[63]

February began with a rather cold night. Again there was about four inches of snow. For three days it was relatively cold, but on the fourth the weather was already much better. Nonetheless, the weather is beautiful every day. The sun shines almost all the time, except when it snows. Then it is hidden, but that usually does not last long.

Here the cattle roam around outside the whole winter.[64] They know how to get the grass even though there may be four inches of snow – which does not happen every year. People who have been here for several years say that four inches of snow is a lot for Alberta. Usually no more than two or three inches will fall.

You can usually tell from the cattle whether or not it will snow. When the cattle come from the north, you can be pretty certain that snow is on its way. The snow always comes with a north wind. In large numbers the cattle then retreat before the wind and steadily drift southward until the river, which flows near here, stops them. However, when it stops snowing, then they go northward again. Why? Because, people say, the further north you go, the more grass you find. A cow likes to graze on tall grass; a horse prefers it a little shorter. Hence here in our vicinity you usually see more horses on the prairie than cattle.

Corr. [George Dijkema] 8 Feb. 1905

---

64 The cattle he refers to are the herds of the ranchers on the open range. Most homestead land in the area was not yet fenced in. The winter of 1906–07 would be severe and thousands of cattle would die on the open range.

Willem Willemsen Jr. and friends at his granary.

LETTER FROM LEAVINGS
(*De Grondwet,* 14 March 1905)

After some days of cold weather, a change has come. On the coldest day in February the thermometer was 34 degrees below zero. Fortunately, the cold lasted only a few days. There was also more snow than has fallen in the last years. There is about six inches. Yet I am still happy that I am in Alberta, in "sunny Alberta," where at present the cold no longer prevails, but gentle mild weather, as if it were already spring. The farmers are already busy ploughing and harrowing and discing. The first half of February was certainly cold and the weather freezing, but the last half has been gentle and mild, with bright sunshine. No, there are no snowstorms here such as they have so often in America. There is no constant severe cold here such as people are familiar with there. Here there is severe cold only for a few days, and snow for a short time.

The Dutch colony has again increased by a few souls. Mr. G[errit] Willemders [Willemsen] came to us with his family, consisting of seven persons.[65] A son was born at the home of Mr. [Evert] Aldus.[66]

I also hear that still more people are coming, both from Holland and from the United States. There is still plenty of land here that is just waiting

---

65 The Garrit and Hendrika Willemsen family with seven children arrived in February from Manhattan, Mont. to join their relatives the Jan ter Telgte and Roelof Van Dyk families. Willemsen is my great-grandfather. The previous November he visited Alberta and filed on a homestead on the Leavings side of the settlement.
66 Louis Aldus was born 13 February 1905.

for the plough, and the young Dutch colony is still not too large. But Rome was not built in a day, and the colony will certainly become larger. We always have good courage, and hope that it may continue to expand.

Corr. [George Dijkema] 28 Feb. 1905

LETTER FROM ALBERTA
(*De Volksvriend,* 23 March 1905)[67]

The Dutch colony in Alberta is gradually becoming larger. A good year ago there were still only six souls;[68] now, a good year later, the number has grown to ninety. Yes, now there are ninety, but who will say how many will yet follow this summer. Not only is it increasing by births, but people are also coming from the Netherlands and the United States. Some are on the way from the old Fatherland and from America. People in Iowa and Wisconsin are getting ready to settle in Alberta.[69] So it appears that Alberta is not as cold as some in the United States imagine. We are not yet frozen to death, like many people imagine happens here.

We've had a few days of cold weather. At some places in the Dutch colony it was 34 degrees below zero, at others 40. It was very cold, but fortunately it lasted only a short time. That was in the first half of February. People (English) who have been here eleven years claim that it has never been so cold here in the last eleven years. But at the end of February people were ploughing, harrowing, and discing; yes, some were already seeding. However, no one believed that the weather would remain so mild. Then on the 9th of March we got a couple inches of snow again, so the field work has once again been postponed for a few days. But the general opinion is that this will not last long.

---

67 This is the first report from southern Alberta to *De Volksvriend,* the Dutch newspaper published in Orange City, Iowa. The correspondent was probably George Dijkema.

68 The six souls were the original Dutch family who arrived in southern Alberta in 1903, Harm and Jantje Emmelkamp and their four children. The second family, that of Hendrik and Maria ter Telgte, did not arrive until the end of 1903.

69 Anne Weerstra, Albert Lantinga, and Gerard Schuitema soon arrived from the Netherlands, the first from Friesland, the other two from Groningen. From northwest Iowa the Koole brothers were expected. From Vesper, Wisconsin, the Nan Dekker family was on their way. A letter from Vesper, dated 21 March, in *De Grondwet* (28 March 1905) reports: "Today Mr. and Mrs. N[an] Dekker, their son Arie and daughter Mrs. John de Puyt left for Alberta, Canada. The last-named accompanied them to help her sickly mother. Their son Thys has been there already for several months, and has already tasted the climate; his fingers at least have already been frozen." Maartje de Puyt apparently returned to Vesper after accompanying her parents to Alberta. The Vesper correspondent is clearly not happy that the Dekkers were leaving and brings out the old saw about a cold climate in Canada.

Horses are much more expensive than last year. That is undoubtedly the case because many more people have arrived, since almost every European nationality is represented here. Not only do Hollanders live here, but Swedes, Norwegians, Danes, Germans, Frenchmen, Belgians, Englishmen, and Scots, even Russians, and they must all get horses for themselves, so they are now more expensive than last year. A year ago you could see a house here and there on the prairie, and many homesteads were still available; now the homesteads are gone, and, last summer, houses sprang up like mushrooms out of the ground.

Land, namely railroad land, is also increasing in price. Last summer one could buy it for $5 an acre; now some has been sold already for $9.50 an acre.

There is joy in the family of Mr. S. Alders [Evert Aldus], because a baby boy was born. Mother and child are in excellent health.

NOTICE IN LOCAL NEWSPAPER
(*Lethbridge News*, 30 March 1905)[70]

Immigration Notes

B[astiaan], L[eendert], and A[rie] Koole, three brothers, are among the recent arrivals.[71] They hail from Iowa, and have brought with them two [railway] cars of effects and stock, consisting of three fine spans of horses and a complete outfit of farm machinery. They have taken land twenty miles west of Lethbridge. These boys mean business; they are settlers of the right sort and they will succeed.[72]

---

70 Only rarely did the local newspapers, the *Lethbridge News*, *Lethbridge Herald*, and *Macleod Gazette* take notice of the Dutch settlement in the area.

71 Bastiaan and Leendert Koole had come to southern Alberta in the spring of 1904, worked for ranchers in the Pincher Creek area, and on 27 September each filed on a homestead on the east side of the Dutch settlement. Each brother also bought a half section of C & E Railway land. Then they returned to Iowa for the winter to purchase farm equipment. A letter from Alton, Iowa, in *Pella's Weekblad* (4 November 1904), reports: "Bastiaan Koole from Sheldon was here in Alton last Thursday. He, with his brother Leonard, just came back from a three-year trip through Washington, Oregon, and Alberta, Canada. They have plans to spend the winter with their parents Mr. and Mrs. Arie Koole west of Sheldon. In the spring they are going also with another brother [Arie] to Alberta, Canada, where they each bought a half section of land." A later letter in the 17 March 1905, issue of the same newspaper reports: "Bastiaan Koole, son of Arie Koole, one of Sioux County's most prosperous farmers west of Sheldon, visited Alton and Orange City friends last week. He will soon leave for Lethbridge, Alberta, Canada, where he will farm with both his brothers next year."

72 Years later Leendert and Arie Koole made a major contribution to Canadian agriculture when in 1917 they invented strip farming as a method to counter the problem of soil drifting.

LETTER FROM LEAVINGS
(*Nieuwsblad van Friesland,* 6 May 1905)

The Climate in Alberta

The climate in Alberta is very different than the climate in Holland. Holland is a land that lies below sea level. There may be some high points in Drenthe or in the Gelderland Veluwe which would not come under water if the sea dikes broke, but the largest part of Holland would be bathed in sea water.

Alberta, however, lies far above sea level, about 3,500 feet, and has a dry mountain climate.

I will try to give you an idea of Alberta's climate by indicating month by month what kind of weather we have here. Let me begin with January.

In January winter usually sets in for good. Almost everyday the weather is clear and sunshiny. You can see the sun almost daily. Sometimes, however, snow falls; most years no more than three or four inches, but this year six inches. When snow has fallen you can always count on it that you will get some days of cold weather. But when the cold weather goes away, then all at once the snow disappears and nature is as mild as if it were already spring.

In February it is the same. You understand that the cattle, which are always outside, sometimes have a hard time eating grass when five inches of snow lie on the ground and it is pretty cold besides. The thermometer falls much lower here than in Holland; if it froze so many degrees in Holland, many people would die. Yet one can very well stand the cold here, because here we have what they call a dry cold.

In March the sun gets warmer by the day. Yet also in March it can still snow heavily. The first half of March is usually like February, alternating between snow and cold and nice warm weather. But the last half sometimes becomes spring-like. The farmers start seeding already before the frost is out of the ground. In March it can sometimes also rain. In January and February not; as far as I know only sometimes a few drops in February. But then comes April with its warm days and cool nights. Sometimes also a snowstorm yet, which the farmers are very happy about because this makes the ground once again good and wet. In April there are many warm dry southwest winds.

May generally brings fine weather and June even more. The days are warm and long, longer than in Holland, the nights short and cool. At night it is always cool here, even in the heart of summer. In June it also rains, which again stands the farmer in good stead.

In July and August there is no rain; always bright sunshiny, warm, sometimes definitely hot, weather. There may be an occasional thunder shower here and there, but in July and August the rainy season is past.

In September the days begin to get shorter again and the farmer begins to harvest his grain. August is not harvest month here, but September.

If there is a lot of snow in the winter and a lot of rain in the spring and summer, then you can break sod the whole summer; otherwise you have to stop in July and August because the ground is too hard. However, at the end of August or beginning of September rain comes again and the ploughing begins anew.

October has splendid, clear, sunshiny weather; warm in the day, but cool at night. Sometimes a little frost, also occasionally in September. Also in October bright sunshine alternates with southwest winds, which are certainly not harmful but they are annoying.

In November every day still has fine weather. The busyness is then about past and some already begin to look forward to winter. December also can still be pretty good. Yet already in November snow sometimes falls; but it remains only a short time. After the snow there is good weather again and it is very good for ploughing.

December is colder, however. By Christmas winter here begins to set in for good.

On the whole Alberta has a lovely, healthy climate. Though it can sometimes be cold in the winter, the cold is no problem; one does not get sick of it and one can delight in the sunshine almost every day. The air here is much thinner than in Holland; that's why one can better stand the cold. Here we never have the dreary, dark, foggy days that are so common in Holland.

Geo. Dijkema   Leavings, Alberta, Canada, March 1905

LETTER FROM LEAVINGS
(*De Grondwet,* 23 May 1905)

It was busy here in the last few weeks. Everyone was busy seeding the land that he had broken last summer or fall. Wheat seeding was done already some time ago and on most farms it's already up above the ground; yes, on some places it's waving in the wind that blows over the land. Also the oats is already coming up. It is no wonder; the ground was moist enough, and the weather warm every day with beautiful sunshine. The grass also is growing fast so that the cows and horses again have plenty to eat. The whole vast prairie is green, except for the scattered patches made black by the ingenious and industrious hand of man. What a difference between last year and now. Then you could see a small house here and there; now almost everywhere. The houses came like mushrooms, as it were, springing up from the ground. Yet there is still room for many more people. Not every 160 acres has a house standing on it. Beautiful land can still be bought here, although there is no chance any more for homesteads.[73]

Several weeks ago some gentlemen came over from Holland, [Gerard] Schuitema and [Albert] Lantinga from Groningen and [Anne] Weerstra from Friesland, so the colony is again enlarged by three adult men. At the same time it was increased by the birth of two, in the Postma [Postman] household, a baby son, and at the home of Venhuizen, a baby daughter.[74]

Next Sunday and the following we will have Rev. Holwerda here from Manhattan, Mont.[75]

Corr. [George Dijkema]

LETTER FROM LEAVINGS
(*Nieuwsblad van Friesland,* 27 May 1905)

The Lay of the Land

As most of your readers well know, Alberta is not yet as populated as Holland. The cities and villages are not as close to each other and there are not as many farms between them. That is not possible. Three to four years ago almost no one lived here. Only here and there had a large cattleman or horse rancher put up his house and the whole prairie belonged to him. But the government gave part of the land away to people who wanted to come here to live.

---

73 The land rush for homesteads occurred in the Leavings district from 1902 to 1905. Thus only the earliest Dutch settlers were able to claim homesteads. The C & E Railroad sections between each homestead section were still available for purchase.
74 The child born to the Postman family was not a son but a daughter Janna, born 13 April. Margaretha Venhuizen was born on 28 March. The Venhuizen family arrived from Manhattan in June 1904. The single men were Albert Lantinga and George Schuitema from Groningen and Anne Weerstra from St. Jacobi Parochie in Friesland. Schuitema settled in the Pearce area south of the Oldman River.
75 The first Sunday that Rev. James Holwerda, pastor of the Manhattan Christian Reformed Church, led a service in Alberta was 14 May. He came to lead worship for two weeks and to baptize two children of parents who were still members of the Manhattan church.

Fifteen to twenty years ago the government of the United States of North America did the same in some states of the union. At that time the states were still thinly populated, and now the land there costs $40 to $60 an acre. Then people could get it for nothing.

Alberta also was thinly populated and the land was good. In order to attract a denser population the government gave the land away.

A Homestead

When someone goes to a land office to take up 160 acres as a homestead and receives proof at the land office that the 160 acres belongs to him, then he has 160 acres of prairie with no house or tree, no canal or well. It may be that he is fortunate enough to find a slough on it, but for the rest he has flat prairie grown over with very good grass. Then he can build himself a house and a fence around his 160 acres of land, because there are no canals here.[76] It would be almost impossible to dig canals since the ground is too hard. Also, in most places no water would go into them because Alberta lies too far above sea level. Rather, people here put a post in the ground every ten or fifteen steps, buy barbed wire, and connect one post to another to enclose the whole area, in order to keep their own cattle in and another's cattle outside the 64 hectares.

You can buy the posts, but you can also get them for nothing. The government gives a permit to cut 500 posts in the hills. Of course, the way there is not very easy. It also takes more time to fetch them than to buy them in town. It is cheaper, however.

Fuel (wood) you can still get for nothing out of the river bottom, but that too will quickly change. Then another way will surely open up to buy wood. Yet coal is also not expensive and is found in many places on the prairie.

But a homesteader is still not ready. He now has a house and a fence around his land, and fuel and horses and cows, but no water for his family or his cattle. He can dig a well, but is he certain of water? Sometimes one finds it at 12 feet, sometimes at 30 feet, sometimes not at all. If one does not live far from a river or creek he can easily haul it, but not everyone lives near a stream. Yet the proverb is still true, "the persistent one wins."

Now a family lives there on 64 hectares of land. No tree and no bush near the house; everywhere bare, naked, open prairie. But can one expect anything different? Imagine that a part of Holland suddenly became like

---

76   In many parts of the Netherlands fences are not necessary because parcels of land are surrounded by canals.

the prairie here; would large trees grow in one year? Would it at once be like it was before? Here too things will change in the course of time.

Trees and bushes grow very well here. Currants and gooseberries, raspberries and strawberries grow wild in the river bottom where there is enough woods; won't they grow then on the rich prairie when it is ploughed and transformed into beautiful gardens? Also, it appears to be good here for apple and pear trees, plum and cherry trees. "Everything will turn out all right," say the Transvaal Boers.

Birds and Wild Animals

Since there are not many trees here, neither are there many birds. In the summer there is a kind of lark. Countless bird nests are then found on the prairie. Here also is a kind of swallow; besides that there is some kind of hawk that is an awfully big chicken thief. You have to pay special attention to them. In the spring and summer there are many wild ducks that live and brood by the small sloughs found everywhere on the prairies. Late in the summer they leave, but come back in the fall in the company of countless wild geese.

In the winter the birds are here the most. By the thousands you can then see them flying close to the ground. The English call them "snowbirds." They very much resemble the Dutch sparrow.

Also rabbits and partridges are found here in great numbers. Here, however, the partridge is twice as big as in Holland. The rabbits are grey in the summer and white in the winter. In mid-March they again take off their winter suit and appear in summer dress.

Here the enemies of the rabbits and partridges are not only people, but there is a kind of wolf (coyote), about as big as a hunting dog in Holland. These wolves lie in wait for rabbits and partridges, and also for chickens. These animals can be very bold sometimes, especially when it is cold. Anyone who has chickens – and everyone has them – has to have a dog to be on guard. The coyote is afraid of a dog. Perhaps it thinks that where there is a dog there will also be people.

Chickens

Having chickens in Alberta is a good thing. Eggs usually fetch a good price. In January and February they cost 40 to 45 cents a dozen; that is, a guilder for 12 eggs. Now they are no longer so expensive; 24 American cents for 12; that is still 5 Dutch cents per egg.

Whoever has a rather large number of chickens can almost make a living from them alone. Also butter fetches a good price. With a pair of milk cows and 70 chickens you get a long ways here.

Every man over eighteen years can get a homestead (160 acres) for almost nothing. If you plough that land and sow wheat or oats or barley, or plant part of it with potatoes, then you have more income than only from chickens and a pair of milk cows. But the free land that the government gave away is almost taken up already. Here and there still lies a homestead, but there are not very many more.

Pre-emption of a Homestead

However, there is still another way to get 160 acres. When one takes up such a homestead, one has to fulfil a few requirements that the government imposes on the homesteader. One must live on it six months of the year and plough part of it every year; otherwise one cannot receive his title papers in three years. There are always and everywhere people who do not fulfil the requirements. So someone can pre-empt his homestead. In this case one goes to the land office and says that this homesteader has not fulfilled his requirements. Then the government gives such a person a period of sixty days to do so yet. If after the sixty days he has not done enough, then his homestead is taken away from him and is given to the person who tried to pre-empt it from him. Such pre-emption is not exactly a pleasant action since the outcome is uncertain. But in this manner one can still get 160 acres for $10.

Geo. Dijkema   Leavings, Alberta, Canada

LETTER FROM GERRIT J. WITHAGE
(*De Wachter,* 14 June 1905)[77]

It seemed good to us to send a piece to our paper, so that there may be some familiarity with this part of the far west, because the proverb "unknown is unloved" is still always true. But fortunately, we are no longer completely unknown and unloved by the churches in America. No, we have wonderfully experienced proof of that in recent weeks. Let us briefly inform to you about it.

77   *De Wachter* was the official weekly of the Christian Reformed Church.

Here we have a Dutch settlement and there is one also about twelve miles closer to Leavings; together they number about 120 persons, adults and children. Of that number 33 belong to the congregation at Manhattan, Montana. Except for one family, they come from that place and because there is no closer congregation, they are still members of that church.[78] The consistory of that congregation was convinced that work must be done here, in spite of the great distance. After corresponding several times with the brothers of that place, who were also very eager to do so, they in cooperation with the Classis and the Home Missions Board sent their minister to us for two weeks.[79] For us it was a wonderful time; many a time we have called to the King and Lord of the Church: O send us one of your servants, who is able and willing to explain your Word to us according to the mind of the Spirit, who can strengthen us by your Word in our way of life. O Lord, visit us with your salvation. And the Lord heard our groans. Is it any wonder that our heart as it were overflowed with praise and thanks now that we, once again after fifteen months,[80] might go up with God's people? It was no beautiful temple where we found ourselves; no, it was only a simple hut, because we still do not have beautiful houses here. Also, we did not have a nice platform; a chest turned bottom up, a 2 × 4 with a small store box on top of it – that was the whole pulpit. But no problem; we heard God's Word. The first Sunday the Reverend preached at this location and then baptized two children who belonged to the Manhattan church; this the classis had approved. In the morning about forty were present, adults and children; in the afternoon at least sixty people. The following Sunday the Reverend preached at Leavings. Then there were not at all as many, because it rained almost the whole day. Also from here and from Leavings a request was sent to the Board for a missionary. Our wish and prayer is that the Lord may gladden us also in this matter. Brothers and sisters who read this, before I end, a request yet. When you pray for you and yours and pray for others, think also of us in your prayers.

Thanking you, Mr. Editor, for the space, I remain your friend and brother, G[errit] J. Withage   Lethbridge, Alberta, Canada

---

78 The thirty-three persons who were still members of the Manhattan Christian Reformed Church included Willem Feller and the families of John Postman, Jan Hendrik ter Telgte, Garrit Willemsen, and Gerrit J. Withage. The Postman family is the only one that had not actually lived for a time at Manhattan; Postman had sent their membership papers to the Manhattan church, since it was the nearest Christian Reformed church.

79 The Manhattan church was part of Classis Orange City, a regional assembly of the Christian Reformed Church. At this time the focus of the Home Missions Board of the Christian Reformed Church was to establish new churches among the groups of Dutch families scattered across America.

80 It was fifteen months since the Withage and J. H. ter Telgte families had arrived in Alberta from Manhattan.

LETTER FROM ALBERTA
(*De Volksvriend,* 15 June 1905)

Slowly but surely the Dutch colony in Alberta is expanding. In March the gentlemen Schuitema and Lantinga arrived from Groningen and Weerstra from Friesland; last week a family came here from Overijssel, a man, his wife, and three children. The brother of J[acobus] Nyhoff came to us with his wife, children, and a friend.[81] So this spring the colony was again enriched by nine persons. Where there was still nothing just over a year ago many buildings are now standing. Who knows how many will come yet this summer or next fall.

Last week and the previous week we had a lovely rain. So the grain is also growing well; it cannot do otherwise. Beautiful warm weather followed the rain, so now everything is thriving. Again there is abundant grass for the cattle and horses. Now also after the rains breaking is going very well. The land here is turning a whole different colour. Last year at this time almost everything was still green; now much of the green landscape is being transformed into farmland. Everyone is busy making the land black in order to seed winter wheat next fall.

On the 14th and 21st of May we had Rev. Holwerda here from Manhattan, Montana. He preached the gospel for us these two Sundays. On both Sundays the weather was rainy, yet almost all the Hollanders were present both times. We have no church yet, but the attendance was still good.

At the Postmas [Postmans] a son was born, and at the Veenhuizens [Venhuizens] a daughter.[82]

LETTER FROM EVERT ALDUS
(*Twentsch Volksblad,* 17 June 1905)

Lethbridge, 20 May 1905

Now that spring has come, I would like to report to our friends and acquaintances in and around Nijverdal something about our lives and our activities. As before, I'll first tell a little about the weather. In my last letter, I reported that we still had thaw days late in the fall, and also many nice days.

---

81 In May 1905 Rense and Aaltje Nyhoff and their three children arrived from Nijverdal. The friend was probably Albert Rutgers, also from Nijverdal.
82 This letter to *De Volksvriend* was probably written by George Dijkema.

At Christmas there was severe cold and snow. After New Year the "Chinook" began to blow; it stopped the freezing and melted the snow. Mild weather remained until mid-January. Then about eight inches of snow fell and it began to freeze very hard. How hard it froze you cannot imagine in Holland. At Macleod the lowest level on the thermometer was 36 degrees below the freezing point, and according to some, 40 degrees (Celsius). It froze through everything. In my well, which is 16 feet deep, the water was sometimes frozen. Yet the well was covered with a three-foot thick layer of sod, and the small opening for drawing water was closed with a hatch and sacks.

When we stoked the stove hard until 12 o'clock at night, many a time the water in the kettles on the stove was turned to ice the next morning. If with such cold it was overcast or foggy as in Holland, then one could not live here. However, the sun almost always shines. If you are properly clothed, with thick gloves on, then you can be outside for a while in the middle of the day. Because the air is drier here, you do not feel the cold as much. But because of that you can get frozen ears, fingers, or nose in a couple of minutes. If there is a strong wind with such cold, then anyone can understand that you cannot go outside the door. Fortunately it was almost always quiet sunny weather. The wind blew for a couple of days. It drove the snow, frozen like dust, in thick clouds over the prairie, so that anyone outside could not see 500 paces ahead. When you go out on the prairie in such weather, you put your life in danger. With such a snowstorm the prairie cattle suffer a lot. The poor animals walk along before the wind, and many a time fall down exhausted and then freeze to death. If they come to the river, they sometimes fall down a steep slope and break their neck or legs. Therefore the ranchers round up their cattle within a fenced-in space, or some sheltered place, when they think a snowstorm is approaching.

In spite of our more or less imperfect dwellings, and clothing insufficient for this climate, I think I can safely report that none of us has had to suffer much from the cold. Though some of us did not have coal, they could keep sufficiently warm with wood. Except for some frozen ears, toes, etc., the winter did us no harm. The colossal stoves and heating apparatuses in private and public buildings, as well as the large mass of coal that is directly hauled across the prairies from the mines in the fall, even to the Indian camps, shows that we can have a cold severe winter here.

The thick layer of snow prevents the livestock from finding grass, so we have to feed hay to the cows and horses. This is too bad, because nine or ten of these animals quickly eat up a load of hay.

The severe winter lasted until the middle of February, a short four weeks, I think. Then we had thaws, so strong that we could begin our fieldwork in the middle of March. Since that time it has sometimes snowed and frozen a bit, but it was never very cold. I think after March 15 we had about seven days when we could not work due to the snow.

In brief, we are able to say this about the past seasons: A cold, late, unpleasant spring; a short warm summer; a long beautiful fall; and a short severe winter. This spring differs from the last one by much milder weather and more nice days, also fewer frosty nights. As a result, the young prairie grass has appeared a month earlier than a year ago. Also, the trees by the river are in leaf a few weeks earlier. The yellow lupines, the red primroses, and other flowers are already in bloom for some time. Last year everything was a month later, so this spring compares favourably with the last one. The rainfall, however, is much less than a year ago. In early May we had a couple of days of rain. Immediately after that the wind began to blow, which sucked up all the moisture from the ground. Now, however, as I write this, the sky is darker and large drops of rain are falling on the dry ground. For this we are very glad; in the first place crops and grass can grow again, and furthermore the rain makes the ground wet and soft, so that we can plough a little prairie, in order to seed it next year.

Our Spring Work

As soon as the frost was sufficiently out of the ground, we began to prepare our land for seeding. First some of us still ploughed a little; others had ploughed enough in the fall. When the prairie is ploughed up, the ground is not yet fit for seeding. The sods are too tough and too hard. They have to be made fine. This is done with a disc. This implement, drawn by three or four horses, cuts and breaks the sod pieces. When the discing is done, then one harrows the land to make it level.

It is necessary to make the land as even as possible. If you leave the thick lumps lie, then in the fall you cannot mow the grain short because the mower may not cut through the lumps. To disc the sod pieces requires a lot of time and work; you have to go over the same piece of land four or more times. And in spite of all the work with disc and harrow, you still do not get the ground nice and fine; the sods are too tough. Everyone can understand that after being worked for some years the land becomes nice and fine, just like the farmland in Holland. Then you do not have as much work.

When the land is prepared as much as possible, it is seeded with the seeder or drill. This implement places the seed evenly in the ground in rows, and also mostly covers it. Some of us dragged an upside down harrow or a beam over the land after seeding, all to get it as level as possible; others rolled with heavy iron rollers that are used for that purpose. Our wheat we seeded mostly in April. It comes up after a couple of weeks, and looks like a field of young rye in Holland. Oats we seeded in the second half of April and in the first half of May. Some is coming up; the later seeded not yet.

Most of us plant potatoes. Some people ploughed them in, others first ploughed the land very deep and made it good and fine. Afterward they planted the potatoes with a shovel. Here one plants potatoes three or four times as far apart as in Holland. In favourable years the yield can be five times as much as by you.

We seeded peas, onions, turnips, cabbage, rhubarb, carrots, lettuce, beets, and other vegetables. We do this in rows, not in beds.

So we are going to meet the summer in the hope that the weather may cooperate to give us a good harvest. As long as the ground does not become too hard and too dry, we can plough for the next year. In connection with the work, most of us have bought a disc and drill.

Last Spring and Now

The change since last spring is great and striking. Then, if one saw a few shacks here and there with a little piece of ploughed land, and saw no life on the prairie because nothing could be worked due to the drought, now it is totally different. There are a large number of houses and shacks, as far as the eye can see. Large stretches of yellow grass have given way to fields of darker green wheat. Everywhere there is activity and busyness. Because every day the "prairie breakers" (ploughs) are driven through the yellow grass to turn it into black land. Or one sees the disc, drawn by four horses, split and break up the tough lumps of grass into small pieces. And besides the fact that the wasteland is being turned into fruitful land, something is also being done for the culture and development of the youth. Between here and Leavings three new schools have been built.[83] Here where we live two school districts have been formed. So next spring two schools will be built here in the neighbourhood.[84] When the required number of children is present in a square of four by four or four by five miles, one can request a school. The school is built as much as possible in the middle of the district, so that those living farthest away have to go only a good hour.

83 The Rose Butte school opened in the spring of 1905, the Rocky Coulee school was built in May 1905 and opened in September, and the Jumbo Valley school opened in April 1905.
84 On the east side of the Dutch settlement there was the Rose Butte school and the Finley School, which opened in January 1906.

Worship Services on the Prairie

On 14 May for the first time we had church on the prairie.[85] Then Rev. Holwerda from Manhattan, Montana, led us twice. Although I am poor at "picturing" things, I nevertheless want to tell a little about it.

The church was a small wooden shack (a polder shed one would call it in Holland) temporarily inhabited by P[ostman]. The pulpit consisted of a large chest turned over, a board nailed vertically against it, and a smaller box nailed on the board with the bottom up. On the large chest stood the "dominie," on the small one attached above the pole lay his Bible. Seating places were made from beams, planks, blocks, chests, etc. This "church" lay on a high point from where you can look over the colony. So an onlooker from there that morning could see the churchgoers coming. A few on foot, as in Holland, but most on wagons or on horseback, a couple even on a prairie sled. Since there was no clock to sound, and not all watches tell the same time, not everyone came on time. A little after ten, however, everyone was present, about 35 adults and some children and babies.

It was something peculiar. Psalm-singing ringing over the prairie from the shack or shed, surrounded by the usual things like firewood, logs, barrels, etc., and also by a number of wagons and other vehicles, with hay eating horses tied to them.

Although there was no persecution to fear, and the psalms were not sung according to the rhyming of Peter Dathenus, yet the whole thing reminded one of the "hedge preaching" from the time of the Reformation.[86] In some things the worship service bore an American character. Thus (as is customary here) some mothers brought along their babies who were freely allowed to enjoy their mother's milk during the sermon, to stop the crying. That is something a young mother in Holland would not do so quickly in church.

In the afternoon Rev. H[olwerda] spoke once again and baptized two little ones (of parents belonging to the [Christian] Reformed Church).[87]

So on 14 May 1905, for the first time God's Word was delivered by Rev. Holwerda of Manhattan, *to those scattered in the land of loneliness,* as the Reverend said, dedicating us to God in his prayer. What words would have expressed the Reverend's impression last year if he had visited us then?

A[ldus]

---

85 Aldus means that, for the first time, an official church service was held, under the leadership of Rev. James Holwerda. He was sent by the Manhattan, Mont. Christian Reformed Church to visit the Dutch settlers in southern Alberta for two weeks since some of them were members of that church. Earlier in the settlement, at least some families gathered together on Sundays in one of their shacks to hold informal reading services where someone read from a Dutch sermon book.

LETTER FROM EVERT ALDUS
(*Twentsch Volksblad*, 1 July 1905)

Farm Machinery

The readers of our paper know that the field work on an American farm is done with different and better implements than in Holland. In the hope that the reader will take some interest in this, I will tell a few things about the farm implements and their use.

The implement that one needs first of all is a plough. Ploughs here are made in all possible sorts and forms. You can properly divide them into "walking ploughs" (ploughs that you walk behind and steer by hand) and "riding ploughs" (which the plougher sits on and are steered by the horses).

As far as I can remember, a plough in Holland consists of a strong beam to which the ploughshare is attached, with the handle on the back end to steer the plough. The plough-beam is supported by two wheels, the large one in front, and the small one running on the unploughed land. You should now imagine that these two wheels are gone, so that the beam with the ploughshare is left. In front under the beam a small wheel is attached, which can be shoved up and down. If you move the little wheel close to the beam it is lowered to the ground and the plough cuts deeper; if you move the wheel farther from the beam, then you do not plough as deep. Instead of one, such a plough has two handles, between which the ploughman walks. Coupled to the front-end of the beam is the tongue which the horses pull. By placing this tongue (to which the harness traces are attached) more to the right or left, you get a wide or narrow furrow. The "cutting" of the furrow is sometimes done by a blade, as in Holland, but usually by a rotating steel disc, which is ground sharp on the edge. The wooden tongue is sometimes replaced by a steel one.*

---

* The description of the Dutch plough given by our respected Canadian correspondent applies only to the plough of the sandy regions (Overijssel, Drenthe, Gelderland, etc.). In the clay regions (Groningen, Friesland, Zeeland, etc.) we use – to judge by the description – exactly the same ploughs as in Canada.

86 Due to persecution early followers of the Reformed faith in the Netherlands in the sixteenth century held secret worship services outside the towns in fields behind the hedgerows.

87 The children baptized were Janna Postman and Jan ter Telgte. Their parents were still members of the Manhattan, Mont. Christian Reformed Church. Aldus often refers to the Christian Reformed Church as the "Gereformeerde Kerk," since that was the mother church of the CRC in the Netherlands. Likewise, he usually refers to the Reformed Church in America as the "Hervormde Kerk," after its parent denomination in the Netherlands.

Beert A. Nauta ploughing at Granum, *ca.*1909. (Courtesy: Annie Nauta.)

A "riding plough" is an implement with three wheels of different size. One of these runs in the old furrow, one in the furrow just ploughed, and one on the unploughed land. On this three-wheel (completely iron) frame the plough-share and cutter are attached or suspended. By means of handles you can lower or raise the ploughshare, if you want to plough deeper or shallower.

In front of this plough a pole or tongue is attached. On both sides of this tongue the horses walk, just as two horses in front of a carriage each walk on one side of the tongue. As the front wheels have a different position when the tongue is moved to the right or left, the plough wheels also have a different position by changing the direction of the tongue. Thus if you steer the horses right forward, then the tongue also moves in that direction, the wheels run well, and so does the whole implement.

Coming to the end of a field one must turn around, and the plough may not cut. You then throw a regular [walking] plough on its side. This does not work with a riding plough. So during the turn you can lift the ploughshare a few inches above the ground either by hand or by pressing your foot on a handle. While working you sit on a seat above the implement.

The advantages of a riding plough over a walking plough are these: In the first place, you only need to steer the horses, not the plough. If you steer the horses well, the plough runs right by itself. Therefore you can use unruly and irregular walking horses for a riding plough; for a walking plough this is very difficult. Second, you don't need to walk, but can sit. Third, the riding plough does better work, just as a sewing-machine does better work than a needle in the human hand.

The ploughs here cut furrows 12 to 18 inches wide. Ploughs that are used to plough prairie are called "prairie breakers," while those used to work old land are called "stubble ploughs." The difference between a breaker and a stubble plough lies mostly in the form of the ploughshare. For most ploughing you can bolt on a breaker- or stubble-share, depending on what you need. For ground with a lot of rocks you use soft tough metal to make ploughshares; for ground without rocks harder material. After it is used for some time, the ploughshare is dull. The blacksmith has to hammer it, which costs 40 or 50 cents.

Besides these types, people also use disc ploughs that differ completely from the others. In these implements the ploughshare is replaced by a slant-ing dish-shaped disc of steel. When the plough is moving, this disc turns, thereby going several inches into the ground, and overturns the soil in this way. Such ploughs run easier, because the cutting motion of the ploughshare is replaced by a turning motion. But you can only use them on old land. Riding ploughs with two shares and disc ploughs with two discs are often used here. Such ploughs cut two furrows at the same time. A walking plough costs about $25, a riding plough about $50. The Hollanders here use both kinds. Because the prairie is tough, usually four horses are necessary to pull the plough.

The Disc

This is an implement to make the ground fine after ploughing. One also uses it to make stubbleland fine without ploughing it first. A disc consists of a long axle to which eight to sixteen steel discs or wheels are attached half a foot apart. These discs have sharp edges and are dish shaped. They are one to two feet in diameter. On this axle with all its discs or wheels a sort of stem is attached on which there is a stool or seat for the driver, as well as a long pole or tongue on both sides of which the horses walk. If you ride a disc over the land, the discs cut the ground into little pieces. The imple-ment is fairly heavy by itself, and is sometimes made heavier by setting on it trays with rocks; then the discs penetrate so much the deeper. If the disc did no more than what I have said, the ground would only be cut into small lumps. But it is also turned over. To achieve this, they have made the axle of this implement in two separate sections, which one can adjust in such a way that they form an obtuse angle, about like the letter V but with a very obtuse angle. When the disc is moved from north to south, the discs turn in a southeasterly and northwesterly direction.

One can best illustrate the working of a disc by a regular saucer that is upright, with its bottom moving a couple of fingers deep in loose sand. But in such a way that the direction of its movement is, for example, north to south, while the diameter of the saucer points northeast-southwest. The hollow side must then be turned southeast. If at the same time you can give the saucer a turning motion, you then have a clear idea of how a disc works.

If you sharpen the angle formed by both halves of the axle, the disc works deeper. This can be done very easily with a handle. Implements with small discs work better than large ones. This is the case because small discs turn more quickly than larger ones, with the same speed of movement, just as the front wheel of a wagon revolves more quickly than the larger back wheel. Discing is heavy work for the horses. Three or four are necessary, though that depends on the size of the implement. A disc costs from $30 to $60.

The Harrow

When the land is broken up enough with the disc, then it is harrowed in order to get it level. I need not say much about the harrow since they have the same form here as in Holland. Usually harrows are manufactured completely of iron. On some of them you can give the teeth a more or less slanting position. A few times I saw so-called spring-tooth harrows. On these the teeth are replaced by bent strings of steel that spring back in rocks, etc.

(to be continued)

LETTER FROM EVERT ALDUS
(*Twentsch Volksblad,* 8 July 1905)

The Seeder

The "seeder" or "drill" is an ingenious implement. Two wheels carry a small 6 to 10 foot long box which is wide on top and narrow on the bottom. In this box you put one or two sacks of seed grain. There are openings in the bottom of the box half a foot apart, through which the seed falls into little pipes that run to the ground. Under each pipe there is a hoof-shaped foot that scratches a little channel through the ground in which the seed then falls (the shoe-drill). Or a sort of knife goes in front of the seed pipe and cuts a little channel in which the seed falls (the hoe-drill). Or in front of each seed pipe runs a small disc (see what I wrote about the disc) and makes a groove for the seed (the disc-drill). With the last two kinds of seeders the grooves are closed by chains dragging behind. If you seed with the first kind, then you must usually harrow afterward. Due to an ingenious apparatus in the seed pipes the seed falls evenly everywhere, just like a sewing machine always makes the stitches an even size, no matter whether you turn it hard or slowly. By pushing a bar up or down you can make the machine seed as thick or thin as you choose. Then you can set the machine for wheat, oats, barley, peas, etc., depending on what you wish to seed. Some seeders also indicate when an acre of land is seeded so that you get to know the area of the farmland with it.

When turning around you shut the machine off, and with a lever lift up the seed pipes above the ground. You can let the implement seed deep or shallow. If the bottom end of a seed pipe hits a rock, then the pipe whips up or backward. If it could not do this, it would break.

Depending on the size, three or four horses pull the seeder. You can sit on some; with the smaller types you have to walk behind. A drill costs from $60 to $120.

The Hollanders here use hoe-drills and disc-drills.

The Binder

Binder is the name of the implement which cuts the different sorts of grain and binds them into bundles or sheaves. Though I saw such a machine working last year during harvest, I see no chance of giving a clear description of this ingeniously thought-out implement.

In my opinion it is one of the most ingenious machines ever invented. As with other machines, however, the binder was first made in a less perfect form. Continued improvements have made it what it is now. I will tell something about it.

This machine runs over the mowed land, just alongside the grain. The stems are cut off with an apparatus that somewhat resembles the instrument a barber uses to cut hair. But this clipper is 6, 7, or 8 feet long, so the machine cuts a strip of that width all at once. The cut off stems fall, neatly with the heads to one side, on a so-called platform. From there they are carried upwards and to the other side of the machine. Here they collect until there is enough for a bundle or sheaf, after which the implement wraps a piece of twine around it, tightens it properly and ties it tight, and finally cuts the twine close to the knot. The sheaf remains in the machine until four or five more are ready; then the implement lets them fall at the same time on the ground. The sheaves are all made equally thick, no matter whether the grain is thick or thin. The machine waits with the binding until the sheaf has the same thickness as the previous one. However, you can make it bind thick or thin sheaves by setting the machine for that.

The machine cuts so fast that two men must work hard to set up the cut sheaves into stooks and keep up with it. Three or four horses pull the binder. The price of such an implement amounts to about $150. We do not own any binders yet, but we hope that we will all have to buy one this fall.

In other parts of America people use so-called "head-cutters." These are very wide machines that cut off only the heads and collect them in a large tank. The straw then remains standing on the ground, and is burned or ploughed under. There is something peculiar about these machines in that the horses walk behind the implement, not in front of it. They do not pull but push it. This has to be the case; otherwise the animals would walk in the grain.

Threshing Machine

Of a threshing machine or "thresher" I cannot say much, since I have never had a good look at one. This much I will offer. The threshing machine is put into motion by a steam engine, which is placed at some distance in order to prevent fire in the straw. The motion is conveyed by a drive belt, like those used in factories.

This machine takes the grain out of the straw, cleans out the dust and dirt, and indicates how many bushels of seed are threshed. The implement also cuts the twine from the sheaves. Some men are continually busy throwing in the sheaves. Others take the full sacks of grain away and hang empty ones in their place. Again others bring straw to the steam engine, because it is fuelled not by coal, but by threshed straw. Fifteen to twenty men are needed for threshing. But inconceivably large masses of grain are threshed in one day. People have told me, more than 50,000 pounds in one day. Above the thresher is a large pipe. Through it a strong stream of air is driven which blows the straw, dust, etc. onto a large pile.

The steam engine can not only drive a threshing machine, but also move forward itself, like an automobile. When the work is done at one farmer, the threshing machine is coupled behind the steam engine, and the latter pulls the former to the next farm. So it goes from house to house.

The price paid to the owner of the machine is calculated according to the number of bushels of seed that are threshed.

Small machines are occasionally driven by twelve horses, and not by steam.[88]

88 According to Willem Stotyn, in 1905 his wheat harvest was threshed by a neighbour Emil Hann, "with a crude type of thresher operated by a team of horses going around and around in a circle all day. The machine had no straw blower and the straw had to be removed and piled by hand." As reported by Jacob Dekker, "Monarch, A Little Bit of Old Holland," *Lethbridge Herald*, 25 June 1955.

Chris T. Withage on binder. (Courtesy: Hilda Withage.)

The Mower

Grass is cut with a "mower." I've heard that such a machine is used in Nijverdal; therefore it is better to go see it there than for me to say something about it. We rake up hay with a "rake," a very large rake with long curved teeth. This machine is on a long axle suspended between two wheels. One or two horses pull it forward so that the teeth with their points drag along the ground. When the rake is full, you press your foot on a pedal; the teeth then rise a couple of feet, the hay remains on a pile, and the teeth again fall down.

Besides the machines that I have mentioned, machines are also made here to plant potatoes. Large potatoes are cut into four.

Digging out potatoes also happens mechanically here. Such a machine can collect the potatoes in a sack. But stones, etc., are also collected. So people usually let the implement throw the potatoes in a row on the ground. Then there are mechanical hay tedders, hay loaders, etc. Also wagons that spread or scatter manure on the land while moving. But I know most of these implements only from the catalogues that one gets. Therefore I cannot report much about them.

A[ldus]   Lethbridge 30 May 1905

LETTER FROM EVERT ALDUS
(*Twentsch Volksblad*, 15 July 1905)

House Moving

Some time ago I wrote how one of us moved his shack with horses. House moving is not unusual in America.

In Holland when people read in the newspaper about something strange or apparently impossible, they say: Surely it happened in America. In reality, however, they do things here that people in Holland cannot do, simply because they consider them impracticable and therefore do not try. A [North] American does not easily say that something cannot be done as long as he has not tried it in every way. Thus we saw a very large three story building being moved in Winnipeg. This house was lifted with jacks, and then placed on rollers that ran on heavy beams. A number of horses again and again pulled it a short distance further. Last week in Lethbridge they were busy moving a large printing shop back about 10 metres to set it on a new stone foundation. This building also stood on rollers. One horse moved it. For this purpose the house was fastened with a strong chain to an apparatus similar to what is used in Holland to pull a ship onto the slip. Without this implement ten horses would have been necessary to move this building. As anyone can understand, it is much easier to move a wooden house than a stone building. Yet in America many a time large stone buildings are also moved.

We too did a similar job this past April. One of us, [Jacobus] N[ijhoff], did not have his house standing in the right place. Since his house was pretty large, 30 × 16 feet, we first had to seriously consider how best to move it 200 metres. It seemed preferable to tow it on heavy beams. But to place a house on beams does not happen by itself. We began shoving one beam, 20 feet long and 6 × 6 inches thick, under the wall from one end. Then we laid a block under the beam as close as possible to the wall. When some of us pressed the long end of this pivot down, we succeeded in lifting the house up a little ways at that point. Someone then immediately shoved a block or plank under it. By raising it in this way at various places and then shoving a block under, we got the house a little ways above the ground. By again and again lifting it up a little higher with the beam and stacking it on the first blocks, the second, the third, etc., the building stood a foot above the ground after one day of work. (During this labour the wife cooked her food as usual.)

When the house was elevated a foot above the ground, we began to make a "sled" under it. Three heavy beams, 20 feet long, were laid under its width.

These beams rested on iron rollers two inches in diameter and these rollers ran on thick planks. When these planks were all laid across under the building, with the rollers on them and then the heavy beams, the blocks were removed and it all rested on the beams. The front ends of the beams were previously rounded, like the runners of a sled. Hooks were also attached to them in order to fasten the heavy chains that the horses had to pull. The rollers made it possible for the horses to get the heavy mass moving. When the house was moving, they naturally rolled out from under it and unto the ground.

Finally, when everything was ready, and the house was prevented from sliding from the beams by strong blocks, we hitched up the horses. Beforehand the heaviest objects were taken outside. But the cat stayed sitting calmly in front of the window during the move.

On each of the outside beams there were two horses, on the middle one four. Next to each pair of horses one man was there to lead them. "All right!" each man called out as a sign that he was ready. And then, to the horses, "Get up, boys!" The strong animals bent their legs, their bellies close to the ground, and the house actually slid forward. Each one of us thought: Well, we will be finished in ten minutes. But wrong. About 25 metres was covered and then the corner of the house struck against a post. This stopped the horses. Certainly, we could have gone past the pole, but to steer eight horses hitched in front of a house does not go as easily as two or four in front of a wagon.

Now what to do? Two more horses were fetched and added at the front. But the ten animals were not able to get it moving again. First we chopped off the post. The beams rested on sand, the rollers no longer under them. There was nothing left to do but to lift up the house once again and lay the rollers and thick planks again under the beams. This caused a delay of a few hours. Finally when everything was ready, the horses were hitched a second time, and actually pulled the heavy load forward again. But not far. The driver on the right side did not lead well, the sled broke, and one beam came out from under the walls. Again stop. Now we decided to make a new sled with two beams under it. This was done. On each beam two horses pulled; thus four in all. Four animals naturally were not able to start moving the heavy mass. Two of us stayed in front of the house to lead the horses. All the others went to the back. Each one shoved a strong bar a little ways under the wall and then put his shoulder under the bar. Then the two men with the horses called out, "Lift up!" and to their horses, "Get up!" The horses pulled, and the men with their bars with all their might lifted the house up a bit and helped push it forward. And to everyone's joy, the four animals pulled the building farther without mishap to its new location.

I calculated that this house certainly weighed no less than 12,000 pounds, so each horse towed about 3,000 pounds over the prairie. There was a little snow on the ground, but under the snow the ground was thawed and wet, so it did not help much. But the horses that did the job were very heavy and strong.

And now a cellar indicates the place where N[ijhoff's] house earlier stood, because we could not drag that along. And two broad tracks in the grass show the path along which the house was moved.

A[ldus]   Lethbridge, 25 May 1905

LETTER FROM LEAVINGS
(*De Grondwet*, 22 August 1905)

For a few weeks I have sent no news, but now I will again write a few words. Some have written me that I am no longer writing in *De Grondwet* because nothing here is worth writing about. That is not the case. I have not written because I am so busy.

The Dutch colony here is growing slowly but surely. This fall a group of eight people will be coming from Holland, and most likely also a few families from the United States.[89]

Some weeks ago we had the privilege of having the gospel preached to us by Rev. Holwerda of Manhattan, Mont. In our midst at present is Rev. F. Stuart who is now leading us. So we have not been forgotten by the Christian Reformed Church of North America.[90]

The grain harvest promises to be good.[91] The winter wheat for the most part is already cut and the spring wheat is almost ripe. Of course, yield from land that was broken last fall in October and November leaves something to be desired. That could not be otherwise. Also land that was broken for the first time in the spring does not promise a good harvest. Oats will grow rather well on such land, but wheat remains very short stemmed. Land that was broken last summer lives up to all expectations.

---

89   The group of eight expected from the Netherlands was probably the family of Rommert Weerstra who arrived with his wife Jantje and five children in November. His eldest son Anne had come to Alberta the previous March. The Leendert Bode and Johannes Gunst families may have been expected from Vesper, Wisc.

90   Rev. Frederick Stuart was a home missionary of the Christian Reformed Church and led services in Alberta for two Sundays on 13 and 20 August.

91   For most in the Dutch settlement 1905 was their first regular harvest. See *Appendix B* for a summary of homestead records.

The land here is excellent and the climate is good. This summer we received rain just on time, though for some crops a little too late; but on the whole we did not have to wait for rain. Hence the harvest promises to be good. Everyone who came here last year is very satisfied with the land, its climate, and its crops.

The hay harvest is about done, but it's about time too, since the spring wheat is waiting for the binder. The oats is also beginning to ripen, so everything this year seems to be early. It appears that the price of wheat is going to be high, so the farmer here has nothing to complain about at present.

This year a lot of land has been broken, which now is ready or is being made ready to be seeded soon into winter wheat. This region is excellent for this crop.

Corr. [George Dijkema]

LETTER FROM LEAVINGS
(*De Volksvriend*, 24 August 1905)

Due to the many rains that have fallen this summer we could break more sod than last year. While last year it was very dry in the months of July and August, this year that was not the case. Last year people could not plough past mid-June, so not much was broken and also not much land could be seeded into winter wheat. It seems that this year will be different. Many farmers here have a good many acres broken that they will soon seed into winter wheat. The little winter wheat that was seeded yet last fall promises a good harvest. That is an incentive for many people to seed their land with this kind of grain. However, land that was broken in June and July and remains unplanted until next spring can also be expected to produce a good crop of spring wheat. But people here generally believe that this region is excellent for winter wheat.

Crops are good throughout all of Alberta. From Macleod to Edmonton everything is doing well. A few places suffered a little damage from hail. The winter wheat is mostly cut already, while the summer [spring] wheat is almost ready for the binder and the oats is beginning to ripen.

Some weeks ago we had the privilege of having Rev. Holwerda from Manhattan, Mont., lead us; now in our midst is Rev. F. Stuart, who will preach the gospel to us. While Rev. Holwerda led us in one of the houses of the Hollanders who live here, Rev. Stuart is enjoying the privilege of preaching in one of the schoolhouses that was built after the coming of Rev. Holwerda.[92] So we are making progress. A few more steps like this and we will have our own church. It is the wish of your correspondent that this will happen as quickly as possible.

[George Dijkema]

LETTER FROM EVERT ALDUS
(*Twentsch Volksblad*, 2 September 1905)

In connection with an item that I read in the 29 July issue recommending caution about immigrating to northwest Canada, which was found in the *Staatscourant* and was included because the Vice-Consul at St. Paul drew attention to the fact that some Netherlanders have left northwest Canada very disappointed,[93] I would like to point out that no Hollanders from this area have gone back disappointed. Certainly our beginning here last year was anything but heartening, but this year, and even last year, we could see and point out things that did not disappoint us but gave us a lot of heart for a good future. Soon I hope to write more about this in a longer piece.

I do not state this as if to say: "Rest assured, you don't need to be cautious," but because no one should have an idea about the part of Canada where we live that is far from the real truth. Perhaps the attentive reader will say: "You live in southwest, not northwest Canada." That is true, but it was precisely the fact that many are unfamiliar with this that made me decide to write these words.

Thank you, Mr. Editor, for the space.
E[vert] Aldus   Lethbridge, 16 Aug. 1905

---

92 Rev. Holwerda led worship services in the home of John Postman on 14 May and in the house of a Dutch family on the Leavings side of the community the following week. On 13 August Rev. Stuart led services in the new Rocky Coulee schoolhouse, which was completed in late May 1905. The next week he led services in the house of the Koole brothers.

93 In the 29 July 1905 issue of the *Twentsch Volksblad*, there was a short item: "Emigrants to Northwest Canada. The Vice-Consul at St. Paul draws attention to the fact that the Netherlanders who left as emigrants some time ago for northwest Canada (Winnipeg) and other places have left that region again very disappointed. This report was taken up in our *Staatscourant*, to which was added: To those who may intend to immigrate to Canada, great caution is therefore recommended."

LETTER FROM EVERT ALDUS
(*Twentsch Volksblad,* 21 October 1905)

Lethbridge, 1 Oct. 1905

In the hope that the reader's interest has not faded, I want to tell something about the last few months, the summer and fall. March, April, and May gave us a lot of nice mild weather, little rain, and fortunately, little wind; June, considerable rain and warm days, the first two weeks of July, severe drought and wind, after that two weeks of rain and warm growing weather. In August it did not rain, and the "Chinook" blew with great force, likewise in September, except for one day of rain in about the middle of the month. Except for a couple of light night frosts in August we had no trouble with frost from 25 May to 15 September. In an earlier letter I reported that in April and May we seeded our wheat and oats, etc. If you simply seed grain in this country, a disease called "smut" later comes into it when the plant has developed. This disease ruins the seed and turns it into a dusty black mass. What the disease is or what causes it, I still don't know.* The cause or germ is not located in the seed, but in the ground or air. Because wheat seeded with healthy seed is also affected by it. This evil is effectively fought with "bloodstone."

* Can this not be the same disease that occurs also in Holland, fortunately only sporadically, here called *brandkoren* or properly speaking *brand* (in the grain)? This disease is caused by a family of parasites, the so-called fire-fungus (*uredinieeën*). *Editor.*

What is bloodstone? What it really is, I also don't know. If you could give pieces of soda a blue colour, they would look like bloodstone. We buy it in the drugstore for 10 cents a pound. We throw several pounds in a barrel filled with water, and then wait until the dust is dissolved in the water. Then we dump a sack full of wheat in the mixture for five minutes, and then pour the wheat into a wagon, for example, to dry it again. Wheat and oats that have undergone this process are protected from smut. We also treated our seed grain in this way. The cost of bloodstone is 2 to 3 cents an acre.

At the beginning of this piece I reported how the weather was this summer. The reader will notice that we can call it very favourable – a considerable amount of rain and warmth, little frost and Chinook wind, except for the last two months. The extra large quantity of grain grown in Canada proves that the weather was very good. "But how is it with you? Have you grown a considerable amount of it?" the reader will ask. Here is the answer.

You will remember that I wrote more than once how we broke small pieces shortly after our arrival in April 1904. One 8 acres, another 5 acres, but a couple did none. The rest of our wheat land we broke in October and November. Some ploughed 15 acres, others 25, a few even 40 acres then. Thus we have grown grain on old land, broken last year in the spring, though only small pieces; and on the other hand on large pieces broken last year in the fall. The wheat grown on the first broken land produced a very good harvest twenty to twenty-five times the seed grain. The wheat seeded in the fall breaking produced a very small yield, two to four times the seed grain. From this it follows that those of us who had a few acres of old land have grown a little bit; the others who seeded only fall breaking received only seed wheat and chicken feed, without anything to sell.

This week the threshing machine threshed our grain. One of us had 3½ acres of winter wheat. (Here there is winter and summer wheat, like winter and summer rye in Holland. The first is seeded in the fall, the second in the spring.) This winter wheat produced more than 30 bushels an acre. A bushel of wheat weighs 60 pounds. Three bushels is something more than a hectolitre. Hence a rich harvest. The summer wheat seed on old ground produced from 15 to 22 bushels an acre. Also a good yield. The wheat seeded on fall breaking produced from 2 to 5 bushels. That is little more than nothing. Good and bad, the average yield of all the Hollanders living around here, taken together, will not fetch 6 bushels an acre. So, in general, little or nothing was earned.

An example may illustrate this. One of us was out working last year and had 33 acres broken in October and November.[94] At $3 an acre this cost about $100. 33 bushels of seed grain at $1 a bushel makes $33. If you calculate the discing of the land, the seeding of the grain, as well as the cutting and stacking at $1 an acre, then it cost this man $166. He harvested about 100 bushels of wheat. Off this goes the threshing costs. We will call this $10, though it is probably more. The wheat is worth 60 cents a bushel now. Consequently, he is getting $60 for 100 bushels. $10 goes off for the thresher. $50 is left. Expenses are $166; income $50. He is $116 short.

This is one of the most unfavourable cases. Now one of the least unfavourable. One of us had 6 acres of good wheat on old land and 29 acres on fall breaking.[95] Together 35 acres. The cost of breaking and discing, seeding and

94 This was John Postman. He was working on traffic bridges at Macleod and elsewhere, and paid Hendrikus Veldhuis to break some land on his homestead.
95 Based on acres of breaking reported in homestead records, this was probably Gerrit Withage.

cutting, in addition to the seed grain, $5 per acre. (This is calculated very sparingly, probably too low.) He got an average of 8½ bushels per acre. At 60 cents a bushel this gives a yield of $5.10. Threshing costs for 8½ bushels are about 50 cents. $4.60 is left. The loss per acre is 40 cents, and for 35 acres $14.

Of course, one need not pay this loss out of pocket; he did the work mostly himself. But if you calculate the value of the work, in addition to sharpening of ploughshares, wear and tear on the machines, the cost of seed grain, etc., then we all come up quite a bit short.

Oats also produced a much smaller yield than we expected. The best produced about 9 bushels per acre; that is, 320 pounds. (One bushel of oats weighs about 34 pounds; a bushel is a measure of quantity.)

In connection with the slight harvest only two of us bought a binder, and with it they cut also for the others. Some wheat was too short so the machine could not bind it. Then there was nothing left to do but to mow it with a hay machine, and to rake it together with a "rake." In this case at least a third of it, whatever is not carried along with the rake, stays lying on the ground, and can be ploughed under.

Potatoes and Garden Produce

"How did it go with these?" many a person may ask. Well, I'll tell you. On about the 25th of May I planted the first potatoes. At the same time I also sowed peas, radishes, onions, carrots, etc. In early June I planted the rest of the potatoes, and I sowed vegetables at a time, so I thought, when the weather would allow it. For my garden I took a piece of land that I had broken and disced already in the spring of last year. This spring I ploughed it again with a "stubble plough" about 8 inches deep. Then I harrowed it often until all of it was fine. I planted the potatoes 3 feet apart. As I said, I planted the first ones in the last week of May. They began to blossom by July 1 and on the 16th of July I dug up nice and large new potatoes that tasted very good. Just six weeks after I had planted them. Since that date I could pick an abundance of radishes, green peas, beets, carrots, and a short time later, also turnips, beans, broad beans, lettuce, etc. That vegetables grow unusually fast here with favourable weather is apparent from the above. I have never heard that anyone could dig big new potatoes 6 weeks after planting. Also this summer some wheat was seeded and cut within 90 days. Usually wheat needs 90 to 110 days to grow. The potatoes are now fully grown. On average I find under each bush five to six potatoes the size of a fist; a few are much larger, others the size of a seed-potato. At the table there are none of what you call little ones. We have not had one potato yet that was not completely healthy or whole.

This past spring I was in town. There I found on the street two large potatoes. To me they appeared to be a good variety, so I cut them into pieces and planted them. When I dug them up, I got back sixty very large potatoes. Thus a 30-fold yield. Both grew luxuriantly. The types grown here have the form of a turnip. I had many with a diameter of about 15 centimetres; the heaviest weighed 2½ pounds. Turnips, lettuce, peas, carrots, onions, and radishes produced a very good yield and grew quickly. Beans and cucumbers produced a mediocre crop, also purslane and endives. Kale did not develop very well due to the dryness of the last few weeks. For me white cabbage was a failure, but that was due to mistreatment. The yield of potatoes and vegetables is greater and the quality is better than I ever had in Holland. I can add, however, that those who did not have their garden on old ground, but on prairie broken up this spring, had much smaller results. Some even had poor potatoes.

As for Dutch seeds sown here, Dutch lettuce, carrots, cabbage, onions, and beets will not grow here. You have to sow the kinds that are native here. Dutch green peas and marrowfat peas do produce a rich harvest. Also broad beans. Bush beans and string beans produced as much as a mediocre yield in Holland. People say that seeds made here produce a larger yield. Next year I hope to prove it. I have succeeded in getting some seed beans dry. I pulled the bushes out as soon as the beans reached full size but were still completely green. By day I let them dry in the sun, and at night I laid them on a barrel and protected them from the frost by covering them. If you do not pick the beans from the bush before they are fully dry, you get good seed beans in this way. String beans got no higher than two to three feet. This is because the Chinook broke the tendrils of all of them as soon as they reached that height. Also it repeatedly knocked the poles down. Therefore next year I will let the beans crawl over branches lying on the ground.

String beans and Dutch varieties of bush beans appear to be unknown here. But certainly there are good varieties of beans here. Of purslane and kale I have yet to see a seed or plant here. I think the latter froze dead in the winter, so one cannot get seed from it for next year. I will try it this winter. For most of the vegetables that I have grown I think this is a suitable country. But not for beans, cucumbers, and purslane. The rhubarb I sowed this spring developed into fine strong plants.

We do not have flowers except sunflowers and marigolds. But in Lethbridge I saw all kinds of beautiful flowers that are sown and grown also by you.

These grew in gardens that were protected from the wind by high fences. I also saw some apples grown this summer in a garden in the same city. They were nice well-formed fruits picked from a four-year-old tree. This spring a farmer here in the vicinity received 2,000 young trees from the government. Anyone can get them completely free. They are seedlings from one to two feet high, four different kinds. Almost all of them grew very well. Furthermore, here one can plant strawberries, raspberries, currants, and gooseberries with favourable results. Except for a couple kinds of apple, I do not think that fruit trees can grow here, such as cherries, pears, etc.

(to be continued)

LETTER FROM EVERT ALDUS
(*Twentsch Volksblad,* 4 November 1905)

(continuation)

What Has This Summer Taught Us?

1 That a large rainfall very much promotes the growth of all plants here, as elsewhere, provided that the rain is combined with enough warm days.

2 That old ground, that is, ground that is good and fine to a proper depth and no longer consists of lumps, remains moist very long, also in a severe drought. This is a heartening sign.

3 That such land has a good capacity for production, for potatoes and vegetables as well as for grain.

4 That on prairie ground broken late in the fall nothing will grow the following year, not even with very favourable weather.

5 That on ground broken in the spring at best a little oats, potatoes, etc., grows, but only under favourable circumstances.

6 That one can only expect a good harvest when the land is broken a year and a half before harvest time; in other words, land broken in May 1904 gives the opportunity for a good harvest in 1905. (By land I naturally mean prairie.)

7 That anyone who comes here in the spring must have patience for a year and a half before he can expect any fruit of significance. If one comes in the fall, then it is two years.

8 What has experience taught about the much-discussed Chinook
   wind? Here are some facts. Early in July a very warm dry
   Chinook blew on a Sunday. In the wheat fields that were nice and
   green in the morning one could see large yellow spots the following morning. In one day the wind draws more moisture from
   the ground than strong sunshine in a week. In August I saw hay
   wagons return empty six times. The wind prevented them from
   getting in one forkful.

Some days the machines could not even cut. The wind blew the hay away in
front of the knives as quickly as it cut the grass. In September the Chinook
made it even worse. Sometimes for a whole week one could not think about
making hay.

Short wheat cannot be cut when the wind is blowing hard. It bends under
the knives and is partly cut off. The wind hampers the stacking of sheaves.
The Chinook very much speeds up the ripening of the seed, which is not bad
in itself. But if you do not cut right away, it threshes for you, that is, due to
the intense movement of the stalks the seeds fall to the ground.

The wind destroys and damages our grain- and haystacks. It is a big
burden when threshing with a steam threshing machine. Among other
things, when this machine threshed at my place the power of the wind again
and again made the large drive belt that connects the steam- and threshing
machine run off the pulleys, immediately stopping the implement. Several
men and several minutes are necessary to get this heavy 150 foot long belt
back on the wheels.

Once, on a Sunday night in the month of August the strength of the
Chinook was extraordinary. Our shacks and everything in them trembled
and shook while the howl and wail of the wind equalled the thunder in
strength. The following morning five wagons with hay racks on them were
overturned. Wagons standing right in the wind were pushed forward a
ways. One of us found his washtub again at the place of another who lives
not quite an hour away. Another person's washtub, three quarters full of
water and laundry, was overturned and blew away. In short, everything
that was not firmly tied down blew away that night. From a large chest I
found only a board here and there in the morning. And I could easily add
to these examples. Now what did I do? I asked people who have farmed here
already a number of years – in the vicinity of Macleod – what they thought
about the usefulness and harm of the Chinook for agriculture. Their answer
was unanimous: "The Chinook does only good for agriculture in that it
moderates the severe climate a bit." When the Chinook blows it does not

freeze at night. In northern Alberta, for example, which does not have this wind, there are more cold frosty nights later in the summer, and the winter is more severe. That's why oats and wheat sometimes freezes there before it is ripe. Also the greater rainfall, which makes the seed ripen more slowly, contributes to that.

Besides this one positive, this wind has a whole lot of negatives, and is a big burden when doing all kinds of work.

Is Our Future Better Than Last Fall?

In a whole lot of ways the answer to this question can be affirmative. We all have seed grain for next year as well as chicken feed, and a little oats for the horses, though some do not have much. Some of us have grown enough potatoes and vegetables, but not all. Last year we faced the winter without anything at all, unless we bought it. And what is most important, this summer enabled us to break large pieces of prairie. This land will be "old ground" next year and thus gives us a very fine chance for a good harvest. In September most of us seeded a part of this land into winter wheat. According to experts, winter wheat has more certainty of success because in the spring this grain can grow right away. So, when the summer wheat seeded in the spring comes up, the winter wheat is already a number of inches higher. Precisely because this wheat is a month before the summer grain it does not dry up. In the first months of spring the ground is moist enough from the melted snow to make the winter wheat grow. Just like winter rye in Holland, winter wheat can also freeze. If this happens, all is not lost; you can disc up the land in the spring and seed oats or summer wheat. If you seed part of your land with winter grain, then you do not need to cut everything in a short time, since this grain is ripe a couple of weeks before the summer wheat.

If next year is not a total failure, most of us have the chance for 50 acres or more of good wheat.

As the reader will understand, the financial pressure throughout this year has not eased. None of us received so much grain that he can make from it an amount of any significance. Those, however, who began with the least capital, feel it the most, and also those who have large families. But it is clear that everyone learns by experience how difficult it is to get something started with little money. Because, like everywhere else, the pressure of circumstances is the greatest for those who possess the least. For example, anyone who bought his horses for cash only needs to feed them. Another who has them half paid or bought them completely on credit pays 8 per cent interest; besides, in the latter case he has to pay much higher prices.

You can safely reckon that you have to pay $125 for a horse that is worth $80 in cash, if you get it completely or half on credit for a year. So there are more things, sometimes merely the result of the course of events, that work against you. Thus the price in the spring, when we bought seed grain, was $1 a bushel, but now that we have a little to sell it is only 60 cents. So he who still has to pay for his seed grain now, for every 6 bushels must give 10 back. Yet those who possess less may be very thankful that one can get machines and tools on credit, and, if you know how, horses (though they are then unbroken, wild) and cows. If one could not do this, it would require a good many guilders to begin here. In what country in Europe would one give a stranger, known recently and only superficially, $500 or even more on credit, with no other guarantee of payment than the fruit of his work in the future? Where does one find so much trust? Actually, in this respect society here offers also those who have less, the worker, a chance for prosperity in the future; this will not be offered to him anywhere else, at least not in Europe. Though it is at high prices and interest, it opens the door, also for those who cannot pay cash.

(to be continued)

LETTER FROM EVERT ALDUS
(*Twentsch Volksblad*, 11 November 1905)

Little Enemies

Here we have to carry on a continual battle with little enemies, namely, gophers or prairie dogs. These rat-like rodents, which live by the thousands on the prairie, eat the grain as soon as it comes up and as long as it grows. And later when the grain comes into head, they very skilfully know how to shake the stems and eat the seeds out of the heads. Due to their large numbers they can devastate large fields. Therefore people try to eradicate them as much as possible. In the vicinity of residences cats hunt these little animals. For children it is a pleasure of the hunt to catch them in traps which they set in front of the holes. Since you can approach them at a short distance it is easy to shoot them with a small calibre rifle. I have certainly shot them with a revolver. The most effective means, however, is to poison them. We did this by dissolving strychnine in warm water and then letting the mixture absorb into a few pounds of wheat. Then you get a strong working "rat poison." You lay some kernels by every hole; the animal eats the food right away and is dead in one minute. If you clear the land in this manner, you can begin again in one or two weeks, since other gophers have come from the prairie to take the place of the previous ones. It is best to put out poison in the spring before the animals bear their young. But there are also innocent victims. Small birds eat the poisoned seed and die an undeserving death. You must also keep the poison outside the reach of chickens and pigs, or else you get no more eggs or bacon.

Potato disease does not seem to occur here. This year I did catch a couple dozen Colorado beetles on the leaves of this crop. As the reader knows, these beetles can completely wreck a potato harvest if they occur in large numbers.

The Threshing Machine

Now that we have had the steam threshing machine, I will tell something about it.[96] This implement consists of a steam engine, which supplies the energy, and the actual threshing machine or "separator." The steam engine has a horizontal boiler, and stands on four wheels. The front two, like the front wheels of a wagon, can turn to the right or left. This implement also serves as a "locomotive;" it can move forward and take along the heavy separator. If the front wheels, or rather their axle, could not be turned, the implement could not be driven. The back wheels are very large. Their diameter amounts to 1.75 metres; the width of the wheel bands 50 centimetres. On the outside of these wheels large edges or lugs are fastened to prevent slipping on the ground. The steam engine looks like a small locomotive; it weighs 2,000 pounds and has 20 horsepower. With the heavy 4,000 pound separator behind it, it drives quickly over the prairie, over loose farmland, up a slope, etc., while the engineer lets it go forward or backward or makes a long or short turn, as necessary.

The separator is an enclosed wagon about 6 metres long, 3 metres high, and 1½ metres wide. Just on the outside I counted 31 wheels or pulleys on which drive belts run. The shafts of these wheels move the insides of the implement. From the steam engine motion is carried to the separator by a broad 150 foot long drive belt.

In front of the separator is a large tank in which the sheaves are thrown. The bottom of this tank moves toward the inside, taking the sheaves with it. (One can compare this bottom to a 3 foot wide drive belt that runs over

---

96 For the harvest of 1905, most crops on the east side of the settlement were threshed by Joe Cox, an earlier settler nearby, who had bought a steam-powered threshing machine.

two rollers.) Above this bottom there are four large serrated knives. They have a backward and downward, and then a forward and upward motion. They cut through the twine on the sheaves.

When the loose sheaves leave the bottom of the "feeder" (that is what the tank is called), then they are threshed. This happens with the "cylinder." This is an iron roller about 50 centimetres in diameter. It is filled with iron needles the size of a finger. In front of the roller there is a flat piece of iron on which are riveted needles of the same size and spaced at a similar distance as on the roller. When the roller turns, its fingers or teeth go exactly between the teeth of the huge "comb" in front of it.

The grain falls on the very quickly turning cylinder, and is taken away by its teeth. Coming to the teeth of the "comb," it is beaten against it with force and is wrung out through the small space between the teeth of the roller and the comb. No kernel then remains in it. Nothing even remains of the heads except the stem or shaft, and the straw is broken into more or less small pieces. If the cylinder is too close to the comb, the kernels of grain are also beaten in two.

After the grain is beaten out of the heads by the cylinder, the seed is separated from the straw, etc., by a system of course and finer sieves. These sieves are continually in motion. The removal of chaff and dust happens by a stream of air. Straw and chaff collect in the back part of the machine. A strong air stream blows it from there through a wide pipe to the outside. This pipe, called a "wind stacker," is several metres long and can be turned higher or lower to the ground and in all directions. Straw and chaff come flying out of it like the jet of water out of the nozzle of a fire engine. With this wind stacker one can blow the straw the height of a steeple. Getting the air stream to remove the chaff from the grain and to blow the straw out of the stacker happens in about the same way as in a chaff- or fanning mill.

The cleaned seed collects at the bottom of the machine. From there it is conveyed to the top of a perpendicular four-metre high pipe. At the top of the pipe the seed falls into a tank a half-bushel in size. When this is full, the bottom pulls out and the seed falls into another duct somewhat wider than the pipe of a stove. You can make this pipe hang more or less at a downward slant and turn it to the right or left. You place it in such a way that its opening is above the wagon, which takes the seed away. Two men hold a sack under the opening while standing on the wagon. When the sack is full, one man sets it aside while the other holds an empty one ready. When the wagon is loaded, the opening is closed with a lid, and while the loaded wagon rides away, an empty one right away takes its place. Everything must go on.

As I said, at the top of the vertical pipe in which the grain is conveyed the seed is measured in a small tank the size of a half-bushel. When this tank is full, the bottom pulls out and it is emptied. This bottom is connected to a wheel mechanism which brings into motion a plate with figures. Three figures are always visible. They indicate the number of bushels that has been threshed. Anyone at the top of the pipe can see how large this number is at any moment. If the number climbs to 999, then the next figure is naturally 1 again. The conveying of the grain happens in about the same way as water is taken up by an auger of a water mill, or it goes on an endless belt with attached cups which empty themselves at the top. The seed comes to the top in the same way as the mud that a dredging machine draws up from the bottom of a river.

The machine that threshed for us was not one of the largest. In one day of regular work about 1,600 bushels can be threshed, that is, 100,000 pounds of wheat, or about a hectolitre in a minute.

The engineer has to pay attention to his steam engine first of all. At the same time he looks out whether everything is running well on the separator. If he notices that anything is not as it should be, he right away gives a warning by means of the steam whistle, and, if necessary, he stops.

The fireman is constantly busy feeding the fire with straw. Straw is a cheap but dangerous fuel. Although the smoke stack is covered with a spark catcher, it resembles, at least in the evening, a volcano in miniature. Therefore the steam engine is placed pretty far (75 feet) from the separator. Yet, many a time a fire is started by the threshing machine. A third man is busy bringing straw (fuel) to the steam engine. He knows how to do this very easily. He has two horses drag along a long heavy beam crosswise, in such a way that the beam carries along an entire mound of straw from the stack. The straw is stuck in front of the beam and is carried away. A fourth man fetches barrels of water on a wagon for the boiler.

Four men are busy throwing sheaves into the machine. One, the "separatorman," is constantly looking whether this machine is working well. If the threshed grain does not have to be transported very far, then two wagons, with two men each, are sufficient to bring it away. If the distance is longer, then three wagons with six men are needed. The sacks are poured out in a barn designated for the grain, a "granary."

The threshing machine that worked on our farms cost new $3,750, altogether. The large belt that conveys the motion from the steam engine to the threshing implement alone cost $175. The price paid for threshing is 5 cents a bushel for wheat and 4 cents for oats. But the threshing machine does not come for less than $15 or $20, even though one has only $5 to thresh.

Here also he who has planted the least experiences the greatest burden. Anyone who has 100 bushels to thresh pays $15, that is, 15 cents a bushel, while another who has 300 bushels pays 5 cents a bushel in this case.

Anyone will understand that the presence of the steam thresher brings lots of busyness and liveliness to our neighbourhood, which is otherwise so quiet. Already days in advance people are on the lookout in order to be ready on time when the machine comes. It's not only busy for the men but also for the women. They must provide a good meal or meals, as long as the machine is on the farm. And for a dozen men this is a lot of work. Mutual help from neighbours is indispensable when threshing. Many hands are needed, and everything goes "full steam."

We certainly have a little pity for the Dutch farmer, when we think how hard he must work for many days with a flail or stick to do what the iron giant does here in a few hours; when we compare the gasping and blowing of the steam engine, the drone of the separator, the howl of the windstacker with the clip-clap of the flails in the Old Country; when we see steam do the work here that is performed only by human power there.

When the work is done by one farmer, then the steam engine serves again as a locomotive. First a wagon (tender) is coupled to it, on which straw and water is carried, and then the heavy separator. So drives the train to the next farm. It is accompanied by the straw hauler with his horses and lime, by the water wagon, and also by the men who seek any place they can find to ride along. Also, each farmer is required to transport a wagon with straw to the next place. This straw serves as fuel so that there is enough to burn until the threshing begins. Thus the thresher marches on, for the whole harvest.

The men sleep on the straw piles or wherever they can find a place somewhere else. Threshing is a happy time for the people in the first place, but also for chickens, pigs, etc. It does not go as carefully as in Holland. Because it goes so quickly, it happens roughly. A mass of seed falls on the ground, especially to the delight of the winged farm dwellers. As proof of how much is lost is the fact that I got 800 pounds of seed from the ground with a rake and broom after the threshing was done. For those of us who did not grow much, this is significant. But if one has a lot to thresh, for example, a thousand bushels, then it does not matter whether a thousand pounds remain on the ground for the chickens. That's America for you.

A[ldus]

Threshing outfit on Willem Van Lohuizen farm. (Courtesy: Joan Hoekstra.)

LETTER FROM LETHBRIDGE
(*De Grondwet,* 5 December 1905)

From this area still not much news is being reported;[97] therefore I thought it would be good to write a little about one thing and another.

The weather is beautiful; now and then a little snow falls, but each time it disappears again.

Our Dutch people are steadily growing in number. Now we are expecting L[eendert] Bode and his family, and J[ohannes] Gunst and his wife from Vesper, Wisconsin. Also the [Rommert] Weerstra family from the Netherlands.[98]

Everyone here is very satisfied, especially now that a railroad is being laid in this district. Also in Lethbridge they are going to build a new station

---

97 The writer was from the east side of the Dutch community closer to Lethbridge in the district later known as Monarch. At this time Lethbridge was a large town of about 5,000 people and had the nearest post office. Apparently this writer did not think George Dijkema, who lived on the west side, was faithful enough as a regular correspondent to *De Grondwet*, or he did not think the east side was being represented well enough. Thus began a regular series of letters from this writer as a correspondent to *De Grondwet*. He was from Vesper and of a Christian Reformed background—probably Teunis Bode.

98 Leendert Bode, his son-in-law Johannes Gunst, and their families arrived on 2 December, the Rommert Weerstra family on 25 November.

that will cost $20,000. So everyone can see that here in the far West there is business activity.

Two weeks ago we had the privilege of having Rev. [Meindert] Botbijl of Pella, Iowa, and Rev. [James] Holwerda of Manhattan, Mont., in our midst. They organized a congregation here. The attendance was good.[99]

Our school building also is making good progress. We hope to open it by 1 January.[100]

There is still room enough for more Hollanders, but the land is already rising considerably in price. There is no lack of fuel; plenty of coal mines in and around Lethbridge. The price is $2.50 and $2.75 per ton. Butter is 30 cents a pound and eggs 40 cents a dozen.

A Reader 23 November 1905

LETTER FROM GERRIT J. WITHAGE
(*De Wachter,* 13 December 1905)

Many readers, especially those who often pray, "Thy Kingdom come," will have thought now and then: How is it going in the far northwest, in the land of John Bull? Will they also get a congregation of our [Christian Reformed] Church there? We can answer, dear readers, that here on Nov. 16 a congregation was established, thanks be to God. I will briefly report a few things about it.

Rev. Botbijl from Pella, Iowa, and Rev. Holwerda from Manhattan, Montana, came to us for that purpose, the former sent as a missionary of the Home Missions Board, the latter fulfilling a classical appointment.[101] After Rev. Botbijl had preached here for two Sundays, there was a meeting on Nov. 16 to find out whether a congregation could be established. At 12 noon the meeting was opened by Rev. Holwerda, who spoke a short encouraging word to us on Luke 12:32a.[102] Then the gathering was informed by the committee[103] that the Classis had received the request from here to organize a congregation and decided after serious consideration to grant our request on the condition

---

99 Revs. Botbijl and Holwerda organized the Nijverdal Christian Reformed Church here on 16 November 1905. It was the first Christian Reformed Church in Canada.
100 The school being built was the Finley school on the east side. The Rose Butte school had opened already in the spring of 1905. The west side of the settlement had the Rocky Coulee school, which opened in September 1905.
101 Christian Reformed classes assigned the ministers in their jurisdiction to spend a Sunday or two visiting churches without a pastor.
102 This verse reads: "Fear not, little flock."
103 This is the organizing committee consisting of Reverends Botbijl and Holwerda.

that we come together at one location on Sundays, the Rocky Coulee school house, until a better middle point is found;[104] this was accepted. Then an opportunity was given to hand in membership papers, which amounted to ten [confessing] members and their children, a total of twenty-six who all belonged to our Church except for one, whose case was handled in the usual way.[105] After that an opportunity was given to those who wished to profess their faith; this was done by six, who were freely accepted after being heard by the committee.[106] Then they proceeded to the election of two elders and one deacon, who were chosen and immediately installed into office.[107] Also those who had made profession were confirmed. The congregation sang God's blessing to them with the singing of a psalm. Then the committee in the name of the Classis expressed their joy that the first congregation of our Church here in Canada was established, wished her the Lord's help, and encouraged her by pointing especially to Luke 12:32: "Fear not, little flock; for it is your Father's good pleasure to give you the Kingdom."

Impressive moments, indeed; it was an hour we will never forget for the Nijverdal church (this is the name of the congregation). And no less so when Rev. Holwerda in the name of our mother Manhattan congregation offered us a beautiful gift, a complete communion set. Yes, we were very glad about it, and now we say to the congregation in Manhattan: Accept our sincere thanks for it. Also the Reverend informed us that he was assigned to be our Counselor, and that the following Sunday, Lord willing, he would administer the Gospel to us and also baptism and the Lord's Supper. After this the meeting was concluded in the usual way.

Now, dear readers, I have reported something of the establishment of the congregation here. Also, we can inform you that two other families of our Church have come here.[108] We request that you remember us in your

---

104 Classis Orange City, the nearest regional assembly of the Christian Reformed Church, met in Sioux Center, Iowa, on 28 September and approved the request from Alberta to organize a church. Because of the distance between the east and west sides of the congregation, there was a concern that worship be held in a central location. For the first year the congregation met at the Rocky Coulee school, but then the Classis allowed the east and west sides to meet separately.

105 Charter members who joined by membership transfer included Willem Feller and the families of John Postman, Jan. H. ter Telgte, Garrit Willemsen, Gerrit Withage, and Mrs. Geert Venhuizen. Mrs. Venhuizen was a member of the Presbyterian church at Manhattan, so she was examined by the committee before her membership was accepted. Actually, counting the children of these families as baptized members, there were a total of forty charter members.

106 Those who became members by profession of faith included Gerrit Bode and his wife Klaasje, Leendert Geleynse, Willem, Hanna, and Aaltje Willemsen.

107 Gerrit Withage and Garrit Willemsen were elected as elders, Willem Feller as deacon.

108 These new families were those of Leendert Bode and John Gunst, who arrived from Vesper, Wisconsin, on 2 December.

prayers, and say to all, a hearty thanks to those who have contributed to the establishment of the congregation. Especially the Classis, the Home Missions Board, and the ministers who visited us here, also all who brought their offerings to the Lord which enabled the Classis and the Board to do their work. Accept our thanks, and let us always remember that, by sacrifices committed to the service of the Lord, what we do in his name to and for his people He will count as done unto him.

G[errit] J. Withage   Lethbridge, Alberta, Canada

LETTER FROM LEAVINGS
(*De Volksvriend*, 21 December 1905)

On Saturday the 25th of November the Weerstras came here, a husband, wife, and five children. Their eldest son had come here already last spring.[109] They came directly from St. Jacobi Parochie, Friesland. They had a good trip. A bit of storm at sea was all they experienced. If they had come a week later it would not have gone so well. At present eastern Canada is full of snow and the trains cannot get through.

Just a week later the Bodes came here from Vesper, Wood County, Wisconsin.[110] They took along some young horses from Wisconsin, which they tied behind the wagon in Lethbridge. The horses did not at all take to that, broke loose, and ran away. For a few days the Bode brothers and a couple of friends looked for them; finally they found them. That was not very pleasant for the Bodes. Had the prairie been clear, not covered with snow, it would not have been so bad; one could then ride faster, but just the previous Sunday about a foot of snow fell and that made looking for the horses so difficult.

And after the snow we got a couple days of cold weather with the thermometer dropping to 16 degrees below zero. Now that weather is also past; a warm Chinook wind has come and the snow is melting by the day. And when it is completely melted, we still hope to plough. True, it is December, but last year and two years ago people ploughed until Christmas. Before this snow people tried to plough, but it did not go very well. The ground was too dry. But if the frost does not set in too quickly, people will be ploughing. They are eager to plough the stubble fields yet.

109 This was the Rommert Weerstra family. Their son Anne had immigrated to Alberta in March 1905.
110 This was the Leendert Bode family. Their sons Gerrit, Teunis, and Barend had settled in Alberta earlier.

The crop was rather good this year. Winter wheat brought in 35 to 45 bushels per acre; yes some got more than that. Spring wheat brought in 20 to 35 bushels per acre, and oats also produced a good yield. Of course land that was ploughed for the first time last fall and this spring and was directly seeded left much to be desired. But the hopes of the farmers were not disappointed. Prices are 60 cents a bushel for wheat and oats pays a cent a pound. Potatoes also promised a good harvest. Those who dug them up on time were fortunate, because in the last half of October we had a hard frost for two nights, so potatoes that were still not out of the ground were completely frozen. A hint to dig them up a little earlier in the future.

Enough for this time. With thanks, Mr. Editor, for the space, I respectfully remain your servant,

Geo. Dijkema[111]

LETTER FROM EVERT ALDUS
(*Twentsch Volksblad,* 30 December 1905)

Now that 1905 will soon belong to the past, I will report a few things from the life of our little circle in the past year. Just as things happen to you in human life and work, so it is here too; we also meet life's circumstances along our way. And since everything in our "small world" is arranged on one's own or with mutual help, every detail makes an impression all the greater; also we tend to view each non-daily event not as ordinary, but as an extraordinary incident.

Perhaps a short description of a couple of these incidents will enable the reader to have an idea, however inadequate, of life in our small society.

The number of people in our colony has expanded considerably this year due to the arrival of Hollanders from the United States or directly from Holland.[112] 128 Hollanders, adults and children, now live here.[113] Forty-nine

---

111 Dijkema sent a similar letter, dated 7 December, to *De Grondwet* (19 December 1905).

112 Those who arrived in 1905 from the United States included the Garrit Willemsen family from Manhattan, Montana, Abel and Walter Vander Burgh and the Koole brothers from Sheldon, Iowa, the Nan Dekker, Leendert Bode, and Johannes Gunst families, and Leendert Geleynse from Vesper, Wisconsin. Those who came directly from the Netherlands were the Rense Nijhoff and Rommert Weerstra families, Albert Lantinga, Gerard Schuitema, Albert Rutgers, and Lucas Steenbergen.

113 Actually, 130 persons can be identified in the Dutch community at the end of 1905. This was an increase of 43 persons for the year. The total included 19 families and 24 single men. 59 persons came directly from the Netherlands, 33 from Montana (most from Manhattan), 17 from Vesper, Wisconsin, 6 from New Jersey, 5 from Sheldon, Iowa, 5 from New Mexico, and 5 were born in Alberta.

homesteads, or about 2,800 hectares of land are now in the possession of Netherlanders.[114] A considerable amount of it is broken.

The number of inhabitants has increased also by birth. Four young Hollanders saw the light of day in 1905.[115]

The birth of a baby is faced with more care here than in a heavily populated country. In a favourable situation it takes several hours before you can get medical help. In winter the weather can be such that it is impossible to fetch a doctor. Therefore you first look for help where it is the soonest available. An old experienced mother in our midst often helps as a midwife, for which she is entitled to the thanks of the happy fathers and mothers.[116]

Not only joyful events like births take place. I also have to mention sad ones. Two of the little children born this year were taken by death from their parents.[117]

With death and burial we also do everything by mutual help. We belong to the Macleod district. There we must give notice of births and deaths, and also go to do burials. But due to the distances, etc., they grant permission here to lay one's deceased to rest on one's own land. This also happened here.[118] The little ones who died were given a resting place on the farmstead of their parents.

One of the neighbours digs a small grave in a corner of the homestead. Another makes the coffin. On the day of the funeral everyone is present. Because how can one refuse to show last respects at the death of a countryman? That is, in a foreign land, where family is absent. When all are gathered in the house of the deceased, one of those present says an appropriate word,

---

114 I can account for only forty-three homesteads at the end of 1905. Aldus is probably including quarters that were purchased.

115 Evert and Christina Aldus had a son Louis on 13 February. Geert and Klaassien Venhuizen had a daughter Margaretha, born on 28 March. Jan and Janna Postman had a daughter Janna on 13 April. And Willem and Hendrika Van Lohuizen family had a son Henrie, born 17 August.

116 Mrs. Theodora Withage often served as midwife for births on the east side.

117 One of these children was Janna Postman, who died in August; the other was Henrie Van Lohuizen who died on 29 September.

118 The first death in the Dutch community was that of five-year-old Hendrikje Van Lohuizen, who died on 21 April 1904, while the family was still living in a tent on the yard of the Emmelkamps. She was buried there in the Oldman river bottom. Later, an infant son of the Huismans died in January 1907 and was buried near a small grove on the family homestead. In the winter of 1907–08 George Dijkema's wife Anna, who was soon to give birth to their first child, fell into the cellar of their homestead shack when the trap door was left open at night to keep the vegetables from freezing, and because of this accident the child was stillborn. It was buried on the yard of the Dijkema homestead. Later, after Anton Fjordbotten bought this land, his wife could hear the child "crying," and insisted that the body be removed. The child was then reburied in the new Granum Christian Reformed Church cemetery in the same grave as Hilda Veenkamp, when this infant died in October 1913. This cemetery opened in March 1911; Albert Ritsema's one-year-old daughter Gerhardina was the first to be buried there. The Monarch CRC cemetery opened in the summer 1909 with the burial of infant Willem Postman.

however inadequate, and prayers. Then, after the coffin maker has opened the little coffin in order to allow one last look at the little one who died, and then has closed it forever, two young men place it on the wagon that serves as a hearse, and the procession begins. First the wagon, followed by the relatives, and then all the guests. They soon reach the little grave. The coffin is lowered in the usual manner, and the gravedigger finishes his work. With an unpleasant sound the lumps of clay fall into the hole, and soon the "last home" is covered. Two little children now rest in the bowels of the earth, in the midst of the small colony, in the far, far west of America.

And when the great day comes, when the dead shall arise, the voice of the Angel will resound also over these plains and be heard in the graves of these young ones who have died.

As for church life, the colony has improved a little this year. Earlier I mentioned that we had a visit by a minister of the [Christian] Reformed Church. After that we again had a minister from the same church in our midst.[119] In November, however, the wish of the members here of the [Christian] Reformed Church was fulfilled – the wish to establish an independent congregation.

Two ministers were sent for this purpose by the higher authorities. The newly established congregation bears the name "Nijverdal," and includes eight male [confessing] members. For the time being two elders and a deacon were appointed. Also the Lord's Supper was held for the first time. At first the worship services will be held in a school located between the two sides of the colony.[120] There is a plan to build a church there later. The members living farthest away are then about three hours from the church. In our colony there is only one Catholic. The Protestants belong to very different creeds.[121]

On 1 January 1906, one new school will open. The other one in our vicinity was built this year.[122] 1905 has not brought us the railroad. Nevertheless, the line was surveyed again in the last few weeks. People say that work on it will begin this winter.[123] Finally, I relate that Alberta was elevated to the

119 In May Rev. James Holwerda visited from Manhattan, Mont.; in August home missionary Rev. Frederick Stuart made a visit.

120 On 16 November 1905 Reverends Holwerda and Botbijl helped organize the Nijverdal CRC. The first regular services were held in the Rocky Coulee schoolhouse; this continued for the first year.

121 Almost all of the Protestants in the settlement were from a Reformed background, but they represented different denominations. Those from the Netherlands were from the Hervormde Kerk or the Gereformeerde Kerken; those from the United States were Reformed or Christian Reformed.

122 The Rose Butte School had opened in the spring of 1905. The Finley School opened in January 1906.

123 This was the railway line between Lethbridge and Macleod, which was finally completed in 1909.

status of an independent province this year.[124] And now, dear reader, as New Year's Day dawns, and you give best wishes or receive them from friends and relatives, or when you go up to the house of prayer to thank God and to pray, then make a little place in your thoughts for your countrymen in the small colony in Canada. They also wish you a happy New Year!

[Aldus]

George Dijkema reading newspaper in his Granum home. (Courtesy: Thelma Durian.)

124 Alberta, which was previously one of the Northwest Territories, became a province on 1 September 1905.

CHAPTER 3

The Years of Growth & Prosperity
1906–09

AFTER THE EARLY YEARS OF STRUGGLE ON THE homestead, there were four years of good harvests, from 1906 to 1909. The Dutch community in southern Alberta continued to grow and began to experience a measure of prosperity. Most of the settlers proved up on their homesteads in these years, some bought extra land, and most families made improvements to their homes.

The letters from this period portray this growth and prosperity from a variety of vantage points. There are twenty-one short correspondent letters from the east side of the settlement, sent from Lethbridge and later from Monarch. From the west side George Dijkema sent nine more letters. Evert Aldus contributed nine more letters, elaborating on the homesteading experience and the crops, the harsh winter of 1906–07, a Christmas celebration, and the development of the community, including the building of new railways and the new towns of Monarch and Noble. From the Dutch settlers near Macleod there are also five short reports. Two articles portray the early growth and prosperity of the towns of Granum and Monarch.

Several persons, including Revs. Botbijl, Borduin, and Vander Mey, students Jacob Weersing and Karel Fortuin, as well as George Dijkema and Geert Venhuizen, offer reports on the early development of the Nijverdal Christian Reformed Church and the construction of church buildings on its west and east sides. Rev. Lammers reports on the founding of the Reformed Church in 1909.

There are also several personal letters that portray a more personal and family perspective on this period. Besides Geert Venhuizen's letter about the west-side families, there are six letters from the Bode-Hartkoorn families, and two from the Dekker family. Hilje Mulder and Beert Nauta present detailed travel accounts of their immigration journeys to Alberta.

LETTER FROM LETHBRIDGE
(*De Grondwet*, 2 January 1906)

Today the weather is beautiful. The last snow we got has as good as vanished.

I reported last time that there were two families on the way. Now I can say that they are in our midst and are busy building. J[ohannes] Gunst had the good fortune in the short time he was here to get a homestead. If anyone wants to know something about this country, his address is J. Gunst, Box 284, Lethbridge, Alberta, Canada.[1]

Also in this district people are very busy making preparations to celebrate Christmas.

Corr. 19 Dec. 1905

REPORT OF REV. MEINDERT BOTBIJL
(*De Wachter*, 10 January 1906)

Home Missions: Iowa, Montana, and Alberta, Canada

You notice from the heading that the mission field west of the Mississippi is expanding farther and farther. Besides the manifold work on our own terrain, under our own flag, a door has opened in Canada in the province of Alberta, under the less beautiful flag of England.

---

1 Johannes Gunst and his wife arrived with the Bode family on 2 December 1905. Having just arrived he would not be the best source for information on farming in Alberta.

The undersigned, one of your missionaries on this great field,[2] will communicate something of his activities in the three above-mentioned places. We will do it this time just in a Jewish way. By saying this, we do not mean to deal in an underhanded way, but to give you a glimpse of this field after visiting it rather than before. First follow me in the spirit to Canada. Canada? Not long ago I spoke with someone for whom Canada hardly existed. And when I said, Canada is a region that lies right next to us, she looked at me so strangely with surprise as if she wanted to say???. She really seemed captivated by this new discovery of hers. Fortunately, her knowledge of Scripture was better than her knowledge of geography.

Now who ever would have thought that we as a church would hear voices like this from England's domain: Come and help us. The old mother always seemed to be quick and ready and very capable of running her own affairs in this region.

Thus it must seem strange for us to hear a voice like this: Can America also help us? But it is a fact; it happened. From under England's flag, from Canada there was a request: America, send us one of your missionaries who may bring us the gospel of salvation. But don't think for a moment that we had to deal with subjects of English blood. No, it was our own people, people of our own stock and faith who called.

Are there Hollanders there? Yes, indeed. They have gone far into the northwest and even across the border. It is now about three years ago that brother Emmelkamp moved there with his family, from Maxwell. He was the first to settle there. He could just choose his homestead, a 160 acres, from many hundreds or thousands of acres where there had never been a plough.

Soon others followed him there. Some directly from the Netherlands, from Nijverdal, and others from the United States. In all there are now about fifteen families, besides a few bachelors.[3] Naturally, the latter also count, but to be called a family first one from Eve's gender must be with them. We hope they may soon have a good choice.

Actually, here we find two settlements, which lie about 12 to 13 miles apart. The one is about 18 miles northwest of Lethbridge, the other 5 miles east of Leavings. This certainly is somewhat detrimental to achieving unity, especially in the area of church life. For some time services were regularly

2 Rev. Meindert Botbijl, as a home missionary of the Christian Reformed Church, visited southern Alberta and preached to the Dutch settlers there two Sundays, 5 and 12 November. Then, with Rev. James Holwerda, he officially organized the congregation as the Nijverdal Christian Reformed Church on 16 November.
3 In November 1905 there were sixteen Dutch families and about twenty single men in the Dutch settlement.

held there on Sundays. They met in one of the houses, and one of the brothers read a sermon.

This was already a pleasure for them. But they felt something more was needed. They eagerly wanted to become organized as a congregation. Last March such a request was then presented to the Classis.[4] It accepted and approved the request, and at the same time it decided to appoint the undersigned and Rev. J. Holwerda of Manhattan to do this work. This task was carried out, as readers have already seen in *De Wachter.*

16 November 1905 is the day when our sister in Canada was born. She got her name from Nijverdal. The little congregation numbers 15 [16] confessing members and 40 in all. This is a first in Canada. May the King of the Church richly bless her.

At the same time this congregation is commended to the churches for prayer. In Montana a new congregation was also established, but about that another time.[5]

Yours in the work of missions,
M. Botbijl

EXCERPT OF LETTER FROM HOMEWOOD, ILLINOIS
(*Nieuwsblad van Friesland,* 13 January 1906)

Homewood, Illinois, 12 Dec. 1905

... A year or more ago the call rang out: "To Canada." I also had a notion to go there, but I really didn't dare. And that was good. In the beginning of August last year, by letter I asked Mr. Geo. Dijkema for information about Canada in the area where he lives. Now I will cite a few things from him, which Mr. Dijkema will certainly not take ill of me.

He wrote, among other things: the homesteads are all gone. There is enough room in the country; it is large and spacious. Whether there is work for you to find I will not guarantee. Maybe there is work for you in one of the big towns; certainly in haying and threshing time there is work. The farmers mostly do their own work, and for a single person it is better than

---

4   The request from Alberta to establish a congregation came, not in March, but to the 28 September 1905 meeting of Classis Orange City, the nearest regional assembly of the Christian Reformed Church. It met in Sioux Center, Iowa.
5   A Christian Reformed Church was established at Farmington, Mont., also in 1905.

for a married worker. Here you have to have a piece of land yourself and then the prospects are good. Too bad you didn't come a year earlier; then you would have been able to get 160 acres of land for only 10 dollars. Still, land here is not yet as expensive as in Illinois. To go there now, says Mr. Dijkema, you have to have about $1,000 in cash; otherwise stay where you are. Groceries here are more expensive than in Illinois. The most necessary items, such as potatoes, turnips, carrots, etc., you can grow yourself, but not fine fruit. The main thing here is grain growing, especially wheat. Barley and oats also grow very well here. I think between 30 and 40 Dutch families live here, and a few more are most probably coming this year.

So says Mr. Dijkema, whom I heartily thank for his warning, because if he had written otherwise, we would have gone to Canada and probably would have found no work and no living there. Now we have it good.

E. Fennema

LETTER FROM LETHBRIDGE
(*De Grondwet,* 23 January 1906)

At present people here are busy building. You see a house rise here and then there. L[eendert] Koole is busy doing this. When he is finished with one building he goes on to another. The school building is also finished. On Monday 8 January it will be put into service.[6]

The Dekker brothers have their well finished, a fine well with water. At Mr. Beagle's place they are busy drilling.

On the 25th of December there was a splendid celebration for the Sunday school children at the house of the Koole brothers. There were about sixty-eight, young and old, and they all went home satisfied. G[errit] J. Withagen was the leader.

Beautiful weather and no snow, so the roads are very good.

Corr. 5 Jan. 1906

---

6 This was the Finley School.

EXCERPT OF LETTER FROM VESPER, WISCONSIN
(*De Grondwet,* 30 January 1906)

… Although it is not my intention to make remarks about my fellow correspondents, yet I am obliged to caution the correspondent from Lethbridge, Canada, not to state the names of persons in *De Grondwet* to whom people may write about what the country is like there, when such persons have been there no longer than seven to eight weeks, as is the case with Mr. J[ohannes] Gunst. This writer has too much respect for him than that you should believe that J. Gunst would allow this....[7]

Corr.

LETTER FROM LETHBRIDGE
(*De Grondwet,* 20 February 1906)

Two weeks ago we had rather severe winter weather for a few days; it soon changed and we are getting beautiful weather, so farmers in this vicinity are out discing.

Since I saw that the correspondent from Vesper, Wisconsin, wants to caution me in a brotherly way not to state names of persons who came here only a short time ago, as with J[ohannes] Gunst, we would assure the Vesper correspondent that we did not steal his name. He approved it himself. Perhaps our friend intends to caution our dear countrymen, especially those who have paid for the trip here and then have no more money left to get established here, as, sad to say, is the case everywhere and also at Vesper. If the Vesper correspondent later hears that J. Gunst misled anyone in a deceptive way, then, he said, you can feel free to strike him off the list of our countrymen. When one reads the correspondence, one should not be too rash since one does not know the writer's intention in advance.

We were also glad to hear that Rev. De Lange took a walk; that is a sign that our beloved pastor is still healthy.[8]

Corr. 5 February 1906

---

7 This was a response to a letter from Lethbridge in the 2 January 1906 issue of *De Grondwet.* Johannes Gunst and his wife had arrived in Alberta from Vesper in early December.

8 The correspondent from Lethbridge was clearly one of the settlers who had come from Vesper and was a member of the Christian Reformed Church there – probably Teunis Bode. Rev. Th. De Lange was the pastor of the Vesper CRC.

LETTER FROM LEAVINGS
(*De Grondwet*, 27 February 1906)

Every day the weather is beautiful. Sunshine almost everyday. Now and then a little snow falls. A few weeks ago about a half a foot of snow fell, but now it seems it doesn't want to fall any more. Usually no more than two inches will fall, but with one good warm day it is gone again. At the end of January each day brought warm winter weather. Some people then could no longer bear their "life of leisure" and began to harrow or disc. It was early, to be sure, but they thought: "What is done, is done."

A week ago Mr. Willem De Jong arrived here from Leeuwarden, Friesland. We give him a hearty welcome to Alberta. He is a carpenter by trade, and will, we hope, be able to help many Hollanders build houses. He also wants to try to take up a homestead, although that will be difficult.[9]

Leavings recently has grown surprisingly. Two years ago there were still only a few houses; today it is beginning to look like a town. The large new hotel of John Arthur [Artun] is almost finished. It is being built a good deal more lavishly than his predecessor built the other one.[10]

Several weeks ago Mr. Willem Willemsen arrived here from Manhattan, Mont. He has built a house for his father, who has a homestead here, and he is even working on getting one yet. He also has plans to buy a piece of land here. Soon he is going back to Manhattan to sell the farm he has there, and as soon as he has sold it he is coming here to settle for good. Our hope is that he may be successful.[11]

Last fall a congregation of the Christian Reformed Church was organized here. We gather once every Sunday. The attendance is pretty good, although it is only a reading service. But soon we expect Rev. [Abel] Brink from Oak Harbor, Wash., to preach the gospel to us.[12]

9   Willem De Jong did not get a homestead or remain in the community.

10   The new Royal Hotel was constructed by John Artun. The earlier Alberta Hotel was built in 1903.

11   A letter from Manhattan, Mont., dated 26 Dec. 1905, in *De Grondwet* (2 January 1906) reported that "Mr. Willem Willemsen and his elderly father have plans to spend the winter months in Leavings, Canada, to which they will leave one of these days." There Willem and his 71-year-old father Arend joined the families of Willem's brother Garrit and two sisters Fenneken ter Telgte and Dina Van Dijk. Another letter from Manhattan, dated 10 April 1906 (*De Grondwet*, 17 April 1906), reported that "Willem Willemsen is again back from Canada, where he spent this winter with his father. The latter, however, stayed there because he has taken up a homestead." In the end, Willem did not return to settle in Alberta until 1910, after he had married and had two children.

12   Rev. Abel Brink visited the Nijverdal church for two Sundays in March 1906. Years later he told a story of this visit, which casts light on the experience of homestead wives and the discouragement of the early years:
"About sixteen years ago I paid my first visit to southern Alberta, where some families had settled not so long before and started the Nijverdal congregation. Among others I visited the family of a certain Mr.

It may be that Mr. J[ohannes] Gunst has not been at Lethbridge, Alberta, long enough yet to give information about the land here, but if there are any *De Grondwet* readers who desire information from someone who has been here longer than a few weeks, let them write to Mr. H. Emmelkamp, Leavings, Alberta. He is willing to provide information to any one.[13]

Corr. [George Dijkema] 14 Feb. 1906

LETTER FROM LEENDERT BODE TO JAN BODE[14]
(1 March 1906)

Lethbridge, 1 March 1906
Dear Brother and Family,

Since I will take up the pen again to write you a letter, first we will let you know that, by the Lord's goodness, we are still in good health, and we heartily hope and wish the same for you. Ja, brother, you'll surely think it strange if you see the address in the heading. We have moved again, about 1,200 to 1,400 miles. I sold my farm in Wisconsin for $2,600 for 80 acres, and now I have 160 acres here for $10, that is, government land. But for three years you have to satisfy the requirement to develop the land and then you get ownership of it. It's prairie land here, flat land without trees. It's very nice land.

[Aldus], who was a teacher in the Netherlands and then was a farmer for the second year on the vast prairies of Canada. When we (an elder and I) approached the house, we heard the woman of the house singing. Her husband was not at home. To my remark that she seemed cheerful, she answered very naively: 'Sometimes one can also sing to forget the sorrow, dominie.' To my question whether she had sorrow, she openly answered, 'Ja, dominie.' And she thought she truly had reasons to feel sorrowful or at least discouraged. She then told us something like the following:

'In the Netherlands we heard of the vast Canada, where thousands of acres of fine land still lay, which the government gave free to immigrants who wished to live on the land and work it. The land could yield a good harvest. The price of grain was good, and after five [three] years we would receive the "deed" and we could sell the land, if we wanted. My husband sat down to do some calculations. A "quarter" of land free. So many bushels of grain per acre; so much per bushel for the grain. This for five years. Then the land is worth so much. After five years in Canada, we could return, if we chose, to the Netherlands with a nice pocketful of money. And now we are sitting here for the second year and still have raised nothing.'

Then I ventured to make the simple remark that her husband had made the mistake only to multiply and add and had evidently not thought to subtract, and that this apparently was necessary also in Canada. Later, when I read in the papers the so promising land advertisements, I always thought of this conversation with this woman." *De Wachter*, 24 Jan. 1924.

The winters are not severe. Sometimes for a day or so it can be cold, but it doesn't last long. Many people living here are from Nijverdal, Friesland [Overijssel]. Perhaps you've heard something about it.

Last fall a Christian church was organized here.[15] We have no minister yet, but every Sunday there's a worship service.

Teunis and Gerrit and Barend [Bode] each have a homestead or government land here too. They all live nearby. They were here a year earlier than we were. We've been here about three months. In the last while I didn't like it any more in Wisconsin, although we had a good living. But to my mind I had to work too hard there. When the three oldest boys left home I was left only with Leendert and he was still only twelve. So I had to do the heaviest work. Here the work is done mostly with horses, because here one grows wheat, oats, and barley.

We live 18 miles or 6 hours from town, but the roads are always good. But in a year or two there is sure to be a closer town, because a new railway is coming past here not far away, and then the other is sure to follow. But enough of this.

A month or so ago I sent three pictures of Teunis to you, one for you, one for Jan Groen, and one for Arie Zwijnenburg on the Kortzij.[16] How are they, brother? Did you receive them? You must write back soon. And how is Antje at Meerkerk and Jan Van der Werff? I've had no letter from [Gerrit] Hartkoorn for a long time.[17] I hope you'll receive this letter in good health. Write back soon. Now my address is: Mr. Leendert Bode, Lethbridge, Alberta, Canada.

Hearty greetings from all of us, and also give our greetings to the rest of the family. Your brother, L. B.

---

13 The last paragraph is a response to the letter from the Lethbridge correspondent to the 19 December 1905 issue of *De Grondwet*, which invites persons interested in Alberta to write Gunst. He arrived from Vesper only in late 1905; Emmelkamp as the earliest Dutch settler had come in 1903. It is apparent that there is some competition between Dijkema and the east-side correspondent.

14 Leendert Bode had grown up on a farm near Noordeloos in the province of Zuid-Holland. In 1889 he and his family immigrated to South Holland, Illinois, and then in 1899 he started farming at Vesper, Wisc. In early December 1905 he moved to the Alberta settlement, after his sons Gerrit, Teunis, and Barend took up homesteads there in the fall of 1904. Leendert's younger brother Jan lived on the family farm near Noordeloos.

15 This was the Nijverdal Christian Reformed Church.

16 Jan Groen was Leendert's brother-in-law, and Arie Zwijnenburg a former neighbour on the Kortzij, a street in the Ottoland district (near Noordeloos) where Leendert's family had lived before emigrating.

17 Antje (Annigje) Bode was Leendert's sister living in the village of Meerkerk. Jan Van der Werff was married to Leendert's sister Wouterina; they were the parents of Herbert Van der Werff. Gerrit Hartkoorn was married to another of his sisters, Jabikje.

LETTER FROM LETHBRIDGE
(*De Grondwet,* 8 May 1906)

Today the weather is beautiful. Recently there has been some rain, so that the grain can grow well. The spring wheat is already standing quite nice above the ground.

Again we have here two visitors from Lynden, Washington, Mr. Elenbaas and Mr. Westrate, who are also looking for land.[18] Most of the Hollanders are well satisfied, except some who become homesick and then secretly leave. This became apparent lately with a person who made his wife and housemates believe that he went out to work and then left secretly to his relatives.[19]

L[eendert] Geleynse has almost finished his house.

Land is rising in price, so if there are still Hollanders who are thinking about coming here, they should not wait long; that is the great fault of the Hollander. Here we also get good prices for our products, such as 30 cents a pound for butter and 18 cents a dozen for eggs.

Corr. 30 April 1906

EXCERPT OF LETTER FROM VESPER, WISCONSIN
(*De Grondwet,* 8 May 1906)

... Last week, on 24 April, we had an auction sale here by Pieter De Boer. Although not many people came, everything sold for a pretty fair price. The cows brought in $33 to over $40, two horses over $100 each, a sow with six pigs sold for $22. Young animals, one-year-old heifers, $12 more or less. The following day, after the sale, Mr. De Boer left for Hinsdale, Montana....[20]

Mr. J[ohannes] Gunst came unexpectedly from Alberta, Canada, back here to his parents. If anyone now wishes information about Canada, one can write him....[21]

1 May 1906

18 Elenbaas and Westrate did not join the southern Alberta settlement.
19 The person alleged to have secretly left was Johannes Gunst. Mrs. Jannigje Gunst was a daughter of Leendert Bode, and at this point the young couple was probably still living with relatives. The correspondent, Gerrit or Teunis Bode, is talking about his own brother-in-law. See the next item.
20 Pieter De Boer was the father of Daniel De Boer who later joined the Alberta settlement in the fall of 1906, coming from Conrad, Mont.

LETTER FROM LETHBRIDGE
(*De Grondwet*, 29 May 1906)

We have recently had a lot of rain. For forty hours straight it rained, so the ground is now soaked. The farmers are again busy at their work.

Mr. McLean [McClain], from California, who bought 18 sections of land here a couple of years ago, is now building a house for over $8,000. His intention is to till the land with a steam plough.[22] It appears that the "ranchers" are too cramped here, because last week Mr. Howe left to the north with 500 head of cattle. J[ohn] Wright sold a carload of horses for $112 a head, and J[oe] G. Graves a carload of horses for $110 a head. So the livestock here are decreasing considerably.[23]

Lethbridge nowadays is building up quickly. Recently a new roundhouse and freight shed.[24] So at present there is an abundance of work. In Macleod also several Hollanders are working for the railroad.

Corr. 19 May 1906

LETTER FROM LEAVINGS
(*De Volksvriend*, 31 May 1906)

For a long time now I have not sent news. That was because I was terribly busy, but since that is now past for the most part and there is nothing left to do but plough, and since that is all but impossible due to the huge rains, there is now enough time to write a piece for the *Volksvriend*. Yes, I spoke about the huge rains. It began to rain here on Tuesday the 15th of May and it rained constantly until Thursday the 17th of May at six o'clock in the

---

21 In the next issue of *De Grondwet* (15 May 1906), the editor included an editorial note: "In connection with an item of correspondence from Vesper, Wis., included in our previous issue, about the actions of Mr. J. Gunst, we deem it necessary to mention that we later learned from a good source that the report about him is wholly and entirely untrue. We hasten to bring this correction to the knowledge of our public. Editor." It is clear that Johannes Gunst went unexpectedly to Vesper, since both the Lethbridge and Vesper correspondents corroborate this, and in early August he returned to Alberta. What the editor may be trying to correct is the circumstances. Perhaps Gunst went to Vesper to sell his farm there, as the 28 August issue suggests.

22 In 1904 Jasper McClain and a partner bought a 36-section block of land from the CPR McClain took the west 18 sections. In 1906 he bought a steam engine that pulled twelve breaker bottom ploughs.

23 With the homestead rush of 1902–05 the earlier ranchers had less open range for their cattle, and the ranching era soon came to an end, especially after the severe winter of 1906–07 killed thousands of cattle.

24 This railroad activity at Lethbridge was due to the decision of the CPR to move the divisional point on the Crow's Nest line from Macleod to Lethbridge. This also led to the building of the high level bridge and a new line to Macleod.

evening. Then it was warm for a couple of days, and on Saturday evening at five o'clock again it poured and thundered like I had never yet experienced here in Alberta. On Sunday the sky was completely dark and on Monday again it rained and rained. For the first few days ploughing is out of the question. The ground is much too wet. The rain has soaked in more than two feet. But, you ask, are you pleased with the rain? O yes, but yet there are some who exclaim with a correspondent from one of the Dakotas: "In dry Alberta we are seriously beginning to long for drought." It is amazing how much water has fallen. Large parts of the prairie are flooded, and wherever there is a low spot there is water, where wild ducks and other kinds of waterfowl quietly swim around. Wild ducks on the prairie, a wonderful phenomenon. And as if that were not enough, in the evenings frogs utter their monotonous sound:

> The frog in the water sings, that little broad man.
> He sings his frog song, as loud as he can.

Strange. Frogs in Alberta. In "Sunny Alberta" that has a reputation with many people of being too dry, so dry that nothing can grow there. Two years ago we had a good crop with little rain; last year the crop was good with less rain, and now we are getting a lot of rain. How will the crop be this year? Everything looks good. Wheat and oats promise to be excellent.

Some days ago J[an] Roos with his family came to us from Michigan.[25] He is well pleased with the country. Yet I think it is plenty wet for him here now; but soon we will have sunshine again and our "Sunny Alberta" will come back, with its warm days and cool nights, with its beautiful, glorious climate.

[George Dijkema][26]

---

25 Jan Roos arrived with his wife and five children from Grand Rapids, Mich., in April. Jan was a brother of Harm Emmelkamp's wife Jantje.

26 George Dijkema sent a similar letter, dated 21 May, to *De Grondwet* (5 June 1906).

27 Though both men bought land south of the Oldman River already in 1906, both families moved to Alberta only some years later, the Leeuwerik family from Hull, Iowa, in 1909, the Zoeteman family from nearby Perkins, Iowa, in 1911.

28 Jacob Weersing had just finished his first year of study for ministry in the Christian Reformed Church at the Theological School in Grand Rapids. He was the first of a number of students in the early years to do a summer assignment in the southern Alberta settlement.

LETTER FROM LETHBRIDGE
(*De Grondwet,* 21 August 1906)

At present the weather is warm here, so everything is growing well. The grain is also ripening fast. A week yet and then we will hear the noise of binders cutting the spring wheat. Earlier we passed on reports from others that harvest prospects are good; now we can bear witness to it ourselves.

Recently two more people came from the Netherlands: [Jacobus] Van Haarlem and Lursen Hull. They were lucky yet to get a homestead, about five miles from our people.

Jan Zoeteman and Jake Leewerik [Leeuwerik] each bought a quarter of land. Both are from Iowa.[27] Also B[artel] Geleynse and J[ohannes] Gunst arrived here from Vesper, Wisconsin. B. Geleynse was very pleased with this district and with the crops that he saw.

Student J[acob] Weersing has left again, after spending five weeks in our midst.[28] Anyone who wants to see this region should come now; then he can be an eyewitness of the harvest.

Corr. 8 Aug. 1906

LETTER FROM LEAVINGS
(*De Grondwet,* 28 August 1906)

This summer a lot of rain has fallen and the crops are excellent. Last year and two years ago it was much drier than this summer; yet crops standing on land that was ploughed on time were good both last year and two years ago. But this year it doesn't make much difference. One can well see, however, that land that was ploughed for the first time in the spring will not bring in as many bushels per acre as land that is well cultivated, but yet it does not take away the fact that also the so-called "spring crop" promises a very good harvest. The grain is almost ripe. Some farmers have already begun cutting. The winter wheat is not particularly good this year. In February the days were too warm and the nights too cold. Most winter wheat was therefore replaced with spring wheat. Some pieces of barley are already cut and the spring wheat is almost ready. The winter wheat is standing in stooks and the oats is also ripening nicely. Everything – oats, wheat, barley, etc. – promises to be good, much better than last year. Every year more land is cultivated here. The homesteads in the neighbourhood of Leavings are all gone, and the so-called "railroad land" is running up tremendously in price.[29]

Student J. Weersing from the Theological School in Grand Rapids has again left us, after preaching the gospel to us for five Sundays. He went from here to Farmington, Montana. However, we hope to see him here once again in the far West. He gained many friends here, both among the Hollanders and among the English. Now we have services again as usual.[30]

Now and then a couple of Hollanders still come. The old Mr. Glaince [Bartel Geleynse] and J[ohannes] Gunst from Vesper, Wisconsin, sold their farms there and will now begin to farm here. One of the sons of Mr. Glaince has already been here a long time, and his second son is coming this fall with his wife and children.[31] So the longer the Dutch settlement is here the more it grows.

The weather is beautiful every day. Always sunshine. A lot of hay has been put up this year. Binders are being used a good deal more than last year.

Corr. [George Dijkema] 14 Aug. 1906

REPORT OF JACOB WEERSING[32]
(*De Wachter,* 12 September 1906)

From Nijverdal, Canada

Since I was busy this summer doing mission work at Nijverdal, Canada, and at Farmington, Montana, I thought it would be good to inform readers of *De Wachter* a little about the state of these small congregations. First, Nijverdal, Canada. This congregation lies about a hundred miles north of the border between western Montana and Canada, sixty miles east of the Rocky Mountains, and approximately two thousand miles from Grand Rapids, Michigan. It numbers eleven families, but this number will increase, Lord willing, when a minister first comes there. There are now about two

---

29 By 1906 c & e Railroad sections in the Leavings area were selling for about $10 an acre; three years later the price rose to about $30 an acre.

30 Services as usual meant reading services where an elder would lead the service and read a published sermon since no minister or student was available to preach.

31 Leendert Geleynse had settled in Alberta in July 1905; his brother Jan later came with a family of six children in October 1906.

32 Jacob Weersing, as a student preparing for the ministry, spent five weeks in the summer of 1906 serving the Nijverdal Christian Reformed Church in Alberta.

hundred Hollanders, who together have about sixty farms of 160 acres each under the plough. Nearly all are willing to support the church financially, and it would not be long before this congregation could support its own minister if a missionary would regularly work there for some time. The land is of the best quality and is still not high in price. It would be very desirable if Hollanders who are seeking a home in the West would settle here. A small number of Christian Reformed brothers would be able to give much support to the congregation here and build it up. This congregation has a lot of promise for the future. This year the land is bringing a heavy wheat harvest, without irrigation. May it please the Lord to make this congregation grow and flourish and to make it become a pillar with others in our Church. This writer will gladly give information to interested persons.

J[acob] Weersing Jr.   Cascade, Montana

LETTER FROM LETHBRIDGE
(*De Grondwet*, 18 September 1906)

At present we are very busy here hauling grain with each other, and there is a shortage of workers. So at present they pay good wages – from $2.00 to $2.75 per day. Two Hollanders have already threshed their winter wheat. R[oelf] Lantinga got 35 bushels per acre and G[eert] Venhuizen 36½ bushels, so that is not bad. Also the winter wheat that was recently seeded is already standing nice and green above the ground.

A[rie] Koole from Sheldon, Iowa, bought a half-section of land here.[33] L[eendert] Geleynse left this morning for Vesper, Wisconsin.[34] D[aniel] De Boer arrived here from Conrad, Montana, to visit friends and acquaintances.[35]

Corr. 11 Sept. 1906

---

33 Arie Koole came to Alberta in March 1905 with his older brothers Leendert and Bastiaan and then took up a homestead.
34 Leendert Geleynse went to Vesper probably to help his brother Jan prepare for the move to Alberta. A letter from Vesper in *De Grondwet* (16 October 1906) reports: "J[an] Geleynse held an auction day on 25 September and did well beyond expectation. The cows brought in $30 a head. Last Friday he had a boxcar loaded with his property. He is leaving to Lethbridge, Canada."
35 Daniel De Boer had moved with his parents from Vesper to Montana in the spring of 1906, so the friends he came to visit were people who had come to Alberta from Vesper. Probably because of this visit De Boer himself decided to move to Alberta.

LETTER FROM LETHBRIDGE
(*De Grondwet*, 4 December 1906)[36]

Today is a bit wintry, a little snow and slight freezing. I came here six weeks ago and found it good here. I am really impressed by the land. I have also witnessed threshing and have seen the grain. It gave a good yield. Wheat averaged 25 to 32 bushels per acre and the price at present is 55½ cents a bushel. Oats brought in 40 to 65 bushels per acre and is 25 cents. Flax brought 13 to 15 bushels per acre. And as for the potato harvest, I have seen it as good as in Wisconsin, in the potato country. My father also had the good fortune to get a homestead close to mine, and Daniel De Boer has also taken up a homestead.[37]

G[errit] J. Withage's family has been increased with a baby daughter.[38]

Thys Dekker went to Humboldt, Iowa, to go fishing there.[39]

We are seeing automobiles riding around the prairie with land buyers.[40]

T[ijmen] Hofman from Westfield, North Dakota, paid us a visit to see the land. He found it very good here.[41]

Also here in Lethbridge a large project has been contracted out – a bridge 1¼ miles long for the railroad that is coming in this district.[42]

Corr. [Jan Geleynse]

36 The new correspondent from Lethbridge was a newcomer from Vesper, Wisc., Jan Geleynse.

37 Jan Geleynse's father was Bartel Geleynse, who arrived in August 1906. That same month Daniel DeBoer visited from Conrad, Mont., and then returned to take up a homestead in November.

38 Gerrit J. Withage's new daughter was Hermina.

39 Thys Dekker spent the winter months in Iowa working.

40 Real estate agents were among the first to use automobiles in southern Alberta. The automobile first appeared in Alberta in 1903.

41 In the fall of 1906 Tijmen Hofman was considering a move west from his farm in North Dakota. A letter from Westfield, N.Dak. in *De Volksvriend* (18 October 1906) reports: "F. [T.] Hofman is thinking about paying a visit to his brother-in-law van der Vaarte [van der Vate] in Montana." During this visit he may have been checking possibilities for land in Montana. It is likely that during the same trip that Hofman visited Montana he also checked out southern Alberta in November. He liked what he saw in Alberta, sold his farm in North Dakota, and in May 1907 arrived with his wife Heiltje and ten children.

42 The railroad bridge was the high level bridge over the Oldman River, allowing a new railway line to run from Lethbridge to Macleod. The bridge was finally finished in 1909.

43 This decision of Classis Orange City reversed its original decision that the Nijverdal congregation must worship in one central location – the Rocky Coulee schoolhouse or some other middle point. For the next two or three years the east and west sides of the congregation each held their own services in a home or local schoolhouse, except for combined services when a minister or student visited.

REPORT OF JACOB WEERSING
(*De Wachter,* 12 December 1906)

Nijverdal, Canada

Though this congregation does not find itself in United States territory, nevertheless there are multiple reasons that call and compel us to formally celebrate the only legal Christian holiday with all our sister congregations, east and west, large and small. The Nijverdal congregation, due to its expanse, is now allowed by the Classis to regularly hold services at two locations,[43] something that makes it much easier for those who like to gather every Sunday in God's house with his people; also others who could not earlier attend due to the great distance now have ample opportunity to do so. Our settlement is growing in number, and land seekers are still always coming here to look at the country in order to settle here later. Hence this congregation also will grow and increase until the number here is large enough that we are able to have our own shepherd and minister. Then this congregation can very soon stand on its own feet. The Classis has also promised to send us a minister for two Sundays. If someone were working here longer and more regularly to gather in the rich sheaves and spiritually build up and encourage those who are growing, then it is possible that now already this would be a strong congregation.

On the spiritual level there is nothing to complain about, and on the temporal and financial level we are all well provided for by our God. Indeed, however dim the way may appear, we always find help and know that he never leaves us. We had a very fruitful season. This fall produced winter wheat well beyond expectation. So for the winter we are well provided for again.

Perhaps the reader is thinking that this is certainly necessary in the cold northwest. Yes, but this fall we have still not had as much cold and snow here as in Michigan. And although it becomes very cold for a day or so in the winter, then the Ruler of nature again sends the lovely warm Chinook wind that makes the snow and cold disappear like "wax before glowing coals." We have reason to be thankful in everything, but we also ask the reader to remember us in spiritual matters before the throne of grace.

J[acob] Weersing Jr.

LETTER FROM LEAVINGS
(*De Volksvriend*, 20 December 1906)

Winter has made its entry into our Sunny Alberta. Already for a couple of days the weather has been dark, and large snowflakes have fallen now and then so that the fields are now covered with four or five inches of snow. It is not yet cold, very cold, and we hope we soon will have nice sunny weather again.

The farm work is done; ploughing is no longer possible now, although many farmers still really wanted to do some ploughing. Threshing is finished; the yield was pretty good. The winter wheat produced from 35 to 40 bushels per acre, although it was almost all frozen; yet a few patches continued growing. This year a lot of it has been seeded again, and we hope that it may survive the winter. So far it appears excellent. This snow is very good for it. And if in February and March we do not get too much warm weather in the day and frost at night, then it will go well. In general people here believe that this is a country for winter wheat. Summer [spring] wheat also thrives well here. Last spring a lot of it was seeded because the winter wheat for the most part froze. It produced from 23 to 47 bushels per acre; 23 bushels was the least I heard of. The average yield was from 25 to 35 bushels. Yet there was someone who got 47 bushels per acre from a 45 acre piece of land. The prices are not very high: 52 to 56 cents a bushel. A lot of oats was also seeded, with a yield from 60 to 70 bushels per acre.

Now that winter has set in and people have to stop ploughing, it is the time to haul grain to town. But, even though Leavings already has two elevators, they cannot take a bushel there because the elevators are full and no [railway] cars are available, since the CPR Co. needs all its cars – people say – to supply the people in Saskatchewan with coal. During the prolonged strike by mineworkers there was no coal, and now that the strike is over the Company needs all its cars to keep people there alive. So we have to wait.[44]

Our Dutch people here are well satisfied. At present no one hears people complain. Everyone is well pleased with the country. And why not? The land is good and the climate is excellent. Here no houses blow over like in some places in the United States that I read about in *De Volksvriend*. Here there are no snowstorms that cost farmers thousands of sheep. Here nature is always calm and mild. Readers of *De Volksvriend*, come, see, and convince yourselves.

[George Dijkema]

LETTER FROM GEERT VENHUIZEN
(*De Wachter,* 26 December 1906)

From the Nijverdal Congregation, Canada

It is now about a year ago that this congregation was established by Reverends Holwerda and Botbijl, with the mandate of Classis Orange City, and for a small, weak, just-beginning congregation this first year has been one of growth and progress. There was a growth in numbers of no less than 100 per cent – that in the short time of one year.

Reading services are held regularly. Last spring Rev. [Abel] Brink of Oak Harbor, Washington, fulfilled two classical appointments here, and during the summer vacation student J[acob] Weersing worked here for five weeks. Had Rev. [John] Schaap, previously of Bemis, South Dakota, not been in such a terrible hurry to move to Michigan, he would also have preached here for two Sundays. At least that was the decision of Classis. Now nothing has come of it.

On the material side our settlement is also making substantial progress. The yields of products were above expectation. If a number of families were to come here from other places, the Christian Reformed Church would soon have a thriving congregation in Canada, able to support its own minister.

G[eert] Venhuizen[45]   Leavings, Alberta, Canada 15 Dec. 1906

LETTER FROM LETHBRIDGE
(*De Grondwet,* 15 January 1907)

At present it is wintry, with a little snow, so it is not very busy. Thus one has time now and then to write.

Transporting grain is not going very fast at present, because all the roads are still slippery. All the grain that is grown in this vicinity is brought to Lethbridge and is sold as No. 1. The Dekker brothers had the misfortune of losing a very good horse.

---

44 In February 1906 the United Mine Workers of America unionized the miners at Lethbridge and within a month called a strike. During the strike, which lasted from 8 March to 2 December, the mines at Lethbridge and Fernie were closed.

45 Geert Venhuizen was not a member of the Nijverdal CRC, although his wife and children were. Yet Geert was an active "friend" of the congregation. For a number of years he served as the local agent for *De Wachter.*

Christmas is past again. The Hollanders here had a pleasant celebration in the Rose Butte schoolhouse. There were about 80 present there, young and old, and after spending the day enjoying singing and talking and some refreshments they all went home satisfied. Festivities were also held in the Finley district, a day before. There also the evening was well spent.

Soon school will begin again; here also in a month an election will be held for "trustees," since we have heard that T[eunis] Bode will no longer serve as a trustee.[46]

Last week some men from the CPR Co. came and bought up from the farmers land on which the railroad will be laid. A town will also come in this vicinity, so we will no longer need to make such long trips.[47] It is thus becoming gradually easier for us here. We have also heard that R. E. Werkman wants to have people come here.[48] We wish him much success and that "Sunny Alberta" will quickly be fully populated!

Corr. 1 January 1907

LETTER FROM EVERT ALDUS
(*Twentsch Volksblad*, 19 January 1907)

It's about a year ago that I last wrote something in your newspaper. Perhaps many readers have thought: "The writer from the Dutch colony at Lethbridge has forgotten his old Fatherland and former residence." I will not deny that these thoughts have crossed my mind. But I can put forward one thing to excuse my delay, and that is that you feel less suited to handle the pen when you work on the farm here in the far west. You feel more at ease with the reins of the horses in hand than at the writing table. However, in the future I will try to compensate for where I came up short in the past.

Now I begin as usual by telling what happened to us in 1906. The winter of 1905–1906 was not very severe but lasted rather long. In November the fieldwork had to be stopped due to snow and frost. On about March 15 we

---

46 This was the Rose Butte school. Each country school was required to have at least three trustees on its board.

47 The CPR was planning to build a new railway line from Lethbridge to Macleod. This line was completed in 1909 and on this line the town of Monarch would appear at the southern edge of the east side of the Dutch settlement. With Monarch nearby the Dutch settlers there would no longer have to haul their grain all the way to Lethbridge.

48 R. E. Werkman was a land agent in St. Paul, Minnesota. For a number of years he sold land in various parts of Montana to Dutch people who wanted to buy farmland in the west that was cheaper than in Iowa.

could begin again by discing the land that had to be seeded. The first wheat was seeded at the end of March, but most of it in April. For everyone this summer began with adversity. As I reported before, we all had seeded a number of acres into winter wheat in September 1905. We bought this seed wheat at a high price, a dollar a bushel. The dry fall weather did not allow the wheat to grow much before the winter, so the little plants were not very strong. If we had had favourable spring weather, everything probably would have gone well. The dry month of April, bleak weather, and the raw Chinook wind made the little plants even weaker, and a large number died. Towards the end of the month, we saw that nothing came of it, so in a hurry we disced up the land and seeded spring wheat there. The last was seeded on the second of May. Some of us used our chicken feed to seed this in place of the unsuccessful fall wheat.

Also, before doing the spring grain and oats the weather was unfavourable until the middle of May. It was cold and dry. Then something happened that many of us would have thought impossible had someone told us before. It rained more or less heavily for three weeks. In that time this area did not deserve the name "Sunny Alberta" that is usually given to it.

During these weeks we saw neither sun, moon, nor stars. No one was ready for such weather, so quickly there were shortages of different things, and it was practically impossible to go to town. So now and then, when the rain was not heavy, you saw someone in a winter coat rushing on horseback over the soaked ground to borrow a batch of flour, some coffee or sugar from here or there. Gradually these trips were extended further. In the last week of the rain a real lack of provisions was becoming prevalent. Everyone's supplies were exhausted. So there were some who used burned wheat to make coffee; others had no flour to bake bread and ate potatoes. Yet another, for want of tobacco, smoked his wife's tea. Toward the end of the rain we could no longer wait. One of us went to town in a light little wagon drawn by two horses and came back the following day with a good quantity of purchases, although in some places the axles of the wagon dragged through the mud. A couple of others put four horses in front of one wagon, and though it required all the strength of the four animals, they also came back safe and sound with a good supply.

Soon thereafter the rain stopped and the need to make do was forgotten. That the rain was unpleasant in some ways is easy to understand. Our cattle had a hard time of it. The stables built of sod and covered with straw seemed totally inadequate. The rain went through the roof and made the stables unusable.

At some places the walls fell in or the roof sagged. One of us had dug a new well but had not yet put in wooden walls. When the rain stopped, the well had completely fallen in. These small disadvantages, however, were doubly compensated by the favourable consequences of the rain for plant growth. All the more because the rain was followed by a warm summer, with a refreshing shower now and then, and little wind.

In June and July the crops grew more luxuriantly than we had ever seen them grow before. Wheat, oats, vegetables and potatoes, prairie grass; everything grew quickly.

At the time when the wheat came into head, some of us saw their grain destroyed completely or partly by a hailstorm that traveled from the northwest to the southeast over the middle of the colony. It is very discouraging to see one's grain field destroyed in a quarter hour. Most of the stems were totally pulverized and lay flat on the ground; others were half broken. Here and there a few still stood upright, but most of the seed pods were knocked off the head. After the hail a garden with vegetables and potatoes showed streaks of green pulp, the only remains of the rows of plants. The northern and southern inhabitants of our colony had no trouble with the hail; those in the centre were most affected by it. One saw his whole harvest worth $400 to $500 completely destroyed.

If only two bought a machine last year to cut their grain, this summer almost everyone of us purchased a binder. Such a machine costs $170 with a cutting width of 6 feet, and $190 when the implement cuts an eight-foot swath. In the first case three horses pull the binder, in the second case four. You pay for such a machine in three annual terms.

Every reader can realize how satisfying it was for us to see the good fruits of our labour for the first time in two and a half years of hard work and much adversity; in other words, even to have need of a binder to cut the extended golden fields. Perhaps some readers will laugh that wheat is not cut first; no, first the machine goes into the oat field to provide the necessary and long desired food for our faithful animals, the horses. Because they have gone through the "lean" years with us, and often have had nothing but what they themselves picked from the prairie.

Although the crops began to grow late because of the rain, the grain was ripe early, thanks to the beautiful summer weather. On 15 August the first wheat was cut, the last about four weeks later. That was a busy time. From early in the morning to late in the evening one heard the peculiar hum made by the machines. Many of us were compelled to hire a man to put the grain on piles, or what they here call "shocks." In harvest time you have to keep working. As soon as the grain field is ripe, it must be cut, because if the wind comes, then some of the seed is quickly lying on the ground.

If the grain is dry enough, which usually does not take long, then it has to be brought to heaps or stacks. If you are alone, then you have to hire a man for this too; for this work two men are necessary. By the 20th of September all the grain was stacked.

All the stacks of grain spread over the fields give the landscape a very different look. Here one makes the stacks, usually four together, in the middle of the cut grain field. Then one can haul the grain together in the shortest possible time. Later the threshing machine moves from one "setting" (four stacks together) to another, leaving behind a huge pile of straw. After finishing the grain at each other's places, we could right away begin ploughing or discing the stubble land, insofar as it will be seeded again the next summer. One has to take care to have the ground ready for seeding in the spring as much as possible.

We had a lot of time for this work, since the threshing machine did not come before about 15 October. This implement needed three weeks to thresh our grain. The steam threshing machine that worked for us this year was much larger than the one last year. The steam engine had 40 horsepower.

In favourable conditions 2,500 to 3,000 bushels are threshed per day. We had to pay 6 cents a bushel for wheat and 4 cents for oats. This price is pretty high, but the thresher himself took care of the food for his crew and horses. He fired his machine with coal.

This steam thresher consisted of the engine with the separator, a water wagon, a cook car in which a man and woman prepared food for the threshers, a large tent to sleep in, a hay wagon, etc. A peculiar sight, when this smoking train moves through the fields, led by the smoking and blowing steam engine.

Many a person will say such a thresher earns a lot of money in one day. That is true, but, on the other hand, there are many costs and expenses related to threshing. Our thresher paid over $60 a day for wages, etc. In addition, one has to consider the maintenance of the machine, interest on the capital that it cost, and that the implement which cost $4,000 is worn out after several years. Also, the thresher has work for only a couple of months a year. If he wants to earn money, he must work during that time.

As soon as daylight comes in the east, well before the sun rises, the steam whistle sounds and thick smoke clouds indicate that the thresher has begun his work. In clouds of smoke and dust the men do their work, the engineer on his steamer, the throwers on the stacks; the separatorman is everywhere

– on, then behind, then in front of his implement, looking after everything, the oil can always in his hand. From twelve to one is meal time, and then work until it is dark.

Day after day these men do their work under these circumstances. Their faces and hands are black, their clothes dirty and covered with dust. But you feel more inclined to take your hat off for these industrious men than for many a dignified gentleman in the "Old Country" who rides around in his carriage.

The presence of the steam threshing machine brings an unusual liveliness and busyness. For us who had our first good harvest threshed it was a happy time. The wheat produced from 17 to 33 bushels an acre, or averaged 25. Oats produced from 35 to 65 bushels. A very good harvest; it should be acknowledged with thankfulness.

A[ldus]

(to be continued)[49]

LETTER FROM LETHBRIDGE
(*De Grondwet,* 19 February 1907)

This winter we are having a severe winter, so many cattle are perishing because about six inches of snow lies hard frozen; that makes it difficult for the animals.[50] Yet for the farmer this is good, especially for the winter wheat.

At present a lot of land here is sold for "crop payments." These are easy terms for a poor man, although land is rising higher and higher in price. A farmer, Freeman Anderson, came here three years ago and bought two sections at $5.10 per acre and now he sold it for $21 per acre with a house and stable and a fence around it.

A couple of weeks ago there were a lot of colds here. A[rie] Koole was not well for a couple of weeks but now he is better again. Two or three weeks ago the youngest child of J[ohan] Huisman died.[51]

Recently we had Peter De Boer from Conrad, Montana, in our midst. He paid a visit to his son and acquaintances here.[52]

---

49 Apparently a continuation of this letter was never published.
50 The severe winter of 1906-07 killed thousands of range cattle on the open prairie. This loss, combined with the rapid settlement of homesteaders, marked the end of the ranching era in the area of the Dutch settlement.
51 Their infant son, several months old, died in January 1907, and was buried on the family homestead.
52 Peter De Boer visited his son Daniel and other acquaintances formerly from Vesper, Wisc.

The price of coal has risen to $3.25 to $3.50 a ton. Yet we still have nothing to complain about, because in other places it has risen to $9 a ton since the strike.

Everything brings in a good price at present. Wheat is 55 cents a bushel, oats 25 cents, flax $1 a bushel, hay $9 to $11 a ton, potatoes $1 for a hundred pounds, butter 30 cents a pound, and eggs 45 to 50 cents a dozen.

Corr. 6 Feb. 1907

LETTER FROM LEENDERT BODE TO JAN BODE
(27 February 1907)

Lethbridge, 27 Feb. 1907
Dear Brother and Family,

I'll take up the pen once again to write a few words. It's the only way we can still hear something from each other. First I will let you know that, by the Lord's goodness, we're still experiencing a large measure of health, and we heartily wish the same for you too. We'd regret to hear otherwise.

A few months ago we had a letter from you, but till now I have not written back. I hope you won't blame me for my neglect. Recently we also had a couple of letters from brother-in-law G[errit] Hartkoorn. I think you know something of his intentions – that he's planning at the beginning of March to come to America, or rather, to us here in Canada. His brother-in-law Frans Vanden Berg and his son will also come along then.[53] Hartkoorn writes that the wives will come in May or June. What his wife Jabikje Hartkoorn is feeling about this we don't know. We think she hasn't completely decided yet. But we'll see what will come of it.[54]

We've had a hard winter here. They say there hasn't been such a hard winter in 20 years. That's obvious; otherwise there couldn't be ranchers here

---

53 Gerrit Hartkoorn was married to Leendert Bode's sister Jabikje. Hartkoorn's sister Klaasje was married to Frans Vanden Berg Sr. Gerrit Hartkoorn actually immigrated to Alberta in May 1907, accompanied by Frans Vanden Berg Jr., his brother Paul, and Cornelis Kamp, all from Rotterdam. Frans Sr. and the rest of his family also immigrated that year.

54 Gerrit's wife Jabikje and their grown sons Arie and Barend were reluctant to emigrate, so they stayed behind in Rotterdam. After receiving two letters from Gerrit, in June or July 1907 Jabikje wrote her brother Jan Bode: "[Gerrit] wrote that he was surprised to see that brother Leendert has such a nice house, 3 stables, 6 milk cows, 9 horses, many young cattle, and a lot of machines, as well as a beautiful piece of land.... In the morning Gerrit milks three cows and so does Leendert. Gerrit also bought 160 acres of land. So, Jan, he too will become an American farmer, and I a Rotterdam saleswoman." It was not until the spring of 1910 that Jabikje and their sons finally immigrated to Canada after Gerrit returned to the Netherlands for a visit.

who never give their cattle feed or shelter. They always have to look for their own food on the prairie. That certainly happens in ordinary winters, as is usually the case, but not this winter, so many cattle have died of hunger and cold, but mostly of hunger. There was about 8 inches of hard snow on the ground because it thawed for a couple of days and then was cold again, so there was no grass to be found.

There are also horse ranchers here, but that goes better in winters like this since horses know better how to help themselves by scraping away the snow with their forefeet in order to bare the grass. Our cattle and horses have no trouble with such winters, because in winters like this they're in the stable, but as soon as possible we send them outside during the day.

Last summer we had a good crop here. I raised about a thousand bushels of oats (84 pounds a bushel) and 200 potatoes. This spring I hope to seed 60 acres of wheat, and then I still have to plough for the oats. Oats here is worth 25 cents a bushel, wheat 55 cents a bushel (60 pounds). We have about 90 chickens, and the egg price here is 20 to 50 cents a dozen. For a time this winter we got 50 cents a dozen; now they are still 40. Butter goes for 20 to 30 cents a pound.

Now brother, I've already written about a few things. We've already had beautiful weather for a couple of weeks. We think we have it good here. It's a nice country here. Land is quickly rising in price.

I hope you will receive this small letter in good health. Let us hear from you soon. Give our greetings to Antje and to Jan Van der Werff and his wife. They also have to write. We get no more letters from Jan Groen, just as we never hear anything from Dirk Hartkoorn.[55] Write about everything in detail. For us it's all new. It's almost eighteen years ago that we left from there.[56] Greetings from all of us. And give our greetings also to all who still ask about us.

L[eendert] Bode, Box 284, Lethbridge, Alberta, Canada

55 Dirk Hartkoorn was the son of Jabikje Bode before she married Gerrit Hartkoorn. He grew up on the farm of his grandparents and uncle Jan Bode, and did not immigrate to Canada.
56 Leendert and Willempje Bode and their family immigrated from Ottoland in Zuid-Holland to South Holland, Illinois, in April 1889.
57 1907 was the fiftieth anniversary of the Christian Reformed Church, which began in Michigan in 1857.
58 No Christian Reformed minister had visited the Alberta settlement since Rev. Abel Brink in March 1906.

LETTER FROM MACLEOD
(*De Wachter*, 24 April 1907)

The celebration of the fifty-year Jubilee of our church here in North America is again behind us.[57] At first we could not bring ourselves to send something to our church paper, because we did not feel in a festive mood for the celebration. The brothers and sisters are spread over an area of 25 miles. For thirteen months we had no administering of baptism or the Lord's Supper, and were almost inclined to hang our harps on the willows.[58] Save the Nijverdal congregation from despondency, Lord! – that is the prayer of this writer. The harvest is great and the workers are few. But now that the celebration has come, the Lord has restricted our focus to all the blessings the King of our church has granted in the last seventy-three years in spite of all scorn and slander.[59]

My family springs from the first seceders in 1834. My godly grandmother was the first to side with the people who were persecuted in those days. Father, when he was alive, often told us how she was hated also by her family, except for her husband and children. Once when there was a wedding in the family circle, all were invited except our godly grandmother. Someone in the family asked her whether she had any regrets about it. She answered: Oh no, because I soon hope to sit down at the heavenly wedding. And so it happened. A year or two later (we don't know exactly) the Lord took her to himself in the prime of her earthly life, not yet fifty years of age. From what our dear parents told us we would be able to say much more about the first days of the secession, but we heartily thank our editor in advance for granting space in our church paper. From the heart we also celebrated with our church in these lands. The Lord has done great things for her; for this we rejoice in him. Praise the Lord, O my soul, that the little mustard seed is becoming a tree. May the Lord bless her still more richly in the future – that is the wish of the

Correspondent[60]   Macleod, Alta, Canada

---

59 The writer is referring to the time since the Secession of 1834 took place in the Netherlands. In that year a group of conservative Reformed people led by Rev. Hendrik DeCock seceded from the liberal Hervormde Kerk that was under state control. In the beginning the seceders were often persecuted socially, legally, and economically. In 1847 and later years many seceders immigrated to the United States, to form Dutch colonies especially at Holland, Mich. and Pella, Iowa. In 1850 the western Michigan group joined the Reformed Protestant Dutch Church (later called the Reformed Church in America). A split from this church in western Michigan in 1857 marked the beginning of the Christian Reformed Church.

60 The correspondent from Macleod was probably Johannes Gunst.

LETTER FROM GEERT VENHUIZEN TO HENDRIK VELDMAN
(25 April 1907)

Leavings, Alberta, Canada
25 April 1907
Dear Friend and future Brother-in-law,[61]

We should have written you long ago, but we always kept putting it off. Today I have time to settle old debts of this kind, because it has been snowing and raining for two or three days so the farm work has to wait for better weather. In addition, spring is already very late. We have had a severe winter and cold, raw, and barren weather the whole spring. So the farm work is far from being done, although it is almost May already. I have seeded 51 acres of wheat and still have to do 28, part of it oats, the rest wheat. I don't know of anything else to write about the farm.

As for family life, we are all in regular good health, except, of course, for some colds. The children are growing well and are full of life and almost endlessly playful. Of course, Hettie often plays master over the others. The little one, of course, cannot play along much yet. They like horseback riding a lot; Hettie is especially eager to go along with me to the field to bring in the horses and then she rides "Sorrel," who is gentle. Ada doesn't like it as much as Hettie; Margaretha is still somewhat afraid of horses and cows. Hettie received home schooling during the winter and with some regularity she is still getting lessons in reading Dutch. She has already made good progress in reading; writing doesn't go so well. But it is not so necessary to teach her that at home; she can learn it at school.[62]

Not the reading of Dutch, of course; this she must learn at home, at least if she is not going to remain ignorant of it. She is five years old and could therefore go to school, but we are keeping her at home for a year yet, both because we live a good distance from school and so that she may have a better opportunity to learn Dutch.[63] If she would go to school now, she would learn

---

61 On 22 June 1907 Hendrik Veldman, a teacher at 't Zandt, married Trijntje Dijkema, a sister of Geert Venhuizen's wife Klaassien and of George Dijkema. Geert Venhuizen was born on a farm at Woltersum, Groningen, in 1876. He wanted to become a minister, but his father insisted that he stay on the farm. In 1898, however, he quietly left with a friend for America and worked in various places, including Texas. In early 1901 he returned to the Netherlands, married Klaassien Dijkema, and in March 1901 the couple immigrated to the United States, first to Maryland and then to the Bozeman-Manhattan area of Montana, where Geert worked for a Dutch farmer and then for a grain elevator at Belgrade. In June 1904 the family moved to Alberta to take up a homestead near Klaassien's brother George Dijkema. The original of this letter is in the possession of Harm Veldman of Ten Post, Groningen.

62 At this time the Venhuizens had four children, Harriet age 5, Ada age 3, Margaretha age 2, and Alice 11 months old.

English there and nothing would come of learning Dutch, because I think learning two languages at once does not go very well for a small child.

A good three weeks ago Anna Mulder arrived here after a good trip, and immediately, on the same day, she married brother-in-law Geert [Dijkema].[64] For a couple of days she was with us; then she moved into her own house. It is going very well with her here, and to begin with, her health is fine. At first she was weary and travelled-out, but a strong man becomes weary from such a trip, so for her it is even less surprising. For Geert it is a big relief to have a wife. The language for Anna is naturally a difficult matter. If she energetically applies herself to learn it, it will, of course, get better, but at first it is annoying not to be able to speak to the neighbours. They have a couple of Hollanders in their vicinity, but most of their neighbours and the closest are Norwegians. As you know, they live five or six miles from us and so we don't get together during the week; but on Sundays they come to us and then we talk about a lot of things before and after the service.

At our home and at a neighbour's, reading services are held in turn on Sunday afternoons,[65] and then during the reading of the sermon I have to deal with the children a lot. Or, better said, I have nothing else to do than to sit dead still in the same position so that I become as stiff "as a door." Because at the beginning I set Ada and Margaretha on each side of me, and as soon as they sit down they fall against me and go to sleep. Then I have to sit still and sort of hold onto them so that they don't tumble off the bench or stool. Hettie can stay awake and take care of herself. On her lap Klaassien has the little one, who pulls on her nose, picks at her hair, sticks a little finger in her mouth, or tears on her hat. So we each have something to deal with.

The Dutch settlement here is not growing fast. The free government land is gone, and those who come here now have to buy land and that will soon run up to $20 an acre. And then quite a bit of capital is required to be able to do that. Opportunities for earning a living here by working out are not at all as good as in Montana, for example, because farmers there are much busier the whole summer due to the irrigation. Since we don't need to do that here we are not so busy in the summer that one man cannot take care of 160 acres by himself. Only during harvest time must one have help for

---

63 The Venhuizens lived over three miles away from Rocky Coulee School.

64 Anna Mulder arrived by train in Macleod and married Geert Dijkema there on 30 March 1907.

65 This letter reveals that separate reading services were regularly held on the west side of the Dutch settlement at the homes of Geert Venhuizen and probably his neighbour Willem Feller. This service was held on Sunday afternoons. Though his wife and family were members of the Christian Reformed Church, Geert was only a "friend" of the church.

a few days if possible; if there is no help, one has to manage on his own as best he can, by working longer hours per day and by spreading the work out over a longer time period, for example, by letting the grain lie in the "swath" until the ripe grain is about ready to take root.

You would meet the following persons in a possible visit to our settlement.[66] [Jan H.] ter Telgte, born at Nijverdal in the province Overijssel, married, has a wife and five children, has an unpleasant and "boorish" appearance and character, associates with none of the Hollanders, and also never comes to church due to a vehement quarrel that he has had with his brother-in-law [Garrit] Willemsen, an elder of the church. Willemsen, is also from Nijverdal, married, has a wife and six children; his elderly father also lives in with him. Of the children Willem is the oldest, twenty years old, can learn well and really likes debating, so he is always at loggerheads with one person or another; has plans to go to Grand Rapids, Mich., a year from this fall to study to become a minister in the Christian Reformed Church. Willemsen himself, a fine elder, is very naïve about almost all business matters, not a bad fellow to live with. His wife is somewhat "bitchy," at least in the house, and acts more or less like his boss.

Willem Feller, from Venhuizen, Noord-Holland, a bachelor, about fifty years old, a good fellow, deacon of the church. This spring he built a new house,[67] and he is expected at some time or another to go to Michigan where he has an "old flame" living, to get married. Albert Lantinga, 24 to 25 years old, a bachelor, from Nieuw Scheemda, where he went through the regular elementary school and the M.U.L.O.[68] A good lad, comes regularly to church although he does not have a church background (former Prime Minister Sam Van Houten is his uncle!);[69] he doesn't talk much, but is somewhat quiet by nature. His brother Roelf, also a bachelor, two or three years older, formerly a non-commissioned officer, talks more than Albert, more boastful, does not like going to church very much, more egoistic.

[Harm] Emmelkamp, 40 years old, married, has a wife and four children, hails from somewhere in the Hoogeland,[70] not very educated, a good worker, a fine farmer, lives right next to us, and we get along well with each other.

---

66 Venhuizen here describes only the Dutch people on the Leavings side of the settlement.

67 Feller earlier lived in a dugout that he dug into the side of a bank; it had a wooden front. His new house was 14 × 28 feet in size.

68 The Meer Uitgebreid Lager Onderwijs was a high school level institution.

69 Sam Van Houten was a prime minister of the Netherlands from 1894 to 1897. He represented the Liberal party and was responsible for an 1896 election reform that expanded the franchise. He is also well known for initiating the 1874 Children's Law that prohibited child labour in factories under the age of twelve.

70 The Hoogeland is a clay-belt region of northeastern Groningen, north of the Dampsterdiep canal.

[Hendrik] ter Telgte, brother of the aforementioned, married, has a wife and four children, lives entirely on his own. A poor worker, he takes life easy. [Lubbert] Van Dellen, 26 to 27 years old, a bachelor, from Burum, a first-class worker, well educated, a good talker. [Rommert] Weerstra, from Sint Jacobi Parochie, married, has a wife and six children, a half-socialist,[71] will have nothing to do with the church and worship, doesn't associate with many people, also because he lives in a somewhat out-of-the-way place, otherwise is well educated and a sociable talker.

Jan Roos, brother-in-law of Emmelkamp, also from the Hoogeland, has a Frisian wife and six children, is not good with language; although he is now still poor he certainly has a future here. Beyond that are people you know, Geert and Anna [Dijkema] and ourselves. That is the total number of Hollanders who live here. Many more are living twelve to fifteen miles east of us, but we do not come into contact much with most of them. We live about in the middle of the western settlement. So you notice that the Hollanders live quite separately from each other. In between us live Canadians, Scots, Norwegians, Swedes, and Belgians. The latter speak Flemish, which however is not easy for us to understand; then we just speak English when we come in contact with these Flemish (Catholics), since they speak and understand it very well.

The land here is prairie which now and then is a bit rolling, but it is almost flat. You come across trees only along streams and rivers. We live a couple of miles from a river. Far to the west you see the snow-crowned peaks of the Rocky Mountains. Twenty to thirty years ago buffaloes flourished around here in countless herds. The horrible slaughters carried out by Indians, half-breeds, and white hunters have exterminated these monarchs of the plains; only far to the north are there a couple of small herds that are protected by the government from total extermination. Now we find only the coyote (prairie wolf) here, an animal the size of a dog, not at all dangerous; only the chickens of the settler are in danger, or young calves, if they are very hungry. There are few rabbits here, but wild geese and ducks are abundant at certain times of the year.

The province of Alberta has 185,000 people (1906 census). How large the province is I don't know, but in any case it is larger than the entire kingdom of the Netherlands. So you see that it is still not overpopulated here; but the population is growing quickly. Immigration to Canada is taking on large dimensions, and the migration is largely to the western provinces, British

---

71 Weerstra as socialist probably refers to adherence to social democratic views.

Columbia, Alberta, Saskatchewan, and Manitoba. Canada now has about six million residents in total.

The provinces of Quebec, Ontario, Nova Scotia, Prince Edward Island, and New Brunswick are already relatively old and heavily populated. And a considerable number of people from these provinces are also making their way to the west. As you know, Quebec (and a part of Ontario as well) is populated by Frenchmen. What the proportion is of the French-speaking part of the total Canadian population compared to the English-speaking portion I do not know; there was certainly a time when the French element was far in the majority. Now that is no longer the case, because the immigrants who now come to Canada, whether English-speaking (English, Scots, Irish, Americans) or others, are assimilated by the English-speaking part of the population. Canada is a bilingual country; French and English stand on equal footing before the law, at least in many respects. The French, however, will slowly be crowded out entirely by the English. And, in my opinion, the French element has itself entirely to blame for this. If the French element (1) had always worked at encouraging emigration from France and Belgium, and (2) had expanded more to the west rather than staying piled up by themselves in the forests of Quebec and Ontario, then this element would have absorbed the immigrants from the other countries of Europe, and then Canada would have become a French-speaking country. Now it is too late for that. The French element now no longer exercises a predominant influence. True, the names of some of the most important men in the political arena are French; thus for example, Sir Wilfred Laurier is prime minister, but with that the most important thing has also been said about the influence of the French element in Canada.

With respect to their populations, Canada and South Africa closely correspond to each other, at least in some respects. Here a powerful party was originally in a commanding position to get the whole population to speak its language, but it failed to take advantage of its dominant position. Over there is also a party[72] that still nowadays finds itself in such favourable circumstances. Time will tell what use this party will make of these circumstances. I now and then fear that it will go the same path there. But I remain hopeful. I will go into this no further now, since I then get on my

---

72 Venhuizen is referring to the Boers of South Africa, who were of Dutch background. He kept abreast of events in the Netherlands by getting a Dutch newspaper, probably the *Nieuwe Provinciale Groninger Courant* to which he had subscribed while living in Montana.

hobby-horse and I would most likely assert things on which you clearly would not agree with me.

We have read in the newspaper, and Trientje has also written us, that next July 1 you will become head of the new school in Ten Post. Hearty congratulations! Considering it is the Netherlands, for once, fortunately, things are going well for you!

It was long ago that you had a letter from us. But this time you are getting a long one. Regarding its contents it is better that I do not comment, but with the length you will be well satisfied.

With greetings,
Your friend G[eert] Venhuizen

LETTER FROM LEAVINGS
(*De Volksvriend,* 9 May 1907)

Last winter a lot of snow fell in our "Sunny Alberta." Already on 15 November the first snow fell and it remained the whole winter. Sometimes it thawed for a couple of days, but then new snow soon came, so you can say that it was on the ground almost the whole winter. Therefore many cows starved to death. You find them lying on the prairie everywhere. But finally winter left us and the sun came to nurse the earth with its friendly beams. The farmers then began seeding, and everything looked very good until we got another snowstorm on 22 April that badly set back the seeding. Yet this snowstorm is very good for the farmers. Everything indicates that we will have a good year again. Some farmers have their wheat seeded, but most had to stop because of the snow.

In the area of church life it is going very well here. Every Sunday we meet at two o'clock. The attendance is very good. This summer we are getting two ministers who will preach the gospel to us, Rev. Bijleveld and Rev. Nagel, and maybe also a student from the Theological School in Grand Rapids.[73]

---

73 At this point the east and west sides of the settlement each held their own reading service on Sundays in a local home. When a visiting pastor or student was available, however, they would worship together for two Sunday services, one week at the Rocky Coulee school, the next at the Finley school. Rev. John Bijleveld was from Edgerton, Minnesota; Rev. Barend Nagel was from Ebenezer, South Dakota. These Christian Reformed pastors were each sent by Classis Orange City to minister to the needs of the Niverdal CRC for two weeks. Student Cornelius Vriesman served for several weeks in July 1907.

The Dutch colony is also expanding gradually, by birth as well as by immigration from Holland. Some weeks ago two young women arrived here in MacLeod from Holland, one of whom married L[ucas] Steenbergen, while the other is married to G[eorge] Dijkema.[74] We wish the young women a happy marriage and much pleasure in this – for them – strange land, and we hope that they will be spared from homesickness. It was a big undertaking for the young women, and so we hope they may feel happy in this foreign land.

At the home of Jan Roos a baby son arrived. Mother and child are very well. Best wishes, Mr. Roos![75]

[George Dijkema][76]

LETTERS FROM ALBERTA
(*Twentsch Volksblad*, 25 May 1907)

In the Nijverdal colony (near Lethbridge in Canada) a men's choir was established, numbering fifteen members. The director is Mr. E[vert] P. M. Aldus. The practices take place on Saturdays.

From a private letter we furthermore take the following:

In our settlement everything is going its usual course. In February the awfully severe cold stopped, and the snow melted. Then we were first busy for more than a month hauling grain to town. Then on 1 April we could begin working on the land. And today I saw that my first seeded wheat is beginning to come up, after lying in the ground for three weeks, thanks to the extra raw, cold spring. I seeded 63 acres of wheat. Now I am busy ploughing oats land.

---

74 This letter may suggest that George Dijkema was no longer the Leavings correspondent. However, it is more likely that Dijkema was simply referring to himself here in the third person. Dijkema married Anna Mulder, and Steenbergen wed Marie Talens. 30 March, the day the young women stepped off the train in Macleod, both couples went to the justice of the peace there and were married.
75 The son born to Jan Roos was their sixth child, Anne, born 16 April 1907.
76 Dijkema sent a similar letter, dated 1 May, to *De Grondwet* (14 May 1907).
77 This mine was at Diamond City, twelve to fifteen miles east of the Dutch community. It opened in 1905.

LETTER FROM EVERT ALDUS
(*Twentsch Volksblad,* 15 June 1907)

In the last months the newspapers told us that severe cold was prevalent this winter and a lot of snow fell in almost every country of Europe and America. Here also we abundantly received our share of it.

On 15 November of last year the first snowstorm came, and after that the winter stayed until 10 February. During almost that whole time the thermometer showed about 40 degrees below zero (Fahrenheit). Snow storms and blizzards followed one another, and the Chinook, which in previous winters visited us every now and then to drive away the snow and frost for a few days, this time let us down.

That such severe weather is very unpleasant is easy to understand, especially in a country like this, because one is then cut off as it were from everything. One does not go outdoors other than to take care of the cattle, and to go haul a little coal or store goods on one of the least cold days. Because none of us had enough coal in stock for such a cold spell that lasted almost three months. Fortunately we did not need to be in want of fuel; about four hours from here a new mine opened last year where we can easily go.[77] To reassure those who think that some of us were half-frozen, I can say that no one had an injury worth mentioning from the cold. Only a young man from Amsterdam was careless enough to walk alone on the prairie. Affected by the snow and his unfamiliarity with the area, he lay down and got his hands and feet frozen. He was tended to in the hospital at Lethbridge.

However, in other areas of America, for example, Saskatchewan and South Dakota, a lot of people froze to death. The snow lay so deep that the trains could not run and supply coal. In such areas it was very common to burn stables, railings, etc. It often happened this winter that two or more families went to live in one house in order to use the empty one for fuel. Also cases were not rare where oats or wheat was burned. In remote parts of the areas mentioned this winter was a life-and-death fight, a struggle against the winter.

In southern Alberta where we live, the cows ranging on the prairie had it very hard. The poor animals walked in long rows from one place to another to find a mouthful of food, which seldom happened since the short grass was buried everywhere under the snow. A sad sight to see such a long, long row of cows walking slowly after each other; living skeletons, with hollow eyes, hunched backs, frozen udders, and cut and bleeding feet from walking in the frozen snow. More than once we saw such a funeral procession (as some of us called it) an hour long. When the animals exhausted by hunger and cold lie down in the evening, there are some that cannot stand up again the following morning. They die slowly, sometimes covered by the falling snow before they are dead. Thousands now lie dead spread over the prairie, sometimes 40 or 50 together. We had a lot of trouble keeping the starved animals away from our farmyard. They broke through everything to get only a handful of straw. Besides, one had to be cautious in chasing them away, since the otherwise not vicious animals now more than once attacked a person. Often they fell down in the attempt, never again to stand up.[78]

On 10 February the cold receded and the Chinook with its mighty breath began to melt the snow. In a few days this changed the look of the whole landscape. Before everything was a monotonous white; now grass and farmland, alternating with large sheets of water. Because the land is rolling, that is, it is not flat but runs slowly up and down so that one point is sometimes forty to fifty feet higher than another that is a quarter of an hour away. This lay of the land contributes much to break the monotony of it. The grain fields that stretch from the valley to the top of the slowly ascending knolls, or lie lengthwise along the valleys, the shacks that are scattered over the heights and in the valleys, the cattle grazing on the slopes all give the landscape a very pleasant look. It all gives the impression, not of the flurried tumult and activity of a city, but of tranquil and calm work. But, to get back to the point in question, because the land is rolling, the water cannot run off and it remains standing in the low places. Thus one of us had a pond that was over 30 acres large on his land; another had to leave his house for a

---

78   Years later Willem Stotyn also described that winter: "He says that the winter of 1906 to 1907 was very severe with heavy snow and cattle from as far north as the Red Deer river had drifted this way from the severe north winds. There was so much snow that it was not possible for these animals to find food and consequently they were near mad from hunger and really dangerous. He says that he had a manure pile and these cattle found it one evening and the next morning the entire pile had been eaten up. A humorous incident was also related such as when two farmers were coming home with a load of hay for their horses. The cattle attacked and they had only time to unhook their team when the cattle were upon them. When they went back the following day not only was their hay gone but the hayrack was completely destroyed from the frantic attempt to get a bite to eat." As told by Jacob Dekker, "Monarch, A Little Bit of Old Holland," *Lethbridge Herald*, 25 June 1955. In later years Jennie Hobbelink, daughter of Willem Van Lohuizen, described how her uncle Jan Van Lohuizen was chased by one of the crazed cows: "There was a little stack of straw against the barn on which he climbed and then onto the roof of the barn, the cow after him. The roof held him, but not the cow, and the animal fell through. He was lucky. We had another neighbor who sat in the outdoor privy nearly all day as there was a wild cow crazy with hunger, and it would not let him out" (*Sons of Wind*, 382). Mary Ronhaar, daughter of Rense Nijhoff, later described her childhood experience of that winter: "I remember when droves of these starving cattle came our way, staggering and bumping against our small house. Dad, axe in hand, stood ready to beat any one of them over the head that might succeed in breaking down the door. When the storm subsided, we could see dead animals dotting the landscape where they had just dropped in their tracks" (*Sons of Wind*, 310).

couple of months because it stood in a couple feet of water.[79] Fortunately the ground absorbed the moisture rather quickly; now most of the water has disappeared.

On 25 February the road dried up enough that we could begin to haul grain to Lethbridge. Till the end of March we were busy with that. In all that time nothing could be done on the land; it froze too hard. On the first of April the work in the field could begin, and one saw the first seeding machine on the land. During that month we could not begin before ten or eleven in the morning because the ground froze every night. Till early May the weather was cold and unfavourable for growing; now it is nice and mild. The wheat is standing nice and green, and oats and potatoes have been seeded and planted. Most people have begun prairie breaking for next year. This spring is better than the last one in one way – there is an abundance of rain so crops have no lack of moisture.

Old friends. Now and then you come across old friends in this land far removed from the Netherlands. Insignificant things sometimes, but no less pleasant when you meet them. In the first place, you see in the stores some things imported from Holland. For example, "Genuine Dutch Gin" in four-sided bottles from the Kuiper firm. Van Houtens Cocoa is also available. One of the stores in Lethbridge even sells Dutch cigars. Alas, they are pretty expensive – 5 cents apiece. And that is cents of the dollar. Some time ago my neighbour came home from town. "Wife," he said, "guess what I brought along." The wife did her best, but she could not guess. And, dear reader, what do you think the man brought home? Yes, don't laugh, then I will tell you. A heath brush. They are sold in one of the stores, something that none of us had found out till that time. How foolish, many a person will say, to be so happy with such a silly thing. But you cannot imagine how many pleasant memories such a barren heath brush can awake. And then, the water. When the thaw suddenly set in in February, large ponds developed. It is hard to believe how attractive and beautiful such a sheet of water is for Hollanders who have not seen them in three years. And when it became warmer in the first days of May, more old friends came out – the frogs. Just as in Holland, every evening and night they gave a concert. And our children, insofar as they were still too small to meddle with frogs when they left Holland, with inquisitive gazes examine how such a green croaker looks, and do their best to catch one of them.

And now some brief news that I will report yet, at the risk of being accused of just bunching together a mix of items, as is usually done in American papers. I will not give the full names, but only write down the first letters.

---

79 The flooded shack may have been that of Aldus himself, since he later mentions moving the shack.

Twins were born to W[illem] J[an] van L[ohuizen], one of whom came into the world stillborn.[80]

The mare of J[ohan] H[uisman] had two nice colts, one of which died after living a day.

When A[rie] K[oole] recently rode home, one of his horses fell down dead in front of the wagon. When he got off to help the animal, it was already dead. It was a horse worth more than $200.

H[endrik] V[eldhuis] is busy building a good house. W[illem] S[totijn] and B[astiaan] K[oole] have likewise built a new little house. E[vert] A[ldus] is getting ready to place his on a large sled and to move it a couple hundred metres with the help of several horses.

J[ohan] H[uisman], H[endrik] V[eldhuis], and E[vert] A[ldus] each bought an additional work horse this spring. W[illem] S[totijn] bought two. J[an] B[annink] and B[erend] N[ijhof] together bought three.

Several weeks ago a Christian men's choir was established. It consists of J[acobus] N[ijhoff], president, B[astiaan] K[oole], secretary, J[an] B[annink], treasurer. E[vert] A[ldus] acts as director. The society presently consists of fifteen members and two aspiring members, young lads under age sixteen. They gather every Saturday evening in a house located at about the centre of the colony.

In April for many of us it was three years ago that we came to Canada and to the homestead. They have now performed the required formalities to get possession of their land.

The number and variety of birds is noticeably increasing. Thus a couple weeks ago for the first time I saw four sparrows hopping on the yard. Also old friends.

A[ldus] Nijverdal (near Lethbridge), 20 May 1907

---

80 The living child was Henrie, born 27 April 1907. He soon died, however, on 10 July.

81 Tijmen Hofman arrived with his wife and ten children in May 1907. He had earlier come to see the area in late 1906.

82 Rutgers had immigrated to Alberta from Nijverdal in March 1905. He claimed a homestead in July of that year but did not take up residence there until June 1907. Because of illness, he spent some time at Brandon, Manitoba, and he also worked in Lethbridge for a while.

83 Besides Cornelius Vriesman, student Nicholaas Dijkema was expected to visit the Alberta settlement in June, but he died before he arrived.

84 With this item a new correspondent appears in *De Grondwet*. He is reporting on a new group of Dutch families who settled south of the Oldman River east of Macleod. Abel and Walter Vander Burgh and George Schuitema were the first Dutchmen to settle there in 1905.

85 Jacob Leeuwerik bought this land in 1906, but then continued farming at Hull, Iowa, until the family moved to Alberta in 1909.

LETTER FROM LETHBRIDGE
(*De Grondwet,* 25 June 1907)

People may well think that the correspondent from Lethbridge has moved, but such is not the case. Busyness and circumstances sometimes make it difficult to write. Now, we have beautiful warm weather here, combined with rain, so there is a beautiful stand of grain and crops. We cannot wish for better. Also, the flax is as good as in, and we have never seen better grass than what we have this year, so the cattle need not suffer shortage.

Now and then more Hollanders come to this colony. Three or four weeks ago T[ijmen] Hofman arrived here from Westfield, North Dakota, with his family; he bought a section of land near our Dutch people.[81] Also, four [men] have come from the Netherlands, G[errit] Harthoren [Hartkoorn], P[aul] Vanden Berg, F[rans] Vanden Berg, and C[ornelis] Kamp. They are all very pleased to be here, although at first it seemed somewhat strange to them to see such a vast prairie without trees or bushes.

At L[eendert] Bode's place they are busy drilling a well. They say they found water at a depth of 90 feet.

T[hys] Dekker is back from his short trip to Humboldt, Iowa.

Arie Koole lost a very good workhorse.

B. Beagle has become a real estate agent and is going to live in town.

Albert Rutgers is once again in our midst.[82]

In the area of church life it is also going pretty well here. The attendance is satisfying. We hope soon to see a minister once again in our midst. We also expect two students here this summer, so distant Sunny Alberta has not been forgotten.[83]

Corr. 11 June 1907

LETTER FROM MACLEOD
(*De Grondwet,* 16 July 1907)[84]

The crops here are doing exceptionally well. The winter wheat is already headed out, and every now and then we receive timely rain.

On the land of Jake Leeuwerik 100 acres is now broken, and his spring wheat promises a good harvest.[85]

Jan Vaale has moved his stable near his house. Piet van der Burgh filled up a well, before something fell into it.

Abel Van der Burgh has tamed "broncos" with his neighbour for the first time.

Last Saturday John Gunft [Gunst] went to the other side of the river. There he visited many of the other Hollanders.

Prairie breaking is again done for this season.

Dick Selmen has again drilled for water, but has still not succeeded in finding it near his house.

A school district was formed here, and now a school will be built soon.

We hope to see the new Lethbridge-MacLeod railway line completed next winter. Rumor has it that a beginning on it will soon be made, from MacLeod.[86]

The price of land here is going up. Now it is already $15 and higher. Every day you see more land being fenced in.

A Reader

LETTER FROM MACLEOD
(*De Grondwet,* 10 September 1907)

The Hollanders here are in a very good mood, and no wonder, because the harvest is excellent. They are busy hauling grain. The wheat harvest is requiring 3 to 3½ pounds of "twine" per acre.

The newly seeded [winter] wheat is already above the ground and is doing well.

Adam Drost, who lived in town, has moved to his homestead.

George Schuitema and three Canadians have bought a threshing machine. He is also going to build a large granary.

Dick Selmen found abundant water near his house at a depth of fourteen feet. So has Piet Van der Burgh, but he had to go somewhat deeper.

In October L[ucas] Steenbergen is expecting his brother-in-law, who is coming over here from Holland to buy land and to farm.[87]

Next month a beginning will be made on building a school in the Big Bend district.

A Reader

---

86 The CPR railway line connecting Lethbridge with Macleod was completed in 1909.
87 Steenbergen's brother-in-law was Jan Tersteeg, who immigrated with his wife Jenneken from North Holland.
88 Since the Nijverdal CRC was part of Classis Orange City, this Classis arranged for occasional visits by pastors to outlying Dutch settlements like that in southern Alberta. Rev. John Bijleveld from Edgerton, Minn., visited in June, Rev. Barend Nagel from Ebenezar, S. Dak. in August, and Rev. Henry Haarsma from

LETTER FROM LETHBRIDGE
(*De Grondwet,* 19 November 1907)

Once again we will send some news from Sunny Alberta. The whole summer we had beautiful weather here; only, in September we had a snowstorm, which, however, caused little damage since most of the grain was already cut.

Last time I wrote about others, but now I can tell of myself; this year I harvested 40 bushels of wheat per acre, and the crop is running from 30 to 48 bushels per acre. So that is not so bad.

This summer the Classis has also been good to us, because first we had Rev. Bijleveld in our midst, then student Vriesman for several weeks, then Rev. Nagel, and finally Rev. Gaarsma [Haarsma].[88] In the area of church life things are also improving here. A committee has been apponted to buy a ten-acre piece of land for a church and parsonage in the middle of our settlement, so that we may have our own minister as soon as possible.[89]

Corr. 1 November 1907

LETTER FROM GERRIT HARTKOORN[90] TO JAN BODE
[December 1907]

Dear Brother-in-law[91] and children,

At the writing of this letter we are still experiencing, because of the Lord's goodness, a large measure of good health, and that is our prayer and hope for you people too. Now you will surely say, is there really a letter? I plead guilty; I promised to write you. On the one hand I now know more about the country.

Lebanon, Iowa in October. Student Cornelius Vriesman had just finished his second year at the Christian Reformed Theological School in Grand Rapids.

89 The committee to purchase land for a church was a committee of the east side of the Dutch settlement, consisting of Leendert Bode, Jan Postman, and Jan Geleynse. The east side would build a church in their midst in early 1909. At the same time the west side made plans to build their own church, also completed in early 1909.

90 Gerrit Hartkoorn was forty-nine when he immigrated to Alberta in May 1907. He left his wife and children behind in Rotterdam. He was related to the Leendert Bode and Frans Vanden Berg Sr. families in the southern Alberta settlement. Later, in late 1909 Gerrit returned to the Netherlands to fetch his wife and sons Arie and Barend. Together they returned to Alberta in March 1910, but within a month they took up homesteads at Hodgeville, Saskatchewan.

91 The brother-in-law to whom Hartkoorn is writing is Jan Bode of Noordeloos, a brother of his wife Jabikje.

Now I will write something about Leen's [Leendert Bode's] family.[92] He still has a fifteen-year-old boy Leen [Leendert] at home and a twelve-year-old girl Geertje, and a girl Cori [Cornelia] who was married this summer to A. Kool [Arie Koole] who lives nearby. His other daughter Janige [Jannigje] is also married to J[ohannes] Gunst, who lives two or three hours from here.[93] They have two children. The men are farmers; each has 160 acres of land. And then there is Gerrit who lives nearby and also is married. They have three children. And Teunis also lives near his father. From Leen to Gerrit is a twenty minute walk and to Teunis the same distance. Maria lives in Chicago. She has three children and her husband [Everett Dudley] one, so that makes four.

Now I will begin again with Leen. This month it is two years ago that he came here. Then he took up a homestead, that is, a farmstead of 160 acres for 10 dollars (25 Dutch guilders). That land he is now farming. The first year he grew 1,100 bushels of oats. Already the second year he had 60 acres in grain, from which he threshed close to 1,700 bushels, and 20 acres of oats, from which he had over 800 bushels. And 250 bushels of potatoes. Now his livestock. He has twelve horses and this summer he milked six cows. But now he has only three. We butchered the others; he sold one that weighed 617 pounds for 6 cents a pound. Late this summer he bought another 160 acres of land for $15 an acre, so now he has 160 acres in front of his house and 160 behind. Also, he has machinery and ploughs, and he rides a nice buggy, as you can see on this card. And he has a wagon. Here you always ride with two horses, and with four or six horses to plough. Such work is manageable here. One man works 160 acres of land. You may say this is not possible. But it is always done with horses; it is not worked by hand as in Holland.

Now about Teunis and Gerrit [Bode]. They came here a year earlier. Each has a homestead, that is, 160 acres. Gerrit raised over 2,100 bushels of grain besides his oats, and Teunis 2,400 bushels and 900 bushels of oats. And the three of them also have 230 bushels of flax. They are busy shipping [their grain]. The prices were 89 cents a bushel, but now just in the seventies. You can figure out how much money these young men make. The oats was 50 cents, but now much less The flax price has been $1.09, but now 80 cents a bushel. Now Teunis has also bought another 160 acres next to his land and

92 Leendert Bode was a brother of Gerrit Hartkoorn's wife Jabikje. Leendert and part of his family moved to the Alberta settlement from Vesper, Wisc., in December 1905, but his sons Gerrit and Teunis had arrived already in November 1904.
93 Johannes Gunst farmed his homestead south of the Oldman River near Macleod.

next to Leen's land that lies in front of his house, also for $15 an acre. I also ventured to do that.[94] We have each sent $360; $120 [is due] over one year and then $300 the following year. We can pay it over ten years. There is another piece with 160 acres between us. It lies next to Leen's land. They say I have the best land of all. Then this week Gerrit also sent $360. If he gets that land, we'll be next to each other. Now, Jan, if you come quickly, you too can still get one or two pieces there. It is excellent land. The land here is going fast.

They are busy laying a railway line, and there is talk that they may build a village nearby.[95] As you well know, we already quickly had a homestead, but we gave it up again.[96] It was so hilly that it could hardly be ploughed. With this land I am pleased, because it lies close to Leen and the boys and is here in a Dutch settlement. Frans [Vanden Berg] and the boys now also have a homestead no less than 100 miles from here – three miles is an hour – and then among all sorts of people.[97] We live here twenty miles from the city of Lethbridge, but if the new town is built, then it'll be only seven or eight miles away.

Now, dear brother-in-law, I think rather often about those young Hollanders who stay there, because there is so much room here. Because I have now seen so much of Canada, I know you can always make a good living here with the blessing of the Lord, and there is a future for your children. Now I don't want to exaggerate. Life here is very different than in Holland – it's much quieter and lonelier. And as for church life, it's a sad thing that they are overly pious here and everything is just fine. I've often said I do not believe that there is one child of God living here. I have already laughed about it. It seems like such a make-believe play.[98] Enough of that.

Now I will still inform you that Gerrit and his family have made a trip to his wife's parents in Wisconsin[99] – that is 1,300 miles from here – and to Maria in Chicago and at the same time to Hendrik [Bode].[100] That little trip

---

94 Gerrit bought a quarter of land (NW 33-10-23 W4) nearby Gerrit Bode's homestead.

95 This is the future town of Monarch.

96 Gerrit Hartkoorn, Paul and Frans Vanden Berg Jr., and Cornelis Kamp had immigrated together to Canada in May 1907, and each took up homesteads on a section about twenty miles northeast of the Dutch settlement, but in September 1907 all four men abandoned them.

97 Frans Vanden Berg Sr.'s wife Klaasje was a sister of Gerrit Hartkoorn. This family had immigrated to the Dutch settlement in Alberta in 1907, their sons Paul and Frans Jr. in May 1907 with Gerrit Hartkoorn. Frans and his sons each took up homesteads south of Burdett, Alberta, in November 1907.

98 Gerrit had been part of the Gereformeerde churches in the Netherlands, but in Canada he did not join an organized Reformed church. He practiced private worship at home.

99 There they visited the Klaas Van Schuur family in Vesper, Wisc.

100 Hendrik Bode was another brother of Gerrit Hartkoorn's wife Jabikje. His family lived in South Holland on the south side of Chicago.

is costing him over $100. Jannigje and her husband [Johannes Gunst] are taking care of the cows and horses for two months. Now they are here too. And this week Teunis bought a nice buggy, as you see here. So Gerrit and Leen and Teunis each have one. You can see that these folks are having a good year. And as I see it, Teunis will soon be married. He is busy courting a Dutch girl.[101] Like us, her father [Tijmen Hofman] arrived here this spring. He bought a whole section (4 times 160 acres) for $16 an acre, and he took up a homestead. Thus he now has 5 times 160 acres of land. You may think that cannot be worked. One piece of 160 is a small farm, they say here, and each 160 acres is 64¼ hectares in Dutch measurement. These people came from Dakota, but they are actually Frisians.[102]

You will probably say, you write everything so confusedly. That's true. I also want to write yet that one of Hendrik's daughters is also living in Canada 300 miles farther than we do here.[103] I have already had a letter from there asking whether or not I wanted to come there, but it is so cold and the winter is too long there. They live 2,000 miles from her father. They live in the city of Edmonton, the capital of Alberta. As long as I've been here, Leen and Hendrik have not corresponded.

And now something else. You will ask, what have you done this summer? First, I pretty much wandered around here, worked with Leen and the boys, and then I hired myself out to a dairy farmer at Macleod for $30 a month, the second month $35, the third month also $35. That month I was there only a week when Teunis and Gerrit wrote asking whether I would come there for the harvest time. I did so gladly, because with that farmer everything was English; that language is quite a pain. Then I earned $40 a month, and I threshed for almost three weeks; I got $2.50 a day and board everywhere. Then I was with Teunis again for a week or so. And now I have hired myself out again for two months for $15 a month to people who have also gone to Wisconsin. Now I have to take care of four horses and thirty chickens. I am now living on their farm and get good food with it.

---

101 This relationship did not last, because Teunis Bode married Pauline DeBeeld on 10 August 1909.
102 Actually Tijmen Hofman had originally come from Doornspijk in Gelderland. A letter from Westfield, N.Dak. in *De Volksvriend* (11 April 1907) reported that "T[ijmen] Hofman is going to leave us and will become a subject of King Edward of England. After a public auction on the 9th he is going to Alberta, Canada. He sold his quarter of land to a Russian for $4,500, buildings of little or no value." A later letter from Westfield (*De Volksvriend*, 9 May 1907) noted that "Tieme Hofman is ready to step on the train with his family to begin the 'trek' to Alberta, Canada."
103 This was Maggelje Bode, married to Frederik Baron. In 1906 they moved from Farmington, Mont. to Edmonton and were one of the first Dutch families there.
104 This makes it clear that Gerrit's family did not wish to accompany him to Canada. It was only three years later that they finally came.

Now, brother-in-law, I have already explained so many things that I may now write you from the bottom of my heart. To my mind I have it good here, and we get along well with each other, but one thing I do not like is living so separated from my wife and children. That bitterness is not outweighed by the sweet, because I firmly believe that with the Lord's blessing we would have a good living here and a good future for our children. There is not one letter in which I can notice that they are inclined to come, and yet I still hope.[104] Now, dear brother-in-law, I must end. Be so good as to write soon. I long from the heart for you people. Give greetings to the family from all of us here, and hearty greetings from me,

G[errit] Hartkoorn

I will write the address above.
[At top of page:] Mr. L. Bode, G. Hartkoorn, Lethbridge, Alberta, Canada, Box 7333.

LETTER FROM EVERT ALDUS
(*Twentsch Volksblad,* 21 December 1907)

1907 is speeding to an end. Before the year concludes, I want to report briefly on something about the past summer.

After a very long and extra cold winter, we had a late and cold spring. The field work could begin only by April 1, and for many days after that one could not begin before ten or eleven in the morning because the top soil froze at night.

The summer was characterized by few hot days, a lot of rain, night frosts in every month, and little wind. We were spared of hailstorms. In September, we were cutting on a Monday in the most beautiful summer weather, but it began to snow the following morning and continued for two and a half days. It is anything but pleasant to be transferred in this way from summer to winter. Binders and grain, all under the snow.

After the storm the still standing wheat and oats lay flat on the ground, and when the snow melted, it could only be cut from one direction, which goes very slowly. After being threshed this grain seemed to be much poorer in quality. But we did not have a lot of damage from it. We were almost finished cutting when the snow fell; a few of us were already done.

The frost which followed the snow did no damage. The potatoes, vegetables, grain, etc., were saved from freezing by the coat of snow. The rest of

September and October had nice weather, but in November the Chinook wind seemed to want to get in its damage. Day and night it stormed like mad and made things very difficult for us.

In spite of the not very favourable weather that caused crop failure in many parts of America, we got very favourable results. Potatoes and vegetables grew in abundance, the wheat was exceptionally good, and oats also produced a good yield. If you take into account the better prices that we have been getting for wheat till now (the wheat price fluctuates between 76 and 90 cents a bushel; last year it was between 52 and 58), it is sufficiently evident that this has been an exceptionally favourable year for us. The night frosts in August did a lot of damage to the wheat in some places; but in our settlement only a little. In Nijverdal alone (the colony near Lethbridge), taken in round figures, 39,000 bushels of wheat were harvested. Calculated at 75 cents a bushel, this has a value of $29,250.

I am not so well acquainted with the yields in the colonies at Leavings and Macleod, so I can give no information about it. The persons hailing from Nijverdal in Holland who now live in Nijverdal near Lethbridge – J[acobus] N[ijhoff], E[vert] A[ldus], W[illem] S[totijn], J[ohan] H[uisman], H[endrik] V[eldhuis], [Gerrit] J[an] W[ithage], R[ense] N[ijhoff], J[an] B[annink], and B[erend] N[ijhof] – together had about 16,000 bushels of wheat, which calculated at 75 cents a bushel has a value of about $12,000. Of course, the price can fall; till now 75 cents is not considered too high.

Everyone will understand that this prosperity very much delights us and stands us in good stead, after the hard years that are past. When this wheat is delivered, most will have their land, horses and other cattle completely paid off, as well as all their machines and tools, or have an amount of debt left that is of little significance compared with the value of their farm. That one meets "contented faces" everywhere is understandable. Prosperity comes fast. The question, "What shall we eat or drink?" worries no single housewife. Everyone has fat pigs or a cow to butcher, or can buy meat. The shortage of clothes has also stopped this fall. Houses are being enlarged or improved, while some of the sod stables have made place to fine wooden buildings.

Some of us have bought additional land. One bought two 160-acre pieces, others 160 acres, and others 80. This land is sold by the railway company for $15 an acre, to be paid in 8 annual installments. Jan Van Lohuizen went back to Holland this summer. He sold his farm to J. [Gerrit Jan] Withage for $4,500. In the sale some horses were included, a set of machinery, buildings, wire fences, the grain standing in the field, etc. It is clear that J. Van Lohuizen made a pretty penny in these few years. Yet, the general feeling is that the land was not too expensive, since the horses and machinery, etc., were included in the sale, and, according to what I heard, the buyer has threshed about 1,700 bushels of wheat from there as well as a little oats.

The highest yield of wheat was 47 bushels per acre. The average, I think, was about 28.

Three threshing machines worked in the colony. One with steam, one with gasoline, and one with twelve horses for power. Those of us who had their grain threshed first have brought almost all of it away, but those whose turn was last are just beginning to haul. In view of the approaching winter they are very badly off. The thresher, however, cannot be everywhere at once. It also happens sometimes that the elevators (grain storehouses) in Lethbridge and Leavings are full, because the railway line cannot place enough railway cars at their disposal. In that case the farmer has a compulsory rest for a few days. Hauling grain to town always remains hard work for man and horses. Usually we leave at about three to four o'clock in the morning and are then at Lethbridge at about ten or eleven, and go back in the afternoon. One can also go one day and come back the next. But this brings the expense of staying overnight for both man and horses. Usually one can go only three times a week. In this period of grain hauling sometimes almost the whole colony is in Lethbridge. That a cheerful tone prevails when we have a noon meal together in the hotel goes without saying. Some have two, others three, and others four horses on the wagon.

When the road is good (that is, dry) we carry from 3,000 to 9,000 pounds, depending on the number and size of the horses. If we did not have to cross the river bottom with its very steep hills before Lethbridge, we could carry much heavier loads.

That we long for the new railway is obvious. They are working on the bridges, so there is a beginning. Yet the farms of two of us, J[acobus] N[ijhoff] and E[vert] A[ldus], are being cut in two by the line, which is not so pleasant for the persons involved.

This summer was exceptionally good for breaking sod. Almost all of our homesteads were converted into farmland. And, if everything succeeds next year as well as this year, there will be even more grain.

The whole summer there was an abundance of work for wages of $2 to $2.50 a day. So Nijverdalers in Holland, if they had been able to take a peek, would have seen [Frederikus] Kamperman Sr. busy helping to empty the grain wagons in the barns, when the thresher was at work, while his son [Gerrit Jan] covered with dust and chaff threw sheaves in the machine or onto the wagons. Anyone who wants work now no longer has to stand in need of work.

With this I will end. In a future piece I hope to tell something about other things than just the material I was exclusively occupied with in the preceding.

A[ldus]   Nijverdal near Lethbridge, 23 Nov. 1907

LETTER FROM MACLEOD
(*De Grondwet*, 31 December 1907)

We are having nice weather, with almost no frost. The roads are good and the farmers are busy hauling grain. Wheat is up today to 75 cents a bushel, and oats 1¼ cents a pound; butter is 40 cents a pound, and eggs are 35 cents a dozen.

Mr. and Mrs. Peter Van der Burgh are on a visit to Iowa.

John Tersteeg has arrived here from Holland. He is already busy building on the land that he bought. Jake Leeuwerik, from Hull, Iowa, bought another quarter section. The land (160 acres) that he bought last year is already broken up.

Jan Gunst is now on the farm of J. [Gerrit] Bode, who is on a visit to Wisconsin. John Koole and Abel Van der Burgh are taking it easy on the farm of P[ieter] Van der Burgh, now that they have water on the yard.

On Sunday December 15 there was a fire again in MacLeod, on Main Street.

A Reader 24 Dec. 1907

LETTER FROM LETHBRIDGE
(*De Grondwet*, 7 January 1908)

Till now the weather has been beautiful. The cattle are still roaming around outside like in the summer, and that at this time of the year. A proof that it is still not very wintry here. We've had a little snow, but it has disappeared again.

On the Second Day of Christmas we had a celebration in the schoolhouse, which is too small for such occasions because many had to stand due to lack of places to sit.[105] The men's choir also gave a performance and the organ of Mr. Aldus came in very handy.

The Nijverdal congregation held a congregational meeting and they discussed the building of a church.[106] A petition for that purpose made the rounds, and pledges were widely made. The building will be 24 × 36 feet in size and 14 feet high. On 1 January people are meeting again to discuss a parsonage.

Gerrit Bode is making a pleasure trip to Vesper, Wisconsin, and is visiting his relatives there.[107] Teunis Bode bought a brand new buggy.

Grain hauling was stopped for a time due to snow and the elevator was full, but now everything is in full swing again. Prices are also good; wheat is 86 cents, eggs 45 cents a dozen, and butter 45 cents a pound.

Almost everyone here arrived with little or no money, and now you hear from most that they bought another 100 [160] acres of land, others a half-section.

They are still busy building the new railroad bridge.[108]

Corr. 28 Dec. 1908 [1907]

LETTER FROM NAN DEKKER TO THE HELDER FAMILY
(3 January 1908)

Lethbridge, Alberta, Canada
3 January 1908
Dear Family Helder,[109]

I am sitting down to answer your letter. First of all I can tell you that we are all quite well, although the older we become the worse we get. My wife

---

105 In the Netherlands *Tweede Kerstdag*, 26 December, was a holy day that usually included a morning worship service and a Christmas program for children. The celebration on the east side was held in the Rose Butte schoolhouse, which opened in the spring of 1905.

106 A separate congregational meeting of the east side of the Nijverdal congregation was held on 17 December 1907 to discuss a church building.

107 A letter from Vesper, Wisc., dated 4 March 1908, reports that "Gerrit Bode and family, from Lethbridge, Canada, were here this winter to visit their parents" (*De Grondwet*, 17 March 1908). Mrs. Bode's parents were Klaas and Jannetje Van Schuur.

108 The new railroad bridge being built was the high level bridge over the Oldman River at Lethbridge.

109 The Helder family lived in Spring Valley, N.Y. They were friends with whom Nan Dekker and his wife Tryntje had stayed briefly when they immigrated to the United States in 1901. The Dekkers then settled at Vesper, Wisc., before coming to Alberta in the spring of 1905, when Nan was sixty-eighty. Their sons Thys and Arie had come earlier to homestead in 1904. The originals of this letter and the other Dekker letters of 29 November 1909 and 16 September 1910 are in the possession of Nancy Zigenis of Pt. Reyes Station, Calif.

has had a pretty good summer, but now with the winter she always has something. We had a very nice summer here, rain at the right time, a lot of grass, and also the grain was very good. We grew two thousand bushels of wheat, and we have sold nine hundred of it, for which we received $750. The potatoes are very tasty here.

Just received a letter from Jan Groot in Holland, and he wrote that he had been at my brother Jan in Valkoog and found him in poor health. The doctor said he has gallstones. He can no longer eat or digest anything. Then I am the only one left of the twelve children.

I'm sure you have already heard that the burgomaster of St. Maarten, Blom, is dead, and that Abram Klerk has now become burgomaster of St. Maarten.[110]

We do not get much rain here in the fall, and also in the winter. The last rain we had was in August. In September it snowed one day and night and also froze. The garden fruits and vegetables were all frozen. Yet we now have a mild winter here, little snow, and no severe cold so far.

The land here is being sold at a high price, because many people from America and other countries are coming to buy land.

They are going to build a church a mile from us, and place a graveyard right by the church. They bought ten acres from the government.[111] And two hours away from us there is going be a railway line, and also a stop that will be very convenient for us.[112] Now we have to bring everything to Lethbridge, and we live fourteen miles away.[113] They are already building the bridge at Lethbridge.

We had a big Christmas celebration here. All the children had a celebration in the school. We made the chocolate. There was a big organ in the school. Many married people were also at the program. It lasted from ten in the morning till five in the evening. The school stands three minutes from us, on my land, as you know.[114]

If the weather is good tomorrow, Thys and Arie are going to Lethbridge. Hearty greetings from us, and a Happy New Year to you all.

N[an] Dekker
T[ryntje] Strijbis

110 Nan Dekker had earlier been the burgomaster of this village in the province of Noord-Holland.
111 The proposed church building was to serve the Christian Reformed people on the east side of the settlement. The parcel of land that was purchased was the southwest corner of a school section (SW 29-10-23 W4).
112 This railway line from Lethbridge to Macleod was completed in 1909. The stop became the village of Monarch. It was about four miles from Nan Dekker's farm, thus about two hours by foot.

LETTER FROM GRANUM, ALBERTA
(*De Grondwet,* 14 January 1908)

Perhaps there are people who think that in Granum (formerly Leavings)[115] nothing much special is happening. That is true. Everything is taking its usual course. Most farmers, who did not do so last fall, are hauling grain. Now a surprising amount of grain is shipped to Winnipeg. The prices there are a little higher than here. One can haul heavy wagonloads since the roads are nice. Last year at this time the roads were bad; then we had almost seven weeks of winter, cold weather and snow. But at present there is little snow and the thermometer only now and then drops below the freezing point. Only twice did it drop below zero, one time 2 and the other time 8 degrees below. It is amazingly nice winter weather. Yesterday I even saw two of our Hollanders lounging on the sidewalk chatting while a third stood by, and that on 3 January. A correspondent from Montana wrote lately that in order to have nice winter weather you do not have to go to California; you can come to him in Montana.[116] I would say: "You can just as well come to our 'sunny Alberta.'" But all jesting aside, it is beautiful winter weather and the roads are as hard and dry as you could wish. The cows and horses are roaming around calmly grazing on the prairie that is still open. Though last winter cattle died of hunger in great numbers, now that is out of the question since there is no snow.

The Hollanders here are all prosperous, and most no longer have enough with 160 acres of land and have bought an additional half or whole section.[117] Ja, our Alberta is good. The crops are excellent this year, but the snowstorm of 10 September did a good deal of damage at many places. So we got less grain from an acre and the quality was lower. Yet we are well satisfied, since prices are high, and although the wheat is not as good as last year, the prices make up the difference.

Corr. [George Dijkema] 4 Jan. 1908

---

113 Actually Lethbridge was about 19 miles from the Dekker farm.
114 This was the Rose Butte school.
115 On 1 October 1907 the town's name was changed from Leavings to Granum.
116 The comment of the Manhattan correspondent appeared in the 17 December 1907 issue of *De Grondwet.*
117 The additional land bought by homesteaders was mostly C & E Railroad land that was available for sale between homestead sections.

LETTER FROM EVERT ALDUS

(*Twentsch Volksblad*, 29 February 1908)

Our Christmas Celebration

As in previous years, we again celebrated Christmas with the children of the Sunday school. Though celebrating with the children was the main purpose, it cannot be denied that this celebration also gave the adults a pleasant day. Almost everyone, young and old, married and unmarried, comes to the school building for such an occasion.[118] The school was then pretty well filled with people. The celebration was held completely in the Dutch manner. There was story telling to the children and singing with them, while chocolate, buns, and all sorts of pastries, etc., were plentifully shared with everyone present. The children each received a little Christmas book to take along home. The men's choir sang some pieces, which, in the judgment of many, were performed rather well.

One of our people who bought himself an organ made it available that day to accompany the community singing.[119] Some pieces, played by one of us on the violin with organ accompaniment, gave the adults some amusement. I think I can freely say that our Christmas celebration gave pleasure to everyone present, and that there was not only plenty of eating and drinking, but also a sufficient change from business to pleasure for the spirit.

As I said, such a celebration bore a Dutch character. Yet there are some things that remind you that you are in a foreign land. So, for example, some children recited a little verse in the English language. They are the ones who went to school in America and have learned to read and write only in English. All costs were paid from voluntary community contributions. Although the Sunday school originates with the [Christian] Reformed church, the Christmas celebration is something in which the others also participate, that is, it is a more general celebration. Everyone contributes and takes part, and also the children who do not go to the Sunday school receive their little book.

Compared to that of a year ago, this Christmas celebration in many ways gave the impression of improvement and growing prosperity on the material level. Also on another level something was achieved – our men's choir is an example.

Earlier I already mentioned that there is an American [Christian] Reformed church or congregation here. Worship services are led by one of the elders in the school. Some time ago the Christian Reformed people decided to build their own church building. For that purpose a pledge list was presented to all inhabitants of the colony.

From what I have heard, on the list are contributions of more than $100 from one person. As can be expected, the members of the church are contributing the most; but also some from a different persuasion have promised a contribution. I heard that the land is already bought and they will soon begin with the building. If I am well informed, they intend to call a minister as soon as possible jointly with the congregation at Leavings, where a church is also being built.[120]

During the past summer the Christian Reformed congregation was repeatedly visited by a minister or student from another part of America.[121] This is a "vacant" congregation where, as much as possible, they are supplied for their services with ministers from other congregations. This, however, is not as easy as in Holland in such a case. Thus one of the students who preached here last summer came from Grand Rapids, Michigan – more than 2,000 miles or 700 hours away. A trip that costs more than $100 alone on the train. One of the ministers came from 1,500 miles or 500 hours away, and the counselor of the congregation lives 400 miles away in Montana.[122] From the above it is clear that the Christian Reformed Churches are doing quite a lot if they send a speaker here several times.

Now a few words about our men's choir. It was established in the spring of 1907. Good progress was made in spite of the unfavourable circumstances one experiences here regarding such things. First of all, the distances. There are some who are an hour away from the meeting place. Then there is little time. As long as the ground is not frozen, one is always busy. Therefore during the summer we meet on Saturday evenings, from eight to ten o'clock. An attempt to come together on Sundays was a failure. Those who attend go to church, and there is catechism and Sunday school outside the time of services. And some young people have to visit on Sundays, which they are loathe to put aside in favour of singing. During threshing time there can be no singing; the [threshing] machine works late, and a number of neighbours are busy at work there. Also with grain hauling, there are often too many who go to town on Saturdays to have singing in the evening. Yet, in spite of all these difficulties, our choir has kept its head above the water, and we hope it will do so long after this.

---

118 This celebration was held in the Rose Butte school.

119 It was Aldus who had the organ.

120 On 22 October 1907, the west end of the congregation decided to purchase land and solicit pledges for a church building there.

121 The Nijverdal CRC received visits from Rev. J. Bijleveld of Edgerton, Minn., Rev. B. Nagel of Ebenezar, S.Dak., Rev. H. Haarsma of Lebanon, Iowa, and seminary student C. Vriesman.

122 The counselor of the Nijverdal Christian Reformed Church was Rev. J. Holwerda of Manhattan, Mont.

On 1 January 1908, the number of Hollanders, young and old, numbered about 200. Including parents and children, about 80 belong to the (Christian) Reformed church, as far as I can trace. For the most part the others are Dutch Reformed.[123]

Among our Dutch settlers here you find those who were earlier, before coming to America: a farmer, carpenter, shoemaker, cigar maker, factory worker, linen-draper, baker, tailor, engineer, butcher, also a former officer in the navy, a theological student from the school at Kampen,[124] a teacher,[125] a non-commissioned cavalry officer,[126] the cargo-master of the station at Johannesburg in the Transvaal, and a station-master from the same country. Both of these Hollanders left there during or after the [Boer] war and came here.[127] Though position and status were different earlier, here everyone is the same, and most have well grasped that in America "work and persistence pave the way to prosperity."

Before ending, I want to say that so far this winter we've had exceptionally nice mild weather. Up to the 24th of January no snow fell, so everyone has brought most or all of their grain to Lethbridge. Since 24 January there has been a little snow, but it is not yet very cold. So to this day the winter is just as favourable for us as the past summer.

A[ldus]   Nijverdal near Lethbridge, 2 Feb. 1908

LETTER FROM LEENDERT BODE TO JAN BODE
(7 February 1908)

Lethbridge, 7 Feb. 1908
Dear Brother and Family,

Since I am taking up the pen once again to write you a letter, first I will let you know that, by the Lord's goodness, we are still experiencing good health, and we heartily hope and wish the same for you too. Ja, brother, again it's a long time ago that I wrote a letter to you, and yet I realize that you shrug off

---

123 Persons from a Hervormde church background in the Netherlands usually joined the (Dutch) Reformed Church when they came to North America. A congregation of this denomination was established at Monarch in 1909.
124 George Dijkema had studied theology at the Theological School at Kampen, but was dismissed for drunkenness.
125 Evert Aldus had been a teacher at the Christian school in Nijverdal.
126 Roelf Lantinga had served in the Dutch cavalry.
127 In 1897 Gerard Schuitema had immigrated to South Africa and worked for the railway there. Later he returned to the Netherlands.

writing more than I do. I sent my last letter to you on 28 Feb. 1907, and I still have no answer. So it's your turn to write first, but I will yield once again.

We've had a mild winter so far. It's a big difference from last winter when we had a pretty severe winter here. Now and then we have a little snow with a bit of frost. Apart from that the weather is nice every day.

A few days ago you must have had a letter from brother-in-law G[errit] Hartkoorn. He is really in his element here. Perhaps you noticed that in his letter. He's become more than 10 years younger here. The only difficulty he now has is whether his wife and their two unmarried sons will come yet. It's too bad they can't decide. Here they could have a good living together. He bought a nice 160 acres of land near here.

The other five Hollanders from Rotterdam – three Vanden Bergs and two others[128] – also think they have it good here. They are earning a lot of money, working on the railway bridge at Lethbridge. The three Vanden Bergs earn about $10 a day; the other two are each earning $2.50 a day. These folks each have a homestead, but a long ways away – about seventy miles from here. How the land is there, I don't know. They say it is nice land, but there are no Hollanders living there yet.

Teunis and Gerrit and I each bought another 160 acres. Perhaps Hartkoorn wrote about that. Gerrit and his wife and three children have been on a trip for about two months about 1,400–1,500 miles from here. First they went to Wisconsin. His wife's family lives there, and then they are still about 300 miles from Chicago, where Maria lives. Then another 20 miles or so and he is in South Holland. Brother Hendrik still lives there. So in one trip he's going to visit the whole family again, except for you. Oversees, perhaps that will be later.

This summer a new church will be built here in the vicinity. The costs also have to be raised by the residents. So far we still always have our meetings in the public schoolhouse.[129]

Now brother, I've written a few things, and I hope you will receive this slim letter in good health. Write back soon. Give our greetings also to the whole family. How is it going nowadays with sister Antje? I've heard nothing from her for a long time. Greetings from all of us, and also from me, your brother,

Leendert Bode

---

128 These Rotterdamers included Frans Vanden Berg, his sons Frans and Paul, Marinus Dykshoorn and Cornelis Kamp. They each claimed homesteads south of Burdett on 19 Nov. 1907. Dykshoorn and Kamp were the first Dutchmen to settle there, in April of 1908.

129 This was the church building of the east side of the Nijverdal Christian Reformed Church. It was actually completed in the spring of 1909. Till then they met in the Finley schoolhouse.

LETTER FROM LETHBRIDGE
(*De Grondwet,* 24 March 1908)

This winter we've had beautiful weather here. If every winter was like this, one would definitely long for winter. In Dakota we often dreaded the coming of winter.

One would wish there were more Hollanders who would come to visit this settlement and see the beautiful prairie land. Wheat here yields 40 to 56 bushels per acre. Last fall my neighbour got 18,000 bushels of winter wheat from 425 acres, even though the previous winter was unusually severe for this area. Although this settlement has been in existence only four years, it already has the reputation of being the most dependable wheat country in Canada. Those who visit Lethbridge must come to see the Dutch settlement before they pass judgment, because there have been some who have let themselves be driven about by this or that land agent to people who were eager to sell and then turned back disappointed, because one can still get a good deal close to the city, but conditions are not good there. For several miles around the city no prairie hay can be cut, while here we cut 80 tons last summer from our own land and had to leave more than 100 tons standing since we lacked the time to finish it. Because we have no irrigation here, one can work a large farm, and also we don't have to pay water rights.

T[ijmen] Hofman[130]

LETTER FROM MACLEOD
(*De Grondwet,* 24 March 1908)

This week I heard that there are Hollanders in the United States who tried to place our colony in Alberta, Canada, in a bad light. Since this is a false perception, I feel called to dispute it. Someone claimed that when he stayed here he was given shelter by a Hollander in a pigsty (or a place not much better) because according to his report it was not much better. Now I would like to know at whose place this could have happened, since here we do not know of such filthy Hollanders in our colony. Also, he had not enjoyed much sleep because of the vermin. I will not exalt the Dutch farms here to the clouds because, as anyone can well imagine, those without money can build

---

130   Tijmen Hofman was not the regular correspondent from Lethbridge.

no palaces here. But I dare say that none of the Hollanders here needs to be ashamed to give shelter. And I believe it would give us all great pleasure to find out where this pigsty can be found here on the prairie, because then it could be improved.

A Reader 18 March 1908

LETTER FROM GRANUM
(*De Grondwet*, 31 March 1908)

Nice weather! Sometimes it blows a bit, but it is still March. Today it is 20 March, and already a few days ago spring made its entry. One of my neighbours worked on the land almost the whole winter, but most farmers have no appetite for that. The winter was unusually mild this year. Your correspondent has already been on the land harrowing for a few days. One of my neighbours has already seeded a few acres.

Our colony is expanding more and more. Next week a son of S[ebo] Lantinga is coming from Nieuw Scheemda, province of Groningen.[131] Also a son of B[eert] Nauta from St. Jacobi Parochi, province of Friesland, is coming next week. Now he is in Iowa. The old man Nauta is coming here directly from the Netherlands in the beginning of May; he is coming with a niece and some other persons.[132]

Horses are scarce and expensive and cost from $350 to $400 a team.

Granum, formerly Leavings, has three elevators, four grocery stores, and many other stores. The Canadian Bank of Commerce is also finished; it is a magnificent building. Four years ago three small houses stood there.

Corr. [George Dijkema] 20 March 1908

---

131 Twenty-nine-year-old Geert Lantinga came to join his brothers Roelf and Albert who had arrived already in 1905.
132 Eighteen-year-old Jan Nauta had immigrated to Iowa in the summer of 1907 before coming to Alberta in March 1908. His sixty-two-year-old father Beert Nauta, a widower, arrived later in October. He was accompanied by two middle-aged women, his niece Renske Riewald and Trijntje Unema, who became his housekeepers. Renske died of pneumonia in 1911 and is buried in the Granum cemetery.

Granum, *ca.*1908, established in 1902. (Courtesy: Granum Drop-In Center.)

LETTER FROM LETHBRIDGE
(*De Grondwet*, 14 April 1908)

At present the weather is nice here. Today, however, it is a bit wintry, but the farmers are already busy at work on the land ploughing, and also seeding has already begun.

Gerrit Bode and his family are back again from their trip to Wisconsin, and two others came along with them, D[irk] Venema and Miss Tena Van Schuur. They are very happy with the land and the vicinity. He told me that he was also in Illinois and there his friends and family were also all ears about Canada.[133] Here it is a beautiful prairie country, good for grain and all crops. Good markets, schools, and a Christian Reformed church. The prices are also decent: wheat 86 to 88 cents a bushel, oats 45 cents, potatoes 55 cents a bushel, butter 30 cents a pound, and eggs 30 cents a dozen.

Also a couple of families are expected again from the Netherlands.[134]

The Geleynse brothers each bought another team of horses. At present horses are expensive here, from $350 to $400 per team.

I hear that the school will soon be opened again.[135]

---

133 Gerrit had earlier lived with his parents at South Holland, Illinois, where his uncle Hendrik Bode still resided. Gerrit's sister Maria Dudley and her family also lived in the Chicago area.
134 The families expected from the Netherlands were probably those of Hendrik Goldenbeld and Ritske Statema, who arrived in May.
135 Because of the weather the country schools were closed in the winter season.

Emil Hann is busy ploughing with his gasoline engine.

R[oelof] Van Dyke is getting somewhat better.

The machine dealers are now busy setting up seeding machines.

At present there are plenty of immigrants coming again from North Dakota. Last week there were nine [railway] carloads in Lethbridge.

T[ijmen] Hofman is building a fine new house.

Corr. 25 March 1908

LETTER FROM LETHBRIDGE
(*De Grondwet*, 5 May 1908)

At present the weather is beautiful, although this spring we've already had quite a bit of wind. Last week we had a nice rain, and also today as your correspondent writes this it's raining. The grain is as good as in the ground, and the winter wheat is doing very well.

Now and then Hollanders come by, among others H[endrik] Master [Matter] and Mr. Gierhart [Adrian Guichard] from the Netherlands.[136] That's great! There is still enough prairie land, but if the immigration keeps going on like this spring, then it will not be long before the whole northwest is populated, because it well appears that the people's desire at present is for the west.

B[ruce] Beagle has his steam engine at home and is busy seeding and harrowing with it.

A beginning has been made on the new railroad that is coming right through our Dutch settlement. This will be very convenient for everyone in this district.[137]

Emil Hann has gone with his gasoline engine to Claresholm where he has to plough 460 acres of land.

Daniel De Boer has done the seeding for R[oelof] van Dyke. The latter is still sick.

This spring there were a lot of prairie fires here. Last week there was still such a fire, which cost T[ijmen] Hofman a lot of effort to save his buildings. Now the grass is standing nice and green again so the danger is past.

At present Dirk Venema is busy with the brooder coop of J[an] Geleynse.

---

136 Both later took up homesteads at Burdett, Matter in June 1908, Guichard in June 1910.
137 The new CPR line ran from Lethbridge to Macleod and was completed in 1909.

Gerrit Harthoren [Hartkoorn] is soon expecting his family from Rotterdam, the Netherlands.

Wheat is 80 cents a bushel, eggs 25 cents a dozen, and butter 35 cents a pound.

The Dekker brothers have bought themselves a gang plough.

A[lbert] Rutgers has his store as good as finished. He also bought a beautiful wagon with which he can pick up eggs and butter and deliver groceries and dry goods. That is a great convenience for our people.[138]

Corr. 27 April 1908

LETTER FROM LETHBRIDGE
(*De Volksvriend,* 7 May 1908)

Today, April 29, it is rainy, although this spring we had dry weather to seed the grain. The grain is as good as in. Last week we also had a wonderful rain. The winter wheat is doing very well.

A week or so ago there was a lot of prairie fire, and some farmers had a hard time saving their buildings, but now the prairie is looking nice and green.

They have begun laying the new railway. The Hollanders will be very pleased with that, if we get a town nearby, since most now live fourteen to twenty miles from town; if the track is finished, a town will be erected in our vicinity.[139]

Dirk Venema, who came from Wisconsin, finds it much to his liking here.

F[rans] Vanden Berg and his sons Frans and Paul are still working on the railroad bridge at Lethbridge.

G[errit] Harthoven [Hartkoorn] is expecting his family to come.

R[oelof] Van Dyke is still on the sick list.

Bruce Brogle [Beagle] and Ch. Noble each have purchased a steam engine and will break a lot of land this summer. Emil Hann's gasoline engine is also performing well.[140]

---

138 In 1905 Rutgers had immigrated from Nijverdal and taken up a homestead (SW 28-10-23 W4) on the east side of the Dutch settlement. The Rutgers store was a 16 × 10 foot addition built onto his homestead shack. This country store was set up before railroad lines opened in the area, thus before the towns of Monarch and Noble(ford) were established.

139 The new railway being built was the CPR line between Lethbridge and Macleod. On this line the high level bridge was being constructed over the Oldman River. As this line was advancing from the west, the town of Monarch originated in July 1908 just south of the east side of the Dutch community. Before then these families lived up to 20 miles from Lethbridge to the southeast and Leavings to the west.

A[lbert] Rutgers will soon begin his business. His building is finished, and he bought a nice delivery wagon; now he will go around the vicinity buying up (farm) products and selling groceries and dry goods. Great! We wish him success.

Now and then Hollanders are still coming, such as Marten [Matter] and Gieshart [Guichard] from the Netherlands. Well, there is still room enough on the prairie, but it is being settled fast.

Horses are expensive here: from $350 to $450 for a team of two.

Wheat is now 80 cents; oats 45 cents; eggs 25 cents; butter 35 cents. So no complaints about that.

LETTER FROM HILLICHIEN MULDER TO HER PARENTS (22 May 1908)

Liverpool, 22 May '08
Beloved Parents and Sister,[141]

We arrived here in this hotel yesterday evening. At seven o'clock we left from Hull and at eleven-thirty we were here. What a day yesterday. At nine o'clock we came into Hull. Our suitcases were checked but not very well, because they did not see the tobacco that Miss Vredenburg had in hers. I did not get seasick from R[otterdam] to Hull. The sea was calm, but the closer we came to England the colder it became. Hull is a filthy city and the women here in England are not very neat and proper. Our beds last night were not very clean, but anyway we slept well last night and that is the most important thing. On board I could not write very well because of the rocking. It is annoying that we cannot speak or understand a word of English. We are both glad that we are together, because alone, we often say to each other, we wouldn't have

140 Bruce Beagle, Charles Noble, and Emil Hann were not part of the Dutch community. In early 1908 Charles Noble, a large-scale farmer and real estate man at Claresholm, purchased 4½ sections just north of the Dutch settlement; a year later he purchased a larger block of land to the east (his Grand View Farm) and in August the family moved there. See Grant MacEwan, *Charles Noble: Guardian of the Soil* (Saskatoon: Western Producer Prairie Books, 1983).

141 Twenty-five-year-old Hillichien Mulder was from Ten Boer in the province of Groningen, where her parents also lived. In 1907 she had a kidney removed, and then she developed pleurisy, an early sign of the onset of tuberculosis, so doctors advised her to move to a drier climate. This is the second of three letters in which Hillichien describes her journey from the Netherlands to Granum, where her sister Anna had immigrated a year earlier and married Geert (George) Dijkema. The first letter from Hull, England, has been lost. She was accompanied most of the way by Cato Vredenburg, whom she apparently met at the beginning of the journey. They travelled in second-class accommodations. In Liverpool they stayed in the Liverpool Continental Hotel. The originals of Hillichien Mulder's letters of 22 May and 11 June 1908 are in the possession of Ralph Poelman of High River, Alberta.

been able to do it. We are all by ourselves as Hollanders; if we had just one Dutch man with us, then it would be better. Miss Vredenburg has booklets in which there are questions and other things; then we sometimes let them read these booklets if we can't manage by sign language.

You know what Miss Vr. says, only the manners of the English are smooth and are like those of the Dutch, because she experienced that already this morning. The food and drink are good. Yesterday we were taken from the boat to the hotel by carriage, where our meal was set before us, fried eggs, bread, radishes, sardines, ham, cheese, etc., etc. The third-class passengers were taken to another hotel, also last evening when we arrived here in Liverpool. This morning I got up at quarter after nine and we will be brought to the boat again at one o'clock this afternoon. For breakfast we had a boiled egg. On the train from Hull to L[iverpool] I lay down on the seat; it was a nice compartment. How many tunnels we came through I have no idea.

Miss Vredenburg is thirty years old and an orphan; she is not from a strong family. Her parents, two brothers and a sister died from consumption [tuberculosis]. She is now all alone. Her family at first was against her going to Canada because they were afraid that the climate there would be unhealthy for her. Then she allowed herself to be examined and the doctors also recommended that she go because it would be especially healthy for her. She also does not look strong.

The Heuving family was so very friendly. Mr. and Mrs. and Aaltje and Dietje brought me to the boat. Would Mom be willing also to thank them sometime for their friendliness? I would find that very nice. Their address is Bergweg 100.

I will send Diet a postcard.[142] Did you receive my letter from Hull? I hope so. At first I wanted to send you also a postcard, but I would not have been able to write everything on it. I hope that we may safely cross the ocean. It is raining here.

Many greetings to all my friends and acquaintances, and tell them what happened. Later more. Many hearty greetings.

Love, Hil

---

142 Diet was Hil's younger sister.
143 Harm was Hil's brother.

LETTER FROM HILLICHIEN MULDER TO HER PARENTS
(11 June 1908)

Granum, June 11, 1908
Beloved Parents,

You will certainly want to hear something from me. The last time I wanted to write you a letter I was prevented from doing so by visits; so I just quickly wrote a postcard because Geert [Dijkema] was going to Granum and it would be a couple of days before he would go there again. You surely received my letter from Liverpool.

On 22 May at one-thirty we were brought to the *Virginian* and at six o'clock we went out to sea. The *Virginian* is a large boat. On Saturday we had calm weather and were not seasick. On Saturday to Sunday night a storm came up, and when we were awakened, we were also all seasick. On Monday Cato and I were still seasick, but on Tuesday we were again well, so we really suffered from seasickness for only two days. There were some who were sick for four and five days. Harm[143] said to me yet in Rotterdam, "Keep the ship good and clean for the first twenty-four hours, then you will feel fine the whole trip." We had heavy storm weather for two or three days. The waves flew over the deck and we had the storm window on the table. We were always on deck, however, and so we were completely drenched with seawater. But I was not in the least afraid or nervous, and we were sorry at last that the sea journey ended so quickly. The fifth day we saw two icebergs. It was sometimes very cold for me at sea, but I really enjoyed the ocean air. When we steamed into the St. Lawrence Gulf and River it was a delightful sight. I have never yet seen so much beauty. Cato said to me, "And now can you see how high the land is to which we are going?" While dikes must be made in Holland to turn back the sea, here everything is nature.

On Saturday 30 May we steamed into Quebec at nine in the morning. There the third-class passengers were set ashore, while we came into Montreal at nine o'clock on Sunday morning. What a hustle and bustle, especially for us two young women who couldn't speak or understand a word of English, since we were the only Hollanders among all the passengers. Anyway we got ourselves cleared [through customs] without a hitch. A steward from the *Virginian* helped us. Cato became nervous in Montreal, but to my surprise I was as calm as can be. Upon the arrival of the boat each passenger had to stand by his own name, I by the letter *M* and Cato by the *V*. We were then separated a short distance from each other. That has to do with baggage. Each person then receives his own back; then the baggage handlers can see where they must go. For me neither my suitcase nor my trunk was opened. Cato's suitcase was checked, but she quickly let them read a letter from her Piet and then they left her alone. In my vicinity it was different; one trunk after another was opened. I was very happy that I was there because Cato still had tobacco in her suitcase, but on the *Virginian* we had sewn that into a velvet bag; now it was exactly like a little cushion and they noticed nothing.

Then we were brought to the station and had to wait there until ten in the evening. In Canada just as in England no trains run on Sunday. The train trip was much more tiring than the boat trip. I could sleep on the boat at will. We then left Montreal at ten o'clock on Sunday evening and arrived at Winnipeg on Tuesday evening at ten, the first station where we had to transfer. At twelve o'clock we left again and at five in the morning came into Kirkella, where Cato left me.[144] Cato had to transfer and I could stay seated. Later that day, I thought, where must I now transfer again; I suppose Dunmore Junction, but I don't know for sure. Then I let the conductor read the letter from Geert [Dijkema]. He then came to me with someone who spoke German (which I could understand very well) and that person made clear to me that I had to transfer at Dunmore Junction at about ten o'clock to Macleod, and that I would arrive there at five-thirty and not until eight o'clock could I leave for Granum. So I had to transfer only twice. You should be aware that I had almost no sleep the last two nights.

On Thursday 4 June at quarter to nine in the morning I arrived in Granum, but there was no Geert or Anne to be seen. It was now such weather that a farmer would not chase his dog out in it. First I waited a little while there, but I began to feel restless. Then I wrote Geert's name on a piece of paper and let someone read it and said to him that Geert was my brother. He went with me to a store, and the people knew Geert well and also knew that I would come. They also made clear to me that [Rommert] Weerstra was there the previous day and also wanted to see whether I was there; and that Geert would come that day to see if I had arrived. A week earlier other Hollanders had also arrived and were in a hotel; so they fetched them and they told me that Geert would definitely come because Weerstra had told them so. And yes, at two o'clock there he was. He was dumbfounded that I was there already, but was very happy to see me. They had thought that, if I arrived at all that day, it would be on the afternoon or evening train. They really thought that I would come a day later, because the other Hollanders also had to travel a day longer than me. So I had a successful journey, but if I had come a day later I could not have come by way of Macleod, neither by train nor by carriage, due to the heavy rain that had fallen there; then the river becomes swollen, and that we had to cross. Then I would have had to make a roundabout trip via Calgary.

Then Geert and I first ate in Granum in the hotel. Was he ever happy, but Anne no less when we arrived here. She thought … [two lines illegible]. I sat like a real Canadian farmer's wife beside Geert on the spring wagon, with two fine trotters in front of it, and on we went through mud and water.

And now I am sitting here in the middle of the prairie and do not feel like a stranger. I still haven't had a moment of homesickness. As I've already written you, I have become thin but otherwise I have still experienced no harmful effects from the trip. Now I really drink milk again and can get as much as I want, and three eggs a day. I may also have more, but I don't want more. Today I have been here exactly a week and I still have no trouble with this climate, but most people at first have a problem with it. The air here is much higher than in Holland. The people here all seem to be very tanned; they say my white skin will certainly also become tanned. Anne walks around with a large hat. We are very cozy with the three of us. I still knew Geert very well. On board I never had any headache; later on the train I had it again. We also had good food on the *Virginian*, apples in abundance and so delicious words can't describe it. So let it be said here that on the trip I took good care of myself.

The Hollanders who were in the hotel in Granum are now with the Weerstras. Yesterday they were here with us for a visit. They are Frisians.[145]

Later I will write you about the surrounding area and the land here. This letter is already long enough. Give the family and acquaintances my hearty greetings, especially the Klunders, and also tell the doctor how the trip went for me and give him my greetings. [two lines blotted out] Many hearty greetings also from Geert and Anne.

Love, Hil

My trunk is not yet here. Monday Geert went to Granum; then it was not there yet. If the weather is good we are going there on Saturday afternoon with the three of us in order to check.

Bye, Hil

Now it is Saturday 13 June. We are going together to Granum to mail this letter. Before long I will write a letter again.

---

144 Kirkella is in western Manitoba near the Saskatchewan border.
145 The Frisians who had arrived at the end of May were probably Jacob Douma and his wife. They later farmed near Macleod.

LETTER FROM MACLEOD
(*De Grondwet*, 9 June 1908)

The farmers here have had their seed grain in the ground for some time and after a ten-day rain the land is looking rosy. The winter wheat promises to be good this year; there is a field of 1,200 acres here where it is already standing 20 inches high. Little by little most have gone ploughing for the next harvest, and now we have had enough rain to be able to plough for three to four weeks.

They have been busy already for some time with the railroad. By July the line from MacLeod to the Oldman river is to be done, so that materials for the bridge can be transported.[146] On the land of J[acob] Leeuwerik and J[an] Zoeteman a railway siding and a station is being built. We now hope to see a grain elevator arise there soon, also stores, etc.[147]

We here are about ten miles from MacLeod by train, in the midst of an agricultural district.

The trustees are thinking about beginning soon with the building of a schoolhouse. They hope to be able to open the school yet this summer.

Corr. 25 May 1908

LETTER FROM LETHBRIDGE
(*De Grondwet*, 23 June 1908)

It is presently raining about every day, so the correspondent certainly has time to write something. It is very wet so not much could be done in the last week; it is raining steadily, and the rivers have risen above their banks. We can almost no longer believe that we are in Southern Alberta. The winter wheat is doing exceptionally well, and the potatoes are also coming up nicely.

At present a lot of prairie land here is being broken with steam ploughs.[148]

---

146 The CPR line from Macleod to Lethbridge was constructed from Macleod so construction materials were hauled from there for the bridge west of Monarch.

147 The making of this siding was the origin of the hamlet of Pearce south of the Oldman River. Grain elevators were built but a town never developed there. In 1911 Peter Koole started operating a general store at Pearce.

148 These were large sod-breaking ploughs pulled by a steam engine.

R[oelof] Van Dyke is getting better. He has been seen outside again. We hope he can soon resume his work. A couple of weeks ago Cornelius Withagen had the misfortune of falling off a horse and breaking his arm, but is now recovering nicely again.[149]

While H[endrikus] Veldhuis was smoking bacon, the whole business caught fire and caused quite a bit of damage.

A baby daughter was born at the home of W. J. Lohuizen [Willem Van Lohuizen]. Also a baby daughter to Mr. T. Hoffman [Tijmen Hofman].

"The wedding bells are ringing." Last week, on 26 May, Leendert Kole [Koole] entered into marriage with Miss Annie Willemsen, and soon Daniel De Boer will follow with Miss Tena van Schuur.[150]

The school opened at the beginning of May and a lot of children are coming.[151]

Soon we are expecting a "dominie" here again.[152] It's about time, because it was about eight months ago that we last had a minister.

The price of wheat has again gone up a little; it is now 90 cents a bushel. Oats is 55 cents a bushel.

The weather now seems to be changing a little. We hope.

Corr. 6 June 1908

LETTER FROM TEUNIS BODE TO JAN BODE
(3 September 1908)

Lethbridge, 3 Sept. 1908
J[an] Bode, Noordeloos
Dear Uncle and Cousins,

I will write you a letter, since I believe I've never written you. By the Lord's goodness, we are all still fit and well, and we wish the same for you.

This year we have a good harvest again. The grain cutting is done, but we haven't threshed yet. I am still a hermit. Uncle [Gerrit] Hartkoorn worked

---

149 Cornelis Withage was the fourteen-year-old son of Gerrit J. Withage.
150 Johanna (Annie) Willemsen was a nineteen-year-old daughter of Garrit Willemsen. Daniel De Boer married Tena Van Schuur on 17 June 1908. Like the De Boers, Tena Van Schuur had come from Vesper, Wisc.
151 Country schools were usually closed in the winter.
152 Student Nicholas Gelderloos, who had just finished his first year at the Theological School in Grand Rapids, served the Alberta church for several weeks in the summer, and then Rev. George Hylkema from Volga, South Dakota, came for three weeks in August.

for me this summer. It's not my plan now to write much about the farm in Canada. Uncle Hartkoorn will write when we have threshed.

But I'll write you some news. If all goes well with my life and health, I plan to come to the Netherlands this winter, or rather, to lead a life of leisure there for part of a year.[153] Of late I've been getting along very well, and now I've rented the farm to G[errit] Hartkoorn for a year, with the horses, machinery, and cows; yes, everything, since I'm heading out. I now have 320 acres of land, 200 of it under the plough. My plan is to leave late in October, if I can at least be ready. But then I'm first going to Chicago for a couple of weeks, because Maria still lives there, and then I want to go to Uncle Hendrik [Bode] again.

Thus, Uncle Jan, if all goes well, you can expect me there once again, and then we can talk about America again. So I won't write much news now. Because I will walk into your yard unannounced and then we can talk. I hope you will write a note back. I don't know any more news. Hearty greetings from me, Teunis Bode, and from the whole family and Uncle Gart [Gerrit Hartkoorn].

My address is:
Mr. Teunis Bode, Box 333, Lethbridge, Alberta, Canada, N. America

LETTER FROM EVERT ALDUS
(*Twentsch Volksblad,* 14 November 1908)

"Where is the correspondent from the colony near Lethbridge?" the readers of the *Twentsch Volksblad* may have asked. Not without reason, since I have written nothing from here for a long time. For those who would like to know how things are going with us here, this was not so pleasant. On the other hand, I now have a considerable amount of material to write. First of all, I will report on things that are of most interest to us.

Last winter, characterized by a lot of mild weather, left us in about mid-March. In the first half of April most grain was seeded. The weather in that month was far from favourable – dry, bleak, and cold. Almost every day the wind blew and drove clouds of dust from the dry land in front of it. Earlier we did not have as much trouble with this; then the ground was mostly

---

153 Apparently, a major reason for the visit was to seek a wife. He met nineteen-year-old Paulina De Beeld, from his hometown of Ottoland in Zuid-Holland. They were married 10 August 1909.

covered with grass. Now almost everything is loose farmland, which gives the Chinook an opportunity to carry vast clouds of dust with it. Besides, many burn their stubble land in the spring. The ash that is picked up makes the dust clouds much blacker and thicker. The rest of the spring and summer there was good weather in general, except for a couple of rather severe night frosts in July, and in the same month a hot dry wind blew for two days. The frost did not impede our grain; however, due to this wind it ripened too quickly, so the kernels were somewhat smaller and lighter. Yet there is no reason at all for dissatisfaction; the yield was almost generally very good. Because the wheat weighed less per bushel, however, most of us received three cents less for a bushel. At present the price is running between 70 and 80 cents; as long as this remains the case, there is nothing to complain about the "three cents less." The grain was ripe much earlier than last year. Already on August 31 the first threshing machine began to work and by the end of September most grain was threshed by three machines. Everyone is now busy hauling their wheat to Lethbridge. We have not made as much progress with this as we expected. We have had a lot of rainy days in October, and now as I write this, a good snowstorm is raging outside.

In our colony (near Lethbridge) about 55,000 bushels of wheat were grown. If the market does not go down and one calculates 60 cents a bushel after deducting threshing fees, etc., then this represents an income of about $33,000 or upwards of 80,000 guilders. About twenty-five farmers raised this grain, on forty-five to fifty homesteads. Added to this, however, is a good amount of purchased land, which can be seeded for the first time only next year. From our earned money we use only a relatively small part for the necessities of life. Most of it is used to buy or pay for horses and machines, to construct or enlarge buildings, etc. No small amount is for payments on land we bought.

This year threshing happened in a somewhat different way than before. We no longer haul the bundles to stacks, but do no more than sit on the sheaves like "guests." The thresher brings along about ten men, each with two horses and a hay wagon. These men haul the sheaves out of the field to the machine. This spares us from bringing the wheat to stacks. For that, however, we have to pay the thresher 9 cents a bushel of wheat, so the threshing bill soon amounts to 200 dollars or sometimes more. If the threshers continue to charge so much, perhaps this will lead some of us to purchase our own machines.

There is sufficient oats grown for our horses. Potatoes and garden vegetables in most cases were poor, I think; the night frosts are mostly to blame.

Now I still have to conclude this short survey. I do this with the remark that this year also has proved that, although our work is often difficult or is made unpleasant by strong wind and dust clouds, night frosts, and snow storms, it is going very well for us in the New World.

Rapid Progress in General

Something characteristic of this summer was the speed at which the prairie has made way to farmland. In and around our settlement only a little un-cultivated land is left, and this will vanish completely in a couple of years. Only the roads will remind one of the earlier prairie country.[154] Not only in a figurative but also in a literal sense the breaking took place "with steam." This summer a half-dozen steam engines were daily at work in our district pulling the plough through the sod.

With the prairie grass hundreds of cows also disappear. We have had count-less troubles with them. These free-ranging animals respect no barbed wire or anything, but constantly destroy the grain of the farmers. The owners in most cases want to do nothing about it. For the most part they are not favourably disposed to the farmers, because "the bread of the farmer is the death of the rancher." The grass goes away, and with it the large public pasture.

The law also is not of much help. In areas like this it is to the advantage of the rancher. If after days and weeks of being aggravated by the cows someone in rage kills one of them, he may have to pay the owner for the animal, if he is caught. Here I do not want to say that a cow has never died due to the use of too much lead; because the strictest law cannot prevent anyone's patience from snapping, when it is finally exhausted.

Now, however, we are rid of this "pest"; this summer the last few cows were brought to another area by the owner.

And now something about our railway line.[155] In the spring they began building the earthen track bed. Hundreds of men and horses worked on it the whole summer. The tents, sheds, and horse stables, everywhere in camps along the track, as well as the work and activity, are something uncommon up to now. The track bed is now as good as done, and from Macleod to the Old Man River the rails are almost laid. When that section is finished, they can bring the ironwork for the bridge and it can be built. On the bridge near Lethbridge they are at work on the superstructure.[156] This bridge is more

---

154 By this time the roads ran along the designated road allowances, but they were still trails and were not upgraded. The road allowances were still all prairie grass.
155 This was the new CPR railway line that was being built between Lethbridge and Macleod.
156 The first bridge is the one over the Oldman River just west of Monarch. The other is the high level bridge west of Lethbridge.

than 350 feet above the water level (that is, almost as high as the church tower at Utrecht) and has a length of about 1,800 metres. People say this is the largest bridge in the world, if as the criterion you take the length multiplied by the height. Perhaps it will still take a considerable time before this giant superstructure is ready. The bridge on the Macleod side of our colony (from which we are a good hour's walk away) is much smaller. It is certain that this bridge will be finished by next fall, along with the railway line to our place. Once that is the case, we can load our grain here.

Often we have asked each other where a station would come in our neighbourhood.[157] No one, however, could find out the right answer until all at once this summer the report made the rounds: "The station is going to be on section 7." There was general joy among the Hollanders. For us there was no better place. Almost all the land around section 7 belongs to Hollanders, so many will be no more than a few minutes from the station.

Soon after the location for the station was determined, the owner of section 7 sold building lots.[158] And, in true American fashion, after a couple of days wagons brought building materials and the construction of the new town began. Now seven buildings are standing there – a livery stable, two stores, a lumberyard, and three other buildings.

On 1 October the grocery and clothing store was opened. The hardware store will be open in a few days, and at the lumberyard many kinds of lumber are available. Industry is also represented, namely, a brickyard. If it had not rained so much this month, the first kiln brick would be baked already. Although work is constantly being done, the "rising out of the ground" of the town will mostly take place after the locomotive can supply the building materials. Another station is being built between here and Lethbridge, and railway lines that shoot off from this line to the north are marked out.[159]

---

157 This marked the beginning of the town of Monarch.
158 A notice about the new town site of Monarch appeared in the *Lethbridge Herald* (13 July 1908): "Townsite Has Now Been Sold: Monarch, Between Here and Macleod, Bought by a Druggist. Claresholm, Alberta, July 13. The townsite of Monarch, east of here between Macleod and Lethbridge, which will be situated on the new railway from Calgary to Lethbridge, has been sold by the CPR through C[harles] S. Noble of this town to D. M. Ross, late druggist here. The price was $55,000." The 17 July issue contains an advertisement for the sale of town lots, which is mentioned in another notice in the 24 July issue: "Claresholm, July 21. The sale of the Monarch townsite lots begins here today, the agents being Milnes and Noble, and sales should proceed merrily as the town looks like springing up like a mushroom once the railroad which is graded past it is completed. It is almost a certainty that the railroad will pass the town, but even if it did not, purchasers are secure as the CPR gave an understanding to refund if such a contingency occurred. Business lots are to be sold from $250 to $450, and residential lots from $100 to $150."
159 The new station between Monarch and Lethbridge was Kipp. From there a new CPR line would be built to the north to Calgary.

Our town was given the name "Monarch" by the railway company. A request by us to determine the name came too late.[160]

In the next letter I want to point out the advantages and changes that all of this will have for us.

A[ldus] Monarch,[161] 21 Oct. 1908

LETTER FROM GRANUM
(*De Grondwet*, 24 November 1908)

We have had a beautiful summer here. In June there was a lot of rain, but after that almost always nice dry weather, so the wheat produced a good yield. The winter wheat brought in 30 to 45 bushels per acre and the spring wheat 15 to 30 bushels. Oats produced 25 to 40 bushels per acre on old land and some got more on new land; one farmer harvested 80 bushels an acre from new land. Potatoes, cabbage, etc. were definitely poor here this year. We got frost in July and again in the beginning of August, and potatoes cannot withstand that very well.

Gradually we are getting a Dutch settlement here. This summer two families came from the Netherlands,[162] and several weeks ago one came here from Michigan, his family consisting of his wife and five children. He immediately bought a farm here.[163]

In the area of church life it is also improving here slowly but surely. Our church name is Nijverdal, but Nijverdal is so spread out that it really must be called East and West Nijverdal. We here in Granum are then in West Nijverdal.

Corr. [George Dijkema] 16 Nov. 1908

---

160 Most of the Dutch settlers at Monarch had requested the name "Nijverdal." Willem Van Lohuizen disagreed, since he thought one should not hold onto Dutch ways in their adopted country.

161 With the closer location of Monarch, the east-side Dutch settlers no longer identified Lethbridge as their address.

162 The related families of Ritske Statema and Jacob Douma arrived at Granum in May. Statema soon took up a homestead at Burdett; Douma settled near Macleod.

163 The Albert Ritsema family arrived from Sullivan, Michigan. He bought Harm Emmelkamp's homestead.

164 The west side church was built on two acres of land donated by Willem Feller on the northwest corner of his homestead. This church building was originally 16 × 24 feet in size.

165 The east side of the congregation dedicated its new building north of Monarch on Ascension Day, 20 May 1909.

166 This letter was probably sent by George Dijkema, who also wrote other letters to *De Wachter*.

Granum Christian Reformed Church, *ca.*1926, after porch and addition added, first built 1908-09.

LETTER FROM GRANUM
(*De Wachter,* 24 February 1909)

From the Nijverdal Congregation, Alberta

On Friday afternoon, 5 February, the first little church building of the oldest Christian Reformed congregation in Canada was put into use. I mean the little church of the western part of the Nijverdal congregation.[164]

Already last year there was a plan to proceed to build, but it appeared it would have to be delayed due to financial difficulties. This year it could proceed, though it was done on a modest basis. It would have been desirable if it was built somewhat larger, but for the time being there is room enough, and if the number of people expands so much that there is not enough space, an addition can always be built on.

As it looks, this just-built little church will not long remain the only one in Canada belonging to a Christian Reformed congregation, because if all goes according to wish, the eastern part of this congregation soon will also put its own building into use.[165]

Now next year a parsonage and then onto the work of making a call. May the day not be far off that the Nijverdal congregation greets its own minister![166]

ARTICLE ON GRANUM

(*Lethbridge Herald* Special Publicity Number, 27 February 1909)

Granum: The Prize-Winning District

Granum (until recently known as Leavings) lies 40 miles west of Lethbridge on the CPR, between Lethbridge and Calgary, in the centre of a well-settled and productive wheat district. The town itself, which is in a healthy condition of growth, has one of the most admirable sites in Southern Alberta. The Willow Creek, a goodly stream, flows one mile to the west, and the neighbouring Porcupine Hills, o'ertopped by snow-crested mountains lend their majesty and picturesqueness to the scene. The town certainly has fallen into the lap of luxury, and plenty has poured its cornucopia on its head.

Little did the roaming Indian or vagrant cowboy think that the plains in the neighbourhood of the "Leavings," where the old police trail left the "Willow," would be the busy scene of the agricultural labours of today. Like the "Sleeping Beauty," the land lay waiting for the magic touch of the faith and industry that should cause it to awake. The old police name, "The Leavings," was discarded when prosperity, like a lover came, with the chinook, awooing, and the name Granum (Latin word for grain) was assumed as most truly descriptive of a district which anyone, gazing upon from the heights of the neighbouring hills, would certainly hail as a land of promise. "Leavings," which the rancher passed by, has become Granum, the prizewinner. It has since justified and proven the aptness of the name by carrying off the laurels. First, at the Lethbridge Seed Fair last spring, where Mr. John Vosburg, of this place, won the silver cup,[167] and again at the Dominion Exhibition, Calgary, where Granum secured first for district exhibit, and Granum farmers also won several individual first prizes on grain, etc.

In 1907 over half a million bushels of wheat were shipped from this point, and the shipments for the crop of 1908 will run close to three-quarters of a million. This will be much exceeded this year, judging by the unusual amount of fresh breaking done last summer. There are four elevators here in the grain trade, besides the track shipping done by the individual farmers. The great difficulty, of course, here, as at other points, is in the shortage of cars, and this condition is likely to be aggravated owing to increased acreage aforesaid, unless new lines of railroad come to the relief of this fertile belt of Southern Alberta.

---

167 An accompanying full page advertisement for the town states that "J. G. Vosburgh, of Granum, won Silver Cup – for best wheat grown in Alberta, at Lethbridge Seed Fair, 1908; Silver Cup – for best wheat grown in Canada, at Dominion Fair, Calgary."

Granum – Past and Present

Four years ago Granum was marked only by a boxcar for a depot. Ranchers had been here for years, but it is only a short time since attention has been given to the growing of wheat. Now it is a thriving village of nearly 400 population, with every line of business represented.

	Canadian Bank of Commerce	1	harness maker
2	good general stores	2	lumber yards
1	gents' furnishing	3	real estate agencies
2	hardwares	2	billiard halls
1	tinsmith	2	concert halls
1	drug store	1	undertaker
2	doctors	2	barber shops
2	hotels	4	churches
2	restaurants	1	two-roomed school
3	implement houses	3	insurance agents
2	livery barns	3	contractors
4	elevators		Government telephone
1	milliner	1	carpenter shop
1	dressmaker	2	furniture stores
2	tailors	1	shoemaker
1	jeweler	2	coal dealers
1	confectionery	2	butchers
2	laundries	1	feed chopping mill
3	blacksmiths		

There are business openings here for the following branches:

1	large flour mill		More banks
1	large general store		More railways – G.T.R., C.N.R., G.N.R.
1	local newspaper		
1	photographer	2	more elevators
1	dentist		Railway stock yards
1	sash and door factory	1	coal dealer
1	skating rink	1	pork-packing plant
1	establishment to manufacture grain cars (for this year's crop)	1	livery barn
		1	creamery
		1	cheese factory

Room for anybody with money.

ARTICLE ON MONARCH
(*Lethbridge Herald* Special Publicity Number, 27 February 1909)

Monarch

Bald Prairie in November, 1908; Thriving Town with Big Prospects Now
In a province like Alberta where new towns and new cities spring up and
prosper with each succeeding year the appearance and foundation of a new
town does not attract the same amount of attention which it would do in a
country possessed of less magnificent possibilities. Unless therefore a town
can truly claim that either from its situation, or from any other reason, or
from any other combination of reasons that it is superior to its neighbours,
or its competitors, it does not secure the attention of the settler, and the
investor, which is very much as it should be, but every now and again a townsite is laid out which when the town springs up, easily out-strips its fellows
and can show a record of substantial progress which leaves the older towns
far in the rear. Whenever this happens there is always the best of reasons
for the occurrence. The records of the progress of some of the towns in
Alberta are phenomenal indeed, but the record of Monarch, the new town
which is situated about twenty-three miles from Granum, on the cut-off of
the CPR between Macleod and Lethbridge which is now being constructed,
has established a record far ahead of any previous performance. Some ten
weeks ago there was scarcely anything in the building line on the site of
this new town. Today there are over twenty buildings erected of which no
less than eleven are used for business purposes, and with each succeeding
sunrise some new portion of a new building appears which was not on the
skyline when the sun went down.

In addition to this, that curse of the new settlement, "the artificial boom,"
has not cast its blighting influence over the thriving town of Monarch.

The firms which have opened up branches in it are some of the oldest, most
prosperous, and most conservative firms throughout the whole Dominion.
The Canadian Bank of Commerce is not noted for its indiscretion in business
transactions; the Massey-Harris Co. has a reputation for solidity, which has
reached from Atlantic to Pacific, and both of these firms have establishments
in the town. The elevator companies are already vying with one another
as to which shall build an elevator first on the track at the earliest possible
moment after the rails have been laid.

Although the lots have hardly been placed on the market, the shrewd and
successful investors of Calgary, Lethbridge, Macleod and other progressive
towns and cities of Southern Alberta have already secured many of the lots

Monarch, *ca.*1912, established in 1908. (Courtesy: Frieda Dekker.)

which lie adjacent to the track and on the main street. It will be noticed that throughout this article the word investors has been replaced, and the word speculators has not been mentioned once. There is the best of reasons for this. A man speculates in property which he hopes to sell at an early date to some other person at an advanced price, regardless of the fact as to whether or not the land, lots, buildings or whatever constitutes the subject matter of the purchase is worth the price paid for it or not. But a man invests his money in property that he believes will bring a profitable and lasting revenue. And the present holders of Monarch property are investors in the best sense of the word. The question naturally arises, why is Monarch superior to other towns on the south line? Why is it that conservative businessmen have seen fit to rush to this town? Why have the farmers of Alberta already contemplated moving their present holdings and are eagerly inquiring what land is available in the neighbourhood?

The reasons are few in number, but they are sufficient:

Monarch is situated within the limits of the best grain country in all Alberta. Within a few miles of the town the record crop of sixty-two and a half bushels of wheat was grown and harvested during the last season.

Monarch lies in the heart of the ranching district of Southern Alberta and will without doubt, secure much of the business that has hitherto been forced to go to Macleod and Lethbridge.

Monarch is directly on the new cut-off railway line of the CPR and there-fore it can boast of perfect facilities for the shipment of grain, cattle and other assets which it produces.[168]

LETTER FROM EVERT ALDUS
(*Twentsch Volksblad,* 26 June 1909)

"So the raw North finally rests from the assault of hail and roar of storm."

In the last few weeks these lines from Borger's beautiful poem came to mind for me many times. We have still had only a couple weeks of summer weather, I think. The winter did not leave us before the 16th of May. In April we could do little work due to frost, snow, and hail. In early May we had a snowstorm which surpassed all previous ones in severity and lasted thirty-six hours. Then, as a change, the weather was good till 15 May. After that, nature changed all at once; we got heat, and rain and thunderstorms often drove us from the field. The result of all of this is that a lot of grain was seeded late. Due to the abundant moisture, however, it has come up quickly, and our crops now look good. Since the weather in the past couple of weeks is also favourable, there is no reason for discontent.

From the big Canadian newspapers we learned that a princess was born to the Dutch queen.[169] Since these papers are published in eastern Canada, it was about five days after the joyous birth that we received word of it. Already some time before, various newspapers, even the *Lethbridge News,* mentioned that "the Hollanders are happy" about what was about to happen in the palace.

On Ascension Day the new Christian Reformed church was dedicated.[170] Rev. Borduin, the minister from New Holland, Montana, came up for this occasion. The Reverend spoke in connection with a text from the second book of Chronicles: "Raise your hands to the Lord, and go up to his temple" [2 Chronicles 6?]. The ceremony was attended by a number of persons, in-cluding some from other churches.

On the evening of May 15 we noticed an earthquake in this area. It oc-curred as a rolling movement, not unlike that of a boat in the water. It lasted only briefly and was not severe. Some of our people felt it clearly.

168 A similar promotional article on Monarch appeared in the *Lethbridge Herald* Special Publicity Number (2 April 1910).
169 On 30 April 1909, Queen Wilhelmina gave birth to her daughter Juliana, who eventually succeeded her as Queen of the Netherlands.

I conclude this piece with a couple of items of a more private nature. The choral society cheered its director with a fine armchair, which he gratefully accepted.[171] J[ohn] Postman and his wife were surprised with the birth of twins, which gives Postman an even dozen.[172]

A[ldus] Nijverdal near Monarch, 6 June 1909

REPORT OF REV. MENNO BORDUIN
(*De Wachter*, 21 July 1909)

Something about Home Mission Work in the Northwest

During the largest part of the month of May we had the pleasure of working in the congregation of Nijverdal, Alberta, Canada.[173] The congregation there numbers about seventeen families. This is already a nice beginning for the far northwest. Too bad that due to the distance it is necessary for them to meet in two groups, so that they had to raise two church buildings. If things go well, this fall or winter a parsonage will be built so that a call can then be made in a later year, Lord willing. With a little help from the Classis, this would present no financial difficulty for our people there, if they join hands. They have large farms there and the land often produces 30 bushels of wheat per acre. The country there is bare, but yet it has its charms. The snow-covered Rocky Mountains offer a beautiful and lofty view from there, especially when they gleam in the bright sunlight. It was also pleasing for me to feel the warm interest in the Lord's service that many there seem to express. The lack of a proper church society life is the only thing some people regret. Besides our people there who are with the congregation, there are more Hollanders, but for most of them religious commitment does not run very deep, so this gives little support to congregational life. We hope that the Lord will grant the brothers and sisters at Nijverdal the grace to be steadfast, that they with their children may remain closely committed to God and his service, and at the same time that they may become strengthened enough to obtain the desired congregational life.

M[enno] Borduin

---

170 This was the east-side church at Monarch, dedicated on 20 May.
171 Aldus was the director of the men's choir.
172 The Postman twins were Dena and Willem, born 31 May 1909.
173 Rev. Menno Borduin, based in New Holland, Mont., was a home missionary of the Christian Reformed Church serving the west.

REPORT OF REV. BAREND LAMMERS
(*De Hope*, 24 August 1909)[174]

At the spring session of the Dakota Classis[175] there was a petition from a number of residents living in the vicinity of Monarch, Alberta, for church organization. As a committee to visit that field, the minister and an elder of the Westfield, North Dakota, congregation was appointed, since that was the nearest congregation.[176]

This committee then spent the last Sunday of July and the first Sunday of August with these people. On both Sundays the undersigned preached twice for these people in a schoolhouse.

On 29 July we met with the people at the home of J. W. [Willem J.] Van Lohuizen to deal with church matters.[177] After the reading of Scripture and prayer we came to the main purpose of the meeting. After inquiry it appeared that there were eighteen members in full communion with evangelical churches, and three made profession of their faith.[178]

Jac[obus] Nijhof and T[ijmen] Hofman were chosen as elders and E[vert] Aldus and J. W. [Willem J.] Van Lohuizen as deacons.

The elected consistory members were installed in their offices in the morning of 1 August. That morning six children were also baptized.[179] In the afternoon the Lord's Supper was held. Thus it was a busy, but we may add, a blessed day.

Provisionally the congregation will bear the name Reformed Church of Monarch, Canada. It consists of 21 communicants and 47 baptized members. Plans were immediately made to acquire land for the church and a building.

About the prospects of our people there we wish to say this: Our people there live in a splendid region; as for the lay of the land we know of no place where it is more beautiful, even Sioux County, Iowa, and Westfield, North Dakota. There are vast fields of prairie with the peaks of the Rocky

---

174 *De Hope*, a church paper published in Holland, Mich., served the Reformed Church in America in the Midwest. Rev. Barend Lammers was pastor of the Reformed Church of Westfield, N.Dak.

175 Classis Dakota, a regional assembly of the Reformed Church in America, met 13–15 April at Orange City, Iowa.

176 Another reason why representatives of the Westfield Reformed Church were appointed is that Tijmen Hofman and his family had immigrated to southern Alberta in 1907 from Westfield and were members of that church. Hofman took leadership among those in the Monarch Dutch community who initiated contact with the Reformed Church in America and requested that it organize an RCA congregation at Monarch. These people, who were not satisfied with the local Christian Reformed church, were mostly from a Hervormde Kerk background in the Netherlands.

177 The original consistory minutes of the Monarch Reformed Church indicate that the organizational meeting took place two weeks later on 12 August, and that the first service was held 15 August.

Mountains in view in the distance, where in clear weather you can discern the peaks crowned with snow. The crops were good and one can easily accept that various fields promised 40 to 50 bushels of wheat. Understand that whoever knows anything about wheat growing does this without irrigation. The wheat stood so thick and even that it was as if it was clipped with shears from above.

Our countrymen there each received homesteads of 190 [160] acres there. But these are now gone. It is amazing how quickly Canada is becoming filled up. As in the United States, you find people from every country of the world there. In the Reformed congregation there are various people directly from the Netherlands, but also some from the United States, from New Jersey, the Dakotas, etc.

If in our Reformed congregations there are those who are looking to better their lot in Canada, we venture to recommend Monarch and vicinity. One can still buy land there, with no rocks, for $22 to $35 per acre. Those who have no means to buy should readily be able to rent there. We refer all who are interested to Mr. E. Aldus of Monarch, Alta., Canada, or Mr. T. Hofman, who are willing to provide the necessary information. The address of the latter is Blayney, Alta., Canada.[180]

We wish to say yet that we are sorry that everywhere in Canada there are small groups of Hollanders who have no church connection, because the numbers are not large enough to have or to establish a congregation; therefore it is better to concentrate in a few places.

From what we are told, the climate for people in Alberta, summer or winter, leaves nothing to be desired. The prayer of the committee is that the Lord may bless this offshoot of our Church in Canada.

B[arend] W. Lammers
J. Wolf
Moose Jaw, Saskatchewan, Canada, 16 August 1909

---

178 Charter members who joined by membership transfer included: Everhardus and Christina Aldus, Hendrik and Lambertha Goldenbeld, Mrs. Geertje Goldenbeld, Rense and Aaltje Nyhoff, Jacobus and Wilhelmina Nyhoff, Hendrikus and Janna Veldhuis, all from the Hervormde Kerk of Nijverdal or Hellendoorn, Willem and Hendrikje Van Lohuizen from the Hervormde Kerk of Heerde, Tijmen and Heiltje Hofman from the Reformed Church of Westfield, N.Dak., and Roelof and Dina Van Dijk from the Reformed Church of Midland Park, N.J. Those who made profession of faith included Hendrika and Geertje Veldhuis.

179 The baptized children included: Paulus Johannes Aldus, Jaantje Hofman, Henriekus Nyhoff, Herman Nyhoff, and Hettie Van Lohuizen.

180 In 1907 John Warnock opened a general store and post office on his land and called it Blayney. It was located a half mile southeast of the town of Barons, which was established in the spring of 1909. Shortly a new post office at Barons replaced the one at Blayney.

TRAVEL ACCOUNT OF BEERT A. NAUTA
(29 August 1909)[181]

Granum, 29 August 1909

Dear Mother!

I would like to let you know that we arrived in New York well and healthy.[182] Even though it was summer, we really did not have such a good trip due to the heavy winds. But, let me start at the beginning.

In Leeuwarden we had to wait for two hours so we went uptown for a bit and said good-bye to Booi. Arriving back at the station, we noticed two men and a woman standing there with two suitcases.

Hendrik asked me, "Do you think those people are going to America too?"

I said, "I don't know, but let's ask them." We asked, and yes, one of the three, a man, was headed for America too.

"Fine," said the lady, "then you can nicely travel together."

I said, "If you are also going via Stavoren and Enkhuizen, we could travel together."

"No," said the gentlemen, "I am traveling with the city train. Are you going second class?"

"Yes."

"Well, then we will see each other again on the boat."

And so we each went our own way.

When we arrived at Rotterdam we rode the electric tram to the Maas [River], took the ferry, changed over our tickets, and brought our baggage to the baggage master. Then we went into the city for a while. That evening, at 11 p.m. we went to the boat and found that our luggage had already been taken to our cabin. When we stood on the pier, we had to put our heads in the back of our necks (as they say) in order to see the railing. Yes, that is some height, and then yet comes the first, the second, and above that the third promenade or strolling deck. Yes, Mother, you really should see a boat like this yet; it is much different than the *Werkendam*.[183] And so we climbed the steps and got on board the boat. They directed us to our cabin; we undressed and our first night on board had begun.

---

181 This is a revised version of a translation of this account by Hilda Withage, a daughter of Beert Nauta. The original is in the possession of Annie and Roy Nauta of Claresholm.

182 Twenty-four-year-old Beert Annes Nauta and his cousin Hendrik Hoekstra, both from St. Annaparochie in Friesland, immigrated to Granum to join Nauta's uncle Beert Geerts Nauta and his son Jan. They sailed on the *Nieuw Amsterdam*, which left Rotterdam on 26 June and arrived at New York on 5 July 1909.

183 In 1891 six-year-old Beert had sailed with his family to the United States on the *Werkendam* to visit relatives in the Paterson, N.J. area.

The next morning we got up at 6 a.m. and went to a higher deck, as things were being made ready for our departure. The third-class people were also on board by now. The cables were loosened, the tugboats were in place, and our boat was towed away from the dock, out to the middle of the river where we began to cruise on our own steam.

And so very soon Rotterdam was out of sight. Soon we reached the Hook of Holland. I said to Hendrik, "Let's go to the right side of the ship so we can see the place where the *Berlin* sank some years ago." We steamed right by the sight but it was quite a bit different now than when we saw it before.

The soft waves kissed the coastline and played with the crab baskets and sticks, etc., in the light of the rising sun. The lighthouse regularly did its duty and soon we passed this by also. Then we saw the sand dunes of Holland disappear on the horizon. "Till we see you again, dear Fatherland. Farewell."

We then strolled up and down the ship a bit and met three men who asked us, "Do you come from Friesland too?"

"Yes, we come from St. Annaparochie."

"I come from Leeuwarden," one said.

And so we had met a friend, a certain [Lise] Arzoni, a brother of the Arzoni who built the new houses on the north road with Jan of Uncle Hijlke. The second man was a certain Mr. [Jacob] Vreeswijk from Zeeland. The third was [Abraham] Rozema from Paterson [New Jersey] who had been in Holland on business.

It was about 8 a.m. and we heard a bell ringing so we thought that it was time to eat. No, first something else; they gave us our places at certain tables. Hendrik and I each got a place together. The chairs had a number on them so everyone had their own number.

Breakfast was at 7:30 a.m. Dinner was a 2 p.m., and supper at 7 p.m. In between meals, they served cocoa or beef-tea [bouillon-tea] and much more. The meals were unusually good, although there were many dishes that we didn't like. I will send you a menu like the ones we got anew at the table every mealtime; also a bulletin from the farewell dinner on the last day on the boat. And also a newspaper, which appeared daily on the boat, with the latest news from all parts of the world.

The first meal we had on board really tasted good. But you don't make a trip like that without paying for it. We no longer got out to sea than "Neptune" was there for his offering, and want to or not, we had to throw up. That can't be helped. Now I can hear you say, "I didn't think that you would be seasick." But it is something you really can't do anything about. However, it only lasted for a short time and then it was better.

At five in the afternoon we could see the French coast come into view. It was a much different view than the Dutch coastline. Large boulders, mountains, valleys, breakers, fortresses, and lighthouses. Also, steamboats and fishing vessels, etc. A beautiful sight for anyone who has an eye and heart for the beauty of nature.

At 5:30 we heard a noise that sounded like thunder. It was the steam whistle of our boat sounding a warning to a small passenger boat from Boulogne that the *Nieuw Amsterdam* was awaiting its arrival on the open sea, so that fellow travelers who came via Boulogne could come on board. However, no small boat showed up. We looked with our binoculars at the harbour, and yes, the small boat of the Holland-America Line with its green-white-green flag (by which boats of that company are recognized) still lay in dock, showing no haste in the least.

"What's the holdup?" I asked.

Someone responded, "Well, I think the train has not come in yet."

Then we noticed a column of smoke on the horizon which was the train they were awaiting. When it arrived at the station, it did not take long and its passengers were on board with us. I think we took on around 200 people there. However, once they were on board, we could not really notice that there were that many more people on the boat and yet they were mostly traveling second class. But such a large ship holds so many, and they told us there were around a thousand people on board. That was not that many, so there was lots of room.[184] Most people who were only with the two of them had a four-bed cabin to themselves. When you think that the ship has a crew of 400 people then you can understand that 600 passengers is not so many.

The boarding was soon finished, the departure signals sounded, and soon Boulogne sur Mer disappeared from view. The band played the French, Dutch, and American national anthems as well as the Frisian anthem.[185] Yes, even the Frisian anthem. I thought that quite unusual, but it did our Frisian hearts good. When we left Rotterdam the band did not play.

Very soon we could see England and its white cliffs, and towards evening we could see the lights on the pier of the city of Portsmouth.

We strolled around the ship some more, looked in the smoking salon, and then spent the first night on the English Channel. We slept well.

---

184 The *Nieuw Amsterdam*, built in 1906 for the Holland-America line, was 615 feet long and was capable of carrying 2886 passengers.

185 The Frisian anthem, "Frysk blut, tjoch op!" is a nineteenth-century nationalistic song with a rousing melody.

The next morning we passed by the Isle of Wight and could see the English coast at all times. At 12:20 we passed Lizard Point and at 3:30 the Scilly islands, which was the last land we saw.

Now there was nothing to see but sky and water and we soon had no interest in that any more. So we sought our pleasure in the smoking salon though we soon tired of that too. Again we went on deck. First one, then the next one and several times up and down to explore. The promenade deck was 93 steps in length. This was how we spent the time.

At twelve noon there was music upstairs and in the evening from nine to ten the string orchestra played in the first ballroom. I cannot possibly begin to tell you in a letter all that there is to tell as that would be too much. It is simply something that one has to see for themselves.

But I would like to tell you, Mother, that the second-class cabins on the *Werkendam* were only on the sides of the ship and the middle was the dining room. It was not that way on the *Nieuw Amsterdam*. Our dining room was just below the deck and below that were the cabins. It was like a maze down there with all little corridors which made it a bit difficult to find your own cabin. There were five different levels that we could use; first the cabins; above that the dining room. Then above that was the smoking salon and ladies' conversation salon, and above that the deck; then the first promenade deck and above that the second promenade deck.

People traveling first class could not go any higher than we could although their upper deck was much larger. Yet their view was quite obstructed by the lifeboats.

The third-class people had only the first deck at their disposal. The women were at the back of the boat and the men at the front. You can understand that third class was the worst place to be when the boat tossed to and fro.

The *Nieuw Amsterdam* was like a wooden shoe in the ocean as was the *Werkendam* seventeen years ago. We were always fighting strong headwinds, and when we got well out to sea the ship did a lot of tossing to and fro. A horrible feeling it was to float up and down like that. Everyone got seasick then, the one more and the other less. And those dirty Russians just vomited anywhere – on the carpet, in the halls, on the deck. We put our heads overboard, but those people did not. We had quite a few Russians traveling second class also – dirty people and they stunk. It was quite bad. Some had such dirty hands that in the evening you almost stuck to the handrails, but in the morning it was all cleaned up again. There were also neat and clean people amongst them though. I am going to send you some photos of a pair of neat Polish girls and of some Russian girls as well. I took the odd photo so I hope they will turn out.

And so we visited around together on the boat. Everyone was the best of friends – Hollanders, Germans, Englishmen, Americans, Polish people, Russians, Frenchmen, Italians and whatever other nationalities. But not to forget, we had already quite soon found our friend whom we met at the train station in Leeuwarden. His name was Biense Hoekstra. He used to live at Hallum and now had been to Holland on a pleasure trip. He invited us both to spend a week at his place in Paterson. I said, "Agreed, that we will do."

And so nine days went by. One day in the middle of the ocean we saw whole schools of fish that sprang up out of the water about ten metres into the air. We asked one of the sailors what kind of fish these were. He said, "Oh, that is the farmer with his pigs. We'll surely get some stormy weather."

"The farmer with his pigs?" We looked around at one another because this seaman's term we had never heard before. I never found out what sort of fish they really were but I think they were "brown fish."

Nevertheless, the next day we did get stormy weather; heavy winds and rough seas, so the water smashed over the front of the ship and we could not stay dry on the promenade deck. There were very few times on the whole trip that we could be out on deck without our overcoats on. It was not always because of the spray of the water, but mostly the cold.

At last, on the fifth of July around ten or eleven in the morning Long Island came into view. Soon after that we passed the lightship and a pilot came on board. Now it would not be long before we would be on land again. However, we first had to steam a little ways up the Hudson River; on its shore is the proud city of New York with its skyscrapers. That was a tremendous and beautiful sight.

The river here was as broad as about from the train tracks to R. Van der Zee's place. Then a small rowboat pulled up beside us with two men in it. Our boat was cruising so slowly that there was almost no wake. They called out to us, "Three cheers for Princess Juliana!" We responded with the same enthusiasm, of course.

We were welcomed with the noise of cannon shots, sometimes enshrouded in gunpowder smoke. You are undoubtedly asking, "How could this be?" Don't be anxious, Mother, because the bullets luckily had no targets. I will explain it all to you. At the entry of the river before the city of New York are naturally the necessary fortresses; that is why the cannons are there. Now take note of the date. It was the fifth of July. On the fourth of July celebrations are held to commemorate America becoming independent, but if the fourth falls on a Sunday, then they take place on the next day. That was how it happened to be and thus all the music. Do you understand?

We were very lucky; everything was so wonderful. The ocean behind us, a mighty river before us, and on its banks an enormous city; below us a huge sea castle surrounded by a charming shoreline beset with beautiful villas; and welcomed by the roar of cannons, all under the warm American sunshine. We approached the Statue of Liberty and I decided I wanted to have a good look at it. However, much to my disappointment it was just at that point that we had to appear before the doctor. That didn't take long; he hardly looked at us and with a motion of his hand he signaled us to move along. That took a load off Hendrik's mind. They asked how much money we had. I said $150 each, and then we could go.

Finally, after all this, the ship approached the landing pier, a huge long and high building built out into the river. We landed at the dock of the Hamburg-America line since our huge ship could not land at the dock of the Holland-America line. I heard people say that the H-A. dock is being prepared to receive larger boats as well.

Our boat was softly moved along by eight tugs, each supplied with soft buffers, until we were properly in place alongside the wharf. Everyone was already standing with bag and baggage, ready to leave the boat as soon as possible. The gangplank was laid on board and two officers took their place. We could leave the boat after giving them our boat ticket and our medical report. We did just that and walked down the bridge and so we set foot, Hendrik for the first time and I for the second time, on American soil.

But really not yet – that was still one level lower. We were on an upper level, but we didn't realize it until we came down on the elevator. This top level was also where all the baggage was unloaded, and everyone could find their trunks in the section that was indicated by the first letter of their last name. The wife of our friend Rozema and also a sister were there to meet him. B. Hoekstra's wife and a son also were there to pick him up. And so after we were introduced to these ladies and gentlemen, we took our baggage through customs (we were not required to unpack anything, not even the large trunk) and then took the elevator down to ground level.[186]

Now we were in Hoboken, and so we took the electric tram uptown to the Erie station and then after going three quarters of an hour by rail we were in Paterson. We went with B. Hoekstra to his home, also by electric tram.

---

186 Along with other first- and second-class passengers they did not have to be processed at Ellis Island, an anxious ordeal that was required of all third-class immigrants.

The electric tram is really an easy way to travel. The B. Hoekstras live in a two-story house; he rents out the lower floor so we stayed for a week on the top floor. We had a very good time at the Hoekstras. They were very amiable people. It gave us an opportunity to relax comfortably and get rested after our difficult trip on the ocean. It was a quiet balmy evening, that evening of July 5th. All nature was still too, but not so in the city.

All around you could continually hear the shooting, all sorts of fireworks, and the rumbling of the cannons. My, oh my, what a noise! "From hearing and seeing you could perish," we would say. We also lit up some firecrackers in honor of America's independence.

After dark I went outside by myself for a walk. Mr. Hoekstra and Hendrik were having a big discussion. The Hoekstra house is not really in the centre of town but somewhat on the outskirts, right behind Haledon Avenue where Akershoek lives. That is quite a coincidence, eh? Well, I walked around a bit and wondered whether something was wrong with my eyes. I didn't know what it was, but every now and then I kept seeing little lights just ahead of me. But I soon realized what they were – they were fireflies that light up at night; they are phosphorescent. You have seen them, haven't you, Mother? I think we were at this same place when we were here before, when we could look over the city of Paterson and see all those lights in the evening. At that time it was out of town but now it is within the city limits.

The following day Mr. Hoekstra took us uptown to see the city. I must say I can't brag very much about Paterson and can only describe it in one word – dirty. I would say it is something like the Amelandsteeg in Leeuwarden, but of course the houses are much wider and higher and neater, although the street in Leeuwarden is cleaner. The street cleaning companies here and also in Hoboken, where we landed, must be in quite a poor state. That is the impression I got, anyway. It's also true that when people have old newspapers, garbage, trash, etc., they just throw it outside wherever it lands, without considering that everything blows around on the street. This makes us disgusted, we Hollanders with a little sense of cleanliness.

However, if you go to the streets or lanes with villas, conditions are much better. They have nice asphalt streets and sidewalks. In the countryside the roads are also poor, except for the lanes of the millionaires. Paterson and Hoboken really disappointed me. The cities I would call "holes," but not the parks, and the churchyards are paradises. It's really something how they have kept such tidiness, cleanliness, and magnificence completely separate here. Now I can understand why Americans admire Holland; conversely, we do that too. Stark contrasts – beautiful buildings and stores, equipped with the latest inventions, everything electric, but surrounded by sloppiness. I don't think that anyone in Paterson knows what cleaning windows is. I have also been in Bocholt in Germany, but I think that city wins the street cleanliness award by far.

The following day, a Tuesday, again we strolled around. Mr. Hoekstra could show us around since he did not go back to work at the factory for the first week after his return. The weather was warm so we enjoyed the odd glass of beer. The beer here is very good and not expensive. You can get a small glass for 5 cents American, but if you wish you can get a medium or large size. I think the large glasses hold almost a litre, and there is quite a bit of alcohol in it.

We arrived at home with Hendrik just a bit unsteady. It was quite funny really; we had each had a couple of glasses, but Hendrik said he could still down another glass. Mr. Hoekstra said, "Then we will buy another glass," and he ordered two small glasses for us and one large one for Hendrik. He had some difficulty with it but managed to finish it all. However, when we got home Mrs. Hoekstra grumbled at us for giving Hendrik too much beer. He really wasn't drunk, but, as I said, he was a bit unsteady.

On Wednesday morning I asked Mr. Hoekstra to show us the way to Midland Park since I wanted to look up old Uncle Pieter [Nauta]. We were too late to catch the train so we walked there. That was rather disappointing since it was rather far – about an hour and a half, I think – but we finally got there after asking here and there where they lived. They live in a nice house and he told us they also own the house next to it. We went around to the back door where Aunt Sjoukje met us. She knew me right away but did not recognize Hendrik.

Aunt Sjoukje was the same thin little lady as always. Uncle Pieter was sitting at the table reading the Bible; they had just finished eating. Well, was the old man ever happy that we had come to visit them! They have a nice organ in the house and also a nice stove; in short, I believe they are quite well off. They have three daughters who work in the factory. Their son Gerrit had been married but was separated from his wife so was living at home again. Uncle Pieter had a bit of land around his house on which he grew some potatoes, and a portion of it was planted to fruit trees. We spent that Wednesday there and in the evening they took us to the train to go back. We arrived at Riverside Station and Hendrik was quite anxious about whether we would find the Hoekstra residence again. That didn't turn out to be too difficult as I had taken mental note of where we had gone, and so after walking and crossing several streets we arrived at our destination.

Hendrik was quite relieved. He had grumbled at me as we were walking that I didn't stop and ask where to go.

On Thursday we all went to New York by electric tram, but we really didn't get to see too much of the city. We arrived there too late and besides Mr. Hoekstra was not very venturesome in New York. Friday and Saturday Hendrik and I spent the time wandering around Paterson. Our friend Rozema's store was our base and we went out from there and also returned back there again. We went to the station and arranged for our train tickets; the station agent helped us to get this all in order. Our friend Rozema did all he could to help us too, which we greatly appreciated.

On Sunday we first went to church with the Hoekstras where we met old friends or rather people who had known Father and still knew you, Mother, but who didn't know us, and we, of course, didn't know them. It was just 400 years ago that Sunday that Calvin was born (10 July 1509) and so the churches here had a special service at seven in the evening to commemorate that event. In the afternoon after eating with the Rozemas we went to church with them and then returned home with them. We were no sooner there when we noticed that there was a fire in the direction of Rozema's store. We all ran over there as fast as we could, because Rozema thought it could well be his store, but, fortunately, that was not the case. The fire was in a furniture factory on River Street. There was an apartment next to it in which several families lived. The fire had just started when we arrived, but already there were eight steam fire engines working to control the fire.

This was for us a brand new experience. They were very nice machines, I tell you, polished and shining like nickel. They were stoked though, which caused them to smoke as much as the fire itself while they were throwing out water. The four horses in front of each engine stood there quietly and calmly until the fire was out. How they race through the streets and how everyone has to get out of the way is something else! Also how the horses on hearing the fire alarm go by themselves to the fire wagons to be hitched up. You have now and then heard about this but we saw it for ourselves. It took about two hours to put the fire out, but sixteen families were homeless, not to speak of the damage. The cause of the fire was not known precisely, as is usually the case by us at home too.

All too soon Sunday was over, and so we faced Monday morning, the day on which we had to continue our trip. The train on which we were to travel west was due to leave at 2 p.m. We gathered our bag and baggage, and after bidding our friends in Paterson farewell, we stepped on the Erie train headed for Chicago. Now our traveling was about to begin. Soon it was evening and all we could do was try to sleep; yes I say try as that was about as far as it went. Finally it was morning; we washed up and about an hour later the train made a ten-minute stop at a station.

This gave the passengers an opportunity to go out to buy something. I went into the station to stock up on some food. There was a dining car at the back of the train but that, we decided, was too expensive for us. There was also a sleeping car but that would have cost us $2 apiece. That would be 10 guilders for the two of us, and that was too much as well; besides young people can overnight quite well on the train. The trains are quite nice and are furnished comfortably, but to brag about the Erie train line I cannot do. The cars are not as wide as our local coaches. There are two seats on either side of the aisle. The customary dirtiness was also much in evidence here, even though the black porter swept away everything three or four times a day. Each time there was more paper and peanut shells and bread crusts, etc., and then not to forget the smoke from the locomotive.

That was exactly the same as the former trip, Mother, making the Erie train very unpleasant especially in the summer when it is hot and the windows are open. The smoke almost always circulated around the coaches, because we were always passing along mountains, rocky walls, and rugged stretches, causing the engine to snort smoke which traveled right along with us. When we were on the other train after Chicago we didn't have any trouble with the smoke since the land there was more level and the wind could blow the smoke away from us.

There were almost no baggage racks and so everything just lay around on the floor. I think there really should have been better facilities for baggage on trains like that. We arrived in Chicago at about 5 p.m. Prior to this the conductor came around and put a little card in each of our hats. When we stepped off the train I asked him where we were to go. He informed me that outside the station there would be someone who would take us where we should go. I thought to myself if that someone didn't suit me that I would soon get in touch with a policeman. We went out of the station and there stood a lot of buses that took passengers from one station to the other. The bus drivers were wearing uniforms and that to us was a sign that they worked for the rail company.

One of the drivers saw from the cards on our hats that we had to go to the station to which he drove, and he took us to his bus. We could climb up on top of the bus; women have to sit inside. However, no one else came so the driver drove away with two negroes riding on top of his bus. Yes, because we were almost as black as negroes from the smoke. There were washbasin facilities on the Erie train but the water was always soon used up and towels and soap always gone. Then what good are these conveniences to the passengers? At first everything was there, but there should have been new supplies at least five times on a trip like that. There was also a drinking cup but because it was not attached to a chain, you can imagine what became of that. The lavatory – you wouldn't dare touch it with the tip of your walking stick – filthy! No, then our Dutch trains are a lot better.

Our driver took us to a large station in a different part of Chicago and told us to step down. We went up a big set of stairs and I finally found the area where the trains stood. We were a bit too early so we had to wait about a quarter of an hour. I had thought that this would be a very busy place but it was quiet compared to the station in Amsterdam. I could manage for myself a lot easier here than I could over there. We must have struck a very quiet time; otherwise I can't imagine that there weren't a lot more people here. The railway yard of the station looked a lot like the one in Zwolle and was probably also about the same size.

The trains stood next to one another with platforms in between and names and directions on signboards on the platform, not on the sides of the train as it is in Holland. I think it is better to indicate also on the coaches which direction the train will go; thus the Dutch way is better. Quite soon I found the train that was to take us to St. Paul. It was the "Wisconsin Central." The name indicated that we would be traveling through the heart of Wisconsin. This train was better furnished than the Erie train, more roomy and cleaner; also, it had double windows making it dust and draft proof. The padding on the seats was like second class on the local at home. These coaches were not quite so wide but they were a bit higher.

I cannot say that the trains here are so much better than in Holland. Of course I don't include the little old coaches that they sometimes use on some of the lines in Holland. I don't think they even have such old coaches in America for the simple reason that everything here is of a later date. Whatever is manufactured in Holland nowadays is just as good as it is here. It is said that America is more advanced than other countries, but I don't believe it. The cities here have structures that could be called the largest and greatest, but the farmland and the farmers do not even compare to that of Holland. As for the culture of the people, they are far behind us. But we were discussing our train trip and so will continue with that.

Very soon the city of Chicago was behind us and we traveled into the night at quite a good clip. Our tickets were first class and so we had the right to a bed for the sum of $2. However, I said to my fellow travelers, "Do you know what? We can easily earn that money. We'll just put our overcoats a bit over our heads and stretch out on the seat – it is nice and soft – and then we'll have a good night of sleep." So said, so done.

The next morning St. Paul stood before us. I forgot to tell you that as soon as we boarded this train, we immediately took the opportunity to wash ourselves. At St. Paul we had to board another train. We were not told but I could figure that much out. Our tickets consisted of seven separate cards, each card for its own segment of the trip – for example, Chicago-St. Paul, St. Paul-Moose Jaw – so by that I could tell that we had to change trains in St. Paul and also in Moose Jaw. It was 8 a.m. when we arrived in St. Paul and here we had to wait two and a half hours. We went into the station. Hendrik wanted to just stay sitting here but I wanted rather to find a restaurant since I was hungry for some breakfast. So we went uptown and had breakfast in a restaurant for 25 cents apiece.

We also bought a few things to eat on the train – some fruit, etc. – and then made our way back to the station. After waiting about a quarter of an hour we could board the train. This time it was the Canadian Pacific that we traveled on – good coaches and nicely furnished. Soon after we left St. Paul we passed by the huge Mississippi River. We did not see any big ships, but we saw logs floating in the water – a broad stream full of logs with an open channel kept down the centre; otherwise it was full of logs. The city of Minneapolis, which lies across the river from St. Paul, consists almost completely of sawmills and sawdust factories – a huge industry in this area. This industry can only be so huge here, because Minneapolis is especially suited for it due to its location on the river which makes its way through immense forests.

We now cut across Minnesota and after that North Dakota. The landscape here was sometimes flat but then again hilly. At one point a long way into this monotony we traveled through a small forest. A little way off the railway I saw a small graveyard with tombstones and crosses that were leaning over and almost choked with wild grass, forgotten and given up to the ravages of time. What had happened there? That day passed rather slowly and again it was night.

The next morning I was awakened early by Hendrik. A man came into the train to inspect our suitcases. We were at Portal on the border between America and Canada. So a customs officer came to check things, but since we had put all our luggage on the train as baggage, we did not have anything to inspect. Our trunks and large baggage were not inspected here either. If they were on the same train as we were – I don't know. Now finally we were in Canada, in the province of Saskatchewan, and we soon arrived in the small city of Moose Jaw.

Here in Saskatchewan the land was flat and as far as the eye could see it was prairie with a little farmhouse here and there. After many stops we arrived at Medicine Hat toward evening. Again we transferred to another train. We spent the night traveling from Medicine Hat to Macleod, arriving there at four o'clock in the morning. Here we had to wait about three hours so we took the opportunity to get something to eat at the restaurant which was right across from the station. At seven o'clock our train came and thus began the last leg of our journey, Macleod-Granum.

Soon enough we were at our destination; at 8 a.m. we arrived at Granum. There was no one at the station to meet us and so we courageously stepped across the street into the little town. We went to a barber and each had a shave, bought a new collar and bow-tie, put them on in the store where we bought them and we were ready to go. Meanwhile I asked around here and there where Uncle Beert [Nauta] lived but no one seemed to know. Finally we saw [cousin] Jan coming with horse and wagon, and then we were greatly relieved.

After riding for an hour and a half we were finally at Uncle's house. We were happy to have our feet on solid ground again; such a train trip of four days and four nights is very tiring. And if I tell you that we had to stop more than a hundred times during the trip, then you can realize that we certainly were not traveling on any kind of speed train. The train between Leeuwarden and St. Annaparochie may be tedious but this train takes the cake!

I have not as yet experienced much here in Canada, but this I have noticed – that nearly everyone is here to make a dollar. That is the spirit of business here. The relaxed, contented way of life that we had in Holland you do not find here. If Father Poot had lived here he certainly would *not* have sung:

"How pleasantly rolls on the life of a contented farmer."

B[eert] A. Nauta

EXCERPT OF REPORT OF KAREL FORTUIN[187]

(*De Wachter,* 29 September 1909)

Something about our Congregations in the Far West

... After all we saw of Farmington, Conrad, and Nijverdal and heard from
trustworthy sources, it seems to us that for farmers renting in more easterly
states who must work hard to bring in the rent from year to year, there is still
a beautiful opportunity, with the Lord's blessing, to obtain their own piece
of land in these places. Looking at many who settled here in the last four or
five years, one has to be surprised at their prosperity. Almost all are already
landowners. As usually happens, so it was with them – when they settled
in these still unknown areas they had as good as no earthly treasures. And
every farmer immediately agreed with us that if the soil was not fertile in
these areas, one would not be able to see such prosperity in such a short time.
The great stumbling block for the churches is not the soil but the number
of members that is still too small. This obstacle cannot be removed unless
bold men from the eastern states settle there. Considering the exceptional
field crops that we saw in all three places, it surprised us very much that
our congregations there are still so small. This can partly be explained
from the sad fact that the Reformed church is everywhere at our heels,[188]
but otherwise at present it remains a riddle for us. In these congregations
church life till now is still very poor, something that naturally will improve
gradually as more people settle here. The lack of their own minister, in my
opinion, makes these congregations still so tender. If the congregations
become strong enough in members to call their own minister, then there
is no fear for the future, because the land is fertile enough....

Fortunately, we can also give a good report about Nijverdal, Canada. Here
too we took pleasure in the beautiful grain fields that for us spelled a fine
harvest. The fact that our congregation, which split in two due to distance,
saw both sides of the Dutch settlement raise their own small church buildings already in the past year, in my opinion well proves the fertility of the
soil, because the earliest settlers have still not been here six years. In the
area of this congregation there are no more homesteads to be obtained from
King Edward, but one can still get a good piece of land here for a relatively

---

187 Karel Fortuin, as a student preparing for the ministry, served the Nijverdal Christian Reformed Church for
  several weeks in the summer of 1909. He also spent some time in the churches at Farmington and Conrad in
  Montana. This report comments on the state of each of these three churches.

188 In most Dutch communities there was not only a Christian Reformed church, but also a Reformed church.
  At Monarch the Reformed congregation was just recently established in August 1909.

moderate price, on easy terms, yes even for "crop payments." If some good families were to join this congregation, it would already be able to call its own shepherd and minister. A small number in these western areas can do wonders, but then one must be able to form a small number. None of us needs to fear that our congregation there finds itself under England's king. The laws for Sabbath observance, for the liquor trade, and for poor relief, for example, are much better there than by us [in the United States]; at any rate they enforce what is put into law a lot more faithfully. Lawbreakers there are not dealt with gently and the mounted police are always carefully on the lookout....

K[arel] W. Fortuin

LETTER FROM GRANUM
(*De Grondwet*, 16 November, 1909)

We have had a nice summer here. Not as dry as last year. The rains came on time and the farmer's hopes were not disappointed. The fall was beautiful! The wind can sometimes rage here in the fall, but this year it didn't give us any trouble. Therefore the threshing didn't need to stop because of the hard wind. The yield was pretty good. Winter wheat brought in 30 to 45 bushels per acre. G[arrit] Willemsen got 49 bushels of winter wheat per acre and R[oelf] Lantinga got 1,900 bushels from 40 acres. R. Lantinga is now on a trip to the Netherlands.[189]

The spring wheat was also pretty good; 20 to 35 bushels per acre. Oats here is usually not so heavy, because people mostly seed it on old land where good wheat crops no longer want to grow.[190] Also potatoes and other garden produce were pretty good this year.

We had the privilege of having Rev. J. Van der Mey from Manhattan, Montana, in our midst for several days.[191] The Reverend really dotted his

---

189 Lantinga visited the Netherlands to visit relatives and to find a wife.

190 "Old land" refers to the land that was broken and had produced crops for several years. It was probably not summer-fallowed, and so was depleted of nutrients and moisture.

191 Rev. John Vander Mey was the new pastor of the Manhattan CRC since 1908. As the nearest CRC minister he served as counsellor of the Nijverdal CRC. He apparently was a stickler about following the CRC church order, insisting, for example, that regular monthly offerings be taken.

i's and crossed his t's here. Our church was built last winter and now we want to build a parsonage. A building committee has already been named and this week yet they will begin to dig the cellar.[192] We hope that next fall we will be able to call a minister.

At the home of Mr. and Mrs. Dijkema a baby daughter was born; also at the home of Mr. and Mrs. Van Dellen.[193]

Corr. [George Dijkema] 8 Nov. 1909

EXCERPT OF REPORT OF REV. JOHN VANDER MEY
(*De Wachter,* 17 November 1909)

... But Canada is especially the land of opportunity. While we write this, we are on Canadian territory, at the church listed in our yearbook as Nijverdal.[194] Our Reformed Hollanders have lived here for five years already. Starting out poor, most of them are now very prosperous. This is well enough evident from what they are venturing to do in the church. Two church buildings have been raised. This fall a parsonage is being put up. Next spring they will try to call a minister at a salary of $1,000. Indeed, a worker in the Lord's vineyard is due here. The congregation meets in three places. Near Granum is the minister's house. Fifteen miles east of the parsonage is church no. 2. Forty miles further east, near Grassy Lake, is a branch of the congregation where one elder and one deacon have just been appointed. In the latter place a minister would very easily be able to fulfill his classical appointments, while dividing his time and labour between the Nijverdal East and West side. Yet one doesn't need to be a prophet to predict that before long three separate churches will develop here.

The land is beautiful and very fertile, and available for $20 to $30 an acre. Wheat is the main product and is also among the best that appears on the world market. It is only because of unfamiliarity with this region that many do not move here.

---

192 The west-side church was built in the winter of 1908–09. The planned parsonage was built on the west-side church property. It was thought that a parsonage would attract a regular minister to the community. The east side and west side agreed to share a minister, but they vied with each other about where he would live.
193 George and Anna Dijkema's daughter Annetta was born 2 September 1909. Lubbert and Japke Van Dellen's first child Jenny was born 9 September 1909.
194 *Jaarboekje ten Dienste der Christelijke Gereformeerde Kerk in Amerika,* 1908. Rev. Vander Mey, pastor of the Manhattan, Mont. Christian Reformed Church, visited the Nijverdal church for two Sundays in October and November 1909.

Many a person will say: But in Canada one is under English rule! Yet, does this have to scare anyone? One enjoys just as much freedom in Canada as in the States. Only the ungodly who want to follow crooked ways feel more at home in Uncle Sam's territory. For example, divorce is impossible here, Sabbath keeping is beyond reproach, and the administration of justice is very much better and more just than by us. A Reformed person in Canada can feel at ease.

Once again, what a land of opportunities! Canada is large, tremendously large. Millions of acres of the best wheat land still wait to be developed. Railways are being built everywhere. A few Hollanders have already penetrated three hundred miles north of Nijverdal. A former elder of our church at Farmington, Mont., now lives near Edmonton, Alberta.[195] Who knows how many Dutch churches will still appear between Nijverdal and Edmonton. Especially due to its climate and fertility Alberta is the most suitable province in all of Canada for Dutch farmers....

LETTER FROM NAN DEKKER TO THE HELDER FAMILY
(29 November 1909)

Monarch, Alberta
29 November 1909
Dear Friends,[196]

We received your letter in good condition. And I can write you that we also received the portrait in good condition. We had been to Lethbridge three times, and they told us, "When it arrives here, we will send it on to Monarch." Finally it arrived there in good condition. Evert brought it, since he was bringing and picking up the mail.

We have been very busy with the wedding of Arie.[197] He was married last week, the 26th of November, and the reception was the 27th. The first people came at two in the afternoon, the last at eight. And how many there were, I will tell you. All the Hollanders, and that was over a hundred. They had figured well, because they had made place for ninety. The married folk left

---

195 In the spring of 1906 Frederik Baron and his family moved from Farmington to Edmonton. His wife was a niece of Leendert Bode and Gerrit Hartkoorn, who farmed at Monarch. As more Dutch families moved to Edmonton, Baron helped organize a Christian Reformed church there in October 1910, the second in Alberta.
196 Nan Dekker wrote this letter to Eva Helder and her family of Spring Valley, N.Y.
197 Thirty-three-year-old Arie was the second son of Nan Dekker. He married twenty-eight-year-old Louisa Stotyn, the sister of Willem Stotyn and Christina Aldus.

at three in the morning and the young people at four. We had beer and wine and lots of food. For four days we had a maid who could bake everything, so the cellar was full of baked goods, and I don't know what all else. They danced and waltzed. A neighbour came with his organ[198] and another with a mouth organ, and those two could play every song. My wife put on her boerenkap[199] and also sat the whole night and laughed at the fun.

Now what else; the school teacher speaks English and the children must also learn English. I think Evert is leaving this week, first to his land and then to his wife, because the work here is done. We have already had winter and snow here. Fortunately, the weather was good for the reception. Ja, it is not as cold here in the winter as in Vesper [Wisc.] Sometimes the snow may be a foot deep, but if a chinook wind comes, it is gone in a day, because the wind is warm.

Yes, Eva, it is nice living here. We have no fruit trees or other trees. It is too dry; they don't like to grow here. Some people plant trees, but I do not. Arie's wife also comes from Holland, from Nijverdal. We have two stoves, a cook stove and a heating stove. We use coal in the stoves. There is enough of it here.

Greetings from all of us, N[an] Dekker

LETTER FROM MONARCH
(*De Grondwet*, 14 December 1909)

We have beautiful weather here, as nice as one could wish. We also had a good harvest. Winter wheat did not yield much, from 15 to 18 bushels per acre; but the spring wheat 25 to 37 bushels per acre. Oats was also good. The price of wheat is 80 cents a bushel, and oats 34 cents. Butter is 30 cents a pound and eggs 30 cents a dozen.

People here are busy figuring out where they want to go to, the one traveling farther than the other.[200] Yesterday there were five buggies and a farm wagon at our new Monarch station, all carrying passengers who were leaving. Four of the travelers went for pleasure to Holland and three others

---

198 Evert Aldus had the pump organ, which he apparently took along to special celebrations in the Dutch community.

199 A boerenkap is a traditional white cap that Dutch women wore on Sundays to church and on other special occasions.

200 Good crops for four straight years in the settlement (since 1906) led to a measure of prosperity so that during the winter season many Dutch settlers began making trips to visit relatives or to find a spouse.

preceded them by a week.[201] The names of those who just left are L[eendert] Bode, G[errit] Hartkoorn, A[lbert] Rutgers, and D. [Hendrikus] Veldhuis. Seven others went to Vesper, Wisconsin, to visit their relatives there. They are Mr. and Mrs. G[errit] Bode with three children, W[illem] Van Schuur, and L[eendert] Geleynse.

Two wedding ceremonies took place here in the last couple of weeks. The newly-married couples are: Arie Dekker with Lizzie Statijn [Stotijn], and Bastian Kole [Koole] with Katherina Huisman.[202] Success!

By all appearances it is going well for the farmers here. The one is making better improvements to his house than the other.

As I understand it now, Mr. and Mrs. D[aniel] De Boer will also pay a visit to their parents in Montana.[203]

Corr. 1 Dec. 1909

LETTER FROM MONARCH
(*De Volksvriend*, 16 December 1909)[204]

Summer and fall left us earlier than usual. While in other years we sometimes had beautiful weather until after Christmas, now snow began to fall in the middle of November, and the Fahrenheit thermometer continually indicates 10 or 20 degrees below zero. This is not pleasant, but it does not matter much. Coal is nearby, cheap, and of good quality. We can buy our necessities in Monarch, in our immediate neighbourhood; we haul our wheat there too.

On the 1st of September the locomotive came there for the first time; on the 20th of the month the first passenger train passed through. Since that time we have had partial service, until regular service began on 1 December.[205]

Our settlement lies in the immediate vicinity of Monarch, while the Lethbridge-Calgary line on which the town of Nobel [Noble] is being built runs on our northeast side.[206] So we have two stations at our disposal.

---

201 The first group of travelers included Jacobus Nijhoff, Berend Nijhof, and Jan Bannink.
202 Katherina (Catherena) Huisman was the eldest daughter of Johan and Hendrika Huisman.
203 Daniel De Boer's parents lived at Conrad, Mont.
204 This is one of several letters that Evert Aldus sent to *De Volksvriend*.
205 The new CPR Lethbridge-Macleod line opened on 23 Oct. 1909. Earlier partial service was only from Macleod.

As in previous years our harvest was very good. Wheat ran from 20 to 38 bushels. Till now the price has been about 80 cents. Oats, potatoes, and vegetables were also grown successfully.

Land here costs $25 to $40 per acre. When I read that land in Iowa and other areas is three to four times as expensive, then I think: "Why don't people buy here?" Very good land and good harvests. One can buy prairie or farms already worked. Even recently I heard of someone who wanted to dispose of his farm of 960 acres, and gladly to the Dutch.

In January of this year the first church was built, the Christian Reformed.[207] In August the Dutch Reformed congregation was established; its plans also to build a church this year were thwarted by the early onset of winter.[208] Rev. Lammers of Westfield, N.Dak. and an elder were delegated by the Synod [Classis] to organize the congregation. The elders are J. [Tijmen] Hofman and Jac[obus] Nijhoff; the deacons J. W. [Willem Jan] van Lohuizen and E[vert] Aldus.

[Evert Aldus]

LETTER FROM GRANUM
(*De Wachter,* 5 January 1910)

From Nijverdal, Canada

The year 1909 has almost ended as I write this. This year again has brought us much that is sweet and bitter. Yet the Lord has again richly blessed us here, in the community as well as in the church. In the church domain we here in the far northwest have again not been forgotten. We had Rev. [Menno] Borduin here last spring for a couple of Sundays. All who heard him were

---

206 The hamlet of Noble originated in 1909, when the CPR built the new Aldersyde line north from Kipp. The *Claresholm Review* (6 May 1909) briefly noted the origins of Noble: "CPR Buys a Townsite and Named It after a Popular Claresholm Man. The town of 'Noble' is the latest. Mr. C. S. Noble has sold [to] the CPR land in 11-13-23 [3-11-23] on the Carmangay-Lethbridge line and it will be surveyed at once as a townsite and will be on the market shortly. The CPR has honored Mr. Noble by naming the town after him and it is understood he will build a fine home in the new town. He has sold his Claresholm house to his partner, Mr. Milnes. The town of Noble to be, is well situated to become an important point. It is expected that an elevator will be built this summer and the CPR will haul grain there this fall." See also MacEwan, *Charles Noble,* chap. 6. In 1913 the name Noble was changed to Nobleford.

207 In early 1909 the Christian Reformed people on the east side of the settlement constructed a church building north of Monarch. It was dedicated on Ascension Day, 20 May 1909, and in the following winter the inside was finished.

208 The Reformed Church of Monarch was organized on 1 August 1909, and its church building was constructed in late 1910.

pleased to hear him, though on one Sunday there were not many for him to preach the gospel to; it was very cold, snowy weather.

During the long vacation for the students of our Theological School[209] we had Mr. [Gerrit] Vande Riet and [Karel] Fortuin. These young men met with better weather than Rev. Borduin. They were here in the summer. Each of them preached for us a few Sundays, and it was a pleasure for us to see them lead us. It is very different than hearing reading sermons. The living proclamation of God's Word goes very far beyond reading sermons. That's why we eagerly long to have our own shepherd and minister as soon as possible. Therefore we are already building our parsonage. Last year we got our church building, this year a parsonage, and next year a preacher we hope, so that our eyes may see our own minister. Finally, we were pleased to have our counselor lead us – Rev. [John] Vander Mey of Manhattan.[210] Because of him we came so far that we are now building the parsonage. This project did not want to float, but when he was for it, it floated very well; all at once it was so clear.[211] A friendly thanks, brother counselor!

At Christmas we had a celebration here. The catechumens eagerly wanted to celebrate. It was then decided to do so, and people told me that it was a good celebration. Everyone enjoyed it, young and old, even though it was only a children's celebration. Everyone was present, except for a couple, and we believe each had a good time, if one can trust facial expressions. Thank the Lord that it was such a success. After the celebration we took up a collection for the insane asylum to be erected in the United States.[212] Our brother deacon has already sent the money to Rev. Jonker.

Now the Christmas celebration is again over, and soon we hope to see Rev. Borduin once again. We hope that the Lord may send him to us soon, so that we may again hear the good news of salvation preached from his mouth. After that the long vacation will again come to our School. Then students are again free to go out, and we hope that again there may be a couple of them for whom it is not too far and too difficult to preach the Gospel to us Hollanders in King Edward's territory. Then we hope that the Lord may send us our own minister to lead us each Sunday. May he grant us the privilege.

G[eorge] Dijkema Granum (Westend Nijverdal), Alberta 28 Dec. 1909

209 The Theological School of the Christian Reformed Church was located in Grand Rapids, Mich.
210 Rev. John Vander Mey, as counselor of the Nijverdal CRC, visited for two Sundays in October-November of 1909.

LETTER FROM EVERT ALDUS
(*Twentsch Volksblad*, 29 January 1910)

"Hours, days, months, years, swift as moving shadows flee." So we may also say, as the year 1909 has gone by. This is the sixth Christmas that we have celebrated here, and on 2 [3] April it will be six years since we settled in Alberta.[213] Of the years that we have spent here, 1909 is the most important. Not only because our harvest was good, but especially because the railway was finished that year, so our isolation and seclusion from the world no longer exist. On the 1st of September the locomotive could be seen and heard for the first time where we live. And, although many readers may find this strange, for us the otherwise unmusical sound of the steam-whistle rang pleasant to the ear.

Then, however, the line was still not finished; this was the locomotive which pushed ahead of itself the large steam machine that laid the ties and rails. Shortly afterward, the line was sufficiently completed so that partial service could begin.

By 1 December everything was far enough ready that regular traffic could commence. Since that time the silence in our vicinity has given way to the moan and whistle blowing of the locomotive, to the rolling of heavy freight trains, the cargo ships on this great sea of grain. And we hope, forever.

Instead of bringing our grain to Lethbridge, we now have to load it onto rail cars at Monarch. Child's play, compared to our old way of doing it.

As proof that the environs of Monarch mean something as grain country is the fact that up until 31 December upwards of 130,000 bushels or 51,000 hectolitres of wheat were shipped from there.

Monarch is expanding all the time. There are two "elevators" (grain storehouses). The school is almost completed.[214]

From Kipp, a station between here and Lethbridge, the line is being laid to Calgary. On this line the laying of rails is already far advanced. A station

---

211 Plans to build a parsonage for the Nijverdal church stalled because of tensions between the two sides of the congregation about whether to locate it on the Granum or Monarch side. The two sides had agreed to share a pastor, but each wanted the pastor to live on their side. In the end the parsonage was built next to the Granum church.

212 In 1909 a society was organized by pastors and laymen of the Reformed and Christian Reformed churches to establish the Christian Insane Asylum in Cutlerville, Michigan. It was later known as Pine Rest Christian Hospital.

213 Aldus is speaking here only of the immigrants from the Nijverdal area who arrived in 1904. They were the core of the east-side of the Dutch settlement.

214 When the Monarch school opened in January 1910, the nearby Dutch families sent their children there instead of to the Rose Butte school.

on this line lies just northeast of our colony. Since Monarch is situated on the southwest side, we live right between there and the station and village on the Calgary line, named Nobel [Noble]. So none of us is far from the railway.

The year 1909 gave us more than the railway train, however. In the beginning of the year the Christian Reformed church was built; this is especially noteworthy, because it is the first Dutch church built in this district.[215]

Then in August the Dutch Reformed Church was organized. Rev. Lammers of Westfield, North Dakota, was in our midst for this occasion. He baptized six little children, and also held the Lord's Supper and admitted some members. The Reformed congregation saw her plan to build a church before winter thwarted by the early onset of cold weather.

All the above is more than enough for us to look back on 1909 with a grateful heart. As in previous years the harvest was very good and the price of wheat remains high to this day, about 80 cents a bushel.

Generally speaking, the weather was favourable, though one night frost in August did some damage. Cold weather and snow visited us earlier than usual; after 15 Nov. it has been winter.

The Christmas celebration was held in the Christian Reformed church in the usual fashion. It wasn't as crowded as in other years, because some have gone to Holland, others to the United States.

Jac[obus] Nijhoff, L[eendeert] Koole, R[ense] Nijhoff each became the father of a child, J[ohn] Postman of two. Of the latter Postman lost one to death, the sole death in 1909.[216] A[rie] Dekker and L[ouisa] Stotijn got married; so did B[astiaan] Koole and C[atherena] Huisman.

I cannot end before expressing my fear that many of you will skip over the content of this letter as old news, since some of those who are visiting Nijverdal from here will undoubtedly have told you all the news. I could have skipped writing, but then perhaps I run the danger of being eliminated by the editor as a correspondent. The more so since my contributions lately have not amounted to much.

A[ldus] Nijverdal near Monarch, 3 January 1910

Our readers are always very pleased with your letters; also, people still like to read in the newspaper what they already know. *Editor.*

---

215 Aldus is referring only to the Monarch district, since the west-side Christian Reformed church was actually the first one built in the settlement.

216 The Postman child was Willem, who died in July or August of 1909.

LETTER FROM MONARCH
(*De Volksvriend*, 10 February 1910)

In my last letter I reported that winter began earlier than usual, midway through November; I can now add that we've had nice mild weather the whole month of January. It hardly froze at all, and no snow fell. Some days were just as nice as the most beautiful spring day. Although such weather is pleasant and advantageous for man and animal, most people think that some snow and frost would be better for the land. Plenty of that can still come, however, before the flower month of May arrives.

Jac[obus] Nyhoff, B[erend] Nyhof, J[an] Bannink, H[endrikus] Veldhuis, A[lbert] Rutgers, H. Boode [Leendert Bode], and Harthoorn [Gerrit Hartkoorn] are making a short pleasure trip to Holland and hope to be back in the spring. The Koole brothers are on a visit to their parents in Iowa.

In 1909 our number increased with some newcomers,[217] while six babies were born. J. Postma [Postman] lost a small child by death. This was the first person buried in the new cemetery by the Christian Reformed church.[218] In the past year B[astiaan] Koole entered into marriage with C[atherena] Huisman, and A[rie] Dekker with L[ouisa] Stotijn.

We are all still living in our first small shacks, except for R[ense] Nyhoff. He had a fine large house built in 1909, while L[eendert] Koole put up a big spacious barn.

The year 1909 was very important for our settlement. The Christian Reformed church was built in the beginning of the year, the first Dutch church in this district. The Dutch Reformed congregation was established. Then came the telephone connection with neighbouring places.[219] And finally, on 1 December regular service began on the new C. P. Railroad, so from that date our seclusion from the outside world has ended.

[Evert Aldus]

217 The newcomers to the settlement in 1909 included Roelof Kingma, Laurens De Koekkoek, Beert A. Nauta, Hendrik Hoekstra, Peter Koole, Nikolaas Van Gaalen, Willem Van Schuur, and Arie Verbaan.
218 Willem Postman, who died in July or August, was the first to be buried in the new cemetery of the east-side Christian Reformed church.
219 Telephone service began in the Monarch area late in 1908 when Alberta Government Telephones constructed a toll line from Macleod to Lethbridge with an exchange in the Monarch post office.

LETTER FROM MONARCH
(*De Grondwet*, 1 March 1910)

We've had nice weather this winter, but now it is real winter once again with snow the last three days.

G[errit] Bode and family have returned from their trip to Wisconsin and have brought with them relatives and acquaintances. It was quite a sight when they got off at the Monarch station, twenty-eight persons in all. They were the families of K[laas] Van Schuur, John van der Woude, Roelof Kooi, Anthony Gunst, Willem Gunst and their mother, all from Vesper, Wisconsin.[220] They like it here very well.

D[aniel] De Boer is also back from Conrad, Montana. A recently married sister visited him for several days. She has again returned to Conrad.[221]

Our church building is finished. This winter it was finished off on the inside. West of the church they are now building the parsonage, 30 × 32 feet large and 16 feet high.[222]

Two quarters of land, close to Monarch, were sold recently for $50 an acre.

The Koole brothers are also back from their trip to Iowa, where they paid their parents a visit.[223]

Corr. 15 Feb. 1910

---

220 Gerrit and Klaasje Bode returned with their three children. With them were Klaasje's parents Klaas and Jannetje Van Schuur, Jan and Antonia van der Woude with their five children, Roelof and Boukje Kooi with their six children, Anthonie and Maria Gunst with their two children, Anthonie's brother Willem Gunst, and their mother Wilhelmina. Actually the Kooi's eldest son Johannes, Willem Gunst, and Willem Van Schuur arrived about four days later by box car with their horses and furniture. An earlier letter from Vesper, Wisc. in *De Grondwet* (16 October 1906) reported on the Kooi family's arrival at Vesper: "Last week on Sept. 25 five families from Chicago arrived here. They all bought land here this summer and now have come here to live. They are Henry Holstein, A. Holstein, T. Holstein, R. Jansen, and R. Kooy with their families, together 24 in number, adults and children."

221 A letter from Conrad, Mont. in *De Grondwet* (8 March 1910) reported: "On February 2 at the home of Mr. and Mrs. P[ieter] De Boer the marriage of their daughter Etty to C. van der Kop was solemnized…. After the wedding the young couple made a trip to Canada."

222 This is the east-side Christian Reformed church. The parsonage was actually being built eleven miles to the west, beside the west-side Christian Reformed church.

223 The parents of the Kooles farmed at Sheldon, Iowa.

224 The hamlet of Noble, which began in the spring 1909, was later called Nobleford.

225 After living in Alberta without his family for two and a half years, Gerrit Hartkoorn visited the Netherlands for the winter of 1909–10, and his wife Jabikje and sons Arie and Barend returned to Canada with him. They were accompanied by a nephew, Herbert Van der Werff, and Jabikje's brother Leendert Bode, who was also returning from a visit. The Hartkoorns stayed with the Leendert Bode family for less than a month and then moved to Hodgeville, Saskatchewan, where they took up homesteads in April.

LETTER FROM NOBLE, ALBERTA[224]
(*De Grondwet,* 8 March 1910)

For two weeks now we've had rather cold weather with snow. Today, however, the wind is from the southwest again. In January it was nice here, and the roads were good. Only seldom snow, which disappeared again in a couple of days due to the Chinook winds. The snow now lying on the ground is preparing the soil for the soon-to-begin spring work.

A week or so ago some thirty persons arrived here from Wisconsin, and we understand that about 50 are coming from the Netherlands.

Wheat does very well here. Thirty bushels per acre is no exception. And the prices for our produce are as high here as anywhere in Canada, because of the coal mines at Lethbridge and the mines and lumber camps in British Columbia. Eggs fetch a high price, regularly 50 cents a dozen this winter and in the summer most always 25 cents; at present 35 cents. Butter is now 30 cents a pound. Potatoes are seldom less than $20 a ton, or 1 cent a pound. Young roosters bring in 50 to 60 cents each in the summer; old roosters and chickens 50 cents.

Corr. 26 Feb. 1910

LETTER FROM JABIKJE HARTKOORN TO JAN BODE
[March 1910]

Dearest Brother and Children,

Since I am taking up the pen to write you a few lines, first we let you know that we are all healthy and we hope the same for you.

We had a very successful trip and beautiful weather. I was rather seasick. So was Arie for a couple of days and Barend a little, but Gerrit and brother L[eendert] not. Now I've caught a very bad cold and I cough a lot. Otherwise, for me the trip turned out much better than expected.[225]

We arrived at brother L[eendert]'s place on 17 March and had a friendly reception. H[erbert] Van der Werff has hired himself out to Gerrit Bode for $25 for the first month and then $30 a month. This morning he has already gone there.

We are having nice mild weather. It hasn't rained the whole winter. They can already be busy working in the fields.

Monarch Christian Reformed Church, *ca*.1926, built 1909.
(Courtesy: Nobleford Christian Reformed Church 1905–1980.)

Now brother, we had a lot to see due to the many sheds and possessions of brother L[eendert], the multitude of horses, and the land he owns. It's a beautiful piece of land, almost too much take in at a glance.

I hope you will write back soon. We are anxious to hear how you are doing, since you were sick. Hearty greetings from all of us, and also from me, your sister and aunt.

Our address is: G. Hartkoorn, L. Bode, Box 8, Monarch, Alberta, Canada.

CHAPTER 4

The Years of Adversity
1910–12

AFTER THE PROSPEROUS YEARS, THERE WERE THREE
years of crop failure. In 1910 it was drought, in 1911 a major hailstorm, and
in 1912 cutworms. The decline in the farm economy quickly spread to a
decline of the nearby towns.

The letters of this period reveal a more sober tone; yet there is usually a
sense of hope for a better next year. Eleven letters from Monarch correspondents and nine longer ones from Evert Aldus describe the developments of
this period. From Granum George Dijkema wrote three more letters. There
are also two short letters from Dutch settlers near Barons.

Rev. Borduin, George Dijkema, Chris Schiebout, Jan Dekker, Roelof Kooi,
and Tijmen Hofman sent eight letters reporting on aspects of church life at
the local Christian Reformed and Reformed churches.

Again, several personal letters illuminate family situations during this
period. These include letters from Leendert and Teunis Bode, Herbert Van
der Werff, Nan Dekker, Jan Poelman, and Gerrit Hartkoorn. The two letters
of Van der Werff reveal the challenges of being a single hired hand.

LETTER FROM MONARCH
(*De Volksvriend,* 23 June 1910)

In order not to neglect my duty completely I now want to say a thing or two about what has happened here lately.

First, six of our people who spent the winter in Holland have returned[1] and have taken with them a large number of newcomers.[2] So, off and on some are still coming from the Netherlands or from the United States, so that the number of Hollanders here is continually increasing. Most of these people have obtained land in the vicinity of Medicine Hat, about 150 miles from Monarch, while a few have bought land here or at Grassy Lake. Most have not yet gone to their homesteads but are working here to earn some money first.[3]

Monarch is continually expanding, although no Hollanders live in the village. Rev. Borduin from Montana was in the Christian Reformed congregation for some time.[4] Rev. Braak preached for two Sundays (29 May and 5 June) for the Reformed congregation, administered the sacraments, and confirmed new members. For some of the upcoming Sundays student Holterink [John Wolterink] from Holland, Michigan, hopes to lead the Reformed congregation. Their worship services are held in the schoolhouse, with the building of the new church to begin soon.[5]

Though for the last five years we rejoiced in having sufficient rains, this year that is not the case. Since July of last year no rain or snow of any significance has fallen here; at least the moisture never penetrated further than about an inch, so it is terribly dry. A considerable part of our grain has not yet sprouted, and what is up – it goes without saying – is very poor. We hope very much that abundant rain will come soon, in which case a partial harvest can still be expected, if it does not freeze too early. Prairie ploughing, till now, has been impossible; the ground is as hard as brick. Meanwhile stubble ploughing is going badly due to the drought, although many are busy with it. Also potatoes and vegetables are for the most part not yet out of the ground. If the harvest fails, many of our people will have a hard time of it. For the time being, however, there is nothing we can do but hope for the best.

[Evert Aldus]

---

1 Actually, all seven of the men who spent the winter in the Netherlands returned to Alberta in the spring. One of them, Gerrit Hartkoorn, returned with his family and then they immediately moved to Hodgeville, Saskatchewan.

LETTER FROM NOBLE AND MONARCH
(*De Hope*, 28 June 1910)

We thought it would be good to report to readers of *De Hope* something about this new Dutch settlement. About six years ago a few Hollanders began to settle in this cattle-rich region, in spite of strong assurances by the ranchers that it was impossible here to grow grain due to drought. However, the alluringly beautiful prairie invited anyone to investigate, and from the beginning the feeble efforts of the mostly poor settlers were crowned with prosperity, so that, after the first three difficult years, most began to become rather independent, and after a couple more successful years some of these people have begun to go back once again to their places of origin for a few days or weeks.

This has not been without consequence for the growth of our settlement; last February some thirty Hollanders from Wisconsin came here, most of whom affiliated with the still very weak Christian Reformed congregation. About a year ago a Reformed congregation was also established by Rev. Lammers and elder Wolf of Westfield, North Dakota; at that time a report about it by Rev. Lammers appeared in *De Hope*. And some from here left last winter for the old Fatherland to fetch family or to seek a wife; this visit was crowned with a very good outcome, so this spring sixty people from Nijverdal, Overijssel, Netherlands, arrived here together at Monarch, accompanied also by fifteen from elsewhere in the Netherlands. Almost without exception they affiliated with the Reformed congregation. Thus far it has held its services in the schoolhouse, but they have already bought the necessary building materials for their own church, so as soon as these are on site they will begin to build.

For a couple of Sundays we had the privilege of having in our midst Rev. P[eter] Braak, missionary of the Reformed Board. Since he especially called on the various families during the week, he did not waste his time. On Sunday 29 May in the morning forty-five were present in the schoolhouse and in the afternoon eighty; the following Sunday, 5 June, the Lord's Supper

2 The seven men from Monarch who visited their former homes in the Netherlands for the winter influenced a large new group of Nijverdalers and others to immigrate to Alberta.

3 Since homestead land was no longer available in the Monarch and Granum districts, most of the new group of Dutch immigrants who arrived in March 1910 took up homesteads northeast of Carlstadt to form a new Dutch settlement.

4 Rev. Menno Borduin, in his capacity as home missionary for Classis Orange City, was in southern Alberta during the early months of 1910.

5 Rev. Peter Braak was from Chicago. The Reformed Church, established in 1909, first met in the Rose Butte school.

Weerstra family picnic in river bottom, 1910. (Courtesy: Johanna Mackintosh.)

was celebrated in the morning and baptism was administered to two small children in the afternoon, with ninety present. The minister Braak has left for his earlier post at Westfield, N. Dak., and now we have student [John] Wolterink for the next few Sundays to carry on this work. So by all appearances in a short time we will have a rather considerable number of members, because there are still persons and families from the Netherlands who continue to arrive here and at Monarch, and because Rev. Braak also visited the Dutch families who live west of Monarch across the river; they had declared they are also prepared to cooperate with us in the congregational domain, so we hope that before long we will have the opportunity one way or another to be able to have a minister lead us.

But it's too bad that this spring it is still so dry here, so there is every appearance that the old ranchers will see their prediction fulfilled this year; there will apparently be no crop, because the time is running short and the air still remains unchangeably dry. Yet it is a wonder how the wheat has kept its green colour so far; but there is no improvement and as a rule we need a full summer here, because the days are usually not as hot as in the States and the nights are especially cool.

With this we will say good-bye this time to the readers of *De Hope*, and we hope that before long we will be able to report a bountiful rain.

Faithfully yours,
T[ijmen] Hofman Noble, Alta., 15 June

EXCERPT OF REPORT OF REV. MENNO BORDUIN
(*De Wachter,* 3 August 1910)

Home Missions in Montana and Alberta, Canada

Readers of *De Wachter* will undoubtedly be curious now and then to hear something from this far western field....[6]

On 24 April I was in Nijverdal East (Monarch), Canada. They have grown in numerical strength. Five families have come from Vesper, Wisconsin, and two from Iowa.[7] This has given them new encouragement in the area of church life. They have also been brought into closer connection with the larger world there. Earlier one had to cover twenty miles by horse and wagon to go from Lethbridge (the nearest station) to Monarch; now one steps off the train at Monarch itself. Not far from Lethbridge the railway line runs over a bridge, which is more than a mile long and more than 300 feet high.

After that Sunday we led the consistory meeting at Monarch. Also the brothers from Nijverdal West (Granum) were present, because Nijverdal East and West together form one congregation although the meeting places of both branches are fourteen miles apart. At this meeting a trio of names was formed, from which they would choose their own shepherd and minister on 17 May. The choice then fell to home missionary Haan.[8] They promise a good salary and free housing. There is a fine parsonage for their minister to live in. Salary and housing are very suitable to give a good impression of their desire and esteem for the regular administering of the Word, though they can still receive this only in part, because the congregation is divided into two branches. The above mentioned items also provide a good testimony of the productive power of the land. The congregation numbers only about twenty families. However, this year is not very encouraging, because it is very dry. Not long ago at Monarch a Reformed congregation was also established; it was strengthened quite a lot this year from Nijverdal, the Netherlands.[9] We do not regret the existence of such a congregation. If there are those who cannot live with us ecclesiastically, then they have a church home and are kept from running completely wild. This does not alter the fact that we would gladly have some of these brothers and sisters with us.

---

6 This report focuses on home missionary Borduin's work in Holland, Montana, where he was based, and in southern Alberta.

7 In early 1910 the Gunst, Kooi, Van Schuur, and Van der Woude families arrived from Vesper. The Cornelis Van Egmond and Coenraad Ferdinand Schiebout families were from Sioux Center, Iowa.

8 Rev. Gilbert G. Haan was a Christian Reformed home missionary serving in Michigan. He declined the call.

9 From the large group of Nijverdalers who immigrated to Alberta in the spring of 1910 a number of families joined the Monarch Reformed Church.

After the just mentioned consistory meeting in which a trio was formed, we went with the brothers to Granum. As in Monarch, we were pleased to meet old acquaintances and get acquainted with others for the first time, because here too the congregation was strengthened by newcomers. Two families came from the Netherlands and one from Manhattan.[10] On the 1st of May we administered the sacraments here, as we had also done in Nijverdal East. It pleased me to be able to leave the brothers and sisters here and in Monarch with the joyful expectation of being edified soon by the work of two students, one of whom would also be working for three Sundays at Grassy Lake.

M[enno] Borduin

LETTER FROM EVERT ALDUS
(*Twentsch Volksblad,* 13 August 1910)

In the hope that the reader's interest will not fade, I decided to send an article again to our newspaper.

In March the men and young fellows came back from their visit to the Netherlands, the latter each bringing a life partner back with them.[11] Along with them arrived a large group of men, women, and children; people who left their fatherland seeking to better their lot in these distant regions. Contrary to the expectation of many, all of them found work, most of the men as hired men for one of us; the carpenters, work in their field.

Since that time people have arrived off and on from Holland. The number of Netherlanders in Canada is continually growing larger; one can find them all over the place from Winnipeg to Vancouver, in colonies or scattered among the rest of the population. After a lot of difficulty and searching, the newcomers in March succeeded in finding land, northwest of Medicine Hat, about 20 miles (6 hours) from the railway, and 50 hours from Monarch. I hear that this land is of good quality, but hilly. Some time ago [Jan] Westera and [Jan] Dekker went there; the others do not live there yet. They are housed by us, or have put up small shacks on the property of some of us.

10 The Roelof Kingma and Laurens De Koekkoek families, who were related, immigrated from Hillegom in the province of Zuid-Holland. The Willem Willemsen Sr. family arrived from Manhattan, Mont.

11 Jan Bannink, Berend Nijhof, and Albert Rutgers each returned from their visit to Nijverdal with a wife.

This year the weather conditions are very unfavourable. Since the middle of last July, thus a year ago, there has been no rain or snow of significance. So it is unbelievably dry. Part of the grain never germinated. Vegetables and potatoes hardly came up. There is no grass for the cattle. And where the time is too far advanced, absolutely no harvest can be expected. The only thing we can still hope for is that part of the grain will grow long enough that it can be cut with a grass mower, in order to feed it as hay to the cattle. If there had been rain yet at the end of June, then we still could have expected a partial harvest. Therefore I waited so long to write, since I would rather send favourable reports than unfavourable ones.

Another result of the drought is that in general there has been no opportunity to break the prairie. Stubble land is extremely bad. Some have more or less finished; others have continually waited for rain, while others have worked to turn over their wheat fields with the plough or cultivator to have the land ready for next year. Gradually the farmers have had to release their hired men. They are now working on the railway or wherever work can be found. In areas like this that depend completely on farming, a bad harvest stops the whole mechanism of society. There is a slowdown in work in all branches of the economy. Due to the things I mentioned it appears that the newcomers are encountering an exceptionally unfavourable year to begin. This year they are missing the high wages and abundance of work during harvest; also help in the form of products that are otherwise abundant, such as potatoes, vegetables, chicken feed, etc., cannot be offered to them.

As for those who have already been here for years, some of them who began in favourable circumstances (for example, with a little capital) can take it well. They are losing several thousand guilders of harvest, but they can go on without difficulty. Where the petition appears in the Lord's Prayer, "Give us our daily bread," this can't mean "Give us plenty of money" in this case. Others who began in less favourable circumstances could not buy their land when it was still cheap, but bought it later at double or triple the cost. Their loss is noticeably greater, especially due to the rather high interest that is lost in a year like this. Like everywhere, here also a national loss weighs largely on those who have the least. In Canada societal relationships are much more favourable than in Europe; yet it cannot be denied that here also the first condition for prosperity is not industriousness and deliberation but capital, or as the social democrats rather rightly express it, "the society is capitalistic." But enough about this. It is unpleasant to see the harvest fail; many feel it hard and will also feel it next year, but there is no reason to lose heart, which no one indeed is doing. With some patience all of this will again turn out all right.

We are not facing this alone; the drought is general across western Canada and United States.

Ministers visited the Reformed and [Christian] Reformed congregations for several weeks, and they administered the sacraments.[12] Our storekeeper A[lbert] Rutgers had a nice new store built in which he carries on his business.[13] At his house and also by B[erend] Nijhof and J[an] Bannink it looks a good deal more homey, since each of them is glad to have a housewife. The new station in Monarch, a fine building, is almost finished. The old one consisted of a railway car without wheels placed alongside the rails. This winter I went with a couple of others to this "station" to catch the night train to Lethbridge. We found the station-master asleep, lying full length on the table between the telegraph machines. He awoke with our rather noisy talking, and said to us, "Please don't talk so loud," pointing to the other end of the car. There in a section closed off by a curtain slept this wife and children. It seems that the talking of night passengers was too annoying; shortly thereafter a second car was placed next to the first one and was set up as a residence for the stationmaster's family. I could tell many more similar examples of life in the "Far West." Perhaps I will do so now and then this winter; now I have no time.

A couple of remarks yet before I end. I advise anyone who wants to come here to wait for awhile, for example, until next year. There is not much work, so there is a chance that one may earn or live on nothing.

It seems that people in Holland think, or at least have been informed, that good land is here for the taking, as was the case five years ago. The fact is, good land is almost or absolutely no longer to be found except 50 to 100 miles from the railroads. Certainly at greater distances, but it has value there only if a railroad comes into the vicinity. In order to find land one often has to spend 100 or 200 guilders on travel by train and by wagon, before he finds any. One should certainly think about that. I write this, not to scare anyone, but to prevent disappointment.

A[ldus] Nijverdal, near Monarch, 16 July 1910

12 Rev. M. Borduin visited the Christian Reformed Church for two weeks in April and May; Rev. Peter Braak spent two Sundays in May and June with the Reformed Church.
13 Apparently on his return from the Netherlands with his new wife Rutgers had the new store built on his homestead to replace the lean-to store that he had added to his shack in 1908.
14 In April Gerrit Hartkoorn and his family moved to Hodgeville, Saskatchewan, and took up homesteads there.

LETTER FROM LEENDERT BODE TO JAN BODE
(15 August 1910)

Monarch, 15 Aug. 1910
Dear Brother and Children,

I will take up the pen to write you a letter. First I will let you know that, by the Lord's goodness, we are still experiencing good health, and we heartily hope and wish the same for you too. A few weeks ago we received your letter and then learned about your good health. That made us glad again, the more so because, when I left, you were not in the best condition.

We are having a remarkable summer here, but not a profitable one because of the drought. We have next to no crop here. As for the weather, it was nice enough, but it was so dry that a lot of seed didn't come up, and what did come up didn't have enough moisture to grow. But now nature has changed a lot. Now quite a bit of rain has fallen already, so a lot of seed that was sown in the spring is now coming up, although it's too late now to get a crop. Yet it's a wanted rain, especially for feed for the animals. And so we live again in the hope for next year.

Brother-in-law [Gerrit] Hartkoorn and his family live about 100 hours from us. Together they have 620 [640] acres of land. He himself has 320 and Arie and Barend each 160.[14] They work with oxen. They have six of them. To work with oxen one almost has to be an ox himself, as far as laziness goes; otherwise one cannot rightly work with these animals. They write that, in their view, they have it good there. There the conditions are also better. As for crops, there's been more rain there than here. Here this summer, when we thought, "now we'll get rain," we had already had it. So we can see that we are dependent in all things.

Teunis [Bode] has already become a father of a daughter. J[an] De Beeld, his wife's father, has also bought land, 320 acres. He lives about twenty-five hours from here.[15] Many people have come here from the Netherlands, mostly from Nijverdal, Overijssel.

You will also find a letter from H[erbert] Van der Werff with this letter. At the moment he's with us. He thinks he also has it good. This is the first letter I've written to Holland since I am back here. I have such an aversion to writing, but you must not take my outlook on writing. You have to let us hear from you.

15 Jan and Aaltje De Beeld and their family immigrated to Alberta in March 1910 and then started farming in the Dutch community south of Burdett.

I hope you will receive this small letter in good health. Give our greetings also to the family. And if you speak to sister Antje, give her our greetings and tell her that, if all is well, I will also write her a letter shortly. Now, brother and everyone, I hope that the Lord may be with you there and with us for time and for eternity. Also, greetings from all of us and also from me, your brother,

L. Bode and family

LETTER FROM HERBERT VAN DER WERFF[16] TO JAN BODE
(16 August 1910)

16 August 1910

Dear Uncle,

With this I will tell you by letter that I'm still fit and healthy, and I hope the same for all of you. It's not so long ago that I left Holland, so I often long for Holland; if you are just here, you still think about Holland now and again. I've already had in mind to go back to Holland, but now I'm over that.

I've already experienced a lot. First I was with my cousin Gerrit [Bode] for six weeks. Then I wandered for fourteen days over the prairie for work. Then I went to Carmangay and found work there. I was there fourteen days. That was on the railway.[17] There I had to work with four mules. I had no mind for that; otherwise I would be a mule myself this fall. Then I left Carmengay by train to Kipp, where I could work again on the railway. I was there fourteen days, and then I got a sore throat. After lying down with that for five days, I had to go to the hospital [in Lethbridge]. When I got there I was operated on at once. Twice they operated on my throat. I was there also for fourteen days before I could work again.

Here we stay in good wagons. They are just like the carnival wagons in Holland. I worked with Russians, Polacks, and Norwegian people, all sorts of people. We can save about $7 a week here. We have to make our own clothes if they go to pieces, and wash them ourselves. That was quite a trick before I was good at it. Then we had to make beds ourselves from boards. I really miss a bed now, because we always sleep here on boards. That makes for a solid sleep.

---

16 Herbert Van der Werff was twenty-one when he immigrated to Alberta from Vuren, Gelderland, in mid-March 1910 with a large group of other Dutch immigrants. He was a nephew of Leendert Bode.

17 In 1910 the CPR railway line from Kipp to Calgary was being extended north of Carmangay.

When I was better, I went to work there again. And now I've had foot problems for six weeks already. I walked for fourteen days, and then I was sent to the doctor and was not allowed to work. I first lay in the railway wagon for fourteen days, and then I had to go to the doctor again and he said I must not work for another fourteen days. Then I quit the job and went to L[eendert] Bode, because I have to go to Lethbridge regularly and I have to buy all sorts of things for my feet. I spent $5 a week and another $4.20 a week for board. That was about $10, which was heavy for me. The doctor said I had swollen feet [gout?], but fortunately that's not true, because my feet began to get better and I don't have swollen feet. This week I'm going back to work, and my feet are just as good as they ever were.

So for a month I've been nice to my feet. I've earned little money this summer, and I still have no land and also no money. I've saved only $50 here. If I'd had no problems with my feet or with my throat, I would have taken up a homestead, but I don't have enough money now to go onto a homestead. I'll wait a year yet. I would have written to Holland if I was coming back, but I will try it a year yet, because now things are bad. There's no work. Nothing at all is growing in Canada. It may well be better next year, and if I go back now I will take a loss. I have no intention to go back with a loss. To my mind I'm doing well now, and I'm not coming back.

Hearty greetings from Herbert Van der Werff, and also greetings from my aunt and uncle and cousins. English is still not going very well, but it will do.

[In corner of the first page]:
Be so kind as to write back. The address is: L. Bode, Monarch, Box 8.
My cousins must also write once. Bye.

LETTER FROM NAN DEKKER TO THE HELDER FAMILY
(16 September 1910)

Monarch, Alberta, Canada
16 September 1910

Dear Family Helder,

With this letter I am letting you hear from us. We are all pretty well. And at the same time I can tell you that on 4 September Arie's wife gave birth to a healthy daughter. They will name the child Tryntje Bennadiena, after both grandmothers.

We've had a very dry summer. It has not rained for ten months and we also had little snow last winter. They could not plough all summer. But on the 6th of August rain came and then a big thunderstorm for three days in a row, but it was too late for everything. Thunderstorms we have had, but no water. Everything here is equally bad; everyone's wheat and oats are poor. Last year we grew five thousand bushels of wheat, but now I think maybe five hundred bushels. And the potatoes are not worth hoeing. Our garden now is nice and green, because everything is coming up now. We are buying the vegetables and potatoes that we otherwise grow ourselves. A big difference, isn't it? Our horses and cows have had to eat straw all summer. Grass is nowhere to be seen. There are many farmers here who burned all of their straw, but fortunately we did not. Ours get fresh straw and oats every day. We have again raised seven colts, so we have thirty head of horses.[18] The twins are just as heavy as the others. The one is dark brown and the other light brown. They are both easy to handle, but not yet harnessed. They are now two and a half years old.

Today the weather is nice. They are hauling wheat home to the stack. Today it can all be home, and then they are going to plough. The land is still full of wheat and oats, but it's too short to cut. The binder can't bind it. It all falls out. Half of it stays lying on the ground for the cattle and young horses for the winter.

Maartje has been home for three months, and her husband with his parents for three months.[19] I don't get much news from Holland; that slows down now. I hope to receive word back from you soon.

Greetings from all of us, N[an] Dekker, T[ryntje] Strijbis

EXCERPT OF LETTER FROM EDMONTON
(*De Grondwet*, 4 October 1910)

... Last week this society again had a meeting. At this meeting there was also a representative from Monarch (Nijverdal, Canada), who was sent by eight future farmers. This representative was here for three weeks to investigate the matter and all of them decided to join in....[20] The land seekers are on a

---

18 Since Nan's sons Thys and Arie lived with him, this number refers to the total number of horses owned by all three.

19 Maartje Dekker was the daughter of Nan and Tryntje Dekker. Her husband Johannes De Puyt was from Vesper, Wisconsin, where his parents lived.

trip to Leeklebie [Lac La Biche?], 120 miles northwest of Edmonton, where there is beautiful land with about 10 per cent bush, while the soil is rich with various minerals.... We have no doubt that next spring a strong Dutch colony will arise there. And that is everything for us Hollanders....

Corr. 10 Sept. 1910

LETTER FROM MONARCH
(*De Volksvriend,* 3 November 1910)

The last time I wrote how we've had great drought this summer; also that we could expect no harvest at all. The latter I did not see correctly, since some got a small harvest of four or five bushels per acre; others, however, got nothing. At the end of August and in September we received quite a bit of rain, so most of our grain has come up since that time instead of in the spring. So we now have good pasture for our cattle for the first time this summer. After the rain everyone is very busy ploughing, etc., because much that was left undone till now due to the drought still has to be done. Many have also seeded fall wheat. Until now winter has not put in an appearance, and we hope that it stays away a long time yet, so that we can finish our "field work."

In September fifteen families or unmarried persons left for their homesteads at Carlstadt. These people came here from the Netherlands in the spring and continued working here during the summer.

In the last couple of weeks some of our people have been connected to the telephone, so the women now have a better opportunity to have a neighbourly chat. Since the Dutch people at Pearce also have a telephone, we can communicate with them by "long distance."

20   A society was organized by Dutch people in Edmonton to form a Christian colony on land away from the city where they could begin to farm. Hendrik Kippers, who had immigrated from Nijverdal to Edmonton in the spring of 1910 and became a leader of this society, wrote from Edmonton to the *Twentsch Volksblad* (2 June 1910): "There is a plan to establish together a Dutch Christian Colony in one of the new districts of Canada with a very mild and short winter and good soil that is suitable for cultivation. Since various Nijverdalers and residents of Twente [the district where Nijverdal was located] are always holding their eyes fixed on Canada, I invite them to correspond with me. Then I, also on behalf of all the Hollanders here, will provide all the desired information. We have already discussed this also with the Nijverdalers who went to Monarch this past March, and we hope, Lord willing, to establish a strong Protestant Dutch colony." Kippers also sent a letter describing this society to *De Grondwet* (13 September 1910). The society did not establish their colony in the Lac La Biche area, but at Neerlandia in 1912. The representative from Monarch who attended the society meeting was likely one of the Nijverdalers who had arrived in March.

Under the direction of carpenter [Arie] Verbaan the Reformed people are busy building their church. In a couple of weeks they hope to finish the building. About that time Rev. [Peter] Braak from Chicago will probably be with us; this would be delightful for the dedication.[21]

There is no further news here except some births, which I will rather mention at the end of the year.

[Evert Aldus]

LETTER FROM EVERT ALDUS
(*Twentsch Volksblad*, 26 November 1910)

Monarch, 25 Oct. 1910

I wrote last time that we had a prolonged drought; now I can report that at the end of August and in September a good amount of rain fell. Some of us were lucky enough to have a little bit of grain harvested, mainly on land worked under the most favourable circumstances. This grain grew without any rain at all. But it is a very little bit. Since the rains, our fields have become green, because almost all the grain only now has the opportunity to germinate. Now for the first time this summer we have good pasture for our cattle. But the main thing is that the rain gives us hope for better results next year. Of late everyone has been very busy, since much work that had to be put off due to the drought must now be done.

In September the people who came to us in the spring from Nijverdal left for their homesteads near Carlstadt. Considering the unfavourable conditions, all of them were fortunate to find and have work. A few others who came later also found land near Medicine Hat, except for a couple who have still not searched, however.

For several weeks the Reformed people have been busy building their church, under the direction of a carpenter. Toward the middle of November they hope to complete the work. This church stands a forty-minute walk from Monarch, on the same road where the [Christian] Reformed church stands ten minutes farther.[22]

---

21 The Reformed church building was actually dedicated on 12 March 1911 in a service led by Rev. John De Beer of Lennox, S.Dak. It was located a half mile south of the Monarch Christian Reformed church.

22 The Monarch Reformed church was built north of Monarch on land donated by Jacobus Nijhoff. The carpenter was Arie Verbaan.

This summer a large hotel opened in Monarch. At the same time a doctor lives there. For several weeks they have been busy drilling for coal with a steam engine near the town.

Some of us are glad to have a telephone connection with each other and with Monarch, and if necessary, with many other towns, so one can talk from home with somebody in Calgary or Winnipeg.

In August we saw once again how unreliable our climate is. On the 21st of the month it snowed large flakes for more than an hour, to the great alarm of all those who had not cut their grain, because snow-flattened grain is lost. Fortunately the snow stopped in time.

E[vert] Aldus

LETTER FROM JAN POELMAN TO WILLEM POELMAN
(26 November 1910)

Wirdum, 26 Nov. 1910
Dear brother![23]

We are still expecting a letter from you. The plan is that we are all coming over except Jakob, at the end of March. You should write to inform us what we must take along. K[ornelis] Veenkamp and Tetje are also going along. H. Veenkamp's fiancé H. Heller from Wornhuizen [Warfhuizen?] will buy Veenkamp's farm. As you can see, our farm is being sold on 19 Dec. If there are no obstacles, we will be in A[lberta] next year. You can certainly get ready and buy land. For the time being, nothing more. We are first waiting for a letter from America. We are all in good health here at the moment.

In expectation, on behalf of the family, your brother,
J. Poelman

P.S. Greetings to the Dijkema family. I am busy learning some English. I have already had a couple of lessons.

---

23 Willem Poelman, arriving in April 1910, was the first of the Poelman family to come to Alberta. Due to tuberculosis, two children in the family had died, so for health reasons the rest of the family decided to join Willem in the drier Alberta climate. Tetje was Willem and Jan's sister; in the end brother Jakob also came with the family. The Poelman farm at Wirdum, about 37 hectares in size (about 91 acres), was a fairly large farm in the province of Groningen; they had no need to come to Alberta for economic reasons. The original of this letter is in the possession of Ralph Poelman of High River, Alberta.

LETTER FROM GRANUM
(*De Grondwet*, 6 December 1910)

Not much news from here. Our colony is still expanding more and more, though not by giant strides. Last spring a few young men came directly from the Netherlands.[24] Also this past summer two more families came from Manhattan, Montana,[25] and this fall a family from Grand Rapids, Michigan.[26] Land is becoming more expensive; it is almost impossible to get it below $35 an acre.

The crop this year was not very good. We got very little rain, so on new land we got only half a crop or not even half, and on old land nothing. That old land was then for the most part "summer fallowed," so that the soil may be in a good condition for next year. Generally speaking, no new land was broken because rain has been denied us. Wheat yielded 10 to 15 bushels per acre: one of my neighbours got 17 bushels of spring wheat an acre. Not much came of the oats; a few got a little, but most got nothing.

A few weeks ago a baby daughter was born at the home of L[ubbert] Van Dellen. Also a baby daughter at the home of G[eert] Venhuizen.[27]

Every day the weather is still nice. The farmers are still busy with farm work, although the time has about come to stop with it.

Corr. [George Dijkema] 22 Nov. 1910

24 One of the young men to come to Granum in the spring of 1910 was Willem Poelman, who arrived from Groningen in April. Another was Jan Dekker, who immigrated from Nijverdal in March.

25 One of the families from Manhattan, Mont. was Willem and Johanna Willemsen and their two children. The other was Evert and Hendrika Schiebout and their two sons. Willemsen, a brother of Garrit Willemsen at Leavings, had farmed for several years at Manhattan before seeking a wife in the Netherlands. A letter from Manhattan, dated 9 November 1906, reports: "W. Willemsen and Derk Palma have now conceived a plan to make a short trip before long to the old Fatherland, with the goal (at least as your correspondent was told) to each get a life partner. That is 'right boys'; no one can say you are too young and inexperienced. When you come back, if all goes well, we expect a good wedding" (*De Grondwet*, 20 November 1906). Another letter from Manhattan, dated 10 April 1907, reports on their return the following April: "D. Palma and W. Willemsen, who made a short pleasure trip to the Netherlands, are back again. The last-mentioned, people say, took along a life-partner from the 'Old Country.' ...Evert Sieborg [Schiebout] arrived here several days ago with his family from the Netherlands" (*De Grondwet*, 16 April 1907). Thirty-five-year-old Willem Willemsen had found his fiancée Johanna Schiebout, the seventeen-year-old daughter of Evert Schiebout. In 1910 the two families moved to southern Alberta.

26 The Pieter and Hilligje Ritsema family arrived from Grand Rapids, Mich. in September 1910.

27 The daughter born to Lubbert Van Dellen was Anna, born 1 September 1910. The daughter of Geert Venhuizen as Ada, born 16 November 1910.

Harm Emmelkamp farm, 1910. (Courtesy: Dorothy DeBoer.)

LETTER FROM GRANUM
(*De Wachter,* 7 December 1910)

As is our custom, again it is time to write something in *De Wachter.* Little by little we are getting in the habit of reporting in our church paper how things are going in our congregation. In the summer we usually make a request for a couple of theology students to proclaim the gospel to us for several weeks. Also this summer we did this, and we had a couple of students who showed us the way of salvation. They were brothers [Peter] De Jonge and [William] Meyer. De Jonge led us three Sundays and Meyer five. We were very very glad to hear these youthful brothers. Just at that time we had called Rev. G[ilbert] G. Haan and we hoped he would come to us so that our congregation might have its own shepherd and minister, but it was not to be. However, we believe that the Lord will send us the man of his will in his own time. Still, it was a big disappointment for us, but by and by we will again make attempts to get a pastor who will lead our congregation.

As *Wachter* readers know, at the meeting of Classis Pacific it was decided to split our Nijverdal congregation in two and to make two independent congregations from it – the east side under the name Monarch and the west side under the name Granum. We are very glad about this. The great distances have been very inconvenient. Now it's going to be a good deal better. Now that each side is becoming independent, the consistory meetings do not need to be held once on this side and then on the other. No, now everything is much easier and more efficient. Burdett (a branch of our congregation) will also be organized as an independent congregation. Rev. Borduin has been assigned to do this. We hope to meet this brother again soon. He is assigned to lead us (Granum) for three Sundays, Monarch three, and Burdett two.[28]

Our parsonage is sufficiently ready that we can call a preacher. However, when we called Rev. Haan, it was just as complete as it is now. Had he accepted, we would have done the finishing touches to complete it, but now it is awaiting a new call.[29]

The crop this year was not very good. The Lord gave us a very dry year. He withheld the rain from us so the fields produced very little.

Our congregation is still small; yet it is expanding little by little. This year four new families came to us.[30] We hope still more may come, so that later the two sides, with the Lord's blessing, may each have their own shepherd and minister.

G[eorge] Dijkema

LETTER FROM MONARCH
(*De Volksvriend*, 26 January 1911)

> Hours, days, months, years,
> Swift as moving shadows flee.[31]

So says one of the most beautiful songs from the *Evangelische Gezangen*. We have again seen the truth of this now that the year 1910 has ended and belongs to the past. For us in this colony this year will probably be long remembered – a year without rain in the spring or summer, with no

---

28 When Rev. Borduin came in February 1911, the Nijverdal church was dissolved, and he helped organize the three new churches.

29 As it turned out, this Granum parsonage was never occupied by a minister, so the finishing work remained undone. In 1916 Rev. Nicholas Gelderloos was the first minister to accept a call as a home missionary at Monarch and Granum, but he lived at Nobleford. In 1921 the Granum parsonage was sold to Garrit Willemsen and removed from the churchyard.

30 Here Dijkema is referring only to the Granum side of the congregation. In 1910 the Willem Willemsen family from Manhattan and Pieter Ritsema family from Grand Rapids joined, as well as the Roelof Kingma and Laurens De Koekkoek families from the Netherlands.

31 These are the first lines of a hymn often sung at year's end. Its English title is "Hours and Days and Years and Ages."

opportunity to get the land ready for 1911; a year without harvest, a year full of disappointment and failure. Will 1911 bring us something better, will it possibly make up for us where 1910 left us short? We hope so; and this hope is not without grounds, since rain already came in the fall and we are now sitting deep in snow. But the latter is usually blown from the land by the "nothing but good" Chinook wind and becomes piled up in deep banks around our homes and barns.

In the past year our colony increased by some persons and families who bought land and came to live here. A considerable number came from the Netherlands and worked here during the summer, but they are now on their homesteads at Carlstadt. New members were added to the families of T[ijmen] Hofman, L[eendert] Koole, W[illem] Stotijn, A[rie] Dekker, J[an] Postman, and R[ense] Nijhoff.

H[endrikus] Veldhuis and his wife were grief stricken by the death of their youngest child.[32]

W[illem] Stotijn and S[tyntje] Hofman were married.[33]

J[ohan] Huisman left us and settled at Grassy Lake.[34] J[ohn] Postman tried to make a trip to investigate the Peace River country, about 600 miles north of here, but after covering half the distance he had to turn back due to the impassable road.[35] Due to the crop failure, not much has been built.

R[oelof] Van Dijk put up a big new house. The church of the Reformed congregation was erected and was first used on the Second Day of Christmas for the children's Christmas celebration. On Old Year's and New Year's Day neither of the churches could hold services because of the cold raw weather.

Monarch did not grow much in 1910. The main buildings that were added were the station, the Methodist church, and the Monarch hotel.

This is about all I have to say, and I end with the wish that 1911 may be an exceptionally favourable year for all readers of *De Volksvriend*.

E[vert] Aldus

---

32 The Veldhuis child who died was their son Gerrit, born in 1908.
33 Willem Stotijn and Styntje Hofman were married on 10 June 1910.
34 The Huisman family had arrived with the group of forty-one in April 1904. In March 1910 Huisman sold his homestead to his son-in-law Bastiaan Koole and moved to the Burdett area where he could get a larger farm of unbroken land near the small Dutch community there.
35 While traveling by horse and democrat north of Edmonton on the way to the Peace River country, two wheels of Postman's democrat broke on the harsh trail and he had to turn back with make-shift skids under the rear axle.

LETTER FROM EVERT ALDUS
(*Twentsch Volksblad,* 28 January 1911)

"All the present becomes the past," says a beautiful song verse. And we also say it now that the year 1910 belongs to the past. The year 1910 with its comets, the first of which we observed shining brightly for many evenings, while the other one, the long awaited, much talked about, and highly praised Halley's comet, scarcely wanted to show us its tail. The year 1910 with its many earthquakes, floods, and other disasters, with its snowless winter and rainless summer in our southern Alberta.

But I suppose, dear readers, that you already know these things; therefore I consider it better to wish all who read my pen scribbling a "happy and prosperous New Year." Also you and I should not forget that we will go our way in this life only once, also in 1911; and therefore we should not pass by opportunities that are offered to us along the way to do anything good for our fellow man or to refrain from anything that may hinder him. Being faithful, as much as we are able, to the example given by Him whose birth we commemorated shortly before the end of the year.

Christmas was celebrated in the usual way where we live, by young and old, by all together. By the Christian Reformed in their church on 27 December; by the Reformed in their just-completed building on the Second Day of Christmas. With this celebration this church was used for the first time.

The lean year did not have the least influence on our celebration, and everyone seems able to provide for themselves in their material necessities and needs. At any rate, the deacons of both congregations thus far belong to the unemployed, as far as providing relief is concerned.

In connection with the failure of the harvest, not as much was done as was expected at the beginning of 1910. A couple of people replaced their "pioneer shack" with a better house. The Reformed congregation built its church; and the [Christian] Reformed congregation at Granum finished its parsonage. In both congregations ministers from the United States preached for several Sundays. Monarch did not grow much; the hotel, the Methodist church, and the station were added.

The number of inhabitants from our Nijverdal grew with several who bought land in our vicinity,[36] and also by the marriage of J[an] B[annink], B[erend] N[ijhoff], and A[lbert] R[utgers], who each brought along a wife from the Netherlands.

The poor times appear to have had no influence on the increased number of children; the birthrate for this year is pretty large. Among others, a baby came to stay at the homes of W[illem] Stotijn, who was married this year, A[ntoon] Stotijn,[37] B[astiaan] Koole, R[ense] Nijhoff, A[rie] Dekker, and J[ohn] Postman.

A couple of days after he returned from his visit to the Netherlands, H[endrikus] Veldhuis lost his youngest child.[38] In the colony near Granum the elderly Willemsen, a man of great age, died,[39] and A[lbert] Lantinga, a young man there, perished in an unfortunate way. When his horses bolted, he broke his leg. Shortly afterward he died of blood poisoning in the hospital at Macleod.[40] It is touching that Lantinga was ready to make a visit to Holland to visit his parents and to get a life partner.

J[ohan] Huisman left us and settled at Grassy Lake. J[ohn] Postman made a trip for many days in his buggy to visit a region located on the Peace River, several hundred miles north of here. People say this area is very good for farming purposes. Postman went there to find out for sure. But he had to give up. After covering more than a hundred hours, over prairie, across rivers, marshes, and forests, his buggy broke down, and he had to turn back. As long as there is no railway connection with the Peace River Valley, farming there is practically impossible.

Now, readers, I have told about all that I consider worth reading for you. I hope I am not mistaken in this. As for us, "hope gives life," and with good hope and full trust we go into the new year.

A[ldus]

36 In 1910 four families who were former Nijverdalers arrived in Alberta by way of the United States. In the spring the Ferdinand Schiebout and Cornelis Van Egmond families came from Sioux Center, Iowa, and each bought land. These brothers-in-law had immigrated to Iowa in 1904. In April 1910 the Willem Willemsen and Evert Schiebout families arrived from Manhattan, Mont. Willemsen had immigrated to Paterson, N.J. with his family in 1892 and then took up farming at Manhattan in about 1899. In the winter of 1906 he visited Nijverdal to find a wife, and returned to Manhattan in the spring of 1907 with his fiancée Johanna Schiebout and her family – that of Evert Schiebout. Evert and Ferdinand Schiebout were brothers.

37 On 10 June 1910 Willem Stotijn married Styntje Hofman. Their first child was Louis, born 6 August 1910. Antoon Stotijn was an older brother of Willem. Their fourth child Herman was born 14 August 1910.

38 Hendrikus Veldhuis had returned from the Netherlands with his mother in mid March. His year-old son Gerrit died the same month.

39 Arend Willemsen died at age 75 on 7 March 1910. Since the Granum Christian Reformed church did not open its cemetery until the following March, he was buried in the Granum community cemetery.

40 Twenty-eight-year-old Albert Lantinga died on 7 November 1910, and was buried in the Macleod cemetery.

LETTER FROM MONARCH
(*De Volksvriend,* 16 March 1911)

Since we do not read much from this area [in *De Volksvriend*], I thought it would be good to send some news now and then, because we noticed that the correspondent from Vesper, Wisconsin, also would like to hear something from acquaintances.[41]

While we saw something from this area a week or so ago, in my opinion that writer forgot some things. There has been family growth also at the homes of Joh[annes] Gunst, Teunis Bode, Daniel De Boer, and G[errit] Bode; also a son to J[an] Bannink and a daughter to A[lbert] Rutgers.

Winter is still not past, though the weather now is good; still, we are not accustomed to such a long winter here.

At present there is a lot of buying and selling of land here. A[lbert] Rutgers sold his 160 acres for $8,000 to J[acobus] Van Leeuwen. Rutgers intends to go to the Netherlands. C[ornelis] Van Egmond and Evert Schiebout each bought a half-section from C[harles] S. Noble at a price of $50 an acre. B[ert] Plomb [Plomp] bought a half-section for $45 an acre. And now there is still more land fever, but about that later.

Horses are still not very cheap. We heard that L[eendert] Bode bought a team for $380.

We were glad to have Rev. Borduin from Conrad, Mont., in our midst for a couple of Sundays.[42] He is now at Burdett, Alta., to organize a congregation. So we see that various congregations are arising also in the far west, in Alberta, Canada.

Thijs Dekker, who left for New York a couple of months ago to meet his better half, came back married a couple weeks ago.[43]

On 9 March there will be a telephone meeting in Monarch to discuss rural telephones. Various farmers have it already, and now most will certainly get it. Then people can also talk with each other more easily.

Leendert Geleynse who was married last fall now also has a fine house.[44]

Joh[annes] Kooi, who was operated on a couple of weeks ago for appendicitis, is pretty well, all things considered, according to what we hear.[45]

---

41 In *De Volksvriend* (16 February 1911) the correspondent from Vesper, Wisc. noted that people there had acquaintances in various places and so they eagerly read the correspondence in this paper from these places. Such comments clearly indicate that Dutch-American papers like *De Volksvriend* helped maintain an ethnic network among Dutch communities across North America.

42 In February Rev. Menno Borduin was present as a home missionary of Classis Pacific to oversee the splitting of the Nijverdal Christian Reformed Church into three separate churches, the Monarch CRC, the Granum CRC, and the Burdett CRC.

REPORT OF REV. MENNO BORDUIN
(*The Banner,* 23 March 1911)

From the Prairies of the Far Northwest

Our congregation Nijverdal in Canada does not exist any more. This is not bad, however, because it developed itself into three separate congregations.

February 8 [9] we organized the congregation at Monarch. The elders elected were: G[errit] J. Withage, J[ohn] Gunst, and R[oelof] Kooi; for deacons, J[an] Geleijnse and J[an] Van der Woude. The clerk is: Mr. G. J. Withage, Noble, Alberta, Canada.

February 17 I had the privilege to organize our people in Granum as a separate congregation. The elders are: G[eorge] Dijkema and A[lbert] Ritsema; for deacons, R[oelof] Kingma and W[illem] Willemsen [Jr.]. The clerk is: Mr. George Dijkema, Granum, Alberta, Canada.

March 6 the congregation Burdett was brought into existence. The elders are: H[endrik] Matter and P[aul] Van den Berg; the deacons, M[arinus] Dijkshoorn and A[drian] E. Guichard. The clerk is: Mr. P. Van den Berg, Burdett, Alberta, Canada.

The congregation Monarch has 14 families; Granum numbers 12, and Burdett 6, but about as many single members. A few families that live there come to the meetings although they do not belong as members to the congregation.

Monarch has a nice church building on 10 acres of land; Granum has a rather small edifice for public worship, but a good nearly ready parsonage on 10 acres of land. Burdett is going to build a church in the near future on one acre of land.

It may be said of all the three congregations that they are in their infancy, but especially of Burdett. In Conrad, Mont., our special field of labour at present, they are building a church on two acres of land. The congregation numbers 22 families. In Farmington, Mont., four members were allowed to the Lord's Supper by confession of faith in January. In Feb. one in Monarch and four in Granum,[46] and in March two in Burdett.

---

43 After Thys Dekker corresponded with Marie Leyerweerd in the Netherlands for some time he sent for her. When she arrived at New York (Hoboken) on 23 January 1911 on the *Nieuw Amsterdam*, she was not allowed to disembark without a family to go to, so they were married the same day aboard the ship.
44 Leendert Geleynse married Anna Plomp, who had immigrated from Nijverdal in July 1910.
45 John Kooi was the elder son of Roelof Kooi.
46 Mrs. Jannigje Gunst confessed her faith in the Monarch CRC; Laurens De Koekkoek, Pieter Ritsema, Lubbert Van Dellen and his wife Japkje confessed their faith in the Granum CRC, and thus became full members of the church.

Financially our farmers did not have a good year last year, but in general it may be said that they gained by it spiritually. Their dependence on God is felt again. It has drawn them nearer to God. Our eternal interests receive more attention. These things are evident in words and deeds.

The church at New Holland, Mont., is still in existence although largely decreased in number of members, and there is a chance yet that it becomes a flourishing congregation. There are more settlements flourishing today that had nearly been wiped from the map on account of the hardships of the beginning.

By these few words I have given the readers of *The Banner* some knowledge of my mission field and labour.[47]

M. Borduin

LETTER FROM MONARCH
(*De Volksvriend*, 13 April 1911)

Finally, in the middle of March, the severe winter left us. It began in December and continued till into March. The enormous snow banks around the stables and barns have thawed pretty quickly. In recent days the land was being worked everywhere, and some began to sow wheat. However, the day before yesterday it began to snow in the morning, and at the moment it is still doing so. So the work is again held up for a few days.

Some time ago Rev. Borduin was at the Christian Reformed church here. The Reformed people were delighted with the presence of Rev. de Beer.[48] Everyone was sorry that this minister suddenly had to leave due to the sickness of one of his children. In this church E[vert] Aldus and Jac[obus] Nijhoff were re-elected as deacon and elder.

---

47 Rev. Borduin sent a similar but shorter report to *De Wachter* (22 March 1911).
48 Rev. John de Beer was at Monarch to dedicate the new Monarch Reformed church building on 12 March. He was the home missionary of Classis Dakota and lived in Lennox, S.Dak.
49 On the Monarch side of the Dutch settlement no adult died before 1911, but on the Granum side seventy-five-year-old Arend Willemsen, Van Dijk's father-in-law, had died on 7 March 1910, and also young Albert Lantinga.
50 Roelof Van Dijk (later spelled Van Dyke) had emigrated to New Jersey from Oosterwolde in Gelderland, and in 1893 he married Dina Willemsen in Midland Park. In the late spring of 1904 the family with four children moved to Alberta to homestead near Dina's sister Fenneken and her husband Jan Hendrik ter Telgte. In September 1910, while building a larger house on the homestead, Van Dijk stepped on a nail that pierced his foot. He never recovered from an infection that set in, and died on 23 January 1911. His sons Henry and Ernest continued on the farm.

Monarch Reformed Church, built 1910. (Courtesy: Frieda Dekker.)

Throughout the seven years that our settlement has now existed no adult has ever died, although a number of small children have.[49] However, 1911 is an exception. In January Roelof Van Dijk died.[50] He came at a youthful age with his parents from Oosterwolde in the Netherlands, and settled in the eastern States. For some years he held the position of janitor in the Reformed church at Paterson, N. J. In 1904 Van Dijk came here to try his luck on a homestead. Like others he made good progress. Yet his life was not rosy; he had a weak and sickly body, and more than once he was near death. At the beginning of this year his slowly festering ailment had weakened him so much that it was undeniable that the end of his life was near. Many of our people went to visit him, knowing that it would perhaps be for the last time. At the end of January his strong spirit left the weak body. He died calmly and peacefully. With an eye to his impaired health here in Alberta, the words that the aged Jacob spoke to Pharaoh are applicable to Van Dijk: "Many [few] and evil have been the days of my pilgrimage" [Genesis 47:9]. Van Dijk also fought through, endured, and lived the first years of anxiety and difficulty with us with a will-power and cheerfulness (in spite of his weak body) that was lacking in many others. However, he was not able to enjoy rest after his work here on earth; the thread of his life was cut off at age 37. Man proposes, etc. [but God disposes]. At the funeral, which everyone attended, [Gerrit] J. Withage spoke, and at the cemetery Th. [Tijmen] Hofman. For the widow Van Dijk her two sons aged fifteen and seventeen can be a comfort. When their father was often not able, they learned early on to work, and now that their father is there no more, they will certainly keep doing this for their mother.

LETTER FROM MONARCH
(*De Volksvriend*, 20 April 1911)

It seemed to us that winter had left us because everyone was busy in the field harrowing, ploughing, and seeding (H. Meibach already had 500 acres in). But we had to stop work again because we got four days of snow; yet now it is as good as gone. The land this spring is in good condition, because last winter we also had a lot of snow, and now with this added, it provides a good outlook.

Also the land market here is not standing still. Wm. Van Schuur and Daniel DeBoer together bought a half-section, at $51 an acre.[51] The first-mentioned has more big plans, but we cannot write about it yet. Wm. Gunst also bought 160 acres, and people say that Koest [Huibrecht Koert] and his son also bought a half-section. As we look at it, we will have a fine Dutch settlement here.

A[lbert] Rutgers left a couple of weeks ago for the Netherlands.

Joh[annes] Kooi is out of the hospital and is nicely getting better; he is gradually becoming stronger.

H[erbert] Vander Werff, who was in Belt, Montana, is here again and is working for C. S. Noble.[52]

J[acobus] Van Leeuwen, our new storekeeper, comes around once a week for orders and brings the goods to the house – a great convenience, especially when one is busy. Van Leeuwen was offered $55 an acre for the land that he paid $45 for a year ago.[53]

H[endrikus] Veldhuis lost a very good horse.

We now have a Dutch blacksmith in Monarch. Now there are two; the other is a German. The first-mentioned came a few weeks ago from Nijverdal, the Netherlands.[54]

---

51 Daniel DeBoer and Willem Van Schuur were brothers-in-law.

52 Vander Werff, a nephew of Leendert Bode, had immigrated to Alberta with the large group of new immigrants in March 1910. Charles Noble was a large landowner in the district, and the town of Noble, later Nobleford, was named after him.

53 Jacobus Van Leeuwen bought Albert Rutgers's quarter section and took over the store that Rutgers had set up.

54 The new blacksmith in Monarch, Gerhart Van den Broeke, was the first Dutch settler to live in the town.

LETTER FROM MONARCH
(*De Wachter,* 26 April 1911)

On Wednesday 15 March a Christian Young People's Society was established here. Perhaps the first of our church in this country.

The number of our members is fifteen. The name of this first-born child is: "Serve the Lord with gladness." Chosen as officers were: Elder R[oelof] Kooi, president; W[illem] Gunst, vice president; C[hristiaan] I. [Theodorus] Schiebout, secretary; C[ornelis] A. Withage, treasurer; M[arinus] Geleijnse, librarian.

If there happen to be Young People's Societies that have too full a library, or wish to dispose of their read books, this newborn recommends itself.

In the name of the officers,
C. I. Schiebout

LETTER FROM EVERT ALDUS
(*Twentsch Volksblad,* 27 May 1911)

This spring it is seven years ago that the first Hollanders settled where the now expanded settlement lies at Monarch. In all these years not one adult died, a fact that may be considered exceptional. However, 1911 has broken this rule. In January Roelof van Dijk died. A slow festering ailment dragged him to the grave. All his neighbouring countrymen and some others showed him last respects. His body was laid to rest in the graveyard next to the [Christian] Reformed church.

Van Dijk only reached his thirty-seventh year. At a youthful age he left Oosterwolde (Gelderland) with his parents and settled in one of the eastern states.[55] In 1905 [1904] van Dijk came here. Along with others without means among us, he made it through the bad times, but was not able to experience the fruits of his labour. He was married to D[ina] Willemsen, who hails from Nijverdal.

We have a long and severe winter behind us. It constantly froze very hard, and a lot of snow fell. The latter would not be so bad if the snow had stayed lying on our fields where it was much needed. However, now and then the "nothing but good" Chinook wind came and blew it from the land

---

55 The Van Dijks had lived in Midland Park, New Jersey.

and piled it metres high around our buildings, where it was a big nuisance for us. To the railway companies this caused a lot of trouble and damage. Wherever the line was dug through hills these excavations were filled with hard packed snow. For many days the traffic was held up, while the snow ploughs worked day and night; often having to begin again after the line was clear for a day or two. This snow ploughing is not a pleasant job; the plough pushed by one to four locomotives is driven forward with all their power. If the snow is very deep, they quickly lose their speed until at last nature defies the power of the steel giants; they can no longer shove the plough, and, as the Americans say, "they begin to spin." That is, the wheels quickly turn along the rail without going forward. Accidents are bound to happen with all this, such as derailments, etc.

By the middle of March the weather was milder and people began to work in the field. On the 1st of April it was winter again until the middle of the month. The snow that fell then melted on the land. Since that time we have seeded our grain, a large part of which has come up. The fact is that there is a little moisture in the ground, due to the rain that fell in the fall and the melted snow this spring. After 15 April the weather has usually been nice. Yet also this spring the sandstorms have not stayed away; they are much more unbearable than the snowstorms in winter. These become worse each spring, because the prairie is continually being converted into loose ground.

At present everyone is anxiously awaiting the spring rains, and it is high time. For our crops and also to be able to plough. So much is left undone from last year that everyone would like to begin.

The Reformed and [Christian] Reformed congregations both had a preacher for several Sundays.

G[Cornelis] J. Van Egmond and E[vert] Schiebout each bought 320 acres of land. A few others bought some as well. In Monarch it is not as busy as it once was. Probably due to the smaller buying power of the farmers. For these reasons not much new is being built.

E[vert] Aldus Nijverdal near Monarch, 8 May 1911

LETTER FROM HERBERT VAN DER WERFF TO THE JAN BODE FAMILY (9 May 1911)

9 May 1911

Dear Cousins and Uncle,

Now I will write you a letter. I must write you that I am still fit and healthy, hoping the same also for you and the others. Dingeman,[56] I received your letter and hope that you may also receive this one. You wrote that you are still a bachelor. Well, you'll surely remain one for a couple of years yet, because in Holland they don't marry as young as here. Here the girls get married at fourteen, fifteen, or sixteen. That doesn't happen in Holland. I too will surely remain a bachelor for a couple of years, because I have no one at all on the line. Well Dingeman, the girls here in Canada are much prettier than in Holland. Where I now work there certainly are girls, but I still have to ask the first one. The girls here are nice. They use up your money and then you can stay away; then they no longer need you. I've never had a girl here yet. That's a real letdown. In Holland I always had a girl, but here I never have one. There are girls here. I will keep looking at the girls here a little more.

And Barend,[57] he is now out of the service. He'd rather be at home than play soldier. He has become quite a chap, and he now has a very nice moustache. Well, if I come over sometime, I will see it, but he can well have his picture taken. He can surely send that. I have no picture; otherwise I would have enclosed one now. You write that your sisters are still single too. You can certainly send one of them over for me. Then you will never see me again in Holland!

And Dirk Hartkoorn,[58] he is still getting along well. He is still big and fat.

You write that it's been a good year. That is fortunate, and the pasture looks good. You say dairy farming was good but the crops were bad.

Your dear uncle Gerrit [Hartkoorn], he is riding around in an automobile.[59]

This year there is little work. The farmers have no money this year to take on a hired man. I have hired myself out again for a month for $35, but after this month it will be a trick to get work. If there is a crop this year, there will be enough work for three or four months. A lot of wheat was seeded

---

56 Dingeman Bode was the second son of Jan Bode and a cousin of Van der Werff.
57 Barend Bode was the eldest son of Jan Bode.
58 Dirk Hartkoorn was a cousin of Van der Werff.
59 At this time Gerrit Hartkoorn was farming at Hodgeville, Saskatchewan. Apparently he bought a car there.

this year. We still had some snow this week, but not enough to plough and also not enough for the wheat. There's no work at all in construction. Everything has stopped.

I must also mention that I was in Great Falls this winter, and I came back with $100 less than when I went. I have little time to write.

Hearty greetings from H. v. d. Werff

Also, hello from everyone, especially from me. And don't forget Griet.[60]

Bye.

LETTER FROM GRANUM
(*De Grondwet*, 11 July 1911)

> "Rain, rain roll,
> Make all the ditches full."

So sang one of the Dutch poets, and so we sing here now. All the ditches are already full. Though last year it was very dry, this year it appears the opposite will be true. Then in general no rain fell, and now, we thought we already had the so-called heavy rains in May; June came and prairie breaking was in full swing, but the heat came and it became very dry, so last week we had to stop breaking. But while I write this (it is the 24th of June), it is pouring rain. Now people can again begin breaking, because now we are getting the heavy rains. We see that our "Sunny Alberta" has changed into "rainy Alberta." The wind is blowing out of the northwest, our rainy corner, so the local showers are over and the whole country is receiving a general rain. It is no longer falling in streaks; every farmer is receiving enough.

The crop is looking nice this year, and barring unusual misfortune we will get a good harvest. Summer [spring] wheat is in excellent condition, in that the cutworms have done it no damage; winter wheat is pretty good, wherever the cutworms have left it stand. Yet, the general sentiment is that the winter wheat harvest will not be heavy. The reason for this, people think, is the dry year of 1910.

---

60 Grietje Bode was the second daughter of Jan Bode.
61 Willem Poelman, who came in April 1910, was the first of the family to come to Alberta. In February 1911 his brother Geert came with his friends Hendrik Ham and Arie Geerds. In June sister Anje and brothers Jan and Fokko arrived. Then in August the parents Roelf and Hilje Poelman came with their sons Jakob and Kornelis, their daughter Tetje and her husband Kornelis Veenkamp who were just married on 12 July. The Poelmans came from Wirdum in Groningen.

Since spring not many newcomers have arrived. A friend, a few brothers, and a sister of W[illem] Poelman are the only ones.[61] Soon, most likely with the guidance of L[ubbert] Van Dellen, the rest of the Poelman family is coming. L. Van Dellen went to the old fatherland to visit his parents there.[62]

The price of land is rising steadily. One of my neighbours was offered $45 an acre, but did not accept it.

Corr. [George Dijkema] 24 June 1911

TWO LETTERS FROM MONARCH
(*De Volksvriend,* 3 August 1911)

It seems good once again to send some news from this area, because the correspondent this summer was pretty busy to write so much. We are having a splendid summer, also for the crops, so there is a magnificent stand of grain. The fall [winter] wheat is already beginning to ripen hard, and the spring wheat also looks promising. The oats as well. This summer we've had plenty of rain, a big difference from last year, when we didn't get much crop. We hear that now in some of the States it is hot and dry.

Here this summer a lot of land has been broken and much has been sumer fallowed. A week or so ago three young men came from Hull, N.Dak., to do harvesting, and we heard from these lads that five more are coming. We can well use them here now.

F[erdinand] Schiebout had visitors from Taber, Alta., [earlier] acquaintances from Sioux Center, Iowa.[63]

Leendert Geleynse was in bed sick with typhoid fever but is nicely getting better.

Bert, the son of John Geleynse, had the misfortune of falling from a horse and breaking an arm.

Mr. and Mrs. L[eendert] Bode are back from their visit to Morse, Saskatchewan.[64]

---

62 Lubbert Van Dellen's parents lived in Burum in Friesland. He accompanied the Poelmans to Canada in August.
63 The Ferdinand and Johanna Schiebout family had come to Monarch from Sioux Center, Iowa, in 1910. In 1908 and 1909 real estate agents from Sioux County, Iowa, advertised land in the Taber area, and offered excursions by train to check it out. By May 1910 three Dutch families lived there, and Rev. M. Borduin paid them a pastoral visit. See *De Volksvriend,* 13 August 1908, 13 May 1909, 1 July 1909; *De Wachter,* 10 August 1910.
64 The Bodes visited their relatives the Gerrit Hartkoorn family at Morse.

Student Wm. Trap of the Christian Reformed Church has again left after working here for seven weeks.[65] And student Schut of the Reformed church is still active here in administering the Word.[66]

Here also we hear of flying machines nowadays. A couple of weeks ago one went up at Lethbridge, and I am told it was a success.[67]

At present picnics are the order of the day. On the 27th of July there will also be an excursion to the mountains, to the Crowsnest Pass, B. C. We hear that many Hollanders will go.

A week or so ago there was joy at the home of C[ornelis] van Egmond because of the birth of their first daughter; at J[acobus] Nijhof also a daughter, and also at W[illem] J. [van] Lohuizen a daughter. People were then also generous with cigars.

Gerrit Bode is a storekeeper in partnership with J[acobus] Van Leeuwen.

At J[an] van der Woude the children have whooping-cough.

A week ago in Barons ten miles north of us there was a big fire. A lumber yard with $35,000 of lumber, and also a hardware store worth $6,000. Certainly a great loss for a small town. Fortunately the Lethbridge fire brigade came to help; otherwise the whole town would have burned.[68]

From another correspondent:

If last summer everything went wrong due to drought, this summer it is just the opposite. Plenty of rain and heat make the crops thrive, and if frost and hail stay away, which they have till now, there is every chance of a good harvest.

Adversity, however, is not staying away this year. In the spring the unwanted Chinook wind blew large patches of grain out of or under the ground, so it had to be reseeded. Then the cutworm also caused considerable damage. Nevertheless, the outlook is good.

---

65 In 1911 William Trap had finished his first year as a theology student at the Christian Reformed Theological School in Grand Rapids, Mich. The summer activities of Trap are reported in *De Volksvriend* (31 August 1911) in a letter from Lynden, Wash.: "The theology students from the school of the Christian Reformed Church, Mr. Trap and Mr. Kuipers, led the congregation here the last two Sundays, after having served the congregations in Montana and Alberta, Canada, during their vacation time; this week they returned to their studies in Grand Rapids, Michigan."

66 Student Henry Schut had finished his second year at Western Theological Seminary in Holland, Mich. He served the Monarch Reformed Church for at least six weeks.

67 In December 1903 the Wright brothers had made their first flight at Kitty Hawk, N.C. In February 1909 John McCurdy made the first airplane flight in Canada when he flew the *Silver Dart* in Nova Scotia.

68 This correspondent from Monarch sent a similar letter, dated 25 July, to *De Grondwet* (8 August 1911).

In both churches a student is speaking for several Sundays; meanwhile, people are busy painting the church of the Reformed congregation.

L[eendert] Koole is building a fine large house.

Jac[obus] Nyhof has again postponed doing so, and is building a new shed to live in, although he laid the foundation for a good house already a couple of years ago.

Gerrit Bode has gone into partnership with the Dutch storekeeper Van Leeuwen.

Van der Broek [Gerhart Van den Broeke], the blacksmith in Monarch is very busy. He is the first Dutch resident in town.

LETTER FROM BARONS, ALBERTA
(*De Volksvriend,* 10 August 1911)

On Thursday P[ieter] Shippers [Schippers] and D. de Haan arrived, both from Boyden.[69] The former will help me during the harvest, the latter will help my brother-in-law A[rie] deValois,[70] which is very gratifying. A big difference from last year.

[Arie Versluys]

LETTER FROM MONARCH
(*De Volksvriend,* 31 August 1911)

Today our colony was struck by a great disaster. Some were just beginning to mow today when a hailstorm came through, which wiped out our beautiful, promising grain fields in a few minutes.[71] Some farms or fields on the northeast side were spared. In the centre of the colony almost all and in the southwest everything was totally destroyed. There and in the town of Monarch the hail was the heaviest. There, besides many stones as big as a

---

69 Boyden, Iowa, was the same district where the Koole brothers had come from. Arie Versluys also had earlier farmed in that area. In 1909 Versluys visited the Kooles at Monarch and in the spring of 1910 he and his family moved there from northwest Iowa. In October of that year Versluys bought land southwest of Barons and settled there.

70 Arie deValois immigrated to Alberta in August 1910 from Piershil in South Holland, and in November he bought a half-section of land northwest of Barons; his family came the following April. Arie was a brother of Mrs. Versluys.

71 The hailstorm struck that district on 15 August.

cherry, also a number of rough jagged pieces fell, some as big as a chicken egg. Not only were north-side windowpanes smashed, but at some places even the curtains were torn.

This unexpected disaster, and the failed harvest of last year, make it extraordinarily difficult for those who were hit. For many the fruits of their eight years of labour and trouble here are totally lost.

EXCERPT OF REPORT OF REV. MENNO BORDUIN
(*De Wachter,* 8 November 1911)[72]

... It was in the evening of that unforgettable day for me and others that Lethbridge was visited with a tremendous hailstorm. Some stones were as large as oranges; one measured five inches in diameter. A man was killed by the hail; some others were injured. Horses bolted. Most windowpanes on the wind side fell down rattling in pieces from the pelting hail. The storm lasted only ten minutes; then nature again became still and peaceful. The enormous streams of water on the street, the thick layer of melting hailstones, the devastated gardens where only some stems of plants stood to languish without leaves, and the broken windows only proclaimed what had happened....

Since the terrible hailstorm at Lethbridge on 15 August I was especially concerned about our two nearby congregations, Granum and Monarch. In connection with the drought of the previous year, it would look pathetic in these congregations if they all had shared in the terrible devastation of the hailstorm. It was indeed a natural matter, but yet a matter on which much would depend for the well-being of the congregations. When we arrived in Granum from Edmonton, we learned that fortunately the situation was not as bad as we had supposed, but yet two families at Granum and five at Monarch lost everything due to the hail. When they later had a more accurate knowledge of things, it was evident that some others had also suffered quite a lot more than was initially thought. Besides, frost and other enemies of a harvest standing in the field caused quite a lot of harm for some. But thanks to God's blessing and protective hand, this year on the whole there is much to be thankful for in regard to the harvest.

The Granum congregation was strengthened by a large family who came from the old Fatherland. They bought four farms for themselves. Too bad

---

72 This is a report of Borduin's visit to Alberta in the summer of 1911. He reports not only on Granum and Monarch, but also on his visits to Burdett, Lethbridge, and Edmonton.

that another family, bought out by this purchase, will now carry out a long considered plan to leave.[73] We were able to establish a young people's society in this congregation, like the neighbouring Monarch congregation already has. There we also led a congregational meeting, which dealt with the calling of a minister and other matters. But due to financial circumstances, they dare not call immediately. However, they decided, with the financial strength at their disposal, to do as much preparatory work as possible and then to ask permission to call a minister at the spring meeting of our Classis. There they also have to deal with a relatively pleasant difficulty – that the church building is quickly becoming too small.

In Monarch, where the church building was originally erected a little larger, they have no need to enlarge it yet, but though ahead of the Granum church building they do not have a parsonage, as the latter place has. Hence they do not seem to be as far in the matter of calling as her nearby sister congregation. People of both sides no longer seem to see much good in a joint call of one minister.

. We were in Granum for two Sundays and in Monarch only one Sunday, because the latter congregation had enjoyed the work of students more than the former. In both congregations we administered the sacraments.

On this mission trip my conversations with our people especially brought two matters to my attention. The first is that so few read the Word of God out of desire. They read it at the table, but mostly out of custom. If they read anything outside the appointed time to look at Scripture at mealtime, then it is mostly another book or a newspaper. Out of desire the Word of God is very seldom opened. This is not only the case for those whom one would suspect of indifference, but also for souls of a more serious nature. What is the reason, I ask myself, that what a certain poet said is also applicable to them: "Reading about the Bible is common; reading in the Bible, that was done in former days."

Another matter that struck me was that in our church – where the doctrines of the unmeritorious nature of our works, and of our universal guilt and inability, are held in such high regard in word and in writing – one still finds so many self-righteous people, who zealously confess that one has to do good works out of thankfulness and not at all to merit heaven, as

---

73 In the spring and summer of 1911 the rather well-to-do Roelf and Hilje Poelman family, which had suffered from tuberculosis in Groningen, came to Alberta for a healthier climate. Willem, the oldest son, had arrived already in April 1910. Roelf purchased a half-section for himself, his sons Jacob, Jan, and Geert bought three quarters, and newly married son-in-law Kornelis Veenkamp bought Geert Venhuizen's homestead. In January 1912 the Venhuizens moved back to Manhattan, Mont., from where they had come in 1904. A major reason was that they wanted to send their children to a Christian school.

is done by Remonstrants[74] and Roman Catholics. It seems strange, and yet it is the case. They do good works because without them they cannot go to heaven, but the impulse of love and thankfulness is completely foreign to them, because they cannot believe that Christ died not only for others but also for them; because they seek to ground their faith on the condition of the soul instead of on God's unchangeable promises. Instead of being joyful, they often go through life moaning and groaning.

M. Borduin[75]

EXCERPT OF LETTER FROM MONARCH
(*De Wachter,* 29 November 1911)

Society Life

During my stay here this summer, I became acquainted with the Young People's Society that was established here this year.[76] I was able to experience a lot that is pleasant and sociable here; such things especially attract you when you have always lived with society life in the Netherlands. I miss one thing, however, that lies at the core of society life. Not that I want to blame the society here, because it is still young and so you can't expect much from it. But, in my opinion, improvements can well be made, especially by a federation. For when a society stands by itself here, it can never do as much as when it lives in an organization with more societies; then it also stands much stronger. Then they can publish a paper that can also contribute a lot to society life....[77]

J[an] Dekker Monarch, Canada

---

74 Remonstrants are followers of the Arminians who opposed Dutch Calvinists in the early seventeenth century.
75 In a later article in *The Banner* (2 October 1913), Rev. Borduin described some of the personal hardships that he as a home missionary encountered as he made pastoral visits to distant churches in Montana and Alberta: "When away from home, we cannot always expect to find lodging in a well-furnished room set apart for company, although as a rule, they try to make it as comfortable as possible. But sometimes we have to sleep with the family in the same room, and besides this, we sometimes meet with troublesome company at night. To be from home so often is not only unpleasant, but makes it hard to fulfill our parental duties. And to be on the road so much is not only tiresome, but makes it hard to find time for study. It is not without danger either to travel over hills and through brooks, creeks, and rivers, but hitherto the Lord has saved me."

LETTER FROM BARONS
(*De Volksvriend*, 21 December 1911)

Piet Punt is an engineer for W. Lucha [Will Luchia] and is getting $6 a day. The fireman gets $4 a day, the other personnel $3 a day; with a team and wagon $5 a day.[78] The snow has as good as vanished; yet even with the most favourable weather the threshing will not be done by 1 Jan. 1912. Our best wishes for the New Year.

LETTER FROM MONARCH
(*De Volksvriend*, 18 January 1912)

Here we already have a lot of winter with about three inches of snow. Until Christmas the weather was fine, except for the winter we had in November. In the meantime a lot of grain was threshed, but there is still a lot left to do; perhaps it will be spring before it is threshed again. This fall there were far too few threshing machines and much delay due to the weather; that's why it was so late. There were three more new machines that came in December.

L[eendert] Geleynse's wife is home again; she was in the hospital for two weeks in Lethbridge and delivered a stillborn child there.

At the home of G. Van Leeuwen a boy was born, the first; and at W[illem] Stotyn also a boy. Congratulations!

L[eendert] and G[errit] Bode are thinking of taking a trip to Washington.[79]

C[harles] Noble and his wife made a trip to England. The goal is to come back in February with a number of land buyers.

At present there is little business going on in the country.

We are now getting a small flour-mill at Monarch, for the convenience of the farmers.

---

76 Jan Dekker is referring to the Young People's Society established by the Monarch Christian Reformed Church in March. At age twenty-one he had immigrated to Alberta with the large group that arrived from Nijverdal in March 1910.

77 Dekker continues to offer an extended argument for a North American federation of Reformed Young People's Societies.

78 The wages were for a threshing crew.

79 The Bodes visited Lynden, Wash. in late January to explore the possibility of moving there.

LETTER FROM GRANUM
(*De Grondwet,* 30 January 1912)

It has already been a long time since you have heard from me, and now that 1912 has arrived I thought it good to report something once again. Though the summer of 1910 was awfully dry, last summer was just the opposite, very wet. Too little rain is not good, but too much is also not good. Due to frequent rains the crops ripened very late. There was a huge amount of straw and too few threshing machines, so in general threshing was very late. In addition, we happened to have a heavy snow storm very early, so they had to stop threshing for a few days. Then an unexpected thaw set in, so people could resume threshing. However, there are still some fields that most likely will have to be threshed next spring. The crops are pretty good. The yields in bushels were excellent, but the quality is not the best. A fairly dry summer is better for us than a wet one. At present it is rather cold with a lot of snow, so the roads are bad. Hauling grain is difficult then.

Our Dutch settlement is increasing little by little. Last summer we got another couple of families; but on the other hand one family also left, to Manhattan, Montana, for the time being.[80] Land is gradually going up in price. Once the new railroad comes through our Dutch settlement, it will quickly go much higher. Here we still have only one railroad, the Canadian Pacific, but last fall the Canadian Northern also surveyed for a new line, which they will begin to build this spring.[81] The new line is coming directly through the Dutch settlement, a half-mile from the church and parsonage, and they say that a new town is coming a mile and half from the church and parsonage. If we come so far that we have a town a mile and half from our church and parsonage, then we are beginning to make a good deal of progress. At present the church and parsonage are eight miles from town. We hope that this railway will be ready by next fall, for then we will need to haul our grain only a few miles. We can then sing, "How pleasantly rolls on the life of a Canadian farmer."

Corr. [George Dijkema] 17 January 1912

---

80 The families who arrived at Granum in the summer of 1911 were the Poelmans and Veenkamps. The Geert Venhuizen family left for Manhattan, Montana in early January 1912.

81 The Canadian Northern Railway planned to build a line from Calgary to Macleod in competition with the CPR track. It was to run seven and a half miles east of Granum, and the townsite was to be called Stroud. The Canadian Northern constructed the grade for this line in 1911, but then scuttled the project.

LETTER FROM TEUNIS BODE TO JAN BODE
(7 February 1912)

Monarch, 7 Feb. 1912

Dear Uncle and Cousins,

I thought I would write a few lines once a year, since I never hear anything from you. It's two years ago in January that I received a New Year's card from Maaike, and it said a letter would follow. The letter is taking a long time to write. By this time it can well be a book, if you have written at least something each day, but delay is dangerous and that is true also in the case.

By the Lord's goodness, we are still fit and healthy, and we wish the same for you. At present we have beautiful weather, and the winter is not at all as severe as last year, although we've had a couple weeks of severe weather after Christmas. In other places in America, especially in the east, they are having a severe winter.

You've surely spoken to H[erbert] Van der Werff who told you a lot about America, but not much good, I suspect.[82] Now he will truly be in his element again, because here it was much too quiet for him. Here he could not indulge enough in excesses. He drifted about here and there a lot, since he could not keep a job. I think there was something wrong with Hab [Herbert] sometimes. But enough of this.

You have surely heard that I was not very lucky the past two years. Two years ago everything was dry, and last year two weeks before harvest everything was destroyed by hail, or almost everything. I still got a thousand bushels of wheat and 780 bushels of oats. Father [Leendert Bode], whose land is just north of mine, had no hail. He had a good harvest.

I can also mention to you that Father is moving from here. As you know when I was in Holland,[83] he and Gerrit [Bode] had plans to go to Washington to look around, but nothing came of it then. But now they have gone, and Father bought a small farm – eight acres with a nice house and barn, electricity in the house, and a large orchard, just outside a large village, for $5,000. Thus, you may think, it is expensive, but beautiful. He says he's never seen such a nice area. The climate there is quite a bit milder than in Holland. 150 Dutch families live there. It's almost all dairy farming there, and the area is very well suited for that. A cow sells for $80 to $125 there. On 80 acres

---

82 After spending less than two years in Canada as a single man, Herbert Van der Werff returned home to the Netherlands.
83 Teunis Bode visited the Netherlands in the winter of 1908–09 as a single man.

(about 34 hectares) you milk 30 cows there. Father's plan is to milk a couple of cows and otherwise retire there. Land there costs $100 to $300 an acre, depending on the buildings and how far it is away from the village. In April he hopes to be there. He rented out his farm here and he's going to sell his household effects at an auction here.[84]

Perhaps Gerrit and I will go there too, but we must first sell here and that doesn't happen so quickly now, after two bad years. We'll probably have to be patient for a year or so. The place is called Lynden. It's located about 3 hours from the Pacific Ocean and 7 hours from a city of forty thousand residents and 20 hours from Seattle, a large port city of four-hundred thousand residents.

How's it going with you? Cheese has become very expensive, I've heard. Is Maaike or Grietje already married? Surely Dingeman is busy courting, or is he already married?[85] Or will he come to America first? Perhaps he'll come along with H. Van der Werff, because he will surely think of America again when he has to go digging with a spade.

We have about 100 chickens and now we're getting about 30 eggs a day. They are worth about 40 cents a dozen. Our little girl is growing well. She's now off the breast. In May she'll be two years old.[86] I look forward to a boy yet, and then we'll be well satisfied, but my wife is already content with one.

As far as I know, things are also going well with Uncle Gart [Gerrit Hartkoorn]. They have written from Holland that Uncle Gart goes begging and Aunt Joukje [Jabikje] is stark mad, but how they came up with these ideas I don't know, because there's nothing to it. It's easy to lie from a faraway land.

I have no more news. And now I hope you will receive this letter in good health and kindly ask you also to write back once. Accept hearty greetings from me and my youthful wife,

Teunis Bode, Paulina Bode De Beeld
Monarch, Box 8, Alberta, Canada

---

84 A letter from Lynden, Wash. in *De Volksvriend* (29 February 1912) noted their visit to the Dutch community of Lynden: "L[eendert] Bode from Monarch, Alberta, Canada, who visited Lynden at the end of January with his son Gerrit and neighbor L[eendert] Geleynse, bought the house of D. De Jong a block south of the Christian Reformed Church." A later letter from Lynden in the 25 April 1912 issue reported on their move: "Mr. L[eendert] Bode, his son Gerrit, and Mr. Verschuur [Klaas Van Schuur] came here from Alberta, Canada, with their families at the end of last month. On 1 April L. Bode took possession of the house and land that he bought earlier from D. De Jong, and De Jong took possession of his new house on Front Street. Gerrit Bode has already bought a 30 acre farm, two miles south of Lynden, and he can also take possession of it soon." Klaas Van Schuur was Gerrit Bode's father-in-law; his sixty-three-year-old wife Jannetje died

LETTER FROM MONARCH
(*De Wachter,* 13 March 1912)

Our home missionary Rev. Borduin was in our midst to administer the Word and the sacraments, and for us that was good. Otherwise we are not very encouraged at the present time. Faith is often so weak and small now that we have to contend with adversity. When we go with the wind, yes, then life seems fine. But when our God quarrels with us and sends us calamities, then it is not so good. Certainly it gives us no cheer that we have been plagued for two years, in 1910 by a huge drought and in 1911 by a crushing hailstorm, so that we've had no harvest now for two years. It is true that a small few were spared, but most ploughed and seeded in vain. That we do not want. Then there is sometimes murmuring and complaining, and in so doing we sin against God's rule that is wise and good. Though we are not all murmurers, people in general are not very cheerful. Is that too our own fault? Are we looking down too much and looking up too little? Looking back sometimes is also good. I mean looking to that cloud of witnesses behind us, such as Abraham, Job, Joseph, Moses, David, and others of old, who sometimes also had to walk along deep and difficult paths. What a chastening! How gloriously they came out of the crucible, God be praised!

Will the outcome be the same for us? Only if we believe that everything that befalls us in this valley of misery is ordained for us as by our Father's hand. Many a time I think then of the following little poem that I learned in my youth:[87]

> Once amidst the ocean waves
> a ship was in distress.
> Engulfed it was by sea on sea,
> the danger reached its crest.
>
> ...
>
> But isn't my Father there above
> and even at the wheel?
>
> ...

---

at Monarch just before he left. These families apparently left Alberta because of the recent crop failures due to the severe drought of 1910 and the hailstorm of 1911, but for the Bodes another factor may have been a strained relationship with the Monarch Christian Reformed Church.
85 Maaike, Grietje, and Dingeman were children of Jan Bode and cousins of Teunis Bode.
86 Gertrude Bode was born 22 May 1910.
87 This poem continues for nine verses.

Yes, so it is; let us remember more that our Father in heaven is holding the wheel and for us no hair shall fall apart from his will. So go forth with courage, with eyes fixed on [God's] command but blind to the future.

Here we would very much like to expand a little, so that we may be able to have our own minister before long. Aren't there some solid families who have a desire to go west? Here the country is large and good, and now is a good time to buy a farm here. Because of two bad years land is now available on easy terms and is not expensive. Take advantage of it. It's in your own interest and at the same time it would be an asset for the Christian Reformed congregation at Monarch.

R[oelof] Kooi[88]

LETTER FROM EVERT ALDUS
(*Twentsch Volksblad,* 30 March 1912)

Monarch, Canada, 10 March 1912

For too long I have put off reporting something from us. The best time to write, winter, is almost past. So it is time for me to make use of the opportunity. Also, I have reason to suppose that what I am going to write will be pretty much known to those who will read it. So I will touch on everything briefly, as I begin with the spring of 1911. It was not an unfavourable spring; that is, our grain was put in the ground on time and it came up. But a powerful wind did considerable damage by blowing some grain almost out of the ground and completely covering other grain. For the most part this damage was restored by a mild rain that followed. After that the grain disappeared very suddenly in large or smaller pieces. There was nothing we could do but to reseed. This was done, but the same thing happened again. An investigation showed that the ground was full of cutworms which gnawed off the young grain. Some left it as it was, others seeded three or four times until finally they gained on the cutworms. From then on things went pretty well; there was a huge amount of rain. It did not stop, as in other years, by the end of June, but rained all the time. Then came the 15th of August. The country was one big field of grain, grain with large heavy heads. We had never seen it so nice. Some fields began to show a yellow tint; cutting time was near.

88   Roelof Kooi was then an elder of the Monarch Christian Reformed Church and clerk of the consistory.

Some had just begun to cut winter wheat or oats. At that time the affliction of the previous year was forgotten. Then, at noon on that 15th of August the hailstorm came. No one of us had ever seen anything like it; and we hope never to see it again. A sound like a coming train announced its arrival. There was scarcely time for those who were in the field to safely find cover. Hailstones, some the size of an egg, others as big as cherries, and all sizes in between, dropped out of the sky, broke windowpanes facing the wind, and made such a noise on our buildings and everywhere that the strongest thunder could not be heard. In less than half an hour it was all over. The sight of the fields was very pitiful; the devastation complete.

The storm came out of the northwest and pretty much followed the railway line in our district. Its width was more than an hour's walk, and it destroyed an area larger than the province of North Brabant. The hail was the heaviest right along the railway. The fields on either side of it appeared to be rolled flat with gigantic rollers. But also farther from the line not much was left.

The damage to broken glass in Monarch and Lethbridge was enormous. Many horses ran away, which cost one man his life. The hail did not come to the northeast part of our colony. There the harvest was spared. But that was not yet the end of the adversities. The hail was followed by heavy night frosts, and a large part of what the hail had left froze and became completely worthless, or had value only as cattle feed. All plans to plough the land in the fall as much as possible to prepare it for the following year were also stopped by the unusually early setting in of the frost. 1911 for most of us was a year of successive adversity and disappointment. Since hail and frost both go by "streaks," a few of us escaped it. So the harvest varied between ten thousand bushels per farm and nothing. By far most, however, have saved very little or nothing. But in the end there is nothing one can do about it; man cannot fight against nature.

This winter was cold until the middle of January; after that we had six weeks of spring weather, but in the last two weeks again there is biting cold. We are eagerly looking forward to spring, so that we can again seed. Before we can do that, we have to do an unpleasant and, I hasten to say, odious work, namely, burn the destroyed and frozen grain.

And now, I suppose, many a reader will ask, what are the consequences for you people there in Canada of two unsuccessful years in a row? I could answer this myself, but I will rather copy the following piece from *The Graingrowers Guide*, the newspaper of the United Farmers of Western Canada.

In the province of Saskatchewan eighteen out of twenty farms (where the owner himself works, thus homesteads) were burdened with a mortgage in 1910. These mortgages were loaned at 8, 9, and 12 percent, an average of 8½ per cent. This is much too high, as is evident from the fact that the provincial government can borrow money on the credit of the province for 3 and 4 percent.

Thus far the newspaper. The situation in Alberta certainly does not differ very much from that in Saskatchewan. Not all loans are taken out to meet the shortage from bad harvests; many were taken out also to make up the shortage of the first three years; others to make it possible to buy additional land. In the main, however, the farmer was forced to take them because till now the farm (the harvests taken together) does not cover the expenses for all necessities. According to the same paper, more than 15 million dollars of mortgage rest on Saskatchewan homesteads. In Alberta it is certainly not much better. The last two years have brought about a rapid shift of these lands, developed with so much care and difficulty, out of the hands of the ploughers and into the grip of those who "reap where they have not sown, and gather where they have not laboured" [Matt. 25:24]. And this shift into the hand of capitalism is certainly the greatest disaster that the last years have brought upon us.

Perhaps someone will ask: Is nothing done by the government to prevent this wrong and deplorable situation? The answer to this question is given in the following item that appeared in the *Calgary Weekly Herald* of 7 March. The article is part of a speech presented by Dr. Worst, president of the agricultural college of [North] Dakota.[89]

Dr. Worst first demonstrates the desirability of replacing the exclusive grain-growing in this area with mixed farming, that is, crops, cattle raising, dairying, etc., together. Then he discusses the possibility of this change and says:

It is of little use for others (non-farmers) to preach the gospel of diversified farming without doing something to bring about such conditions as would make its practice profitable and expedient. Under present conditions it is impossible for the great majority of the farmers of this country to engage in diversified farming and make a living. The natural conditions are favourable, but the

---

89 Dr. Worst presented the speech to the Canadian Club of Winnipeg at the beginning of March. The *Calgary Weekly Herald* report on it is headlined, "Diversified Farming in Canadian West."

artificial conditions, conditions which are due mainly to legisla-
tion and the privileges which certain favoured interests enjoy under it, are unfavourable. A man who desires to farm properly, to
keep cattle and to produce beef, milk, and butter, finds himself a
prey for all kinds of exploiters. When he buys lumber and cement
for his buildings, when he buys his implements and his wagons,
his pump, his household necessities, and indeed practically
everything that is necessary to his business, he is required to pay
exorbitant prices enhanced by the protective(?) tariff and unnec-
essarily high transportation charges. When, as is at present the
case, he cannot obtain sufficient young stock or milch cows in this
country to fill his barns, he must pay duty also to import them.
When he needs to borrow money to finance his undertakings, he
is required to pay a rate of interest three times as high as his bank
will pay when he has money on deposit. And when the farmer has
produced his milk or butter, his beef or pork, he must pay freight
or express charges which are altogether unreasonable in order to
get his product to a market in which he receives, in most cases,
barely half what the consumer in the same city pays for it.

Those Canadians who are anxious to see the farms of Canada
properly tilled and scientific agriculture made a permanent
source of prosperity for the towns and cities as well as the rural
areas, should give evidence of their sincerity by helping to remove
the restrictions and burdens which prevent the general adoption
of diversified farming. Give the farmer his agricultural implements, his building materials, his clothing, his food and
everything else that enters into the cost of production free of duty;
give him cheaper freight and express rates; give him a chance to
use the good land near the railways and the cities which is at present held out of use by speculators; give him capital at a low rate of
interest; give him market conditions under which he will receive
the value of his product after the work of distribution has been
done at cost; and give him access to the nearest and best foreign
markets for such of his products as cannot be consumed at home,
and he will then be able to make diversified farming pay.

Thus far the *Herald*. I think, dear readers, that I have written about enough.
This piece is an enumeration of a number of unpleasant things, and I do not
write it with pleasure. But I must stay faithful to the truth. Apart from this

article, I have seldom written about anything else than our experiences in this settlement.

For now I will leave it at that. Yet I hope one day to write something more extensive about all sorts of things concerning this country, but not now. I think the time has not yet come to be able to pass a fair judgment. Especially in these adverse times one's judgment would be somewhat wrong or too harsh.

P.S. Now and then we read something from Monarch and Carlstadt, but we hear nothing out of Edmonton. Come on, writer from Edmonton, show us that you are still alive; tell us how it's going there!

A[ldus]

LETTER FROM MONARCH
(*De Grondwet,* 2 April 1912)

Summer is again around the corner and soon everyone will be busy enough. It is our hope that the year 1912 will make us forget the last two years, and that everyone's work this year may be richly rewarded, because the past two years were bad years. 1910 was a failure due to a severe drought, and in 1911 we were ravaged by a hailstorm and frost which destroyed thousands and thousands of acres of grain. And then also the cutworms. They eat off the grain cleaner than a cow can. Hopefully this year we will have no cutworms, because otherwise the situation looks sad for everyone. Hence some have already given up on farming and left for somewhere else or have begun something else, so there is sufficient land to buy or rent. At present the price of land is $25 to $35 an acre.

This week Mr. [Leendert] Bode and his son G[errit] left again. They went to Lynden, Washington, after selling their horses and machinery. We were surprised how expensive the horses sold for. So there is one sale after another here.[90]

Correspondent

---

90 Another Dutch family who left was that of Anthonie Gunst; they had moved to Monarch from Vesper, Wisc. in early 1910. A letter from Vesper in *De Volksvriend* (21 December 1911) reported that "Anthonie Gunst and his family are here for a visit from Alberta, Canada. They are thinking of going back in February." A few months later another letter from Vesper in *De Volksvriend* (14 March 1912) reported that "A[nthonie] Gunst sold his 40 acres to J. Scholten. Gunst will now stay here on his mother's farm. Hence he will not go back

LETTER FROM MONARCH
(*De Grondwet,* 16 April 1912)

Today the weather is nice and there is no frost. But on Friday 5 April we had a heavy snowstorm which forced everyone to stay home. The next day the weather was good again and the snow almost disappeared.

R[ense] Nijhoff, son of K.[?] Nijhoff, bought 160 acres of land for $40 an acre. A. Alders [Evert Aldus] bought 160 acres for $38 an acre, so they have not yet completely lost heart.

G. B. van Leeuwen and his son have taken up land at Carlstadt, and soon hope to take possession of it. W[illem] Gunst rented the farm of G. B. van Leeuwen. W. Verschuur [Willem Van Schuur] has also left for his homestead.[91]

Mr. [Charles] Noble, who went to England last fall and wanted to sell his land here, is back and was not successful in the sale, so he has his hands full of work again.

LETTER FROM MONARCH
(*De Grondwet,* 30 April 1912)

Today a sad accident happened here. While the eleven-year-old son of J. G. of Baarns [John Warnock of Barons] was discing, he somehow fell under the disc and was injured so seriously that he had to be taken immediately to the hospital at Lethbridge. His condition is very critical.[92] A warning for all to be careful, especially with children.

The farmers are in good spirits again. It has rained again and the weather is good every day, though the sky is mostly cloudy.

Mr. E. Klomp [Egbertus Plomp] has left for his homestead at Carlstadt, where a large number of Hollanders are already living.[93]

Correspondent 18 April 1912

---

again to Canada." A later letter from Vesper in the same paper (31 October 1912) noted that "A. Gunst is again living on the old homestead, the place where his parents settled fifteen years ago."

91 Willem Van Schuur left to his homestead at Orion east of the Dutch settlement at Burdett.

92 In this accident young Harry Warnock's leg was cut off just below the knee. Courageously he was able to drive his team of horses on to a neighbour for help. The Warnocks were not part of the Dutch settlement.

93 In the spring of 1910 Egbertus Plomp had immigrated to Monarch from Nijverdal with other Dutch families and individuals who soon settled northeast of Carlstadt. The Plomps were one of the later families to leave Monarch to join the group homesteading there.

LETTER FROM MONARCH
(*De Volksvriend,* 27 June 1912)

Winter left us later than usual this year. It was a few days into April before we could begin with field work. The wheat that was first seeded and planted in well-worked ground came up nicely and is growing well so far. But what was seeded in stubble has not done much till now, partly due to the drought that prevents it from germinating. Also the cutworms have wiped out large fields. Yesterday was the first rain of significance, so there is still a chance for a moderate harvest.

It is quiet in the country and in town, a result of bad times. But our blacksmith [Gerhart] van den Broeke is very busy. He does his best not to let the farmers wait for their ploughshares, something the earlier blacksmiths certainly did. Several days ago van den Broeke bought a large blacksmith shop where he now works, no longer in the small workplace. He is the only Dutch resident in Monarch.

Rev. [John] de Beer of Lennox, South Dakota, is with the Reformed congregation for some time, leading the Sunday worship services.

Also in the Christian Reformed congregation there has been a minister for some time.[94]

The two Bode families and a Verschuur [Van Schuur] family left us this spring and bought or rented land in Washington where they have settled.

Mrs. Verschuur and Mrs. Dekker were taken by death.[95] Both were very old. They were laid to rest in the small piece of land by the church, where the grim reaper gathers his harvest, in spite of hailstorm or drought. Happy is the one who spends his days wisely.

LETTER FROM GERRIT HARTKOORN TO JAN POSTMAN
(Morse, Saskatchewan, Late Summer 1912)

Friend Postma,

Well, my friend Postma, the other day I received your letter. I am pleased that one of my boys was in Moose Jaw; otherwise I would not have gotten the

---

94 Rev. Tjeerd Jongbloed, a Christian Reformed home missionary based in Edmonton since 1911, made several visits to serve the Monarch and Granum churches in the summer and fall of 1912.

95 Sixty-three-year-old Jannetje Van Schuur died in early 1912. Seventy-five-year-old Trijntje Dekker died on 23 May 1912.

letter. The address on it was wrong. Now by the Lord's infinite goodness we are still in good health, and we wholeheartedly wish that for you folks too.

In your letter you want me to inform you a little about the matter that I have been going through with Jh [Johannes] Gunst.[96] You know that Gunst has my land for $30 [an acre]; that is $15 for myself, eh?[97] That was in 1909. Then I received a payment of $1,000. It was sold for three payments, just as he had sold his homestead across the river.[98] In 1910 there was no crop due to the drought. Then I received nothing. 1911 was the time of the last payment. Thus it was that altogether I still had $1996 coming from him. It was the same also with the sale of his homestead. In October 1911 I received a letter from him that the man who lives on his homestead could not pay. Then I wrote him back that I would gladly take $1,500 and leave $500 until the year 1912 when there might be a crop. I figured that he could well pay me that; he had a good crop. That was obvious; he had 3,500 bushels. Since I received no answer at all to that letter, I was really perplexed about it. You know just as well as I do that when you begin all kinds of things are needed. Then several weeks later he wrote me again that the man across the river had a little money, that he could well pay him off, and then he thought he would hand over his [title] papers to him. Then he would pay me off, if I would accept $400 or $500 less. I wrote him back that I would not do that, because the previous year I had received nothing due to the crop failure and it was money that is owed to me. After that he had me come to the bank at Morse on two occasions. If I would accept $400 to $500 less, then I could get my money. That I absolutely did not want. And then again a third time to the bank. There was a $700 loss on his homestead. [He asked] whether I would bear half of it; if not he would abandon the land. He knew just as well as I do that I could not take it back. With that he put a seal on it. What must I do now? If my eyes pass over this iniquity, I will receive about $1,700 of the $1996. Now, friend Postma, judge for yourself what is right. For myself I have lost that money. He has purposely pierced it through my nose. He well knew that now was the time to strike the iron while it was hot.

---

96 Johannes (John) Gunst was the husband of Hartkoorn's niece Jannigje Bode.

97 Hartkoorn had bought his quarter of land (NW 33-10-23 W4) in 1907 for $15 an acre. It was located near Postman's homestead. Apparently Hartkoorn sold his quarter to Gunst just before he left to the Netherlands in late November 1909. The following March Hartkoorn returned to Monarch with his family, but they soon settled at Hodgeville, Saskatchewan, southeast of Swift Currant.

98 In December 1905 John Gunst had claimed a homestead quarter (SW 18-10-24 W4) south of the Oldman River. After fulfilling the homestead requirements he received his patent on this quarter in October 1909. He immediately sold it and bought Hartkoorn's quarter. Now Gunst and his family could live next to their Bode relatives.

And now I have become a stinker to the family there.[99] That you can well imagine. [They think] I should not have made it public. I should have called the evil good. They are writing that I forced him. If I had known that, I would certainly have received my justice. He had to come from across the river to play Elder there. I have said now and then that they may be glad that they have such an Elder there.[100] Now, friend Postma, I will end. I think you will well understand it now.

We are now having beautiful weather for the crops, and till now they are doing extremely well. The wheat is standing five feet high and thick, especially on new breaking. We each have a half-section.[101] On that I have 60 acres of flax and 20 acres of oats – a delight to see. Arie has 30 acres of wheat and 20 of flax; Barend 41 acres of wheat. If all goes well, there can surely be a heavy crop. Now, my friend, I'm going to end, and hope that you may receive this in good health. Hearty greetings from all of us.

G[errit] Hartkoorn Morse, Sask., Box 140

LETTER FROM MONARCH
(*De Volksvriend,* 16 January 1913)

During the fall we were not burdened much by snow or cold. But in the last couple weeks of the year the west wind blew with mighty force so we were troubled by a lot of dust. This continued until 3 January, when it began to snow and winter set in. Now it is freezing 35 degrees below zero. We had enough time in the fall, however, to do all sorts of work, so the snow does not hinder us much.

Due to lengthy drought in the spring, cutworms, rain for too long in the fall, as well as frost at night, the harvest in 1912 was very uneven. That is, a few had a good harvest, others half, and some got next to nothing.

1912 was not a good year. Besides, the price of wheat is low this year. Indeed, that times are not good is clearly evident in Monarch, where the doctor, druggist, and butcher have left. Last year one hardware store sold

99 Hartkoorn was related to the Bode family at Monarch.
100 In 1911 John Gunst became an elder and president of the consistory (council) of the Monarch Christian Reformed Church. Hartkoorn would find easy sympathy from Postman, since Postman was to be excommunicated by this consistory on 24 November, for insisting on catechism teaching in "the language of the land" and for neglecting the devotional life of his family.
101 Gerrit Hartkoorn and his sons Arie and Barend each homesteaded a quarter of land and bought another quarter at Hodgeville, Saskatchewan.

Young men at the horse barn of the Granum Christian Reformed Church.

out, and now the other, so soon we will probably have to buy our hardware somewhere else.

Several children were born in 1912, such as at the homes of A[rie] Dekker, J[an] Bannink, B[astiaan] Koole, L[eendert] Koole, H[endrikus] Veldhuis, H[endrik] Goldenbeld, and J[an] Postman.

Mrs. J[acobus] Nyhoff and this writer received news from Holland that their mother passed away,[102] and shortly before the end of the year the Koole brothers lost their father by death. So they have now gone to Boyden, Iowa.[103]

A couple of weeks ago the fast train killed two horses of B[astiaan] Koole and injured a third.

In conclusion I report that the Christmas program was celebrated with much cheer on 26 December by the Dutch Reformed church and the following day by the Christian Reformed congregation.

E[vert] Aldus

---

102 Jacobus Nyhoff's wife Wilhelmina was a younger sister of Evert Aldus. Their mother Johanna Aldus died at age 63.

103 The Koole brothers from Monarch were Bastiaan, Leendert, and Arie. A letter from Boyden, Iowa, in *De Volksvriend* (2 January 1913) reported: "On Friday Mr. A[rie] Koole died, at age 70. He had been ailing already for a long time, and now a cold that settled in his lungs suddenly put an end to his life. The deceased was one of the best farmers in Sioux County, and with the help of a number of sons he acquired a stretch of land here. Three of his sons who live in Canada are here to attend the funeral. Besides his spouse the deceased leaves behind seven sons, three of whom are married."

CHAPTER 5

The Years of Renewed Stability
1913–14

AFTER THE THREE BAD YEARS, THERE WERE BETTER harvests and the Dutch farm settlement at Granum-Monarch-Nobleford slowly recovered. As the community approached the end of its first decade, most Dutch farmers were quite well established and ties to the Old Country were becoming weaker. Life in the settlement was becoming more routine, and there was less news. So there are fewer letters in the year or two before World War I. A few correspondent letters from Monarch and Barons, and from Evert Aldus and George Dijkema, reveal something of the renewed spirit of this period. In a final letter Aldus reflects on the changes brought about in the first decade of the settlement.

LETTER FROM GRANUM
(*De Wachter,* 5 February 1913)

As usual, on the Second Day of Christmas we got together to celebrate with the children of the congregation. It is our custom to make a joyful day for the small catechism children. With these small children also come the parents with the rest of the children, and so we have all the families of the congregation together. Besides, the unmarried are not often conspicuous by their absence, so we see the whole congregation united, as it were.

Although the weather was not very pleasant that day, almost everyone was present. One family could not completely come due to illness, and another was absent because of the weather. Yet we had a celebration. Our young people's society provided recitations.[1] Our choral society could not perform because its director was absent due to illness. But in its place the choral society from neighbouring Monarch was present with their director to oblige us with a few pieces. This society was invited to spend the evening at the annual program of our young people's society, but since we had our celebration that day they decided to be present the whole day, which pleased us very much. Celebrating without music can hardly be done, so we were very glad that Monarch's society was here, since ours couldn't be. To the joy of all of us, the director, as often as he was asked, said they were ready to oblige us with one of their songs.

Our congregational life is going slowly, but we believe it is certainly making headway. A couple of years ago we built a parsonage and tried to get our own shepherd and minister, but our attempts were not crowned with success. Now at the congregational meeting we decided to make the parsonage ready and, Lord willing, to make efforts once again to get our own preacher.[2] May the King of the Church then bless our efforts, so that it may be said also of our congregation: "Your eyes shall see your own minister."

Geo. Dijkema

---

1 This typically included a recitation of poems or short literary pieces.
2 In November 1912 the Granum CRC decided to call a minister jointly with the Monarch congregation.
3 Egbertus Plomp and his family immigrated to Monarch in 1910 and then moved to the Dutch settlement at Carlstadt in early 1912.

LETTER FROM MONARCH
(*De Grondwet*, 4 March 1913)

Monarch has not died out, although one does not hear very much from here. On the contrary, everyone is very glad about the past year. On the whole we harvested a good crop, and I am sorry that I cannot write all about it. A few people harvested only a little, but everyone is full of hope about the year 1913, and each has his land in good condition. There is still a lot of land to buy for $25 to $40 an acre.

Today E[gbertus] Plomp is at the home of his brother-in-law Mr. Gelense [Leendert Geleynse] here and found that family in good health.[3] The weather is nice today; the snow is gone, and the chickens are showing that they are already pleased with spring by laying plenty of eggs. For a week already Mr. Gelense has been getting 16, 18, and 20 eggs a day from his chickens.

Corr. 16 Feb. 1913

LETTER FROM EVERT ALDUS
(*Twentsch Volksblad*, 30 March 1913)

Monarch, 1 March 1913

I have waited already too long to write, and many no doubt will think that I have forgotten my old place of residence and also my obligation to the newspaper. However, it is becoming ever more difficult to write about something that is "news," so I will now be able to supply little more than a report of very ordinary things.

Hence I will begin by telling about what is most important to us during the last year, our work. The spring gave us dry weather until 15 June. So a lot of grain did not come up or it came up unevenly. After that it rained a lot, and in the fall too much and too long. More than once there was hail, but it did not do much damage. Also the cutworms destroyed an enormous amount of grain. So, when fall came, some took in a good harvest, a large number had half a harvest, and many received much less than that. Besides, there was a lot of poor-quality grain, since it came up unevenly and therefore also ripened unevenly.

Also, the Chinook wind blew for a day with unusual force, and cast thousands of bushels on the ground. For the majority of the population 1912 was hardly more favourable than the two previous years. It is no wonder that the consequences of these failures are clearly noticeable. Many of the small towns that depend mainly on farmers for their prosperity are half depopulated. Also in Monarch this situation is visible. In turn the doctor, druggist, saddle maker, butcher, and a storekeeper have left. A hardware store sold out last year; the second and last one is doing so now. So our village is terribly marred by empty buildings.

Yet, in spite of all this, we soon hope to take our drills into the fields again; perhaps the result will be better for us than in previous years. However, it cannot be denied that for many farmers it is necessary that things improve; many are in circumstances that cannot endure much more decline.

It seems to me that people on the outside think more favourably about this region than reality may allow; certainly large and small speculators in land and town property are not without fault. Beyond all criticism, they boast intending only to fill their pockets with capital or by the work of others.

The population of our colony remains about the same. A couple came here from elsewhere, and some left us and went to the United States.[4]

Also in church life there is not much news. Both congregations are content with reading sermons all the time, except for a few Sundays when a minister visits us. Christmas was celebrated as usual in both churches. These celebrations are always very sociable and exciting, and everyone attends. In almost all respects they are good Dutch celebrations.

A[ldus]

LETTER FROM BARONS
(*De Volksvriend*, 9 October 1913)

We like it well here. Our district has an excellent harvest. The threshing proceeded well; only at night a little snow and now somewhat colder. We finished the threshing a week ago, and threshed 8,000 bushels of wheat from 320 acres. The yields varied a lot, from 10 to 40 bushels an acre. The best-worked land brought the most. Those who threshed early got a good price; those who threshed late will get at least 10 cents less. I have contracted 7,000 [bushels] at 70 cents a bushel. So much grain is being brought to Barons that you sometimes have to wait two hours at the elevator before getting the opportunity to unload your load.

Arie Versluys

Beert G. Nauta stooking on his Granum farm. (Courtesy: Annie Nauta.)

LETTER FROM MONARCH
(*De Grondwet,* 21 October 1913)

The threshing is almost done, and everyone has his grain in the bin, so that it may be shipped by railway car as soon as the busyness has let up a bit. People are satisfied with the harvest this year. Some farmers here harvested 46 bushels of wheat per acre. Certainly proof that Monarch is the feather in Alberta's cap. The land is also rising regularly in price.

We had the great privilege of having Rev. Rottschaffer in our midst for a couple of weeks.[5] Everyone regrets that his stay here was so short, but he also had to be in Carlstadt.

E. Alders [Evert Aldus] lost one of his best horses.

At the home of C[ornelis] van Egmond there were a couple of tense days. Their youngest [Alice], an only daughter, was very sick and they feared the worst, but we can report with joy that the danger is past and she is getting better.

Everyone here has a phone in the house, which is a great convenience for the farmers.

Corr. 5 Oct. 1913

4 In 1912 several single men arrived in the settlement, including Klaas and Berend Poelman, Arie Verwoerd, Willem Van Os, Hendrik van Huizen, Krijn Gortsema, Andries and Antoon Krijthe, and Cornelis Bannink. The Geert Venhuizen family moved to Manhattan, and the Leendert and Gerrit Bode families and Klass Van Schuur moved to Lynden, Washington.

5 Rev. William Rottschaffer from Oak Harbor, Wash. was making a pastoral visit to the Monarch Reformed Church.

LETTER FROM BARONS
(*De Volksvriend*, 29 January 1914)

Till today the weather has always been nice; now it is snowing, but it is not cold.

Last week someone from eastern Canada held a public auction here of milk cows imported from there; prices from $65 to $87 were paid. Butter is now 30 cents and eggs are 40 cents and pigs 6½ cents. Our hog sellers will send their grunters to Seattle in the future, and show in this way that they still do not need millionaire Pat Burns.[6] Mr. B[astiaan] Koole of Monarch delivered 22 pigs to Barons last week.

My brother G. Versluys, now in the Netherlands, writes of "rain, mist and mud. This evening the socialists will announce their doctrine of discontent in a new way. They appear to be men with much advice but little benefit. One thing is certain, they are very zealous."

With esteem, Arie Versluys

LETTER FROM MONARCH
(*De Volksvriend*, 14 April 1914)

The winter has left us and was rather severe, except for the first half of March when the weather was mild. Everyone is ready to start seeding, but we cannot begin since the ground is too wet. This has never before happened in all the ten years that we have been here, and it occurred because the snow thawed where it fell, instead of blowing from the land, as in other winters, and piling up where it is not needed, causing a nuisance. As I write this, it is raining, a phenomenon that can be called unusual here before April. Considering everything, there is plenty of moisture in the ground to make the grain grow for a long time, so at least we have a good beginning.

J[an] Postman went with most of his children, stock, and possessions to the Peace River district, 400 miles north of Edmonton, where he bought

---

6 Pat Burns had a large packing plant in Calgary and monopolized the market.
7 John Postman left Monarch with nine of his thirteen children in August 1913, and the trip to the Peace River district took them over two months via the notorious Edson trail. The other four children joined them in March and July 1914. In later years most of the children returned to Monarch. The interesting saga of the Postman trips and experience in the Peace River country is told in Hofman, *Strength of Their Years*, 125ff.

land. A couple of his children are still here and are also thinking about going there in May.[7] The [Cornelis] Van Egmond and [Roelof] Kooi families also want to go to Peace River in the fall.[8]

T[ijmen] Hofman and his wife are just back from their trip to Lynden, Washington, where they visited family and friends. J[an] Withage and his wife, as well as W[illem] Nijhoff, made a trip to Holland, and brought along a family and a young man.[9]

Mrs. [Christina] Aldus was in the Lethbridge hospital for six weeks and underwent an operation, but is now home again and getting better.

The Christian Reformed congregation made a call, but the minister declined.[10] A short time ago Rev. [Arend] Guikema from Washington visited the congregation, and the Reformed church soon hopes to see Rev. [John] Roggen of Conrad, Montana.

A baby girl came to stay at the home of R[ense] Nijhoff, and some time ago W[illem] Stotijn had a boy.

LETTER FROM EVERT ALDUS
(*Twentsch Volksblad*, 16 May 1914)

Monarch, Alberta, Canada 15 April 1914

At the beginning of this month it was ten years ago that we settled in this area.[11] That a lot can be done in ten years is certainly evident here. Where nothing but vast grassy plains were apparent every day, now everything is farmland, intersected by roads, and almost all the houses spread everywhere are connected with each other and other places by a huge telephone network. We no longer see the caravans of covered wagons and carts; they have been

8 Their sons John Kooi and Gerrit Van Egmond were first to join the Postmans in the Peace River district in February 1914. But they did not like it there and returned after about three months. The families never went.
9 The family that returned with Gerrit Jan Withage was that of Jan and Hermina Konynenbelt and their four children from Nijverdal. Hermina was a sister of Withage. The young man was Dirk Van Os, who was returning to his farm at Granum, where he had lived since 1910. Also returning with them was Jan Koole from Pearce and his fiancée Johanna Zeylmans.
10 An attempt in 1913 to call home missionary Rev. Menno Borduin to southern Alberta for two years was unsuccessful.
11 Aldus is referring to the group from the Nijverdal area who arrived in 1904 and settled in the Monarch district. The same issue of the *Twentsch Volksblad* contains a general article about Canada based on reports in the London *Times*. This article reports on the latest Canadian census of 1911, according to which the Canadian population numbered 7,206,643, of whom 54,986 were Dutch. 2,851 Hollanders lived in Alberta, 2,684 in Saskatchewan, and 2,853 in Manitoba.

replaced by the locomotive which pulls long trains east and west of our colony. This writer and a few others who planted some young trees a few years ago are seeing them grow up to three or four metres in height.

That ten years is a long time we can also see from the children who made the trip with us; most of them are grown up, and some are already married. And many of us, who were relatively young when we left, are now beginning to turn gray.

And so things take their natural course here. The number of children has much increased in recent years, and the small piece of ground behind the [Christian] Reformed church (where everyone who stays living here will rest at some time or other, no matter whether they have occupied many or few acres of land) is already showing a number of small mounds.

Also as a result of the less than favourable conditions of the last years, the churches are not making rapid progress; that is, none of the congregations has a minister yet. The [Christian] Reformed made a call recently, but without the desired result.[12]

The weather in the last couple of years seems to be returning to earlier conditions; at any rate in 1912 and 1913 it was good enough for a harvest. The main cause for failure was the cutworms, especially in 1912.

On the basis of the last ten years, the climatic conditions in this region are not unfavourable for farming, that is, for growing grain. Cattle-breeding has the drawback that relatively little grass will grow here. Therefore the generally depressed conditions that prevail here, also in the towns, cannot just be blamed on the unsuccessful years. A large part of it is the fault of speculators; by bragging and lies to the rest of the world, they force up the value of land and building sites here far too high, in order to fill their own pockets. These and all other sorts of capitalist parasites view new areas like a fat milk cow, from which they get all they can, and the government silently leaves them alone.[13]

12 The Granum and Monarch Christian Reformed churches together had called Rev. Gilbert G. Haan in 1910, but he declined. In January 1914 the Monarch CRC on its own called Rev. Cornelius Vriesman of Zillah, Wash. and then in March Rev. Karel Fortuin of Harderwyk, Mich.; both declined. It was not until 1916, after more declined calls, that Rev. Nicholas Gelderloos came to serve both Monarch and Granum as a home missionary of Classis Pacific.

13 There was a land speculation frenzy in prairie towns and cities in 1910–12, followed by a real estate slump in 1913.

14 This was Evert Aldus's last letter from Alberta. Later in 1914 he and his family moved to Colorado.

We are now busy seeding; we began a little later than other years, because the ground is very wet this spring, so there is every chance for a good beginning.

Like elsewhere, here too it is best to persevere as long as possible. I often neglected to write in the last couple of years, but I will try to do better from now on.

A[ldus][14]

Epilogue

THE PERIOD 1903–14 REPRESENTS ONLY THE FIRST
chapter of the Dutch-Canadian presence in southern Alberta. The Dutch
settlement in the Granum-Monarch-Nobleford district has persisted for a
century, though growth has been restricted by the size of farms. Part of the
community now resides in the local towns. Many descendants of the early
Dutch settlers still live in the area.

Before World War II, growth among the Dutch in the region was slow.
After 1907 a Dutch farm community took root south of Burdett. By 1910
there were several families at Taber, as well as in Lethbridge. Many in the
1910 wave of new immigrants took up homesteads at Carlstadt, northwest
of Medicine Hat, but due to persistent crop failures in this arid region, this
Dutch community dispersed by 1925 to Monarch, Washington state, and
elsewhere.

Beginning in 1947, a large influx of post-war Dutch immigrants brought
new blood to the existing Dutch communities and also established a new
Dutch presence in other parts of southern Alberta. Some of the new immigrants were sponsored by farmers in the Granum-Monarch-Nobleford
district and eventually bought farms or married girls of the local Dutch
community.

Scores of new immigrant families found work in the sugar-beet fields in the irrigation districts of Iron Springs, Picture Butte, and Taber, and many of them settled there. Other Dutch farm communities emerged at Brooks, Vauxhall, Coaldale, and High River. Even more of the new immigrants took up residence in the cities of Calgary, Lethbridge, and Medicine Hat, and engaged in various urban trades.

Elsewhere in the province major concentrations of Dutch-Canadians developed out of pre-war communities at Neerlandia, Edmonton, and Lacombe.

The pre-war Dutch community in Alberta acculturated to Canadian society rather slowly. Use of the Dutch language remained strong among families, and especially in the church, through the thirties and early forties. And just as they were going over to English, the influx of post-war immigrants gave the older community a new infusion of the Dutch language and culture. The post-war immigrants, however, tended to adopt English more quickly. By the sixties most church services were in English.

Dutch ethnic identity in southern Alberta has been perpetuated especially through their two major institutions, the church and the Christian school. The locations and founding dates of these churches and schools reveal concentrations of the Dutch throughout the southern part of the province, especially since the war. Though all are part of the broader Reformed tradition, a multiplicity of denominations also reveals the religious fragmentation of the Dutch community in southern Alberta, reflecting church splits among the Reformed in the Netherlands and the United States.

The Christian Reformed Church remained the largest religious group. After the Nijverdal CRC was organized in 1905 and reorganized in 1911 into the Granum, Nobleford, and Burdett churches, many later CRCs were established after World War II in Iron Springs (1949), Lethbridge (two churches, 1950, 1975), Taber (1951), Calgary (seven churches, 1952, 1956, 1956, 1978, disbanded 1989, 1988, 2001, 2003), Brooks (1952), Vauxhall (1952, disbanded 1995), High River (1952), and Medicine Hat (1953).

The Reformed Church in America (RCA) did not establish as much of a presence in southern Alberta. After the Monarch Reformed Church was organized in 1909, RCA churches were started at Carlstadt in 1912 (moved to Bottrel in 1926), and in Calgary (two churches, 1954, 1986, disbanded 1995). A recent split in the Monarch church led to the formation of the Westminster Chapel in Lethbridge (2001).

After World War II, Canadian Reformed Churches were instituted in Coaldale (1950), Calgary (1964), and Taber (1991).

Netherlands Reformed Churches were established in Lethbridge (1951), Calgary (1954), Fort Macleod (1961), and Picture Butte (1999). A group separated from the Macleod church in 1966 to form the Reformed Congregation in North America at Monarch, and another split in the same church gave rise to the Heritage Reformed Church of Fort Macleod in 1998.

Members associated with the Gereformeerde Bond in the Netherlands formed the Bethel Reformed Church of Monarch in 1988. Initially it affiliated with the RCA, and then it joined the Free Reformed Churches in 2000.

A conservative segment that separated from the Christian Reformed Church in the early nineties soon formed United Reformed Churches in Lethbridge and Calgary in 1995.

Dutch-Canadians in the Reformed tradition have generally been strong advocates of Christian education, but in southern Alberta they did not have the numbers or resources to set up Christian schools until the 1960s.

Members of the Christian Reformed churches established Immanuel Christian School at Lethbridge in 1962, and added a high school in 1976. They opened schools at Taber in 1984 and at Medicine Hat in 1982. The Calgary Christian School opened in 1963 and high school in 1976; also in Calgary, the Trinity Christian School was launched in 1993.

Canadian Reformed people started Tyndale Christian School in Calgary in 1994. The Netherlands Reformed churches opened the Calvin Christian School at Monarch (1979), and people of the Bethel Reformed Church started Providence Christian School, also at Monarch (1994).

Dutch Catholics and non-churched immigrants have tended to assimilate quickly into Canadian society, and they have not developed a Dutch community identity. It has been in the larger Dutch community of Reformed heritage that Dutch ethnic identity has been most strongly preserved.

Still, over the decades there has been a gradual assimilation of this Dutch community, especially economically. The Dutch have generally prospered in Alberta. There is now more and more openness to connect with broader Canadian society, but even today there is a reluctance to marry outside ethnic circles. The persistence of Dutch ethnic identity for a century in southern Alberta, nourished by post-war immigration and preserved especially in the churches and schools of Reformed persuasion, carries forward the heritage of the early Dutch settlers of the pioneer era.

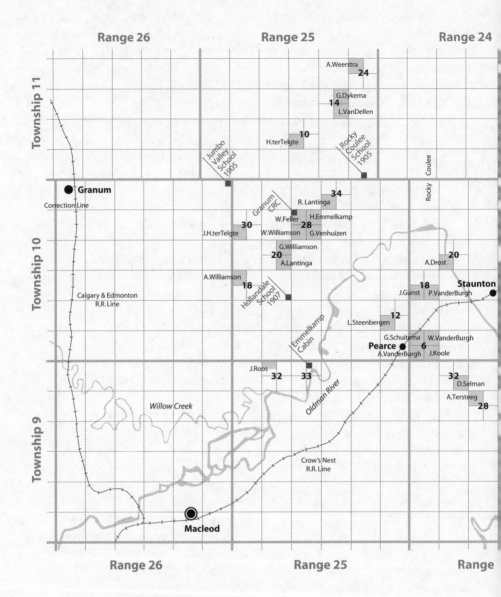

DUTCH HOMESTEADERS IN THE ALBERTA SETTLEMENT

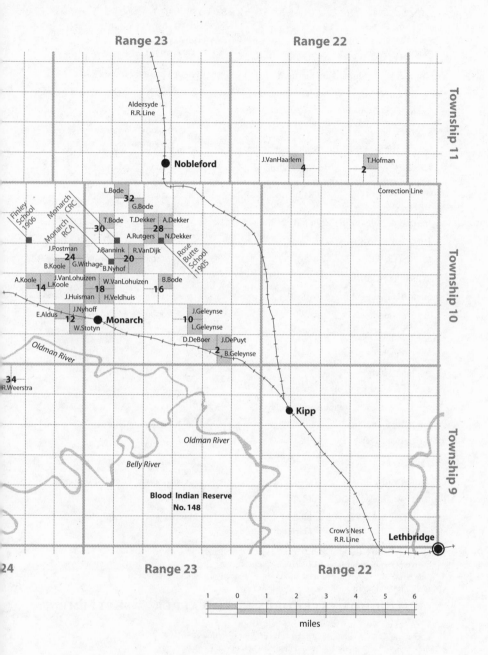

Range 23

Range 22

Township 11

Aldersyde
R.R.Line

● Nobleford

J.VanHaarlem
4

T.Hofman
2

Correction Line

Finley
School
1906

Monarch CRC

Monarch RCA

L.Bode
32
G.Bode

T.Bode   T.Dekker   A.Dekker
30   A.Rutgers   N.Dekker
28

J.Postman
24
B.Koole   G.Withage   J.Bannink   R.VanDijk
20
B.Nyhof

Rose Butte School 1905

A.Koole
14   L.Koole   J.VanLohuizen
18   W.VanLohuizen   B.Bode
16
J.Huisman   H.Veldhuis

Township 10

E.Aldus   J.Nyhoff
12
W.Stotyn   ● Monarch

J.Geleynse
10
L.Geleynse

D.DeBoer   J.DePuyt
2   B.Geleynse

Oldman River

34
R.Weerstra

● Kipp

Oldman River

Belly River

Township 9

Blood Indian Reserve
No. 148

Crow's Nest
R.R.Line   ◉ Lethbridge

24

Range 23

Range 22

1   0   1   2   3   4   5   6

miles

Appendix A: *The* DUTCH SETTLERS 1903–14[1]

Name	Arrival in the[2] Settlement	Arrived from
Harm & Jantje Emmelkamp & children	Jan or Feb 1903	Raton, NM
Hendrikus & Maria ter Telgte & children	late 1903[3]	Manhattan, MT
Lubbert Van Dellen	Feb 1904[4]	Montana
George Dijkema	Feb 1904	Manhattan, MT
Jan & Fenneken ter Telgte & children	3 Mar 1904[5]	Manhattan, MT
Gerrit & Theodora Withage & children	3 Mar 1904	Manhattan, MT
Everhardus & Christina Aldus & children	3 Apr 1904	Nijverdal, Overijssel
Johannes & Hendrika Huisman & children	3 Apr 1904	Nijverdal, Overijssel
Jacobus & Wilhelmina Nijhoff & children	3 Apr 1904	Nijverdal, Overijssel
Jan & Janna Postman & children	3 Apr 1904	Den Ham, Overijssel
Willem Stotijn	3 Apr 1904	Nijverdal, Overijssel
Willem & Hendrika Van Lohuizen & children	3 Apr 1904	Heerde, Gelderland
Hendrikje Van Lohuizen (widow)	3 Apr 1904	Heerde, Gelderland
Jan Van Lohuizen	3 Apr 1904	Heerde, Gelderland
Hendrikus & Janna Veldhuis & children	3 Apr 1904	Nijverdal, Overijssel
Willem Feller	Apr or May 1904[6]	Manhattan, MT
Roelf Lantinga	Apr or May 1904	New Mexico
Roelof & Dina Van Dijk & children	May or Jun 1904	Midland Park, NJ
Geert & Klaassien Venhuizen & children	Jun 1904	Manhattan, MT
Jan Bannink	Jun 1904	Nijverdal, Overijssel
Berend Nijhof	Jun 1904	Nijverdal, Overijssel
Thys Dekker	Nov 1904[7]	Vesper, WI
Teunis Bode	Nov 1904[8]	Vesper, WI
Gerrit & Klaasje Bode & child	Nov 1904	Vesper, WI
Garrit & Hendrika Willemsen & children	Feb 1905[9]	Manhattan, MT

1   This information is based on family histories, letters, ship manifests, church records, homestead records, Dutch emigration records, and Dutch population registers. In the later years the list may not be complete. Some families and individuals lived in the settlement only a few months before moving elsewhere, *e.g.*, the March 1910 immigrants who moved to Carlstadt.
2   This is the date when the family or individual settled. In a number of cases the person earlier visited Alberta and filed on a homestead, but returned later to settle.
3   Hendrikus ter Telgte had visited Alberta in July 1903.
4   Lubbert Van Dellen had visited Alberta and filed on a homestead in August 1903.
5   Jan ter Telgte had visited Alberta and filed on a homestead in August 1903.
6   Willem Feller had visited Alberta and filed on a homestead in August–September, 1903.
7   Thys Dekker had visited Alberta and filed on a homestead in September 1904.
8   Teunis Bode had visited Alberta and filed on a homestead in September 1904.
9   Garrit Willemsen had visited Alberta and filed on a homestead in November 1904.

Name	Arrival in the Settlement	Arrived from
Willem Willemsen Jr.	Feb 1905	Manhattan, MT
Bastiaan Koole	Mar 1905[10]	Sheldon, IA
Leendert Koole	Mar 1905[11]	Sheldon, IA
Arie Koole	Mar 1905	Sheldon, IA
Anne Weerstra	Mar 1905	St. Jacobiparochie, Friesland
Gerard Schuitema	Mar 1905	Groningen
Albert Lantinga	Mar 1905	Nieuw Scheemda, Groningen
Nan & Trijntje Dekker	Mar 1905	Vesper, WI
Arie Dekker	Mar 1905	Vesper, WI
Maartje Dekker	Mar 1905	Vesper, WI
Abel Vander Burgh	Apr 1905	Hull, IA
Walter Vander Burgh	Apr 1905	Hull, IA
Cornelia Vander Burgh	1905 ?	Hull, IA ?
Barend Bode	Apr 1905 ?	Vesper, WI
Rense & Aaltje Nijhoff & children	May 1905	Nijverdal, Overijssel
Jacob De Vries	Jun 1905 ?	Netherlands
Leendert Geleijnse	Jul 1905	Vesper, WI
Albert Rutgers	Jul 1905	Nijverdal, Overijssel
Rommert & Jantje Weerstra & children	25 Nov 1905	St. Jacobiparochie, Friesland
Leendert & Willempje Bode & children	2 Dec 1905	Vesper, WI
Johannes & Jannigje Gunst	2 Dec 1905	Vesper, WI
Arend Willemsen (widower)	Jan 1906	Manhattan, MT
Pieter & Annette Vander Burgh & children	Jan or Feb 1906	Sheldon, IA
Jan Koole	Feb 1906	Hull, IA
Willem De Jong	Feb 1906	Leeuwarden, Friesland
Jan & Rensche Roos & children	Apr 1906	Grand Rapids, MI
Lucas Steenbergen	May 1906 ?	Groningen
Jacobus & Mrs. Van Haarlem & children	Jun 1906	Amsterdam
Lurson Hull	Jun 1906	Netherlands
Bartel Geleijnse (widower)	Aug 1906	Vesper, WI

10 Bastiaan Koole had visited the settlement and filed on a homestead in September 1904.
11 Leendert Koole had visited the settlement and filed on a homestead in September 1904.

Name	Arrival in the Settlement	Arrived from
Dick Selmen	Sep 1906	Nebraska
Jan & Dena Geleijnse & children	Oct 1906	Vesper, WI
Daniel DeBoer	Nov 1906[12]	Conrad, MT
Frans & Klaasje Vanden Berg Sr. & children	1907	Rotterdam
Anna Mulder (married George Dijkema)	30 Mar 1907	Ten Boer, Groningen
Maria Talens (married Lucas Steenbergen)	30 Mar 1907	Groningen
Jacobus Van Leeuwen	spring 1907	?
Tijmen & Heiltje Hofman & children	May 1907[13]	Westfield, ND
Frans Vanden Berg Jr.	May 1907	Rotterdam
Paul Vanden Berg	May 1907	Rotterdam
Gerrit Hartkoorn	May 1907	Rotterdam
Cornelis Kamp	May 1907	Netherlands
Adam & Mrs. Drost & children	Jun 1907 ?	Stettler, Alberta
Marinus Dykshoorn	summer 1907	?
Jan & Jenneken Tersteeg	Oct 1907	Noord-Holland
Frederikus & Jansje Kamperman	Jul 1907	Nijverdal, Overijssel
Gerrit Jan Kamperman	Jul 1907	Nijverdal, Overijssel
Jan Vaale	1907	?
Teun Zoeteman	1907	Perkins, IA
Albert Tersteeg	early 1908	North Holland
Jan Nauta	Mar 1908	Iowa
Dirk Venema	Mar 1908	Vesper, WI
Tena Van Schuur (married Daniel DeBoer)	Mar 1908	Vesper, WI
Geert Lantinga	Mar 1908	Nieuw Scheemda, Groningen
Louisa Stotijn (married Arie Dekker)	Mar 1908	Nijverdal, Overijssel ?
Adrian Guichard	Apr 1908	Netherlands
Hendrik Matter	Apr 1908	Netherlands
Willem Kruyt	spring 1908	Netherlands
Ritske & Maria Statema & child	May 1908	Dordrecht, Zuid-Holland
Jacob & Mrs. G. Douma	May 1908	Friesland
Hendrik & Lambertha Goldenbeld & children	May 1908	Nijverdal, Overijssel

12 Daniel De Boer had visited Alberta in August or September 1906.
13 Tijmen Hofman had visited Alberta in November 1906.

Name	Arrival in the Settlement	Arrived from
Geertje Goldenbeld (widow)	May 1908	Nijverdal, Overijssel
Hillichien Mulder	4 June 1908	Ten Boer, Groningen
Lijzebeth De Haas & children (widow)	Jun 1908	Nyssa, OR
Beert G. Nauta (widower)	Oct 1908	St. Jacobiparochie, Friesland
Renske Riewald	Oct 1908	St. Jacobiparochie, Friesland
Trijntje Unema	Oct 1908	St. Jacobiparochie, Friesland
Grietje Matter & children (family of Hendrik Matter)	fall 1908	Netherlands
Leida Kruyt & children (family of Willem Kruyt)	fall 1908	Netherlands
Albert & Susanna Ritsema & children	Nov 1908	Sullivan, MI
Marinus Van Staalduine	1908 or 1909 ?	Netherlands
Roelof Kingma	Feb 1909	Hillegom, Zuid-Holland
Laurens De Koekkoek	Feb 1909	Hillegom, Zuid-Holland
Jan & Wobbegiena van Kooij & child	May 1909	Nijverdal, Overijssel
Theodoor Haverkate	May 1909	Nijverdal, Overijssel
Beert A. Nauta	16 Jul 1909	St. Annaparochie, Friesland
Hendrik Hoekstra	16 Jul 1909	St. Annaparochie, Friesland
Jacob & Leentje Leeuwerik	1909[14]	Hull, IA
Peter Koole	1909	Hull, IA
Aria Koole	1909	Hull, IA
Hilje Nienhuis (married Gerard Schuitema)	1909	Groningen
Nikolaas Van Gaalen	1909	Sheldon, IA
Willem Van Schuur	1909 ?	Vesper, WI
Wouter Van Dam	1909 ?	?
Paulina DeBeeld (married Teunis Bode)	1909 ?	Ottoland, Zuid-Holland
Arie Verbaan	1909 ?	?
Gerrit & Mrs. Oldenhof & children	Dec 1909 ?	Wapenveld, Gelderland

14 Jacob Leeuwerik had bought land in the Pearce district in 1906 and 1907.

Name	Arrival in the Settlement	Arrived from
Antoon & Hermina Stotijn & children	1910 ?	Almelo, Overijssel
Wilhelmina Gunst (widow)	Feb 1910	Vesper, WI
Anthonie & Maria Gunst & children	Feb 1910	Vesper, WI
Willem Gunst	Feb 1910	Vesper, WI
Jan & Antonia Vander Woude & children	Feb 1910	Vesper, WI
Roelof & Boukje Kooi & children	Feb 1910	Vesper, WI
Klaas & Jannetje Van Schuur	Feb 1910	Vesper, WI
Jakob Van der Klooster	1910	Vesper, WI
Katholientje Kingma & children (family of Roelof Kingma)	Mar 1910	Hillegom, Zuid-Holland
Elizabeth DeKoekkoek & children (family of Laurens DeK)	Mar 1910	Hillegom, Zuid-Holland
Hendrik & Lina Baan & children	Mar 1910	Netherlands
Johanna Baan	Mar 1910	Netherlands
Arend & Johannes Balster	Mar 1910	Nijverdal, Overijssel
Hendrik Bargboer	Mar 1910	Nijverdal, Overijssel
Pieter & Roelofina Berkhof	Mar 1910	Netherlands
Jan & Aaltje DeBeeld & children	Mar 1910	Ottoland, Zuid-Holland
Jan Dekker	Mar 1910	Nijverdal, Overijssel
Johannes Harink	Mar 1910	Nijverdal, Overijssel
Hendrik & Mrs. Hilberdink & children	Mar 1910	Nijverdal, Overijssel
Mannes & Frederika Hobbelink & children	Mar 1910	Nijverdal, Overijssel
Gerrit Janssen	Mar 1910	Netherlands
Leendert Kamp	Mar 1910	Rotterdam
Berendina Leyerweerd (married Berend Nijhof)	Mar 1910	Nijverdal, Overijssel
Albert Nijhof	Mar 1910	Nijverdal, Overijssel
Egbert Nijhof	Mar 1910	Nijverdal, Overijssel
Hermannus & Mrs. Ponsteen & child	Mar 1910	Nijverdal, Overijssel
Jan & Wilhemina Rientjes & children	Mar 1910	Nijverdal, Overijssel
Francisca Rutgers (married Albert Rutgers)	Mar 1910	Nijverdal, Overijssel
Mannes & Gerritdina Rutgers & children	Mar 1910	Nijverdal, Overijssel
Gerritdina Scholten (married Jan Bannink)	Mar 1910	Nijverdal, Overijssel
Albertha Schotveld	Mar 1910	Nijverdal, Overijssel
Berend Ter Stege	Mar 1910	Nijverdal, Overijssel

Name	Arrival in the Settlement	Arrived from
Herbert Vander Werff	Mar 1910	Vuren, Gelderland
Hendrina Veldhuis (widow)	Mar 1910	Nijverdal, Overijssel
Luite Visscher	Mar 1910	Nijverdal, Overijssel
Willem Voortman	Mar 1910	Netherlands
Gerrit Warmink	Mar 1910	Nijverdal, Overijssel
Jan Westera	Mar 1910	Nijverdal, Overijssel
Jabikje Hartkoorn (wife of Gerrit)	Mar 1910	Rotterdam
Arie and Barend Hartkoorn	Mar 1910	Rotterdam
Arie & Mrs. Versluys	spring 1910[15]	Northwest Iowa
Cornelis & Harmina Van Egmond & children	Mar or Apr 1910	Sioux Center, IA
Ferdinand & Johanna Schiebout & children	Mar or Apr 1910	Sioux Center, IA
Evert & Hendrika Schiebout & children	Apr 1910	Manhattan, MT
Arend Willem & Johanna Willemsen & children	Apr 1910	Manhattan, MT
Hendrikus & Johanna Tyhuis & child	Apr 1910	Nijverdal, Overijssel
Hendrik Van Leeuwen	Apr 1910	Heerde, Gelderland
Willem Poelman	Apr 1910	Wirdum, Groningen
Egbertus Plomp	May 1910	Nijverdal, Overijssel
Barend & Bertha Van Kerken	Jun 1910	Nijverdal, Overijssel
Fijkje Plomp & children (family of Egbertus Plomp)	Jul 1910	Nijverdal, Overijssel
Antonetta Plomp (widow)	Jul 1910	Nijverdal, Overijssel
Anna Christina Plomp (married Leendert Geleynse)	Jul 1910	Nijverdal, Overijssel
Arie DeValois	19 Aug 1910	Piershil, Zuid-Holland
Leentje Kamp	Aug 1910	Rotterdam
Pieter & Hilligje Ritsema & child	Sep 1910	Grand Rapids, MI
Hein Van Tol	1910	Huigsloot, Noord-Holland
Pierkje Feenstra (married Anne Weerstra)	1910	Prince Albert, Sask.
Geertje Dijkema (married Roelf Lantinga)	1910	Saaxumhuizen, Groningen
Huibrecht Koert & son Adriannus	1910	Rotterdam
Marie Leyerweerd (married Thys Dekker)	Jan 1911	Almelo, Overijssel

15 Arie Versluys had visited Monarch in 1909.

Name	Arrival in the Settlement	Arrived from
Geert Poelman	Feb 1911	Wirdum, Groningen
Hendrik Ham	Feb 1911	Garrelsweer, Groningen
Arie Geerds	Feb 1911	Appingedam, Groningen
Elsje Warmink & child (family of Gerrit Warmink)	Mar 1911 ?	Nijverdal, Overijssel
Johanna Japin (married Luite Visscher)	Mar 1911 ?	Nijverdal, Overijssel
Taeke Dijkstra	Mar 1911	St. Annaparochie, Friesland
Gerhart & Hendrikje Vanden Broeke & children	Mar 1911	Wierden, Overijssel
Johanna DeValois & child (family of Arie DeValois)	Apr 1911	Piershil, Zuid-Holland
Jan, Anje, & Fokko Poelman	Jun 1911	Ten Boer, Groningen
Jan & Piechia Zoeteman & children	Jun & Jul 1911[16]	Perkins, IA
Arie & Maria Van Gaalen & child	Jul 1911	Papendrecht, Zuid-Holland
Pieter Schippers	Jul or Aug 1911	Boyden, IA
D. De Haan '	Jul or Aug 1911	Boyden, IA
Roelf & Hilje Poelman	Aug 1911	Ten Boer, Groningen
Jacob & Kornelis Poelman	Aug 1911	Ten Boer, Groningen
Kornelis & Tetje Veenkamp	Aug 1911	Ten Boer, Groningen
Hugo Hooft	1911	Hendrik Ido Ambacht, Zuid-Holl.
Geertje Van Schuur (married Willem Van Schuur)	1911 ?	?
Pieter Punt	1911 ?	?
G. & Mrs. Van Leeuwen & son	1911 ?	?
Petronella Hooft (wife of Hugo Hooft)	1912	Zevenbergen, Noord-Brabant
Andries Krijthe	Jan or Feb ? 1912	Northwest Iowa ?
Antoon Krijthe	Feb 1912	Oldehove, Groningen
Jacobus Dekker	Mar 1912	Nijverdal, Overijssel
Cornelis Bannink	Mar 1912	Nijverdal, Overijssel
Arie Verwoerd	Mar 1912	Bodegraven, Zuid-Holland

16 Jan Zoeteman had bought land at Pearce in August 1906 and visited in 1907, when he bought more land.

Name	Arrival in the Settlement	Arrived from
Hendrik Van Huizen	Apr 1912	Middelstum, Groningen
Berend Poelman	Apr 1912	Bedum, Groningen
Klaas Poelman	Jul 1912	Manhattan, MT
Willem Van Os	Jul 1912	Bodegraven, Zuid-Holland
Krijn Gortsema	Aug 1912	Grand Rapids, MI
Pieter De Wit	1912	Klundert, Noord-Brabant
Arie De Koning	28 Feb 1913	Maasdam, Zuid-Holland
Jan & Franciscus Plomp	Mar 1913	Nijverdal, Overijssel
Atze & Wietske Krol & children	Mar 1913	Dokkum, Friesland
Hessel & Pietje Talma & children	Mar 1913	Rinsumageest, Friesland
Jacob Feddes	Mar 1913	Manhattan, MT
Dirk Van Os	Apr 1913	Lynden, WA
Dirk Kamp	Jun 1913	Rotterdam
Jan & Hermina Konynenbelt & children	Mar 1914	Nijverdal, Overijssel
Johanna Zeylmans (married Jan Koole)	Mar 1914	Rotterdam
Rochus Krol	May 1914	Kollum, Friesland
Catharina Mekkes (married Klaas Poelman)	Jul 1914	Bedum, Groningen
Abraham Segboer	1914	Fijnaart, Noord-Brabant

Appendix B: HOMESTEAD RECORDS *of the* DUTCH SETTLEMENT[1]

Name	Entry obtained	Homestead location	House built	Size of house	Began residence	Acres broken 1st year
Everhardus Aldus	14 Apr 1904	NW 12-10-24	Apr 1904	12×38	Apr 1904	1904: 21
Jan Bannink	27 Jun 1904	NW 20-10-23	10 Dec 1904	10×14	23 Dec 1904	1904: 0
Barend Bode	21 Sep 1904	NE 16-10-23	1 May 1905	10×12	3 May 1905	1904: 0
Gerrit Bode	16 Sep 1904	SE 32-10-23	Nov 1904	16×16	4 Nov 1904	1904: 0
Leendert Bode	15 Apr 1905	NW 32-10-23	Dec 1905	16×24	1 Jan 1906	1905: 5
Teunis Bode	16 Sep 1904	NE 30-10-23	Dec 1904	12×18	11 Mar 1905	1904: 0
Daniel De Boer	21 Nov 1906	NW 2-10-23	1 Apr 1907	12×16	17 Apr 1907	1906: 0
Arie Dekker	16 Sep 1904	SW 28-10-23	abandoned 20 May 1905			
Arie Dekker	5 Jun 1906	NE 28-10-23	none[2]			1906: 15
Nan Dekker	18 Aug 1905	SE 28-10-23	Apr 1906	24×24	10 May 1906	1905: 0
Thys Dekker	16 Sep 1904	NW 28-10-23	Dec 1904[3]		Mar 1905	1904: 0
Johannes De Puyt	Sep 1904?	NE 2-10-23	abandoned 1905?			
Jacob De Vries	24 Jun 1905	NE 20-11-20	Dec 1906	14×20	1 Dec 1906	1905: 0
Arien Doornbos	1903?	NE 14-11-25	abandoned 8 Mar 1904			
Adam Drost	17 Jun 1907	SW 20-10-24	Jul 1907	14×24	15 Aug 1907	1907: 1
George Dykema	25 Mar 1904[4]	NE 14-11-25	Mar 1904	14×16	25 Mar 1904	1904: 15
Harm Emmelkamp	21 Apr 1903	NE 28-10-25	Feb 1904	12×24	1 Feb 1905[5]	1903: 15
William Feller	2 Sep 1903	NW 28-10-25	Jul 1904[6]	14×28	Jul 1904	1903: 0
Bartel Geleynse	20 Nov 1906	SE 2-10-23	Apr 1907	12×12	1 May 1907	1906: 0
John Geleynse	6 Apr 1906	NE 10-10-23	Oct 1906	16×24	14 Oct 1906	1906: 0
Lenard Geleynse	14 Jul 1905	SE 10-10-23	15 Jan 1906	14×16	15 Jan 1906	1905: 0
John Gunst	12 Dec 1905	SW 18-10-24	Aug 1906	12×32	8 Aug 1906	1905: 0
Gerrit Hartkoorn	25 May 1907	NE 1-12-21	abandoned 26 Sep 1907			
Tijmen Hofman	6 Sep 1907	NE 2-11-22	none[7]			1907: 0
Johannes Huisman	14 Apr 1904	SW 18-10-23	May 1904	24×24	5 May 1904	1904: 20
Cornelis Kamp	25 May 1907	NW 1-12-21	abandoned 26 Sep 1907			
Gerrit Kamperman	23 Oct 1907	NW 6-12-21	Mar 1908	14×16	1 Mar 1908	1907: 0
Arie Koole	12 Dec 1905	NW 14-10-24	none[8]			1905: 0
Bastiaan Koole	27 Sep 1904	SW 24-10-24	none[9]			1904: 0
John Koole	16 Feb 1906	SE 6-10-24	Mar 1907[10]	14×16	21 Mar 1906	1906: 45
Leonard Koole	27 Sep 1904	NE 14-10-24	none[11]			1904: 0
Albert Lantinga	11 Jul 1905	SE 20-10-25	Aug 1905	12×14	26 Aug 1905	1905: 0
Rudolph Lantinga	17 Sep 1904	SW 34-10-25	Feb 1905	16×24	15 Feb 1905	1904: 12

1 Alberta homestead records are available at the Provincial Archives of Alberta in Edmonton.
2 Resided with his father Nan Dekker on his homestead.
3 Moved his shack to his father Nan Dekker's homestead in 1906.
4 Dijkema filed on his homestead on 9 March 1904, but did not obtain entry until after Doornbos' abandonment of this homestead was processed.
5 The Emmelkamp family earlier resided in the Oldman River bottom in a log cabin on NE 33-9-25.
6 Feller first lived in a dugout in the side of a bank. In the spring of 1907 he built a new 14 × 28 foot house.

Acres cropped 1st year	Acres broken 2nd year	Acres cropped 2nd year	Acres broken 3rd year	Acres cropped 3rd year	Acres broken 4th year	Acres cropped 4th year	Date of Patent
1904: 7	1905: 40	1905: 61	1906: 20	1906: 81	1907: 4	1907: 84	31 Jul 1907
1904: 0	1905: 10	1905: 10	1906: 30	1906: 40	1907: 65	1907: 75	10 Sep 1907
1904: 0	1905: 10	1905: 0	1906: 5	1906: 10	1907: 60	1907: 15	19 Oct 1909
1904: 0	1905: 25	1905: 25	1906: 40	1906: 25	1907: 20	1907: 65	9 May 1908
1905: 0	1906: 37	1906: 25	1907: 75	1907: 80	1908: 0	1908: 95	6 Oct 1909
1904: 0	1905: 40	1905: 8	1906: 35	1906: 40	1907: 35	1907: 90	5 May 1908
1906: 0	1907: 10	1907: 10	1908: 10	1908: 20	1909: 20	1909: 20	4 Feb 1910
1906: 0	1907: 40	1907: 15	1908: 40	1908: 55	1909: 65	1909: 100	6 Oct 1909
1905: 0	1906: 20	1906: 0	1907: 0	1907: 20	1908: 20	1908: 40	26 May 1909
1904: 0	1905: 20	1905: 20	1906: 10	1906: 30	1907: 15	1907: 30	26 May 1908
1905: 0	1906: 0	1906: 0	1907: 80	1907: 0	1908: 0	1908: 80	18 Mar 1912
1907: 0	1908: 1	1908: 1	1909: 20	1909: 1	1910: 0	1910: 21	20 Sep 1911
1904: 15	1905: 35	1905: 50	1906: 30	1906: 80	1907: 20	1907: 100	17 Sep 1907
1903: 0	1904: 20	1904: 15	1905: 40	1905: 50	1906: 25	1906: 85	27 May 1907
1903: 0	1904: 20	1904: 12	1905: 25	1905: 20	1906: 25	1906: 45	25 Nov 1907
1906: 0	1907: 12	1907: 12	1908: 25	1908: 25	1909: 90	1909: 50	14 Mar 1910
1906: 0	1907: 30	1907: 20	1908: 70	1908: 40	1909: 0	1909: 110	29 Jan 1910
1905: 0	1906: 15	1906: 0	1907: 30	1907: 45	1908: 61	1908: 45	6 Oct 1909
1905: 0	1906: 0	1906: 0	1907: 58	1907: 15	1908: 40	1908: 58	20 Sep 1909
1907: 0	1908: 10	1908: 0	1909: 20	1909: 10	1910: 0	1910: 30	24 Feb 1911
1904: 0	1905: 40	1905: 20	1906: 40	1906: 60	1907: 0	1907: 100	3 Sep 1907
1907: 0	1908: 65	1908: 5	1909: 45	1909: 65	1910: 5	1910:105	10 Jan 1911
1905: 0	1906:100	1906: 0	1907: 0	1907: 100	1908: 30	1908: 100	6 Jul 1910
1904: 0	1905: 35	1905: 0	1906: 0	1906: 35	1907: 20	1907: 35	27 May 1908
1906: 15	1907: 30	1907: 45	1908: 40	1908: 75			5 May 1909
1904: 0	1905: 35	1905: 0	1906: 65	1906: 35	1907: 10	1907: 95	27 May 1908
1905: 0	1906: 6	1906: 6	1907: 45	1907: 50	1908: 70	1908: 120	13 Mar 1909
1904: 0	1905: 90	1905: 57	1906: 35	1906: 102	1907: 20	1907: 92	7 Feb 1908

7   From 28 May 1907 resided on purchased land (sect. 21-11-23, purchased 25 May 1907), first in a tent, then in a 14 × 28 foot shack.
8   Resided with brother Bastiaan from 12 December 1905; from 1 March 1907 lived in 16 × 16 foot shack on purchased land (E½ NE 23-10-24, purchased 1 October 1905).
9   From 15 June 1905 resided in 14 × 16 foot shack on purchased land (E½ 13-10-24, purchased 30 September 1904).
10   Previously lived in his barn.
11   From May 1905 resided in 16 × 16 foot shack on purchased land (NW 13-10-24), and in Mar 1907 moved shack to purchased land (SE 23-10-24); both quarters purchased 15 October 1904.

Name	Entry obtained	Homestead location	House built	Size of house	Began residence	Acres broken 1st year
Berend Nyhof	27 Jun 1904	SW 20-10-23	10 Dec 1904	14×18	25 Dec 1904	1904: 0
Jacobus Nyhoff	14 Apr 1904	NE 12-10-24	May 1904	14×32	Apr 1904	1904: 40
Rense Nyhoff	5 Jul 1904	SE 20-10-23	15 May 1905	18×18	1 Jun 1905	1904: 0
John Postman	26 May 1904	NE 24-10-24	15 Apr 1905	14×16	15 Apr 1905	1904: 35
John Rose (Roos)	14 Apr 1906	N½ NW 32-9-25	May 1906[12]	20×30	1 Jun 1907	1906: 5
Albert Rutgers	12 Jul 1905	SW 28-10-23	Oct 1905	12×16	1 Jun 1907	1905: 0
Gerard Schuitema	11 Jul 1905	NW 6-10-24	Jul 1905	12×14	20 Jul 1905	1905: 0
Dick Selman	25 Sep 1906	SE 32-9-24	Feb 1907	14×36	4 Mar 1907	1906: 0
Lucas Steenbergen	21 May 1906	SW 12-10-25	Aug 1906	16×40	15 Sep 1906	1906: 0
Willem Stotyn	14 Apr 1904	SE 12-10-24	Jun 1904	12×14	15 Jun 1904	1904: 10
Albert Tersteeg	11 Jul 1908	NW 28-9-24	1907?[13]	14×16	10 Jul 1908	1908: 43
Hendrikus ter Telgte	12 Aug 1903	SW 10-11-25	Jan 1904	12×24	Feb 1904	1903: 0
John H. ter Telgte	29 Aug 1903	SW 30-10-25	1902[14]	28×28	Mar 1904	1903: 0
Lubbert Van Dellen	18 Aug 1903	SE 14-11-25	Mar 1904	14×14	Mar 1904	1903: 0
Frans Vanden Berg	25 May 1907	SW 1-12-21	abandoned 26 Sep 1907			
Paul Vanden Berg	25 May 1907	SE 1-12-21	abandoned 26 Sep 1907			
Abel Vander Burgh	10 Apr 1905	SE 6-10-24	abandoned 8 Jan 1906			
Abel Vander Burgh	20 Jan 1906	SW 6-10-24	Apr 1906	14×24	15 Apr 1906	1906: 22
Peter Vander Burgh	10 Apr 1905	SE 18-10-24	Dec 1905	16×22	5 Feb 1906	1905: 0
Walter Vander Burgh	4 Apr 1905	NE 6-10-24	Dec 1905	16×24	6 Feb 1906	1905: 0
Roelof Van Dijk	15 Jul 1904	NE 20-10-23	Dec 1904	12×24	25 Jan 1905	1904: 0
Jacobus Van Haarlem	26 Jun 1906	NW 4-11-22	Jul 1906	14×20	5 Jul 1906	1906: 0
Jan Van Lohuizen	14 Apr 1904	NW 18-10-23	Jun 1904	14×20	1 May 1904	1904: 55
Willem Van Lohuizen	14 Apr 1904	NE 18-10-23	May 1904	12×14	May 1904	1904:40
Hendrikus Veldhuis	14 Apr 1904	SE 18-10-23	1 May 1904	12×12	1 May 1904	1904: 10
George Venhuizen	15 Aug 1904	SE 28-10-25	Jul 1904[15]	12×30	15 Jul 1904	1904: 25
Anne Weerstra	16 Aug 1905	NW 24-11-25	Oct 1905	12×14	25 Oct 1905	1905: 0
Rommert Weerstra	1 May 1906	SE 20-8-25	abandoned 11 Jun 1906			
Rommert Weerstra	8 Sep 1906	SW 34-9-24	Jan 1907	14×18	25 Sep 1907	1906: 0
Arend Williamson	19 May 1905	NW 18-10-25	Dec 1904[16]	10×14	15 Apr 1906	1905: 80
Garrit Williamson	14 Nov 1904	NE 20-10-25	Mar 1905	14×28	15 Mar 1905	1904: 0
William Williamson	1 Mar 1905	SW 28-10-25	none[17]			1905: 28
Gerrit Withage	14 May 1904	SE 24-10-24	Jun 1904	12×14	Jun 1904	1904: 40

12 The Rose family first lived in a log cabin.
13 A shack was built by the previous homesteader who abandoned this quarter.
14 The house was built by the previous homesteader Herbert Stewart who abandoned this quarter in February 1903.

Acres cropped 1st year	Acres broken 2nd year	Acres cropped 2nd year	Acres broken 3rd year	Acres cropped 3rd year	Acres broken 4th year	Acres cropped 4th year	Date of Patent
1904: 0	1905: 10	1905: 10	1906: 30	1906: 40	1907: 60	1907: 70	12 Sep 1907
1904: 7	1905: 40	1905: 50	1906: 20	1906: 80	1907: 0	1907: 100	15 Oct 1907
1904: 0	1905: 12	1905: 0	1906: 48	1906: 60	1907: 52	1907: 60	5 Aug 1908
1904: 0	1905: 40	1905: 45	1906: 80	1906: 80	1907: 0	1907: 150	25 Nov 1907
1906: 0	1907: 5	1907: 5	1908: 10	1908: 10	1909: 20	1909: 20	17 Feb 1910
1905: 0	1906: 0	1906: 0	1907: 5	1907: 0	1908:125	1908: 5	28 Sep 1910
1905: 0	1906: 50	1906: 15	1907: 50	1907: 60	1908: 0	1908: 85	23 Nov 1908
1906: 0	1907: 60	1907: 25	1908: 35	1908: 60	1909: 15	1909: 95	21 Apr 1910
1906: 0	1907: 20	1907: 20	1908: 45	1908: 65	1909: 35	1909: 85	15 Sep 1909
1904: 10	1905: 15	1905: 25	1906: 3	1906: 25	1907: 60	1907: 37	15 Apr 1908
1908: 10	1909: 30	1909: 43	1910: 0	1910: 70	1911: 35	1911: 60	20 Aug 1911
1903: 0	1904: 30	1904: 10	1905: 20	1905: 30	1906: 15	1906: 50	3 Oct 1907
1903: 0	1904: 60	1904: 25	1905: 45	1905: 65	1906: 25	1906: 105	29 Aug 1907
1903: 0	1904: 20	1904: 20	1905: 30	1905: 50	1906: 40	1906: 90	22 Aug 1907
1906: 0	1907: 30	1907: 22	1908: 10	1908: 52			7 Apr 1909
1905: 0	1906: 20	1906: 20	1907: 40	1907: 60	1908: 20	1908: 60	14 Apr 1909
1905: 0	1906: 20	1906: 20	1907: 20	1907: 40	1908: 12	1908: 52	2 Apr 1909
1904: 0	1905: 10	1905: 5	1906: 20	1906: 30	1907:110	1907: 55	22 Oct 1907
1906: 0	1907: 8	1907: 0	1908: 35	1908: 35	1909: 0	1909: 5	1 Dec 1909
1904: 10	1905: 35	1905: 65	1906: 30	1906: 94	1907: 0	1907: 45	28 Jun 1907
1904: 5	1905: 40	1905: 50	1906: 50	1906: 80	1907: 0	1907: 70	9 Jul 1907
1904: 10	1905: 35	1905: 35	1906: 55	1906: 40	1907: 0	1907: 100	4 Sep 1907
1904: 0	1905: 50	1905: 40	1906: 37	1906: 75	1907: 44	1907: 104	7 May 1908
1905: 0	1906: 80	1906: 23	1907: 30	1907: 80	1908: 0	1908: 110	23 Dec 1908
1906: 0	1907: 90	1907: 0	1908: 0	1908: 90	1909: 0	1909: 90	10 Dec 1909
1905: 0	1906: 27	1906: 80	1907: 0	1907: 107	1908: 0	1908: 107	24 Sep 1910
1904: 0	1905: 15	1905: 15	1906: 45	1906: 15	1907: 50	1907: 60	16 Jun 1908
1905: 0	1906: 20	1906: 28	1907: 20	1907: 48			16 Jun 1908
1904: 0	1905: 60	1905: 40	1906: 45	1906: 100	1907: 0	1907: 105	22 Nov 1907

15 Began residing on homestead before entry obtained, since paperwork for the previously abandoned homestead was not yet complete.

16 A shack was built by the previous homesteader who abandoned this quarter in February 1905.

17 From 1 October 1905 resided with father Garrit Williamson on his homestead (NE 20-10-25).

SELECT BIBLIOGRAPHY

NEWSPAPERS/PERIODICALS

The Banner. Grand Rapids, MI. Calvin College Library, Grand Rapids, MI.

De Grondwet. Holland, MI. Joint Archives of Holland, Holland, MI.

De Hope. Holland, MI. Joint Archives of Holland, Holland, MI.

De Volksvriend. Orange City, IA. Northwestern College Library, Orange City, IA, and Calvin College Library, Grand Rapids, MI.

De Wachter. Grand Rapids, MI. Calvin College Archives, Grand Rapids, MI.

Lethbridge Herald. Lethbridge, Alberta. Lethbridge Public Library.

Nieuwsblad van Friesland. Heerenveen, Friesland. Provinciale Bibliotheek van Friesland, Leeuwarden, Netherlands.

Twentsch Volksblad. Almelo, Overijssel. Overijsselse Bibliotheek Dienst, Nijverdal, Netherlands.

REGIONAL AND LOCAL HISTORY

Berton, Pierre. *The Promised Land: Settling the West, 1896–1914*. Toronto: McClelland and Stewart, 1984.

Bowman, Ronald F. *Railways in Southern Alberta*. Lethbridge: Historical Society of Alberta, 1973.

Byfield, Ted, ed. *Alberta in the 20th Century*. Vol. 1, *The Great West before 1900*. Edmonton: United Western Communications, 1991.

Byfield, Ted, ed. *Alberta in the 20th Century*. Vol. 2, *The Birth of the Province, 1900–1910*. Edmonton: United Western Communications, 1992.

Down the Trail of Memories. Monarch: Dorcas Ladies' Aid of the Monarch Reformed Church, 1963.

Fort Macleod – Our Colourful Past: A History of the Town of Fort Macleod from 1874 to 1924. Fort Macleod: Fort Macleod History Book Committee, 1977.

Friesen, Gerald. *The Canadian Prairies: A History*. Lincoln: University of Nebraska Press, 1984.

Hofman, Bernice, et al., eds. *Monarch Reformed Church: 75 Years, 1909–1984*. Lethbridge, [1984].

Hofman, Tymen. *The Strength of Their Years: The Story of a Pioneer Community*. St. Catharines: Knight Publishing, 1983.

Leavings by Trail, Granum by Rail. Calgary: Granum History Committee, [1977].

Nobleford Christian Reformed Church, 1905–1980. Lethbridge: Anniversary Book Committee, 1981.

75 Years of God's Grace: Granum Christian Reformed Church, 1905–1980. Lethbridge, 1980.

Sons of Wind and Soil. Calgary: Nobleford-Monarch History Book Club, 1976.

Treaty 7 Elders and Tribal Council, with Walter Hildebrandt, Sarah Carter, and Dorothy First Rider. *The True Spirit and Original Intent of Treaty 7.* Montreal and Kingston: McGill-Queen's University Press, 1996.

Wheat Heart of the West: A History of Barons and District. Calgary: Barons History Committee, 1972.

DUTCH IMMIGRANT HISTORY

De Vries, Klaas and Reindert. *Leaving Home Forever.* Windsor: Electa Press, 1995.

Ganzevoort, Herman. *A Bittersweet Land: The Dutch Experience in Canada, 1890–1980.* Toronto: McClelland and Stewart, 1988.

Ganzevoort, Herman, trans. and ed. *A Dutch Homesteader on the Prairies: The Letters of Willem De Gelder 1910–13.* Toronto: University of Toronto Press, 1973.

Ganzevoort, Herman, trans. and ed. *The Last Illusion: Letters from Dutch Immigrants in the "Land of Opportunity," 1924–1930.* Calgary: University Calgary Press, 1999.

Hofman, Tymen. *The Canadian Story of the CRC: Its First Century.* Belleville: Guardian Books, 2004.

Krijff, J. Th. *100 Years: Dutch Immigration to Manitoba in 1893.* Windsor: Electa Press, 1994.

Kroes, Rob. *The Persistence of Ethnicity: Dutch Calvinist Pioneers in Amsterdam, Montana.* Urbana: University of Illinois Press, 1992.

Lucas, Henry. *Netherlanders in America: Dutch Immigration to the United States and Canada, 1789–1950.* Grand Rapids: Eerdmans, 1955.

Sinnema, Donald. "Dutch American Newspapers and the Network of Early Dutch Immigrant Communities." In *Dutch Enterprise: Alive and Well in North America,* edited by Larry Wagenaar and Robert Swierenga, 43–56. Holland, MI: Association for the Advancement of Dutch American Studies, 2000.

INDEX